ARCTIC OCEAN

Barents Sea

Kara Sea

Laptev Sea

Norwegian Sea

S i b e r i a

Iceland

Oslo
Stockholm
St. Petersburg
A S I A
Sea of
Okhotsk

North
Sea
Glasgow
Copenhagen
Hamburg
Minsk
Moscow
Lake Baikal

Dublin
Amsterdam
Warsaw
Kiev
Shenyang
Sapporo

London
Brussels
EUROPE
Prague
Odessa
Caspian Sea
Beijing
Sea of
Japan

Paris
Vienna
Budapest
Aral Sea
Lanzhou
Seoul
Tokyo

Bordeaux
Lyons
Belgrade
Bucharest
Black Sea
Xi'an
Osaka
Kitakyushu

Barcelona
Rome
Sofia
Ankara
Chengdu
Shanghai
East China
Sea

Lisbon
Madrid
Naples
Istanbul
Izmir
Kabul
Chongqing

Casablanca
Rabat
Algiers
Athens
Beirut
Damascus
Tehran
Lahore
Kunming
Guangzhou
PACIFIC OCEAN

Tunis
Mediterranean Sea
Baghdad
Delhi
Hanoi
Hong Kong

Tripoli
Alexandria
Amman
Persian
Gulf
New Delhi
Dhaka
Rangoon

Cairo
Riyadh
Arabia
Karachi
Arabian
Sea
Calcutta
Bangkok
South
China
Sea
Manila

AFRICA
Bombay
Bay of
Bengal
Ho Chi
Minh City

Dakar
Bangalore
Madras
Medan
Singapore

Abuja
Colombo
I n d o n e s i a

Ibadan
Lagos
Addis Ababa
Jakarta
Surabaya

Abidjan
Nairobi
Mogadishu
Bandung

Kinshasa
Dar es Salaam

Luanda
INDIAN OCEAN
AUSTRALIA
Brisbane

Madagascar
Perth
Sydney

SOUTH ATLANTIC
OCEAN
Johannesburg
Maputo
Adelaide
Canberra
Melbourne

Cape Town

DISCARDED

ANTARCTICA

EXPLORERS & DISCOVERERS

From Alexander the Great to Sally Ride

Volume 7

Nancy Pear
•
Daniel B. Baker

Edited by Jane Hoehner

AN IMPRINT OF THE GALE GROUP

DETROIT · SAN FRANCISCO · LONDON · BOSTON · WOODBRIDGE, CT

Explorers & Discoverers

From Alexander the Great to Sally Ride

Nancy Pear and Daniel B. Baker

Volume 7

Staff

Jane Hoehner, *U•X•L Senior Editor*
Carol DeKane Nagel, *U•X•L Managing Editor*
Thomas L. Romig, *U•X•L Publisher*

Cindy Range, *Production Assistant*
Evi Seoud, *Assistant Production Manager*
Mary Beth Trimper, *Production Director*

Pamela A. E. Galbreath, *Senior Art Director*
Cynthia Baldwin, *Product Design Manager*
Barbara J. Yarrow, *Graphic Services Manager*

Shalice Shah-Caldwell, *Permissions Associate*
Margaret Chamberlain, *Permissions Specialist (Pictures)*

Marco Di Vita, Graphix Group, *Typesetter*

ISBN 0-7876-3681-9
ISSN 1522-9947

Contents
of Volume 7

Reader's Guide vii

Introduction ix

Picture Credits xvii

Maps xix

Biographical Listings

Carl Johan Andersson (1827–1867) 1
William Balfour Baikie (1825–1864) 7
Daisy Bates (1859–1951) 14
Saint Brendan (c. 484–c. 577) 23
John Byron (1723–1786) 28

Pedro Álvares Cabral (c. 1467–c. 1520) 37

Eugenie Clark (1922–) 44

Luigi Maria D'Albertis (1841–1901) 52

Semyon Ivanovich Dezhnev (1605–c. 1673) 60

Alice Eastwood (1859–1953) 66

Linda Finch (1951–) 77

Mel Fisher (1922–1998) 83

Birute Galdikas (1946–) 92

Ernest Giles (1835–1897) 100

Hanno (c. 500 B.C.–?) 107

Thor Heyerdahl (1914–) 113

Abu Abd-Allah Muhammed
al-Sharif al-Idrisi (1100–1166) 122

Gonzalo Jiménez de Quesada (c. 1501–c. 1579) 126

Wilhelm Junker (1840–1892) 133

Elisha Kent Kane (1820–1857) 138

Kintup (c. 1849–?) 145

Jacob Le Maire (1585–1616) 151

S.S. *Manhattan* (1969) 159

Dervla Murphy (1931–) 167

National Air and Space Museum (1976–) 175

Nearchus (c. 360 B.C.–312 B.C.) 181

Helen Thayer (1938–) 188

Karen Thorndike (c. 1942–) 197

William of Rubruck (c. 1215–c. 1295) 204

Hermann von Wissmann (1853–1905) 212

Chronology of Exploration 217

Explorers by Country of Birth 229

Cumulative Index to Volumes 1–7 235

Reader's Guide

Explorers & Discoverers: From Alexander the Great to Sally Ride, Volume 7, features thirty biographies of twenty men, eight women, one museum, and one ship that have expanded the horizons of our world and universe. Beginning with an ancient Carthaginian navigator and extending to a present-day aviator, *Explorers & Discoverers, Volume 7,* presents the lives and times of well-known explorers as well as many lesser-known women and non-Europeans who have also made significant discoveries. Who these travelers were, when and how they lived and traveled, why their journeys were significant, and what the consequences of their discoveries are are all answered within these biographies.

The thirty biographical entries in *Explorers & Discoverers, Volume 7,* are arranged in alphabetical order. More than eighty photographs, illustrations, and maps bring the subjects to life as well as provide geographic details of specific journeys. Additionally, sixteen maps of major regions of the world lead off the volume, and a cumulative chronology of exploration by region, a list of explorers by country of birth, and a cumulative index conclude the volume.

Comments and Suggestions

We welcome your comments on this work as well as your suggestions for individuals to be featured in future volumes of *Explorers & Discoverers*. Please write: Editors, *Explorers & Discoverers,* U•X•L, 27500 Drake Rd., Farmington Hills, Michigan 48331-3535; call toll-free: 800-877-4253; or fax: 248-699-8066.

Introduction

Explorers & Discoverers, Volume 7, takes the reader on an adventure with men and women who have made significant contributions to human knowledge about the earth, plant and animal life, and ourselves. Journeying through the centuries, we will conquer frontiers and sail uncharted waters. We will trek across treacherous mountains, scorching deserts, steamy jungles, and icy glaciers. We will plumb the depths of the ocean, travel the skies in a vintage airplane, and share in intriguing rituals and customs of unfamiliar peoples. We will accompany Arctic caribou on their centuries-old migration to northern calving grounds, and live among the elusive orangutans that dwell in the rainforests of Indonesia. Encountering isolation, disease, and even death, we will come to know the grave sacrifices that discovery sometimes exacts. But we will also experience the joys of achievement!

Before joining the explorers and discoverers, however, it is worthwhile to consider why they venture into the unknown. Certainly a primary motivation is curiosity: they want to find out what is on the other side of a mountain, or they are intrigued by rumors about a strange new land, or they simply enjoy wandering the world. Yet adventurers often—indeed, usually—embark on journeys of discovery under less spontaneous circumstances.

Many explorers were commissioned by the rulers or governments of their countries to lead expeditions with a specific purpose. The Spanish governor of the South American coastal colony of Santa Marta, for instance, instructed conquistador **Gonzalo Jiménez de Quesada** to explore territories further inland, and also to look for the legendary Indian kingdom of El Dorado, famous for its wealth and splendor. In the highlands of the Andes Mountains, the explorer discovered just such a civilization: he conquered the Chibcha Indians and claimed their great riches and land (named New Granada) for Spain. Sponsored by Great Britain's Foreign Office, naval doctor **William Balfour Baikie** led two trade expeditions up West Africa's Niger River. His pioneering use of the drug quinine to prevent and treat malaria made travel on the swampy river much less deadly, and the trading posts he established eventually led to British control of the waterway and its surrounding territories (which would become Nigeria). Pursuit of trade was also the motivation behind the 1500–1501 sailing expedition of Portuguese nobleman **Pedro Álvarez Cabral.** After explorer Vasco da Gama discovered a successful sailing route to India in 1498, King Manuel I of Portugal rushed to send Cabral on a follow-up trip to the East to set up direct trade relations with rich Indian ports before other European powers did the same. Not only did Cabral succeed in his trade mission, he also claimed the territory that would become Brazil—one of Portugal's most important colonial possessions—when temporarily blown off course during his outward voyage. In a similar rush to beat competing nations, British naval officer **John Byron** led a secret expedition to the south Atlantic in 1764–1765. It was believed that a great southern continent and other large islands were located there; any country that claimed these lands would have an important base from which to travel to the Pacific, either by way of Africa's Cape of Good Hope or South America's Cape Horn. Byron took official possession of the strategically located Falkland Islands for Great Britain just as France was establishing a colony there—igniting more than two centuries of conflicting claims over ownership that culminated in the 1982 Falklands War.

Explorers also received backing from private sponsors or were motivated by economic self-interest. Amsterdam merchant Isaac Le Maire, for example, was intent on breaking the trade monopoly that the Dutch East India Company enjoyed in the Orient. The company controlled the two known sailing routes to the Pacific, and Le Maire organized an expedition—led by his son **Jacob Le Maire**—to find an alternative route there. While Jacob Le Maire did just that, discovering and rounding Cape Horn at the tip of South America, he was still arrested for monopoly violation by disbelieving Dutch East India Company officials. After Jacob Le Maire's death in captivity, his father fought a court battle for the trading freedom his son had earned. Also failing to receive the recognition he deserved for his explorations was Australian **Ernest Giles.** Sent by Victoria-based sheep farmers and businessmen to explore western Australia in search of new pasturelands, he was the first individual to make an east-to-west crossing of the continent's harsh, desertic interior and then return. While his remarkable achievement was appreciated around the world— and the camels he used made the animals the accepted form of transportation in Australia's arid interior—Giles was not honored in his own country during his lifetime because he failed to discover the type of land his sponsors needed for sheep raising. No such lack of appreciation followed the glamorous discovery made by American treasure hunter **Mel Fisher** in 1985, however. After years of searching the waters off Florida's Key West, he located the treasure-laden Spanish galleon *Nuestra Señora de Atocha,* which held an estimated $400 million worth of precious metal and jewels. He became an instant celebrity; four books, a documentary, and a television movie retold his tale of discovery. The fame turned sour, however, when Fisher was accused of mishandling his wealth, unfairly repaying the investors who had financed his search, and participating in other shady business dealings.

Religious dedication has long been a strong motivating force behind exploration and travel into unknown lands. **Saint Brendan,** an Irish monk who had founded monasteries in Ireland and converted local populations to Roman Christianity in other parts of the British Isles, led a legendary missionary voyage west sometime around 566–573, into the forbidding Atlantic Ocean. With no navigational tools to guide them, Brendan and his seventeen companions wandered the sea in search of legendary islands said to exist there by ancient writers; it is believed that the men eventually made their way to Bermuda or the North American mainland. The success of Brendan's voyage, in fact, kept alive the hope—during the Middle Ages—that unknown lands lay waiting to be discovered across the vast Atlantic. Also fired by missionary zeal was **William of Rubruck,** a Franciscan friar sent on a religious quest by King Louis IX of France to the court of Mongolia's Great Khan to convert the ruler and his followers to Roman Christianity. While failing in his religious mission, William made a detailed record of his journey into Russia and central Asia that is now considered one of the most valuable travel accounts written by a medieval Christian. Salvation of souls was not the only motivation behind the friar's trip to Mongolia, however; King Louis had hoped that the converted Mongols would cease their westward conquests into Europe, and form an alliance with European powers against threatening Muslim forces.

Explorers have been inspired, too, by the quest for scientific knowledge. Self-taught botanist **Alice Eastwood,** for instance, spent a lifetime collecting rare and unknown wildflowers and other native plants in the mountains, fields, and deserts of the American West. In a time when women rarely traveled alone, the scientist journeyed solitarily by horse and on foot through the rugged frontier, eventually establishing an outstanding herbarium of 340,000 specimens at the California Academy of Sciences in San Francisco, where she served as curator of botany. Even the great California earthquake of 1906, which destroyed the academy and most of its collection, could not dampen Eastwood's passion for gathering plants. Similarly devoting much of her life to her scientific passion is marine biologist **Eugenie Clark.** The scientist has spent years studying the lives and behavior of tropical fish, particularly sharks. While conducting long-term studies of captive sharks, Clark learned that these lower vertebrate predators—mistakenly labeled "stupid"—had surprising memory and learning capabilities. Studying the creatures in their natural habitat, she found that few species of these feared "man-eaters" attack humans, and that they play a vital role in the ocean's complex food cycle. Years of study were also required for Canadian scientist **Birute Galdikas** to gain a clear understanding of the life and habits of the orangutan, the most elusive of the great apes. Living among the animals in the jungles of Indonesian Borneo, the scientist devoted extraordinary time and patience to learning more about the shy and solitary creatures, who live their entire lives in the treetops, nearly 100 feet above the ground. Nonetheless, over many years, Galdikas was able to gather enormous amounts of new information about orangutan mating habits, reproductive cycles, young-rearing, diet, and methods of communication. With their population decreasing alarmingly over the years, Galdikas has also been actively engaged in conservation efforts to save the animals from extinction.

And sometimes it is the puzzle of our own, human past that inspires journeys of exploration. **Daisy Bates,** a British governess who traveled to Australia as a young woman, became engrossed with Aborigines, the country's primitive native inhabitants. She spent a lifetime traveling and living among the various tribes of western Australia, carefully recording their rich history, which was filled with complex rituals, customs, legends, and beliefs. She felt compelled to capture a portrait of their ancient way of life—unchanged until Western civilization had come to Australian shores—because by the early twentieth century it was fast disintegrating before her eyes. Fascination with ancient legends and practices also spurred Norwegian scientist **Thor Heyerdahl** to take extraordinary actions. Noting the shared beliefs and customs of ancient civilizations located oceans apart, Heyerdahl was convinced—contrary to accepted anthropological beliefs—that ancient peoples made migratory trips across the seas. To prove his theories he undertook ocean voyages in replicas of primitive sailing craft: he traveled from

Chile to Polynesia on a balsa raft, and from Egypt to South America in a papyrus reed boat. Despite the success of his journeys, Heyerdahl's theories remain controversial, because more evidence is needed to confirm them.

But perhaps the foremost motivation to explore is the desire to be the first to accomplish a particular feat. American aviator **Linda Finch,** who restores and flies vintage airplanes, decided to duplicate and complete the around-the-world trip that legendary aviator Amelia Earhart was attempting when she vanished in 1937. Locating and meticulously rebuilding a rare Lockheed Electra 10E—which Earhart had piloted on her unfortunate flight—Finch successfully circumnavigated the globe (at or near the equator) in the sixty-year-old plane, becoming the first woman to repeat Earhart's journey in the same kind of craft. Finch said she undertook the flight to celebrate Earhart's courageous spirit, and to encourage young people to follow their dreams. American sailor **Karen Thorndike** was following her dream when she undertook a solo journey around the world in her thirty-six-foot yacht *Amelia* in 1996. Such a trip had been completed by only six other women before her, and it would take Thorndike more than two trying years before she would become the first American woman to do the same. Circling the world in open oceans around the five great capes of the Southern Hemisphere, Thorndike endured towering waves, driving wind and rain, and—at one point—an emergency rescue at sea. Also no stranger to hardships is **Helen Thayer,** an adventurer and veteran outdoorswoman who decided to become the first woman to travel alone to either of the world's magnetic poles. In 1988 she set out for the North Magnetic Pole, traveling by foot and on skis and bringing only the provisions she could pull behind her on a sled. During her 27-day, 364-mile Arctic journey, Thayer withstood frigid cold, polar storms, and attacks from hungry polar bears before reaching her goal. Subsequent Thayer adventures would include kayaking through the Amazon and trekking through the Sahara Desert.

By concentrating on biographies of individual explorers in this book we seem to suggest that many of these adventurers were loners who set out on their own to singlehandedly confront the unknown. But, as a rule, explorers rarely traveled alone and they had help in achieving their goals. Therefore, use of an individual name is often only shorthand for the achievements of an expedition as a whole. Explorers were often accompanied by large groups of servants, porters, and native guides. Sometimes it was on these indigenous inhabitants and their knowledge that survival depended: it is unlikely, for example, that Helen Thayer could have fought off the assaults of polar bears without the fearless efforts of Charlie, an Arctic husky dog that her Inuit trainers insisted she take along for protection on her journey.

Explorers & Discoverers, Volume 7, tells the stories of these men and women as well as those of others motivated by a daring spirit and an intense curiosity.

A final note of clarification: When we say that an explorer "discovered" a place, we do not mean that she or he was the first human ever to have been there. Although the discoverer may have been the first from his or her own country to set foot in a new land, most areas of the world during the great periods of exploration were already occupied or their existence had been verified by other people.

Picture Credits

The photographs and illustrations appearing in *Explorers & Discoverers, Volume 7,* were received from the following sources:

On the cover: John Smith; **The Granger Collection, New York:** Beryl Markham and Matthew A. Henson.

Archive Photos. Reproduced by permission: pp. 1, 10, 19, 32, 35, 92, 123, 137, 140; **Photograph by Nigel J. Dennis. Photo Researchers, Inc. Reproduced by permission:** p. 3; **The Granger Collection, New York. Reproduced by permission:** pp. 7, 9, 23, 39, 126, 133, 138, 180, 205, 206, 212, 213; **The Library of Congress:** pp. 27, 37; **National Maritime Museum. Reproduced by permission:** p. 28; **Photograph by Andreas Rechnitzer. Reproduced by permission:** p. 44; **Photograph by J. Hides. From *New Guinea: The Last Unknown.* Copyright © Gavin Souter, 1963. All rights reserved:** pp. 52, 55; **Photograph by Jeff Foot. Imapress/ Archive Photos, Inc. Reproduced by permission:** p. 64;

Photograph by G. A. Eisen. Special Collections Library/ California Academy of Sciences. Reproduced by permission: p. 66; **Photograph by J. T. Howell. Special Collections Library/California Academy of Sciences. Reproduced by permission:** p. 72; **Photograph by Rob Robbins. AP/Wide World Photos. Reproduced by permission:** p. 77; **Photograph by J. David Ake. Archive Photos, Inc. Reproduced by permission:** p. 81; **AP/Wide World Photos. Reproduced by permission:** pp. 83, 88, 169; **Photograph by Denise Tackett. Tom Stack and Associates. Reproduced by permission:** p. 94; **Photo Researchers, Inc. Reproduced by permission:** p. 102; **Photograph by Mitch Reardon. Photo Researchers, Inc. Reproduced by permission:** 109; **J. W. Cappelens Forlag. Reproduced by permission:** p. 117; **Photograph by Dan Guravich. Reproduced by permission of the Literary Estate of Dan Guravich:** pp. 159, 161, 162; **Photograph by John Reeves. Reproduced by permission:** p. 167; **Photograph by Wesley Boxce. Photo Researchers, Inc. Reproduced by permission:** p. 176; **Corbis-Bettmann. Reproduced by permission:** p. 182; **Photograph by Francois Gohier. Photo Researchers, Inc. Reproduced by permission:** p. 185; **Helen Thayer and Associates. Reproduced by permission:** p. 188; **Photograph by Gustavo Fazio Stringer. AP/Wide World Photos. Reproduced by permission:** p. 197; **Photograph by Bob Grieser Stringer. AP/Wide World Photos. Reproduced by permission:** p. 202; **From** *Marshall Cavendish Illustrated Encyclopedia of Discovery and Exploration,* **Volume 2:** *Beyond the Horizon* **by Malcolm Ross MacDonald:** p. 204.

Maps

The World

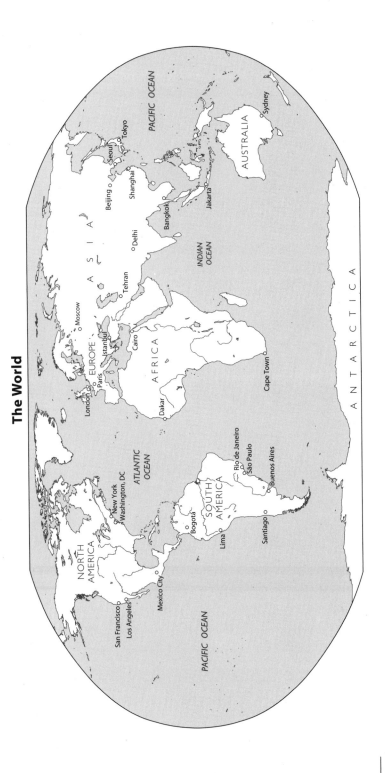

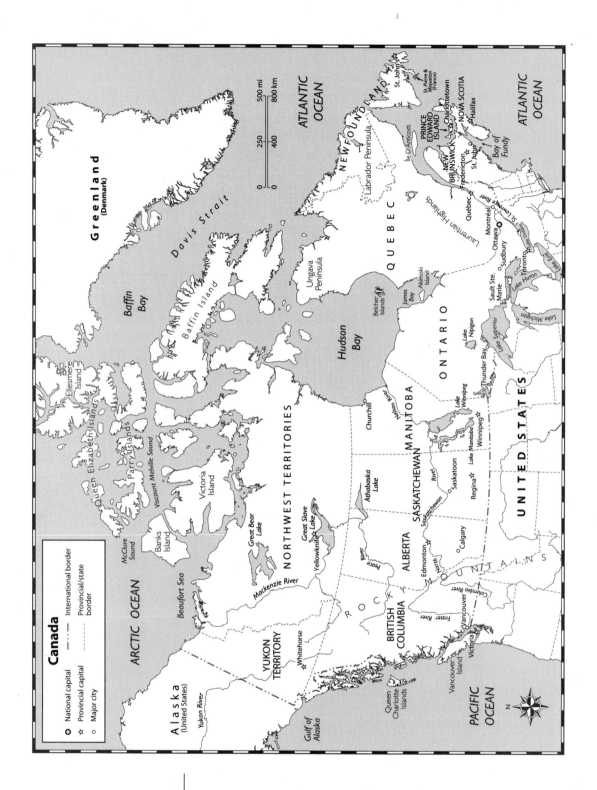

Canada

- ✪ National capital
- ☆ Provincial capital
- ○ Major city

— · · — International border
— — — Provincial/state border

ARCTIC OCEAN

Greenland (Denmark)

ATLANTIC OCEAN

PACIFIC OCEAN

UNITED STATES

Alaska (United States)

Baffin Bay
Davis Strait
Baffin Island
Ellesmere Island
Queen Elizabeth Islands
Parry Islands
Viscount Melville Sound
Victoria Island
Banks Island
McClure Sound
Beaufort Sea
Gulf of Alaska
Queen Charlotte Islands

Hudson Bay
Ungava Peninsula
Labrador Peninsula
Belcher Islands
James Bay
Akimiski Island

NEWFOUNDLAND
St. John's
St. Pierre & Miquelon (France)
Île d'Anticosti
PRINCE EDWARD ISLAND Charlottetown
NOVA SCOTIA Halifax
NEW BRUNSWICK Fredericton
St. John
Bay of Fundy
Laurentian Highlands
Québec
Montréal
Ottawa ✪
Sudbury
St. Lawrence River

QUEBEC

ONTARIO
Lake Nipigon
Lake Superior
Lake Huron
Lake Michigan
Lake Erie
Lake Ontario
Toronto
Sault Ste. Marie
Thunder Bay

MANITOBA
Lake Winnipeg
Lake Manitoba
Winnipeg ☆
Churchill

SASKATCHEWAN
Saskatoon
Regina ☆
Saskatchewan River

ALBERTA
Edmonton ☆
Calgary
North Saskatchewan River
Peace River

NORTHWEST TERRITORIES
Great Slave Lake
Great Bear Lake
Athabaska Lake
Yellowknife ☆
Mackenzie River
Nelson River

YUKON TERRITORY
Whitehorse ☆

BRITISH COLUMBIA
Fraser River
Columbia River
Vancouver Island
Vancouver
Victoria ☆

ROCKY MOUNTAINS

Yukon River

0   250   500 mi
0   400   800 km

N

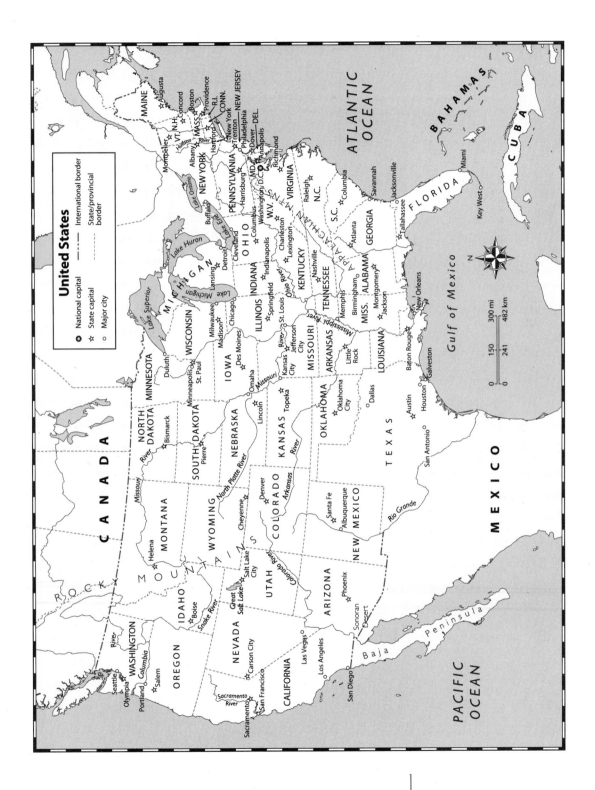

United States

National capital ⊛
State capital ☆
Major city ○

International border — ⋅ —
State/provincial border - - -

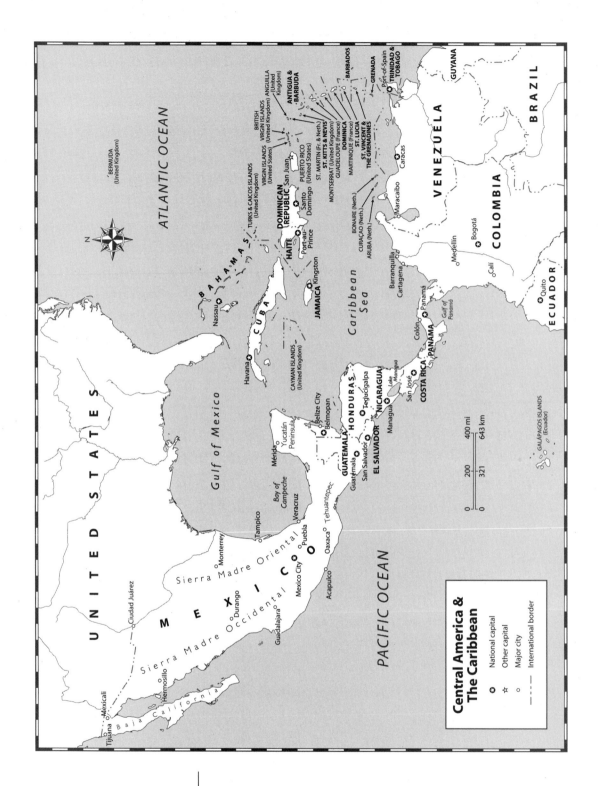

**Central America &
The Caribbean**

⊛ National capital
☆ Other capital
○ Major city
–·–·–· International border

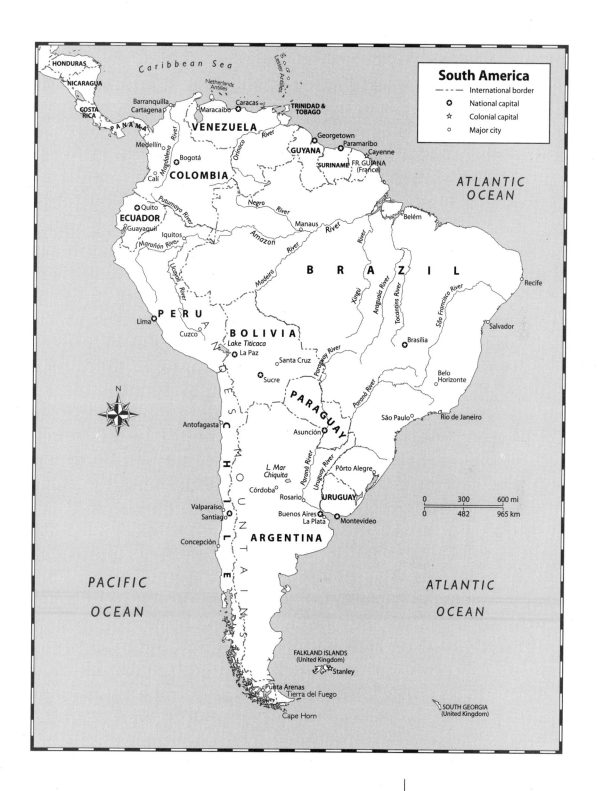

Caribbean Sea

HONDURAS

NICARAGUA

COSTA RICA

P A N A M A

Netherlands Antilles

Lesser Antilles

South America
- - - International border
⊛ National capital
☆ Colonial capital
○ Major city

Barranquilla
Cartagena

Maracaibo

Caracas

TRINIDAD & TOBAGO

VENEZUELA

Medellín

Bogotá

Magdalena River

Orinoco River

Georgetown

Paramaribo

Cayenne

GUYANA

SURINAME

FR. GUIANA (France)

Cali

COLOMBIA

ATLANTIC OCEAN

Quito

Putumayo River

ECUADOR

Guayaquil

Iquitos

Marañón River

Negro River

Manaus

Amazon River

River

Belém

Ucayali River

Modero River

B R A Z I L

Recife

PERU

Xingú

Araguaia River

Tocantins River

São Francisco River

Lima

Cuzco

BOLIVIA

Lake Titicaca

La Paz

Santa Cruz

Sucre

Brasília

Salvador

Belo Horizonte

A N D E S

PARAGUAY

Paraguay River

Paraná River

Antofagasta

L. Mar Chiquita

Asunción

São Paulo

Rio de Janeiro

M O U N T A I N S

Paraná River

Uruguay River

Pôrto Alegre

URUGUAY

Córdoba

Rosario

0   300   600 mi
0   482   965 km

Valparaíso

Santiago

Buenos Aires

La Plata

Montevideo

Concepción

ARGENTINA

N

PACIFIC

OCEAN

ATLANTIC

OCEAN

FALKLAND ISLANDS (United Kingdom)

Stanley

Punta Arenas

Tierra del Fuego

SOUTH GEORGIA (United Kingdom)

Cape Horn

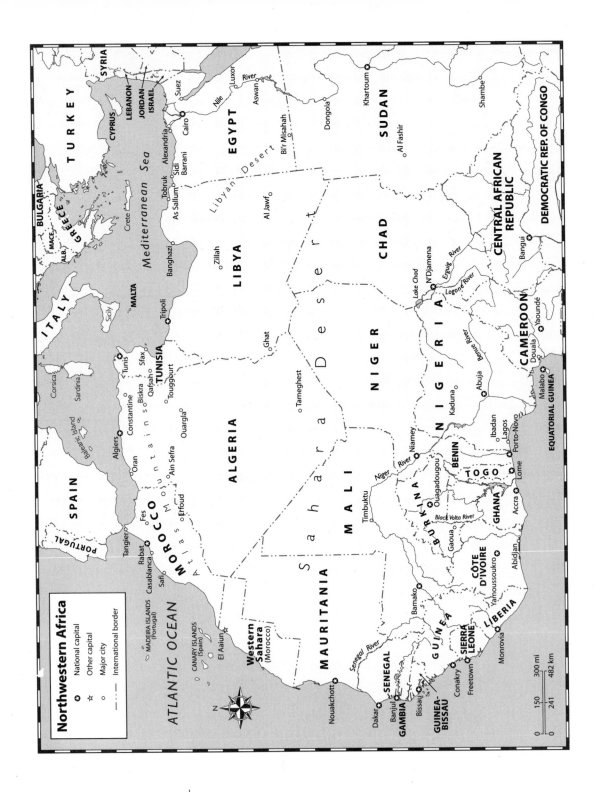

Northwestern Africa

✪ National capital
☆ Other capital
○ Major city
—·—·— International border

ATLANTIC OCEAN

Mediterranean Sea

PORTUGAL
SPAIN
ITALY
MALTA
GREECE
BULGARIA
MACE.
ALB.
TURKEY
SYRIA
LEBANON
CYPRUS
JORDAN
ISRAEL

Corsica
Sardinia
Sicily
Crete
Balearic Island

MADEIRA ISLANDS
(Portugal)

CANARY ISLANDS
(Spain)

El Aaiun

Western
Sahara
(Morocco)

MOROCCO
Tangier
Rabat
Casablanca
Safi
Fes
Effoud
Atlas Mountains

Oran
Algiers
Constantine
Ain Sefra
Ouargla
Tunis
Sfax
Qafsah
Touggourt
Biskra
TUNISIA

Tripoli
Banghazi
Zillah
Ghat

LIBYA

Sahara Desert

Libyan Desert

Tobruk
As Sallum
Sidi
Barrani
Alexandria
Cairo
Suez
Nile
Luxor
River
Aswan
Bir Misahah
Al Jawf

EGYPT

Khartoum
Dongola
Al Fashir
Shambe

SUDAN

ALGERIA

Tamenghest

MALI
MAURITANIA

Nouakchott
Dakar
SENEGAL
Banjul
GAMBIA
Bissau
GUINEA-
BISSAU
Conakry
GUINEA
Freetown
SIERRA
LEONE
Monrovia
LIBERIA
Bamako
Gaoua
Abidjan
CÔTE
D'IVOIRE
Yamoussoukro

Timbuktu

Senegal River

Niger River

NIGER

Niamey
BURKINA
Ouagadougou
GHANA
Accra
TOGO
Lome
BENIN
Porto-Novo
Black Volta River

NIGERIA
Kaduna
Abuja
Ibadan
Lagos

CHAD
N'Djamena
Lake Chad
Erguig River
Logone River
Benue River

CAMEROON
Douala
Yaoundé
Malabo
EQUATORIAL GUINEA

CENTRAL AFRICAN
REPUBLIC
Bangui

DEMOCRATIC REP. OF CONGO

N

0   150   300 mi
0   241   482 km

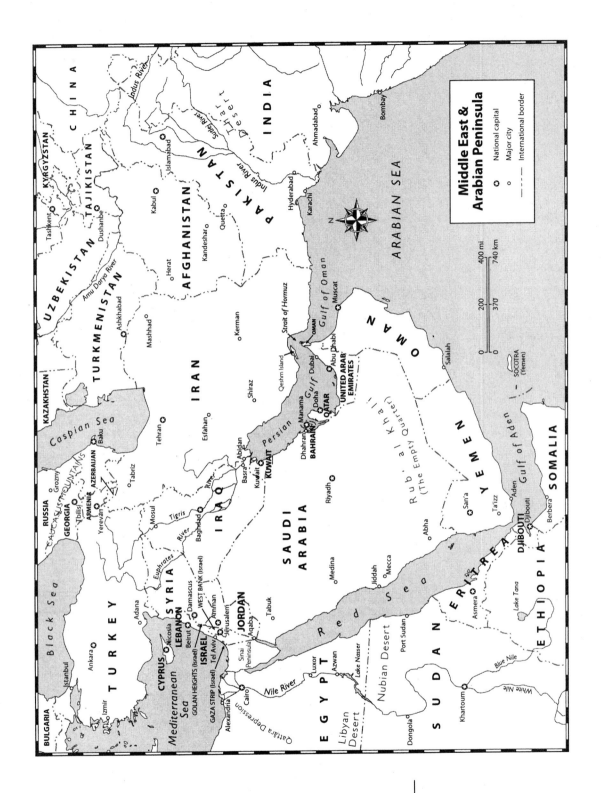

Middle East & Arabian Peninsula

⊕ National capital
○ Major city
–·–·– International border

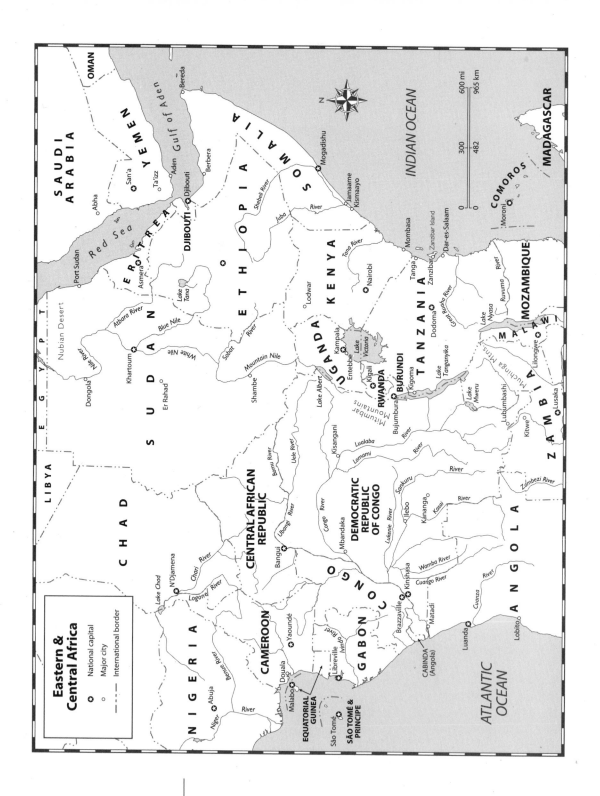

Eastern & Central Africa

✠ National capital
○ Major city
–·–·– International border

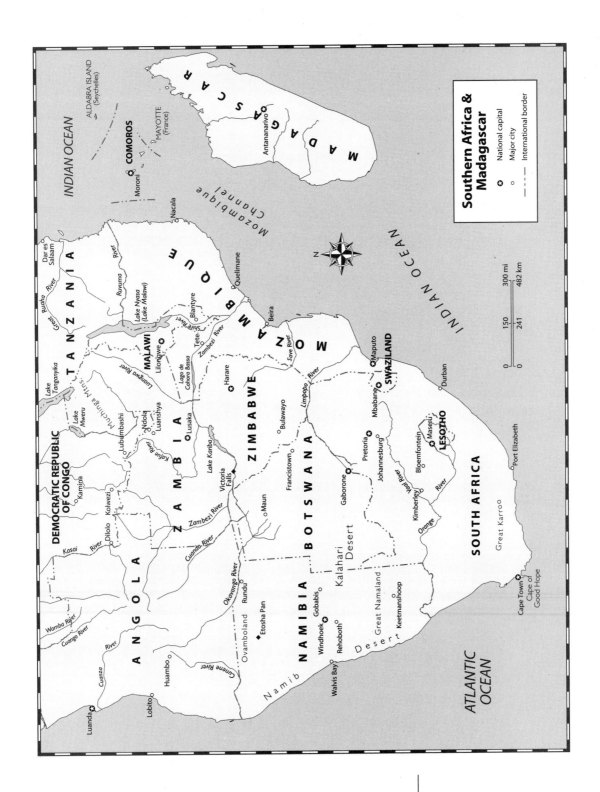

Southern Africa & Madagascar

✪ National capital
○ Major city
–··– International border

| 0 | 150 | 300 mi |
| 0 | 241 | 482 km |

INDIAN OCEAN

ALDABRA ISLAND (Seychelles)

COMOROS
Moroni ✪

MAYOTTE (France)

MADAGASCAR
Antananarivo ✪

Mozambique Channel

TANZANIA
Dar es Salaam ○
Great Ruaha River
Ruvuma River
Lake Tanganyika

DEMOCRATIC REPUBLIC OF CONGO
Kamijna ○
Kasai River
Wamba River

ANGOLA
Luanda ✪
Lobito ○
Huambo ○
Cuanza River
Cuango River
Cunene River

ZAMBIA
Lusaka ✪
Ndola ○
Luanshya ○
Lubumbashi ○
Dilolo ○
Kolwezi ○
Lake Mweru
Kafue River
Luangwa River
Muchinga Mtns.
Lake Kariba
Zambezi River
Cuando River
Okavango River

MALAWI
Lilongwe ✪
Lake Nyasa (Lake Malawi)
Shire River

MOZAMBIQUE
Nacala ○
Quelimane ○
Blantyre ○
Beira ○
Tete ○
Lago de Cahora Bassa
Save River
Limpopo River

ZIMBABWE
Harare ✪
Bulawayo ○
Francistown ○
Victoria Falls
Zambezi River

NAMIBIA
Windhoek ✪
Walvis Bay ○
Rundu ○
Gobabis ○
Rehoboth ○
Keetmanshoop ○
Etosha Pan ◆
Ovamboland
Namib Desert
Great Namaland
Kalahari Desert

BOTSWANA
Gaborone ✪
Maun ○

SOUTH AFRICA
Pretoria ✪
Johannesburg ○
Bloemfontein ✪
Kimberley ○
Durban ○
Port Elizabeth ○
Cape Town ✪
Cape of Good Hope
Great Karroo
Vaal River
Orange River

SWAZILAND
Mbabane ✪
Maputo ✪

LESOTHO
Maseru ✪

INDIAN OCEAN

ATLANTIC OCEAN

N

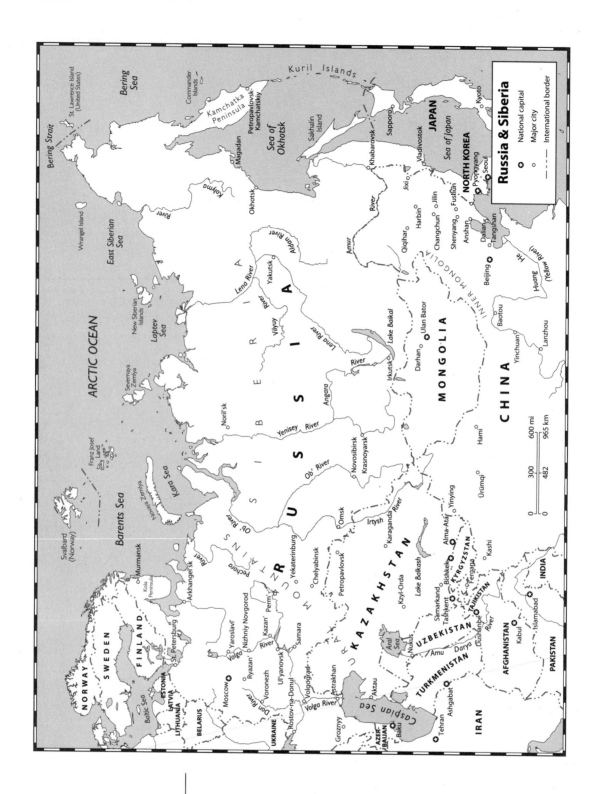

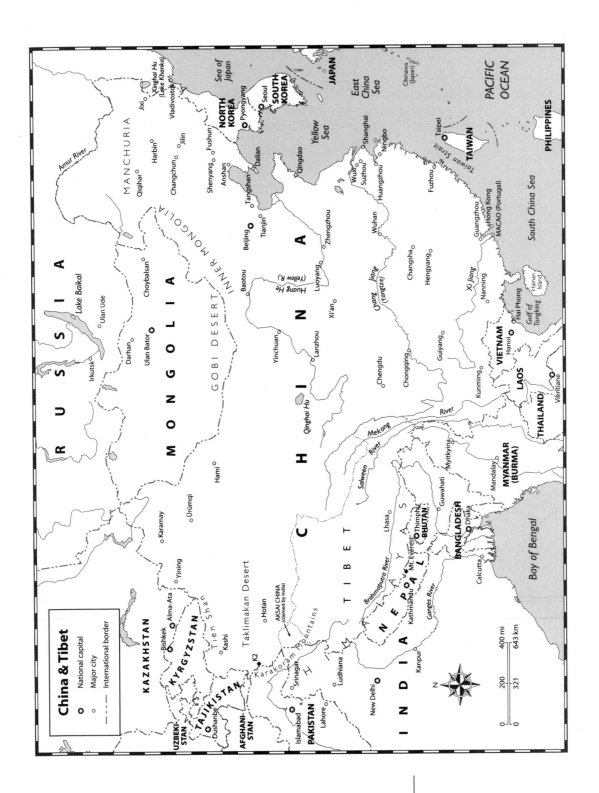

China & Tibet

- ⊕ National capital
- ○ Major city
- --- International border

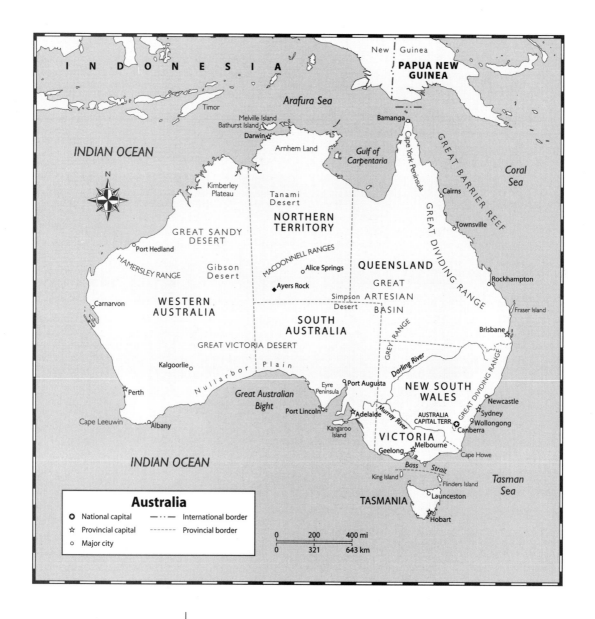

INDONESIA

New Guinea

PAPUA NEW GUINEA

Arafura Sea

Timor

Melville Island
Bathurst Island

Darwin

Bamanga

Cape York Peninsula

INDIAN OCEAN

Arnhem Land

Gulf of Carpentaria

GREAT BARRIER REEF

Coral Sea

Kimberley Plateau

Tanami Desert

NORTHERN TERRITORY

Cairns

GREAT SANDY DESERT

GREAT DIVIDING RANGE

Townsville

Port Hedland

HAMERSLEY RANGE

Gibson Desert

MACDONNELL RANGES

Alice Springs

QUEENSLAND

Rockhampton

Ayers Rock

GREAT ARTESIAN BASIN

Carnarvon

WESTERN AUSTRALIA

Simpson Desert

Fraser Island

SOUTH AUSTRALIA

Brisbane

GREAT VICTORIA DESERT

GREY RANGE

Kalgoorlie

Darling River

NEW SOUTH WALES

Nullarbor Plain

Perth

Eyre Peninsula

Port Augusta

Newcastle

Great Australian Bight

Port Lincoln

AUSTRALIA CAPITAL TERR.

Sydney
Wollongong
Canberra

GREAT DIVIDING RANGE

Cape Leeuwin

Albany

Kangaroo Island

Adelaide

Murray River

Cape Howe

INDIAN OCEAN

VICTORIA

Geelong

Melbourne

Bass Strait

Tasman Sea

King Island

Flinders Island

TASMANIA

Launceston

Hobart

Australia

✪ National capital
☆ Provincial capital
○ Major city

– · – · – International border
– – – – Provincial border

| 0 | 200 | 400 mi |
| 0 | 321 | 643 km |

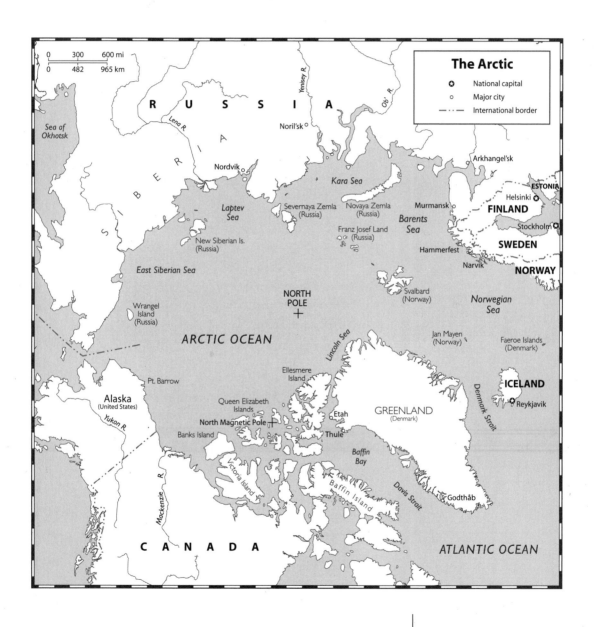

The Arctic

- National capital
- Major city
- International border

0   300   600 mi
0   482   965 km

RUSSIA

Sea of
Okhotsk

S I B E R I A

Lena R.

Yenisey R.

Ob' R.

Noril'sk

Nordvik

Kara Sea

Arkhangel'sk

ESTONIA
Helsinki
FINLAND

Laptev
Sea

Severnaya Zemla
(Russia)

Novaya Zemla
(Russia)

Murmansk

Barents
Sea

Stockholm

New Siberian Is.
(Russia)

Franz Josef Land
(Russia)

SWEDEN

East Siberian Sea

Hammerfest

Narvik

NORWAY

Svalbard
(Norway)

Norwegian
Sea

Wrangel
Island
(Russia)

NORTH
POLE

ARCTIC OCEAN

Jan Mayen
(Norway)

Faeroe Islands
(Denmark)

Lincoln Sea

Pt. Barrow

Ellesmere
Island

ICELAND

Alaska
(United States)

Queen Elizabeth
Islands

Etah

GREENLAND
(Denmark)

Reykjavik

Yukon R.

North Magnetic Pole

Thule

Denmark Strait

Banks Island

Baffin
Bay

Mackenzie R.

Victoria Island

Baffin Island

Davis Strait

Godthåb

C A N A D A

ATLANTIC OCEAN

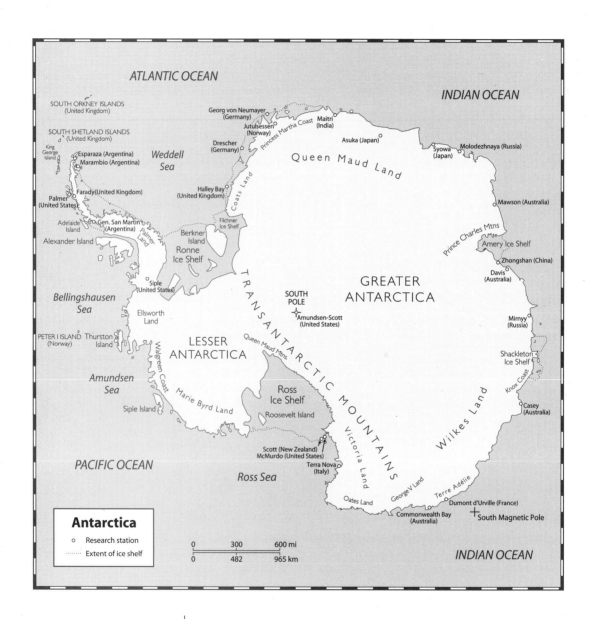

ATLANTIC OCEAN

INDIAN OCEAN

SOUTH ORKNEY ISLANDS
(United Kingdom)

Georg von Neumayer
(Germany)
Jutulsessen
(Norway)

Maitri
(India)

SOUTH SHETLAND ISLANDS
(United Kingdom)

Princess Martha Coast

Drescher
(Germany)

Asuka (Japan)

Syowa
(Japan)

Molodezhnaya (Russia)

King
George
Island

Esparaza (Argentina)
Marambio (Argentina)

Weddell
Sea

Queen Maud Land

Faraday (United Kingdom)

Halley Bay
(United Kingdom)

Mawson (Australia)

Coats Land

Palmer
(United States)

Prince Charles Mtns

Adelaide
Island

Gen. San Martín
(Argentina)

Filchner
Ice Shelf

Amery Ice Shelf

Alexander Island

Palmer
Land

Berkner
Island
Ronne
Ice Shelf

Zhongshan (China)

Davis
(Australia)

Siple
(United States)

GREATER
ANTARCTICA

Bellingshausen
Sea

SOUTH
POLE

Ellsworth
Land

Amundsen-Scott
(United States)

Mirnyy
(Russia)

PETER I ISLAND
(Norway)

Thurston
Island

LESSER
ANTARCTICA

Queen Maud Mtns.

Shackleton
Ice Shelf

Amundsen
Sea

Walgreen Coast

Marie Byrd Land

Ross
Ice Shelf

Knox Coast

Siple Island

Roosevelt Island

Wilkes Land

Casey
(Australia)

Scott (New Zealand)
McMurdo (United States)

Terra Nova
(Italy)

Victoria Land

PACIFIC OCEAN

Ross Sea

Oates Land

George V Land

Terre Adélie

Dumont d'Urville (France)

South Magnetic Pole

Commonwealth Bay
(Australia)

INDIAN OCEAN

Antarctica

o   Research station

......   Extent of ice shelf

0	300	600 mi
0	482	965 km

EXPLORERS & DISCOVERERS

Carl Johan Andersson

Born 1827, Vänersborg, Sweden

Died July 7, 1867, Ondangwa, Namibia

C arl Johan Andersson was born in 1827 in the town of Vänersborg in Sweden. His father, Llewellyn Lloyd, was a hunter and author who was a native of Wales. His mother, Kajsa Andersdotter, was a Swedish farm woman. Because his parents never married, Carl used a version of his mother's family name as his surname.

Swedish explorer, hunter, and amateur naturalist Carl Johan Andersson was the first European to visit many areas of northern Namibia and Botswana.

Decides to travel to Africa

In 1847 Andersson entered the University of Lund in Sweden to study zoology. He was forced to leave after a year, however, because of financial difficulties. So, like his father, he became a professional hunter, working in Sweden. After two years, he decided to travel to Africa, to try his luck hunting more exotic animals. In order to finance his trip there, Andersson went to England, where he sold some zoological specimens and two live bears he had captured.

While in England, Andersson met Francis Galton (1822–1911), an English hunter and amateur scientist. Andersson decided to travel with Galton, who planned to go to the southwest coast of Africa and then proceed inland to Lake Ngami, in the hopes of opening up a trade route along the way. Located deep in the heart of southern Africa—in what is now Botswana—the lake had been discovered with great difficulty by Scottish missionary and explorer David Livingstone (1813–73) in 1849.

Andersson's first attempt to find Lake Ngami fails

Andersson and Galton arrived at Walvis Bay—the only natural harbor on the coast of what is now Namibia—at the end of 1850. From there they set out by wagon, planning to reach Lake Ngami by making their way east across the Kalahari Desert. They traveled through the Okahandja region of present-day Namibia before hostile tribes forced them to alter their course and head in a more northerly direction. This took them to the land of the Ovambos, a tribe that had never before been visited by Europeans. (Today, the Ovambos comprise the largest ethnic group in Namibia.) Andersson and Galton stopped at the artesian wells (underground water that flows naturally to the surface) located at the eastern end of a swamp area called the Etosha Pan. On May 26, 1851, they came to the town of Tsumeb, and found they could go no farther. So they turned around and headed back to the coast.

During the winter of 1851 Andersson and Galton set out on another expedition. They headed east, reaching the site of Windhoek—the present-day capital of Namibia—on August 30, 1851. They made their way as far as the western edge of the Kalahari Desert, to the town of Gobabis, before heading back to the coast. Upon their return, Galton decided to leave Africa. But before he departed for England in 1852 he offered Andersson financial support so that the Swede could continue his explorations.

Reaches destination alone

After Galton left, Andersson ventured into the African interior alone. In April of 1853 he reached Namibia's Nossob River, and then continued on to Gobabis. This time he did not stop, but proceeded through the Kalahari Desert, reaching the western shores of Lake Ngami by the end of June. He spent several weeks there, collecting biological specimens and studying the customs of the local Tswana tribe.

Andersson traveled back to Walvis Bay and then on to Cape Town in what is now the Republic of South Africa, where he presented his biological specimens to the local museum. He also became engaged to a woman named Sarah Jane Aitchison, whose brother was postmaster-general of the territory, then called British Cape Province. While in Cape Town, Andersson received word that his father was ill, so he set out

The Kalahari Desert. Carl Johan Andersson and Francis Galton made their way across the great desert on their search for Lake Ngami.

to Sweden to see him. Along the way, in November of 1854, the explorer stopped in London and gave a lecture to the Royal Geographical Society about his successful venture to Lake Ngami. There Andersson was introduced to the great English naturalist Charles Darwin (1809–82), to whom he presented his notes about his African expedition.

Discovers Okavango River

In 1857, following the recovery of his father, Andersson returned to southern Africa. For a while he ran a mine at Walvis Bay, but when it failed he turned to exploring again. In 1859 he traveled north in an attempt to reach the Cunene River, which now forms the boundary between Angola and Namibia. Along the way he became the first European to see and describe the course of the Okavango River, which flows eastward before it seems to disappear into a large marshy depression (which was once a prehistoric lake). Called the Okavango Basin, the swamp is today located in northern Botswana. While traveling along the shore of the Okavango River, Andersson was gored in the thigh by a rhinoceros. This injury forced him to stay in camp for several months to recuperate.

Leads battle between native tribes

Following his recovery, Andersson traveled back to Cape Town, where he married Aitchison in July of 1860. He and his wife then moved to Namibia, where the explorer worked in the ivory and cattle trade and supplied elephant hunters with provisions. While living in northern Namibia, Andersson became friends with members of the local Herero tribe and eventually was made a chief. When the Namas—an enemy tribe that lived farther south—raided the Herero village, the explorer led his friends in combat on June 6, 1864. In the fight that became known as "Andersson's Battle," the Hereros emerged victorious. Andersson was badly wounded—hit by five bullets, one of them smashing his right leg below the knee. It took nine months before he could travel again. During his convalescence, the one-time zoology student made a com-

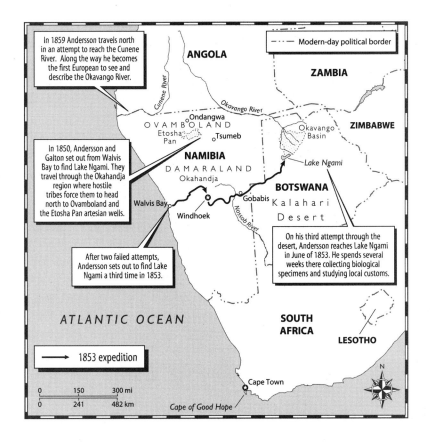

In 1859 Andersson travels north in an attempt to reach the Cunene River. Along the way he becomes the first European to see and describe the Okavango River.

Modern-day political border

ANGOLA

ZAMBIA

ZIMBABWE

In 1850, Andersson and Galton set out from Walvis Bay to find Lake Ngami. They travel through the Okahandja region where hostile tribes force them to head north to Ovamboland and the Etosha Pan artesian wells.

OVAMBOLAND
Ondangwa
Etosha Pan
Tsumeb

NAMIBIA

DAMARALAND
Okahandja

Okavango Basin

Lake Ngami

BOTSWANA
Kalahari Desert

Walvis Bay
Gobabis
Windhoek

On his third attempt through the desert, Andersson reaches Lake Ngami in June of 1853. He spends several weeks there collecting biological specimens and studying local customs.

After two failed attempts, Andersson sets out to find Lake Ngami a third time in 1853.

ATLANTIC OCEAN

SOUTH AFRICA

LESOTHO

1853 expedition

0   150   300 mi
0   241   482 km

Cape Town
Cape of Good Hope

prehensive scientific study of the birds of Damaraland in central Namibia.

Andersson and his wife left Namibia in May of 1865, traveling to Europe to get medical advice about his badly damaged leg. But he decided not to undergo surgery there, and returned to Cape Town, where he stayed at his brother-in-law's seaside home for a while, still recuperating. There he compiled a scientific catalog describing the birds of Namibia. Although not fully recovered, he left Cape Town in May of 1866, traveling to Walvis Bay and then north into the Namibian interior to collect and sell ivory, cattle, and ostrich feathers. While well-supplied with goods after successful trading, Andersson lost some of his property during a raid by Nama warriors. This may have led to his decision to travel farther north—beyond the Cunene River—to trade with the Portuguese who had settled in what would become the country of

Angola. Along the way Andersson became ill from his old wounds and died at the village of Ondangwa in northern Namibia on July 7, 1867.

Specimen collection proves valuable

The specimens of birds and other animals that Andersson had collected during his time in Africa were sent to museums in Europe and South Africa. They provided valuable information about the animal life of Namibia and inspired further scientific studies. He discovered several previously unknown bird species, which were named in his honor. Included among them is the lark *Tephrocorys anderssoni*.

Sources

Baker, Daniel B., ed. *Explorers and Discoverers of the World.* Detroit: Gale Research, 1993.

Explorers and Exploration, Volume 8: *Africa and Arabia,* written by Geoffrey Nowell-Smith. Danbury, CT: Grolier Educational, 1998.

William Balfour Baikie

Born August 27, 1825,
Kirkwall, Orkney Islands, Scotland

Died December 12, 1864, Sierra Leone

The history of Great Britain's exploration of Africa's great western river—the Niger—is one of extreme hardship. Rising in present-day Guinea near the Sierra Leone border, the river sweeps in a giant curve through what is now Mali and Nigeria where it forms a huge inland delta (a large triangular area where a river divides before it enters a larger body of water), full of channels and inland lakes, before it empties into the Gulf of Guinea and the Atlantic Ocean. One of the greatest challenges explorers of the Niger faced was the unhealthy climate of its vast, swampy delta. During the first half of the nineteenth century, countless sailors died as they tried to make their way up the river, usually victims of the ravages of malaria, a parasitic disease carried by infected mosquitos.

William Balfour Baikie, a naval doctor who led an expedition up the Niger in 1854, markedly improved the future of British exploration on the river. His use of the drug quinine to prevent and treat malaria made travel on the Niger less deadly.

William Balfour Baikie was a Scottish naval doctor who led an expedition up the Niger River. He later repeated his river journey, and became the first European to set up permanent headquarters in the interior of West Africa.

He helped turn the river into a navigable trade route that—along with its tributaries—reached far into the continent's western interior. Later, he would set up trading posts along the river and live at one of them, becoming the first British settler in West Africa. Great Britain would subsequently increase its presence in the region, eventually controlling trade on the Niger River and taking possession of territories that now comprise the country of Nigeria.

The son of a British naval officer, Baikie was born on August 27, 1825, in the Orkney Islands off the northern coast of Scotland. He attended the University of Edinburgh, studying foreign languages, the natural sciences, and medicine. He graduated with a medical degree in 1848, and—like his father—joined the Royal Navy.

Baikie served as an assistant surgeon on a Royal Navy ship. He was then assigned to a hospital in London. Eager to get back to sea, he asked to join an expedition to the Niger, then being planned by the British Foreign Office. He was granted the position of expedition physician and naturalist, under the command of John Beecroft (1790–1854), a British official and veteran Niger River traveler who was living on the British-occupied island of Fernando Po in Africa's Gulf of Guinea.

Leads successful expedition up Niger River

In 1854 Baikie made his way to Fernando Po aboard the *Pleiad,* a specially designed boat that was both a sailing ship and a steam-driven riverboat. He arrived on the island to find Beecroft dead, and command of the expedition was transferred to Baikie. He headed up the Niger River in June of 1854 with a crew of twelve Europeans and fifty-four Africans. The expedition's assignment was to make contact with British-sponsored German explorer Heinrich Barth (1821–65)—who was somewhere on the upper Niger River, having traveled there by way of the Sahara Desert—and to conduct trade on the river.

By giving regular doses of quinine to himself and his men, Baikie lost no crew members during the four months he traveled the Niger, a staggering accomplishment at that time.

Although the plant from which the drug is extracted—the cinchona tree—had been discovered in South America by Spanish explorers three centuries earlier, using quinine to prevent or treat the devastating fevers contracted in tropical climates had only recently been tried. With a healthy crew, Baikie was able to sail easily up the Niger and conduct successful trading at native villages along the way; at one stop he bought 620 pounds of ivory in one day. The *Pleiad* traveled to what is now central Nigeria, to the place where the Niger is joined by its main tributary, the Benue River.

Baikie found no traces of Barth, who had by that time headed west to the great trade center of Timbuktu and then had continued through the Sahara Desert to Tripoli on Africa's northern coast. But the Scotsman continued to travel up the Niger, proceeding 250 miles farther than any other previous expedition before heading back. The *Pleiad* returned to England in February of 1855. While Baikie had not been completely successful in his mission (for he had not met up with the German explorer Barth), he had managed to acquire a valuable cargo of ivory. Better yet, through his pioneering health practices, he had made it possible to travel the Niger without the devastating loss of lives. Through his efforts, Africa's western interior was at last open to British trade and settlement.

German explorer Heinrich Barth. Baikie's assignment in 1854 was to locate Barth somewhere on the upper Niger River and to trade with his expedition.

Heads second river journey

It was not long before the British Foreign Office planned a return trip to the Niger River to establish Great Britain's presence in the area. Baikie was chosen to head another Niger expedition, commanding the steamship *Dayspring*. He sailed from Liverpool, England, and arrived at the mouth of the Niger in May of 1857. His mission was to set up trading stations along the banks of the river.

Elephant tusks–a valuable cargo of ivory–ready for shipping. Baikie and his expedition gathered large amounts of ivory during their journey along the Niger.

At the Niger's mouth, Baikie established a trading station which he called Lairdsport, leaving eight of his men there to run it. He then proceeded up the river, to the spot where the Benue joins the Niger. There he spent three weeks setting up another trading station, which would come to be known as Lokoja. With these posts, the British would be able to access the city of Kano, the most important trading center in Africa's western interior (in what is now north-central Nigeria). Up until that time, the city had only been reached from the north, by way of a Sahara caravan, in a journey that took more than fourteen months. From Lokoja, the trip would require just thirty days.

Boat accident strands expedition members

From Lokoja, the *Dayspring* continued up the Niger for another 300 miles. But on October 7, 1857, it ran into a hidden rock in the river and was wrecked. The expedition—which consisted of Baikie, fifteen Europeans, and thirty-eight Africans—was stranded on the east bank of the Niger for 364 days. When a British relief vessel finally arrived to pick the travelers up, all were still alive. This showed that Europeans could actually live in the steamy tropics of West Africa if proper health practices were followed.

During the time that they were stranded, Lieutenant J. H. Glover, Baikie's second-in-command, explored some 700 miles of the lower Niger River region, traveling by canoe. He reached the Bussa rapids where the Scottish explorer Mungo Park (1771–1806)—the first European to discover the Niger River—had died. The lieutenant bought Park's nautical almanac from the chief of a nearby village. (The almanac is now in the museum of Great Britain's Royal Geographical Society in London.)

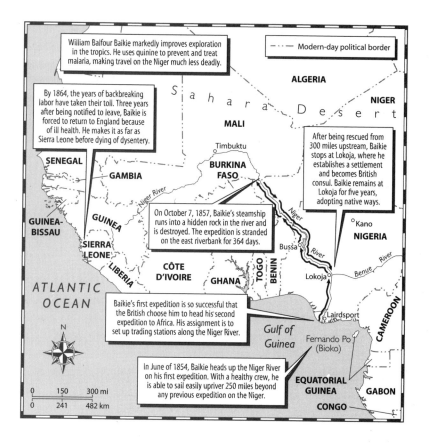

Modern-day political border

William Balfour Baikie markedly improves exploration in the tropics. He uses quinine to prevent and treat malaria, making travel on the Niger much less deadly.

By 1864, the years of backbreaking labor have taken their toll. Three years after being notified to leave, Baikie is forced to return to England because of ill health. He makes it as far as Sierra Leone before dying of dysentery.

After being rescued from 300 miles upstream, Baikie stops at Lokoja, where he establishes a settlement and becomes British consul. Baikie remains at Lokoja for five years, adopting native ways.

On October 7, 1857, Baikie's steamship runs into a hidden rock in the river and is destroyed. The expedition is stranded on the east riverbank for 364 days.

Baikie's first expedition is so successful that the British choose him to head his second expedition to Africa. His assignment is to set up trading stations along the Niger River.

In June of 1854, Baikie heads up the Niger River on his first expedition. With a healthy crew, he is able to sail easily upriver 250 miles beyond any previous expedition on the Niger.

Establishes first British settlement in West African interior

The relief vessel sailed back down the Niger and Baikie disembarked at Lokoja, where he went to work establishing a settlement and became British consul of the area. Through him, Great Britain had made its first official claim over the Niger River region and its first move toward colonization. Baikie remained at the settlement for five years, adopting native ways. He lived in a mud hut, set up house with a local woman, and had several children. He cleared 100 acres of farmland and often worked fourteen-hour days. He studied the region's animal and plant life, and raised native species on his farm. He also studied local languages and dialects, translating the Bible's Book of Genesis and the Anglican Book of Common Prayer into Hausa, the predominant language of West Africa.

Lokoja was located in an area that still had an active slave trade. During his stay there, Baikie did what he could to try to stop the practice. He often bought slaves himself in order to free them, or gave refuge to captives who had escaped. These activities, of course, angered local slave traders, and Baikie sometimes went months without supplies when hostile natives stopped riverboats from reaching him. The Scotsman even went so far as to ask the British Foreign Office for a gunboat to patrol the river, but the request was refused. Conditions improved, however, when Baikie befriended the Emir of Nupe—a powerful local chief—and later became his political advisor. The threats from slave traders stopped then and, after that, Lokoja prospered.

In 1861, the British Foreign Office decided to have Baikie return home, for his mission of establishing inland trading posts on the Niger was complete. The order did not reach Lokoja for a year, however, and even then Baikie delayed his departure for another two years, unwilling to leave the settlement that he had worked so hard to develop. But by 1864 the years of backbreaking labor had taken their toll, and ill health forced Baikie to return to England. He left Lokoja in October on a paddle-steamer that had brought a new British official to serve as consul there. Baikie made it as far as Sierra Leone on the west coast of Africa before he died of dysentery on December 12, 1864. His journal, filled with valuable information collected during his years as a settler in the African interior, was sent on to England. Great Britain's Queen Victoria (1819–1901) wrote a personal letter to the Emir of Nupe to inform him of Baikie's death and to ask for the emir's continued assistance in putting an end to the slave trade in West Africa.

Sources

Baker, Daniel B., ed. *Explorers and Discoverers of the World.* Detroit: Gale Research, 1993.

Gramont, Sanche de. *The Strong Brown God: The Story of the Niger River.* Boston: Houghton Mifflin, 1976.

Perham, Margery and J. Simmons. *African Discovery: An Anthology of Exploration.* Chicago: Northwestern University Press, 1963, reprint, 1971.

Waldman, Carl and Alan Wexler. *Who Was Who in World Exploration.* New York: Facts on File, 1992.

Daisy Bates

Born October 16, 1859, Tipperary County, Ireland

Died April 18, 1951, Adelaide, South Australia

Irish-born Daisy Bates was a self-taught anthropologist who spent much of her life living among western Australia's native Aborigines, studying and recording their disappearing way of life.

Before the arrival of British settlers in Australia, its native inhabitants—the Aborigines—led a simple existence. They wandered from place to place, living off the land by hunting, gathering plants, and digging up roots for food. They gathered boughs from bushes and trees to make simple shelters, or slept in dug-out hollows in the ground. Their social structure and religious practices were surprisingly complex, however—rich with legends, rituals, and customs. Some 300,000 Aborigines, living in different tribes, were believed to exist in Australia before British colonization.

The coming of Western civilization in the early 1800s radically changed the Aboriginal way of life. The settlers fenced in the land, and cattle and sheep grazed the grasslands, eliminating native hunting and food-gathering grounds. Aborigines who did not obey the laws that governed the new colonies were dealt with harshly, and their numbers were threatened by the new diseases that Europeans brought to their shores. At that time, Australia's Aborigines were considered the most primitive type of human—with few rights—and they were often exploited and made to perform the most menial tasks under terrible conditions.

In 1899 Daisy Bates, a British citizen and journalist who had lived in Australia, read reports in the London *Times* describing cruel treatment of Aborigines by western Australian settlers. Already planning a return trip to Australia, she offered to investigate the situation for the *Times* and report her findings. Thus her lifelong work began, studying the various native tribes of western Australia. Bates would eventually live among them, observing their way of life, learning their languages, and witnessing their secret ceremonies. She would marvel at ingenious Aboriginal methods of survival in the difficult environment. Bates wanted to gather as much information about the indigenous culture as she could, because she had little hope for its survival. Even when British settlers treated the Aborigines with kindness—establishing missions, schools, and hospitals for them—their ancient way of life was slowly being destroyed.

Bates was born Daisy May O'Dwyer on October 16, 1859, in the Irish county of Tipperary. She was one of many children born into a Catholic family. Both of her parents died before she reached the age of five, and she and her siblings were left in the care of relatives in rural Ireland, which was still recovering from the ravages of the great famine that had occurred two decades earlier. When she was nine, she was sent to England for a time to live with the widow of an Anglican clergyman. After returning to Ireland she completed her education. It is believed that she then worked as a governess in England for several years. (Because Bates always presented herself as an upper-class Englishwoman—when in reality she wasn't—information about her early life is meager.)

Arrives in Australia

At the age of twenty-one Daisy traveled to Australia for the first time. She had somehow obtained free passage there, and arrived in January of 1883 at Townsville in north Queensland. She worked as a governess in the town of Charters Tow-

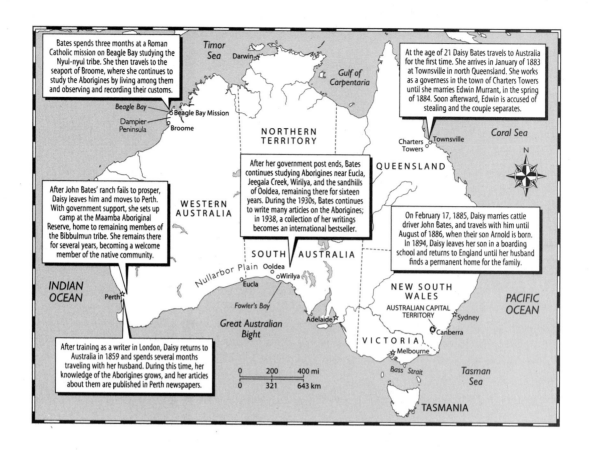

Bates spends three months at a Roman Catholic mission on Beagle Bay studying the Nyul-nyul tribe. She then travels to the seaport of Broome, where she continues to study the Aborigines by living among them and observing and recording their customs.

At the age of 21 Daisy Bates travels to Australia for the first time. She arrives in January of 1883 at Townsville in north Queensland. She works as a governess in the town of Charters Towers until she marries Edwin Murrant, in the spring of 1884. Soon afterward, Edwin is accused of stealing and the couple separates.

After John Bates' ranch fails to prosper, Daisy leaves him and moves to Perth. With government support, she sets up camp at the Maamba Aboriginal Reserve, home to remaining members of the Bibbulmun tribe. She remains there for several years, becoming a welcome member of the native community.

After her government post ends, Bates continues studying Aborigines near Eucla, Jeegala Creek, Wirilya, and the sandhills of Ooldea, remaining there for sixteen years. During the 1930s, Bates continues to write many articles on the Aborigines; in 1938, a collection of her writings becomes an international bestseller.

On February 17, 1885, Daisy marries cattle driver John Bates, and travels with him until August of 1886, when their son Arnold is born. In 1894, Daisy leaves her son in a boarding school and returns to England until her husband finds a permanent home for the family.

After training as a writer in London, Daisy returns to Australia in 1859 and spends several months traveling with her husband. During this time, her knowledge of the Aborigines grows, and her articles about them are published in Perth newspapers.

ers until she married another recent immigrant from England, Edwin Murrant, in the spring of 1884. Not long afterward, her husband was accused of stealing, and the couple separated.

On February 17, 1885, Daisy was married again, this time to Australian cattle drover (driver) John Bates, who worked in New South Wales. She traveled with him on his drives until August of 1886, when their son Arnold was born. The couple had no home of their own, and while John continued his roving lifestyle, it is believed that Daisy worked as a governess and companion at homesteads in New South Wales and Tasmania to secure lodgings for herself and her son. Finally in 1894, fed up with the arrangement, she left her son in a boarding school and returned to England. She did not plan to go back to Australia until her husband found a permanent home for their family. During the ten years she spent in Australia struggling to take care of herself and her young son,

Daisy Bates had not shown much interest in the Aborigines (known there as blackfellows).

Trains as a writer

In London, Bates found work in the office of William Thomas Stead (1849–1912), a well-known journalist. When in 1899 she offered her reporting services to the *Times* to investigate Australian Aboriginal exploitation, she had learned enough about the craft to consider herself a "lady journalist." She was already planning to return to Australia, for her husband had recently sent word that he was about to purchase land in western Australia, putting down roots at last.

As luck would have it, on her voyage to Australia Bates met an Italian priest, Dean Martelli, who had spent some time working with the Aborigines of western Australia at a monastery located on Beagle Bay. She learned a great deal about Australia's indigenous people from him. When she arrived at the western seaport of Perth, Bates was reunited with her son and husband, who had bought a cattle ranch in northwestern Australia near the Dampier Peninsula. For the next several months she traveled with John Bates as he acquired cattle for the property, which did not yet have living quarters. During that time her knowledge of Australia's native population grew as she listened to stories told by settlers, or dealt with local Aborigines herself. She investigated the charges of their mistreatment by colonists but could find no evidence of it. She wrote articles about her inquiry, which were published in Perth newspapers.

Fascinated by Aborigines during mission stay

At the completion of their voyage together, Father Martelli had introduced Daisy Bates to the Catholic bishop of Perth, Matthew Gibney. At the bishop's invitation she decided to travel to his mission on Beagle Bay, which ministered to the Aborigines of northwestern Australia. Bates spent three months at the monastery there, getting to know members of the Nyul-nyul tribe and other local Aborigines. The Nyul-

nyuls were a primitive group that engaged in activities that shocked Bates: some wore bones through their noses, they practiced infant cannibalism, and many of the men treated their wives like animals. But Bates tried to push her own Western ideas of what was "right" aside, and think like an Aborigine. She was eager to learn more about the unique beliefs and customs of these strange native people.

Begins field studies of Australia's native inhabitants

Bates next traveled to the northwest seaport of Broome, which was a leading pearl-gathering center. Aborigines from all over journeyed there to work on the pearling luggers (boats). It was an ideal place to learn more about different native tribes and their beliefs. Conveniently, Bates's husband had recently gotten a new job near Broome, managing a cattle station. So, with her own family left in the care of a housekeeper and a cook, Bates would frequently make trips through the countryside around Broome and beyond, camping with the natives she encountered. She was one of the first Aborigine researchers to live among her subjects (engaging in what is called "participant observation"): sometimes she would be gone for days, gathering food with the women, caring for the children, and making friends with the old men, who were her best source of information about what native life was really like before the arrival of Westerners. For, already, many of the old Aboriginal customs had faded.

Bit by bit, Bates's knowledge of Aboriginal life in western Australia grew. She carefully recorded all she learned in notebooks. She compiled a dictionary of various native dialects and she wrote about Aboriginal tools and weapons. She learned about the indigenous diet, and was amazed at the natives' thorough knowledge of the plants and animals on which they subsisted. (Bates partook of some native foods, trying roasted grubs and baked lizards.) The Aborigines of western Australia employed clever methods of hunting and trapping game in their harsh environment. She also learned about na-

tive diseases and their remedies, which sometimes involved the use of plant extracts.

In her notes, Bates also described the complicated social system that defined kinship within families and amongst tribes. She learned how marriages were arranged. She recorded Aboriginal songs, dances, and ceremonies, and came to know native beliefs concerning religion, death, burial, and the hereafter. And—by convincing her male hosts that she was a supernatural being—she was even allowed to witness their secret rituals, from which all women were excluded. For example, she observed how boys were initiated into manhood. Over time, Bates was able to paint a comprehensive picture of Aboriginal life in western Australia, from infancy to old age. (Much of the information contained in her notes would not be published until long after her death: *The Native Tribes of Western Australia,* edited by Isobel White, appeared in 1985.)

Australian Aborigines perform the ¨Corroborree¨–an ancient ceremonial dance. Daisy Bates witnessed many such Aboriginal ceremonies and rituals.

Undertakes government research project

In the meantime, the cattle ranch that John Bates had purchased failed to prosper. Unhappy with her husband's inability to earn a secure living, Daisy Bates finally left him and moved to Perth. There she supported herself by writing for newspapers and other publications. She sometimes lectured on the Aborigines of northwestern Australia. In 1904 the government of western Australia commissioned her to work on an ambitious project: she was to research and write a report on the languages, culture, and social practices of the Aborigines of that state. Because she had no formal training in anthropology, Bates read everything she could about the methods and practices of the science, as well as former studies about Aborigines. In order to gather information, she sent out questionnaires all over the state—to settlers, local government officials, and missionaries.

This method of gathering data, however, proved unsatisfactory to Bates, who realized that she would need to return to field research if she was to get the information that she wanted. With government support she set up camp at the Maamba Aboriginal Reserve, located outside of Perth. Established in the 1890s, the reserve was home to the remaining members of the Bibbulmun tribe—the largest Aboriginal group in Australia, who had once lived in the Perth area—as well as to other Aborigines of southwestern Australia. Most of these native populations had dispersed, and the reserve was inhabited largely by old men and women. It was from them, Bates knew, that she would find what she wanted: memories of ancient Aboriginal myths, practices, and beliefs that were fast being replaced by Western culture. She would add what she learned from these southern tribes to the knowledge she had already gathered in the northern part of the state.

Work with Aborigines makes personal and professional impact

Bates became a welcome member of the native community in which she lived and worked. She tended the sick, acquiring a reputation as a healer, and secured food for the hungry. Due in part to her anthropological work, interest in western Australia's Aborigines grew, and in 1910 two scientific expeditions arrived in Perth to do field work. Bates accompanied the English expedition (the other was from Sweden) to the northwest part of the state, an area with which she was well acquainted. But the all-male team dismissed her expertise because she was a woman and had no formal training in anthropology. Expedition leader Alfred Reginald Radcliffe-Brown (1881–1955) even suggested that her years of notes be published only as a part of his book. Bates was insulted, and flatly refused.

By 1912 Bates had gathered three full volumes of notes on the Aborigines of western Australia. But by then there had been a change in the state government, and the new officials put an end to her project and dropped plans to publish her work. Bates had counted on its publication to establish her reputation as a professional anthropologist. With her government post gone, she again struggled to support herself with her writings.

Engages in field studies at more native camps

But Bates kept studying the Aborigines. For a while she occupied a friend's home near Eucla, on the southern coast, and came to know the native tribes there. Later she moved to a desolate water hole at Jeegala Creek—living in a tent—so that she could explore Aboriginal life on southern Australia's Nullarbor Plain. After that she stayed at a camp at Wirilya, west of Fowler's Bay. She then moved to the sandhills of Ooldea, near the new transcontinental railway line in western South Australia. Like the pearl industry of Broome, the railway had attracted Aborigines from all over, and Bates found her Ooldea location an excellent place to learn more about various native tribes. She remained there for the next sixteen years, staying in a small tent near a large Aborigine camp. As Bates shared the lives of Australia's indigenous inhabitants, she could observe their culture disintegrating before her eyes. The only way to save it, she thought, was to keep Aborigines in isolation from Western culture—an impossible solution.

Writes autobiographical bestseller

Bates continued to write articles about the Aborigines and what could be done to help them, and published them in newspapers and scientific journals. She lectured in the South Australian city of Adelaide from time to time. Bates was an intriguing figure, always appearing elegantly dressed when she came to town; even in camp, she always wore a prim white blouse and long dark skirt. In 1933 she was invited to Canberra, Australia's capital city, to discuss the future of the Aborigines. A year later she received her greatest honor when she was made a Commander of the British Empire. Soon after, she wrote a series of articles called "My Natives and I," which appeared in Adelaide's leading newspaper, the *Advertiser.* The writings were so popular that they were reprinted in major newspapers throughout Australia and were published in book form in London in 1938. Titled *The Passing of the Aborigines,* the collection became an international bestseller.

In 1941 Bates sold her field notes and other scientific papers—which filled fifty manuscript boxes—to the National Library in Canberra. A few years later she moved to Adelaide. Her health had become frail after decades of living in the bush, and she suffered from malnutrition and periodic blindness. She had few possessions and no savings, having spent most of the money she earned on food and medicine for needy Aborigines. Bates died in 1951 in a rest home in Adelaide.

Sources

Marcus, Julie, ed. *First in Their Field: Women and Australian Anthropology.* "Daisy Bates: Legend and Reality," written by Isobel White. Melbourne: Melbourne University Press, 1993.

Tinling, Marion. *Women Into the Unknown: A Sourcebook on Women Explorers and Travelers.* Westport, CT: Greenwood Press, 1989.

Saint Brendan

Born c. 484, Tralee, County Kerry, Ireland

Died c. 577

During the fifth century Christianity blossomed in Ireland. Until that time it was largely a pagan country, but through the missionary efforts of Saint Patrick—a British Christian who became a monk while in France—and other traveling priests, the island was converted. (Christianity had actually been introduced to the British Isles by the Romans centuries earlier.) Monasteries were founded across Ireland, and from there missionary groups were sent out to further spread the teachings of Christ and the Church of Rome. The first converts were in nearby territories, in places like England and Wales. But the Irish religious (members of a religious order, such as monks) also established Christian communities in France, Germany, and northern Italy. Many monasteries in Ireland kept records of these missionary ventures, giving us valuable information about early Irish explorers.

As the Irish religious looked to continue their missionary efforts, they turned their sights west, toward the forbidding Atlantic Ocean. Although ancient classical writers had described

Saint Brendan was an Irish monk and missionary who made a legendary voyage into the Atlantic Ocean.

beautiful lands located far off in the sea, no Europeans had traveled any farther west than the Madeira Islands, off the northwest coast of Africa. The Atlantic Ocean appeared to extend forever, and few sailors who journeyed beyond the sight of land ever returned. People at that time also had many fearful suspicions that kept them from traveling west: they thought that terrifying monsters inhabited the sea, and—if the world was flat—that they might fall over the edge if they sailed too far. No navigational charts or instruments were available to Europeans at that time. So it was the brave traveler, indeed, who ventured into the vast unknown that was the Atlantic Ocean.

By the sixth century, Irish monks—looking for unknown lands in which to build quiet monastic communities, serve God, and convert the local population—took to the sea. They traveled in simple boats known as curraghs, or coracles: broad, round-bottomed boats with wood or wicker frames, covered with animal hides. While not a sturdy vessel, the curragh maneuvered well in the water, riding lightly above the waves. It could be rowed or sailed. The boat could be built large enough to carry several men, goods, and livestock—all essential for long trips to unknown places.

Performs missionary work in British Isles

Irish monk Brendan rode such a vessel as he traveled on religious missions throughout the British Isles. Born around 484 in Tralee, on the southwest coast of Ireland in County Kerry, he was ordained a priest in 512. He founded a monastery at Ardfert, north of Tralee, and another at Clonfert in Galway, Ireland, around 553, where he served as abbot (monastery head). Historical records show that he also did missionary work in Cornwall (southwest England), Wales, Brittany (northwest France), the Hebrides (islands off the west coast of Scotland), and the Shetland Islands (off Scotland's northern coast).

Undertakes legendary voyage into Atlantic

In several medieval works, most notably the Latin *Navigatio Sancti Brendani* (*The Voyage of St. Brendan*), more exten-

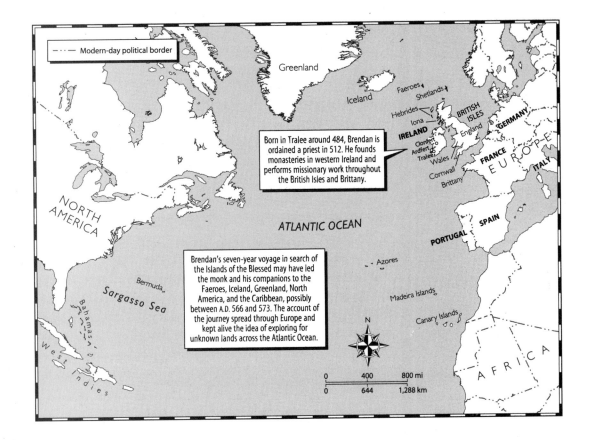

Modern-day political border

Born in Tralee around 484, Brendan is ordained a priest in 512. He founds monasteries in western Ireland and performs missionary work throughout the British Isles and Brittany.

Brendan's seven-year voyage in search of the Islands of the Blessed may have led the monk and his companions to the Faeroes, Iceland, Greenland, North America, and the Caribbean, possibly between A.D. 566 and 573. The account of the journey spread through Europe and kept alive the idea of exploring for unknown lands across the Atlantic Ocean.

sive travels are attributed to the abbot. The *Navigatio,* which is believed to have been written by an Irishman early in the tenth century, tells of the adventures of Brendan and seventeen other monks as they journey in a thirty-foot curragh through the Atlantic Ocean. Supposedly searching for the legendary Islands of the Blessed, which had been described by ancient writers, the travelers visit many strange places and encounter innumerable unusual sights over the course of their seven-year voyage (possibly taking place between 566 and 573).

The account of Brendan and his companions—text meant for religious instruction—is filled with fantastic details that give the journey a mythic quality. However, the *Navigatio* also conveys enough realistic details to intrigue historians, some of whom have worked to identify the real geographical places or odd sights that the abbot and his men encountered. In the *Navigatio,* the travelers come upon islands with giant white sheep and talking birds; these islands may have been the present-day Faeroes, situated in the North Atlantic Ocean between Scotland and Iceland. The pygmies the travelers meet may have been Eskimos off the coast of Greenland. And the remarkable "sea-cats" they observe might well have been walruses.

In the narrative, Brendan and his companions spend five years traveling among the islands of the Atlantic. During that time they are visited every Easter by a friendly whale named Jasconius; and the text describes how they celebrate Easter Sunday mass on the broad back of the whale. The travelers cross a place where the ocean looks like a "thick, curdled mass." This may be a description of the Sargasso Sea, a place in the North Atlantic Ocean that is so still that it is covered by a vast accumulation of floating seaweed. Farther on, the travelers reach large, flat islands surrounded by clear water; these may be the Bahamas. According to the narrative, there the expedition leaves one monk behind—to serve as a missionary for the native population.

Travelers reach destination

The *Navigatio* conveys that Brendan and his companions then sail north, where they soon encounter a large land mass, perhaps the North American continent. The expedition members believe they have reached their destination at last, and they go ashore. After exploring the place for fifteen days, they come upon a large river. There, the *Navigatio* reports, an angel appears to them and tells them that the region's inhabitants will be converted to Christianity at a later time, and that Brendan and his companions are to return to Ireland. The men do as they are instructed. On the voyage home they pass a tall crystal covered with a silver veil. This stunning sight may have been an iceberg, covered by fog.

Voyage inspires future expeditions

During his later years, Brendan worked with Saint Columba, a monk from northern Ireland who had founded a monastery on Iona, a tiny island off the west coast of Scotland. Iona became an important early religious center, for it was used as a base from which Irish missionaries could travel to the British mainland. Word of Brendan's voyage spread throughout Europe, and for many centuries a "St. Brendan's Isle" appeared on medieval maps. However, it was placed at various locations in the Atlantic Ocean: off the west coast of Africa or Portugal, in the West Indies, near Ireland, or beyond Iceland. The most popular modern interpretation of the abbot's travels is that he did, indeed, reach the Western Hemisphere, and landed either on one of the islands of Bermuda in the western Atlantic or on the North American mainland—preceding the arrival of Christopher Columbus (1451–1506) by some 900 years. During the Middle Ages the story of Brendan's journey kept alive the idea that unknown lands lay waiting to be discovered across the Atlantic Ocean. Along with the tales of the Vikings—Scandinavian warriors and sailors who reportedly traveled to Greenland and North America during the ninth, tenth, and eleventh centuries—the legend of Saint Brendan spurred the voyages of European explorers like Columbus during the Age of Discovery. Brendan became known as Brendan the Navigator, the patron saint of sailors.

Christopher Columbus. It is believed that Brendan may have reached the Western Hemisphere, and landed on Bermuda or the North American mainland, long before the famed Italian explorer did in 1492.

Sources

Bohlander, Richard E., ed. *World Explorers and Discoverers.* New York: Macmillan, 1992.

Delpar, Helen, ed. *The Discoverers: An Encyclopedia of Explorers and Exploration.* New York: McGraw-Hill, 1980.

Marshall Cavendish Illustrated Encyclopedia of Discovery and Exploration, Volume 2: *Beyond the Horizon,* written by Malcolm Ross MacDonald, Freeport, NY: Marshall Cavendish, 1990.

Waldman, Carl and Alan Wexler. *Who Was Who in World Exploration.* New York: Facts on File, 1992.

John Byron

Born November 8, 1723, Nottinghamshire, England

Died April 10, 1786, London, England

John Byron was an English naval officer who laid claim to the Falkland Islands for Great Britain and then completed a voyage around the world.

During the eighteenth century, political and commercial rivalries among European nations—including Spain, the Netherlands, Great Britain, and France—led to frequent outbreaks of war. These maritime powers often fought over possession of lands and wealth that still lay unclaimed in little-known parts of the world.

John Byron was a British naval officer whose career reflected these international colonial conflicts. As a young man, he joined a 1740 British expedition sent to attack Spanish territorial possessions in the Pacific; Byron was shipwrecked on the South American coast and suffered five years of hardships trying to make his way home. In 1764, as a British naval commander, Byron led a secret expedition into the South Atlantic Ocean to claim the strategically located Falkland Islands for Great Britain. While near the islands, he passed a French ship pursuing the same mission, and conflicting claims of ownership would involve many nations (the French claim was transferred to Spain, which in turn passed to Argentina) for more than two centuries.

Joins Anson expedition

Byron was born November 8, 1723, on his family's baronial estate, Newstead Abbey, in Nottinghamshire, England. He joined the Royal Navy at a very young age—by fourteen he was an "able seaman" on a government ship that escorted merchant vessels across the Atlantic Ocean, from Lisbon, Portugal, to Newfoundland in North America. At sixteen he was chosen to be midshipman on the *Wager,* a small warship that was part of a British fleet of six ships commanded by Commodore George Anson (1697–1762). At the time, Spain and Great Britain were at war, and Anson's mission was to attack Spanish settlements on the west coast of South America.

Shipwrecked on South American coast

The expedition set sail from England in September of 1740. The six ships reached Cape Horn, on the southern tip of South America, in March of 1741. Because of stormy weather, it took a month for Anson's ships to pass around the cape and into the Pacific Ocean. The waters were so rough that early in the morning on May 14, one of the ships, the *Wager,* was wrecked on the desolate shores of what is now southern Chile.

The *Wager* survivors were stranded in the harsh environment and could find little to eat. By October a desperate group of them—against their captain's orders—decided to take the ship's longboat and try to reach Brazil by sailing east through the Strait of Magellan. Those who stayed behind, including Byron, made their own attempt at escape in December, by sailing north in a small canoe. Unable to make any progress against the heavy seas, the men were forced to return to their camp. There they were finally rescued by a small party of Native Americans who took them to the nearest Spanish settlement, located off the coast at Chiloé Island.

The *Wager* crew stayed on Chiloé until January of 1743, when they were taken to the Spanish colonial seaport of Valparaiso and thrown into prison. From there they were transferred to another colonial port, Santiago, where they were forced to remain until late December of 1744. Byron and his fellow crew members were then shipped to Europe on a French vessel. They finally reached England in March of 1746. A year earlier, Commodore Anson had returned there with a single ship and just 250 of the nearly 2,000 men he had set out with years before. But Anson's expedition had not been a total disaster, for he brought back with him a captured Spanish galleon filled with millions of dollars worth of treasures. Byron wrote about his South American ordeal in *The Narrative of the Honourable John Byron, Containing an Account of the Great Distresses Suffered by Himself and His Companions on the Shores of Patagonia,* which was published in 1746. It was a great literary success.

Because Byron had conducted himself with honor during and after the ill-fated voyage, he was promoted to captain in 1746 and went on to command various ships. He participated in naval actions during the War of Austrian Succession (1740–48) and the Seven Years War (1756–63), during which colonial rivalry between Great Britain and France escalated. In 1758 Byron led an attack that destroyed a French fleet, which was carrying troops and supplies to Quebec City—the capital of New France in North America—which the British had besieged. This and other distinguished military actions earned him the rank of commodore in the British Royal Navy.

Heads expedition into South Atlantic

With peace declared between France and England in 1763, each nation turned to exploration, hoping to discover and lay claim to unknown parts of the world. In 1764 Byron was given command of one such exploratory expedition. Reportedly headed for the East Indies, the expedition's real destination was the South Atlantic. It was believed that a great southern continent, known as Terra Australis, might be found there. Large islands—like the Falklands—were also thought to exist in the region. The European nation that claimed these lands would possess an important base from which to travel to the Pacific, either east by way of Africa's Cape of Good Hope or west around South America's Cape Horn.

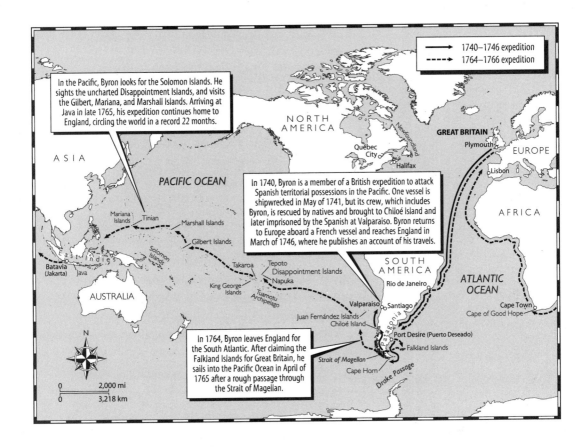

In the Pacific, Byron looks for the Solomon Islands. He sights the uncharted Disappointment Islands, and visits the Gilbert, Mariana, and Marshall Islands. Arriving at Java in late 1765, his expedition continues home to England, circling the world in a record 22 months.

In 1740, Byron is a member of a British expedition to attack Spanish territorial possessions in the Pacific. One vessel is shipwrecked in May of 1741, but its crew, which includes Byron, is rescued by natives and brought to Chiloé Island and later imprisoned by the Spanish at Valparaiso. Byron returns to Europe aboard a French vessel and reaches England in March of 1746, where he publishes an account of his travels.

In 1764, Byron leaves England for the South Atlantic. After claiming the Falkland Islands for Great Britain, he sails into the Pacific Ocean in April of 1765 after a rough passage through the Strait of Magellan.

Byron was further instructed to sail to the west coast of North America, to New Albion (California), which English explorer Sir Francis Drake (c. 1540–96) had discovered in 1578. Byron was then to lead his expedition north to try to find the long-sought-after Northwest Passage—an Arctic sailing route in the Western Hemisphere connecting the Pacific and Atlantic oceans. It was hoped that such a passage might be more easily discovered when approached from the west rather than the east.

In the summer of 1764, Byron left Plymouth, England, with two ships under his command. The frigate *Dolphin* carried a crew of 190 officers and men. The boat was a sturdy vessel, with its hull covered in copper—one of the first of its kind. The second ship, the sloop *Tamar,* had a crew of 115. The expedition reached Rio de Janeiro, the capital of present-day Brazil, and then sailed south along the South American coast. In late

November it stopped at Port Desire in southern Patagonia. Earlier visitors to the region had claimed to see huge footprints in the dirt there ("patagonia" means "big feet" in Portuguese). In Europe the area had come to be known as a land of giants, and even Byron and his men found the natives to be quite large. But most likely the exaggerated footprints reflected local dress—Patagonian inhabitants wore large boots stuffed with straw for protection against the harsh terrain.

Claims Falkland Islands

From the coast of Patagonia, Byron sailed westward to the Falkland Islands—exploring and naming various capes and bays—and he took formal claim of the islands for Great Britain on January 12, 1765. While he was there he was surprised to see a French ship in the same waters; it was commanded by naval officer Louis-Antoine de

Louis-Antoine de Bougainville, who set up a French colony on the Falkland Islands, just as Byron was claiming them for Great Britain.

Bougainville (1729–1811), who—unknown to Byron—had just established a French colony on one of the islands. Great Britain's claim to the Falklands would be the source of conflicts for the next two centuries. It would result in the Falkland Islands War of 1982 (Great Britain still claims possession today).

With the most important part of his mission accomplished, Byron decided not to proceed to North America. Instead, he wanted to look for the Solomon Islands, the elusive southwestern Pacific island group that had been discovered in 1567 by Spanish explorer Alvaro de Mendaña (1541–95). After a brief return to Patagonia for provisions, Byron and his expedition headed through the Strait of Magellan. But because of bad weather, this short sail lasted more than seven weeks. Byron's expedition finally entered the Pacific Ocean on April 9, 1765. Concerned about the condition of his ships and his crew after the ordeal, Byron changed his route, heading northwestward to the Juan Fernández Islands off the coast of what is now central Chile.

What went wrong with the Anson expedition?

When British naval officer George Anson (1697–1762) was assigned a fleet of six ships in 1740 with which to sail into the Pacific and seize Spanish colonial possessions, he was already programmed for disaster. Many of the vessels he was given were in poor condition from the start, and his crew of nearly 2,000 men included many young recruits with no sailing experience and elderly veteran sailors whose advanced age or years at sea had ruined their health and made them unfit to serve. With unsound ships and an unskilled and already weakened crew, it was no wonder that shipwrecks, scurvy, and other hardships took their toll on the expedition. When Anson had completed his world-circling voyage in 1744, he had just one ship remaining and only 250 men.

The expedition showed that such a major voyage required careful preparation, including adequate provisions and foods to prevent scurvy. It also illustrated that ships and crews should be in the best possible condition, in order to withstand the rigors of long travel under unpredictable circumstances. When John Byron—a shipwreck victim of the Anson expedition—led his own voyage around the world in 1764–66 he took great care with the health of his crew, and very few members died. Some years after his ill-fated journey, Anson became First Lord of the Admiralty, and introduced reforms that greatly improved the efficiency of the British navy.

Discovers unknown Pacific islands

Weather conditions forced Byron off course and he missed his destination. However, he did come upon other Pacific islands groups. He sighted several uncharted islands in the Tuamotu Archipelago (island chain), and named two of them Disappointment Islands (present-day Napuka and Tepoto) because he was unable to anchor there. On June 7, he and his men encountered the wreckage of a boat left by Dutch navigator Jacob Roggeveen (1659–1729), who had visited the island of Takaroa in 1722. Farther west, Byron named the King George Islands in honor of Great Britain's monarch, and in the Gilbert group the explorer named Byron Island after himself. At many of these Pacific islands he was able to stop and get food and fresh water. Surprisingly, he discovered that coconuts prevented scurvy, the nutritional deficiency that so often weakened and killed sailors who had long been at sea.

Byron and his men also visited the Marshall and Mariana island groups. On July 31, 1765, they stopped on the Mariana island of Tinian, where they remained for nine weeks, recovering from their months of travel while repairs were made to their ships. Weary of exploring, Byron planned to follow the quickest route back to England.

Completes fastest voyage around the world

Continuing to sail west, the *Dolphin* and *Tamar* reached Batavia (now Jakarta)—capital of the Dutch East Indies on the island of Java—in late 1765. Byron and his crew then sped on to Cape Town, at the southern tip of the African continent, arriving there in just three months. They proceeded to England, arriving on May 9, 1766. Byron and his men had made the fastest voyage (just twenty-two months long) around the world, setting a record that would stand for a long time. While the expedition had made no major discoveries, it had been one of the safest; few crew members had died, and none of them had died from scurvy.

The year following his return, Byron published a narrative of his journey, *Account of a Voyage Round the World in the Years 1764, 1765, and 1766.* He advised the Royal Navy about South Pacific exploration, and was appointed colonial governor of Newfoundland in 1769, serving there for three years. But with trouble stirring in the North American colonies (which would soon become the United States), Byron returned to work at sea. He served as a rear admiral for the British Royal Navy beginning in 1775 and he became a vice-admiral in 1778, engaging in naval battles against the French, who were helping the Americans during the American Revolution (1775–83).

Seafaring adventures recalled in writings of famous grandson

During his long naval career, Byron had earned the nickname "Foul Weather Jack" because of his history of running into bad weather at sea. His bad luck continued when he was commanding a fleet carrying British troops to North America to help put down the colonists' rebellion there. He ran into a series of some of the worst storms ever recorded on the Atlantic, and his ships were scattered off the coast of North America. Byron had to retreat to Halifax, Nova Scotia, leaving the French in control of colonial shores to the south. John Byron's grandson, the great Romantic poet George Gordon Byron (Lord Byron; 1788–1824), would call upon his grandfather's experiences of shipwrecks and stormy seas for his poetry, especially for his most famous work, *Don Juan*.

From North America, John Byron traveled to the Caribbean, where he had more military confrontations with the French. As a result, he became Britain's naval commander-in-chief of the West Indies. On July 6, 1779, he was defeated in battle by French admiral Jean Baptiste Charles Henri Hector d'Estaing (1729–94) in the southern Windward Islands. Afterward he left the Caribbean and returned to England to retire. Byron had married Sophia Trevanion in 1748 and they had two sons. He died in London on April 10, 1786.

John Byron's famous grandson, the Romantic poet Lord Byron. Some of what appears in Byron's poetry came from hearing about his grandfather's seafaring experiences.

Sources

Baker, Daniel B., ed. *Explorers and Discoverers of the World.* Detroit: Gale Research, 1993.

Bohlander, Richard E., ed. *World Explorers and Discoverers.* New York: Macmillan, 1992.

Explorers and Exploration, Volume 3: *Europe's Imperial Adventurers,* written by Paul Brewer. Danbury, CT: Grolier Educational, 1998.

Marshall Cavendish Illustrated Encyclopedia of Discovery and Exploration, Volume 7: *Charting the Vast Pacific,* written by John Gilbert. Freeport, NY: Marshall Cavendish, 1990.

Waldman, Carl and Alan Wexler. *Who Was Who in World Exploration.* New York: Facts on File, 1992.

Pedro Álvares Cabral

Born c. 1467, Belmonte, Portugal

Died c. 1520, Santarém, Portugal

Around the turn of the fifteenth century, great geographical discoveries had been made that opened up ocean routes between Europe and Asia. In 1488 Portuguese explorer Bartolomeu Dias (c. 1450–1500) had discovered and rounded the Cape of Good Hope at the southern tip of Africa. In 1498 Portuguese nobleman Vasco da Gama (c. 1460–1524) had sailed around southern Africa as he made his way to India, a land known for its precious jewels, finely made goods, and rich spices. Manuel I (1469–1521), king of Portugal, wanted to maintain the trade advantage that da Gama's journey had given him, and he rushed to send out another expedition to the East before other European nations did the same.

Because da Gama was still recovering from his difficult voyage, King Manuel chose nobleman Pedro Álvares Cabral to lead the second, more ambitious expedition. The fleet Cabral commanded was much larger than da Gama's; it was comprised of thirteen well-armed vessels that carried a far greater supply of quality goods for serious trading. Although Cabral had little

Portuguese nobleman Pedro Álvares Cabral led his country's second major expedition to India. Along the way he discovered Brazil.

sailing experience, he managed to successfully complete his mission, setting up direct trade agreements with rich Indian ports. (Until that time, Europeans had obtained goods from the East indirectly, from Arabs, who maintained a trade monopoly there.) Cabral returned to Portugal with his ships laden with treasures, including the richest cargo of spices Europe had ever seen. What is more, on his trip to India, he was blown off course and thus he explored the eastern coast of the territory that would become Brazil, which would become one of Portugal's most important colonial possessions.

Cabral was born around 1467 on his family's estate in the village of Belmonte, located in the center of Portugal near the Spanish border. His noble family had wealth and power, as well as ties to the royal court. In 1483 Cabral traveled to Lisbon to serve as a page in the court of King John II (1455–95). When the monarch died, Cabral remained at court as a council member under the new king, Manuel I, and went on to become a knight of the Order of Christ, a devotional society.

Leads trade expedition to India

In 1499, soon after Vasco da Gama's return from India, Cabral was chosen to command the follow-up trip to India's southwest Malabar Coast to establish trade relations. He set sail from the Tagus River in Lisbon on March 9, 1500. His large fleet carried some 1,200 men, which included soldiers, merchants, missionaries, and even convicts to do the hard labor. Although Cabral had never before commanded a voyage, he was accompanied by two seaworthy veterans, navigator Bartolomeu Dias and Nicolau Coelho, a captain who had journeyed with Vasco da Gama. Instead of sailing south along Africa's western coastline as earlier explorers had done, Cabral tried to follow da Gama's route.

The fleet traveled south from Portugal and reached the Canary Islands on March 18. It then passed the Cape Verde Islands on March 22, beginning a westward sweep that would allow it to take advantage of favorable winds at sea. At a point farther south those winds would carry the ships around the Cape of Good Hope and into the Indian Ocean.

Discovers Brazil when fleet blows off course

But the ocean winds and currents pushed Cabral and his expedition farther southwest into the Atlantic than da Gama had traveled; farther, in fact, than any European explorer had yet sailed. On April 22, 1500, Cabral and his men sighted land: Monte Pascoal (Mount Pascal), located in what is now eastern Brazil. The following day they anchored off the coast of present-day Caravelas and sent a boat ashore, claiming the territory for Portugal. A few days later, at Pôrto Seguro (now Baia Cabrália), Cabral disembarked and took formal possession of the new land, which he named Terra da Vera Cruz, or Land of the True Cross. He and his men explored some fifty miles of the Brazilian coast—about midway between the present-day cities of Salvador and Rio de Janeiro—before resuming their journey to India. The expedition left behind two convicts at Terra da Vera Cruz to learn more about the land and its people. (The territory would quickly become known as Brazil, once traders began exporting brazilwood, a forest product used to make red dye.)

Pedro Álvares Cabral takes possession of Brazil in the name of Portugal in 1500.

News of Cabral's find was immediately relayed to Portugal on one of the ships. While most historians think that Cabral's discovery of Brazil was accidental, a few believe that he may have had secret orders to sail farther intentionally, to explore the western part of the global territory granted to Portugal for exploration in the 1494 Treaty of Tordesillas. Although Spain had been given dominion over the Americas in the treaty, the eastern tip of South America fell into Portugal's domain, along with Africa and Asia. Was Cabral sent to claim land that Portugal already knew existed? Scholars debate that question.

Another matter of dispute is Cabral's right to claim Brazil as his discovery: by the time Cabral had reached the territory, at least three other explorers—Spaniards Alonso de

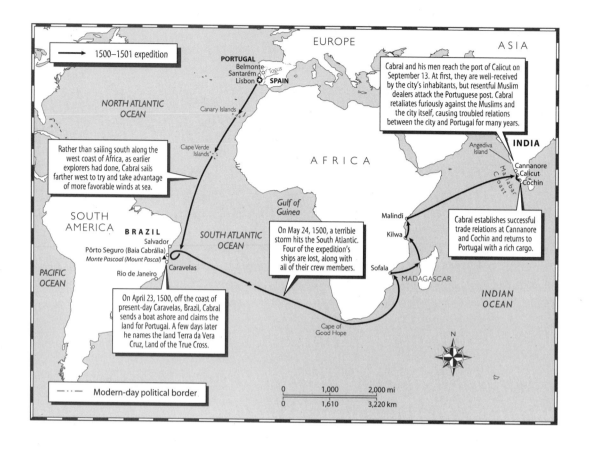

1500–1501 expedition

PORTUGAL
Belmonte
Santarém
Lisbon · SPAIN

NORTH ATLANTIC
OCEAN

Canary Islands

Cape Verde
Islands

EUROPE

ASIA

Cabral and his men reach the port of Calicut on
September 13. At first, they are well-received
by the city's inhabitants, but resentful Muslim
dealers attack the Portuguese post. Cabral
retaliates furiously against the Muslims and
the city itself, causing troubled relations
between the city and Portugal for many years.

AFRICA

INDIA

Angediva
Island

Cannanore
Malabar Coast
Calicut
Cochin

Rather than sailing south along the
west coast of Africa, as earlier
explorers had done, Cabral sails
farther west to try and take advantage
of more favorable winds at sea.

Gulf of
Guinea

SOUTH
AMERICA
BRAZIL
Salvador
Pôrto Seguro (Baía Cabrália)
Monte Pascoal (Mount Pascal)
Caravelas
Rio de Janeiro

SOUTH ATLANTIC
OCEAN

On May 24, 1500, a terrible
storm hits the South Atlantic.
Four of the expedition's
ships are lost, along with
all of their crew members.

Malindi

Kilwa

Sofala

MADAGASCAR

Cabral establishes successful
trade relations at Cannanore
and Cochin and returns to
Portugal with a rich cargo.

INDIAN
OCEAN

PACIFIC
OCEAN

On April 23, 1500, off the coast of
present-day Caravelas, Brazil, Cabral
sends a boat ashore and claims the
land for Portugal. A few days later
he names the land Terra da Vera
Cruz, Land of the True Cross.

Cape of
Good Hope

N

— · — Modern-day political border

| 0 | 1,000 | 2,000 mi |
| 0 | 1,610 | 3,220 km |

Ojeda and Vicente Yáñez Pinzón, and Italian Amerigo
Vespucci—had already sighted the northern coast of what
would become Brazil. Still, Cabral is credited with the find
because he found land where it was unexpected; the other explorers had just continued and extended investigations of
South America's northern coast. In addition, Cabral and his
men had actually gone ashore.

Stormy seas bring tragedy

Regardless, Cabral was more interested in his voyage to
India than in his South American discovery. On May 2, 1500,
his fleet set sail again, heading for the Cape of Good Hope.
Ten days later the travelers saw a comet shoot across the sky,
which was then considered a sign of bad luck. Indeed, a terrible storm hit the South Atlantic on May 24. The expedition

lost four of its ships and all their crew members, which included Bartolomeu Dias. The rest of the vessels were separated, and for twenty days they were tossed by stormy seas—the crew members unable to raise the ships' sails. Eventually, Cabral was able to round the Cape of Good Hope and touch land on Africa's southeast coast, at what is now Sofala in Mozambique. Only two other ships accompanied him. On June 20, at the port of Mozambique, he met up with more of the expedition's vessels. (One lost ship rejoined the fleet the following year, on Cabral's return journey.)

What remained of the fleet continued the journey to India, sailing up the east coast of Africa. Madagascar, the large island off the continent's southeast coast, was discovered by Cabral and his men as they made their way north. They stopped at the African ports of Kilwa (in present-day Tanzania) and Malindi (in present-day Kenya) before heading across the Indian Ocean. On August 22, as they neared India's Malabar Coast, they came upon the small island of Angediva. The expedition members remained there for fifteen days, resting and repairing their ships before undertaking their important trade mission.

Trade mission takes disastrous turn

Cabral and his men reached the great Indian commercial center of Calicut on September 13. At first, he and his party were well-received by the city's *zamorin* (overseer) and inhabitants, and the Portuguese explorers were allowed to establish a settlement and begin trading. But Muslim dealers, resentful of European interference with their trade monopoly along the Indian coast, attacked the Portuguese post and killed about fifty of Cabral's men, including three Franciscan priests. Cabral retaliated furiously, burning ten Arab trade ships and killing their crews. He then turned the firepower of his ships on the citizens of Calicut and bombarded the city. Cabral wanted his show of force to make clear that Portuguese traders would not be bullied away from India. The uncontrolled attack on Calicut, however, would result in troubled relations between that city and Portugal for many years to come.

Enjoys success in other Indian ports

Because Cabral had not been able to trade for the goods he wanted in Calicut, he continued to sail south along the Indian coast. He stopped at the port of Cochin, whose zamorin was an enemy of the city of Calicut. The leader of Cochin was pleased to hear about Cabral's attack on the great port to his north and eagerly assisted the Portuguese traders, helping them set up a post and agreeing to a direct trade treaty. Cabral's ships were loaded with valuable merchandise and the zamorin of Cochin even offered to help the Portuguese fight off the large fleet that was coming from Calicut for retaliation. Although Cabral, with his superior ships and weaponry, would have won the confrontation with the Calicut Indians, he was eager to return to Portugal with his rich cargo. Cabral and his fleet moved on—stopping at the Malabar port of Cannanore to establish trade relations and acquire more goods— before setting sail for home on January 16, 1501.

On the return journey, another of Cabral's ships was lost, off the coast of Africa. But when he reached the Cape Verde Islands, he was rejoined by one of the vessels that had been separated from the fleet during its stormy trip around the Cape of Good Hope the year before. At the islands, Cabral also met up with explorer Amerigo Vespucci, who had been sent by King Manuel to investigate Cabral's recent claim in South America.

Cabral and the ships that comprised his remaining fleet arrived in Lisbon harbor in July of 1501. The expedition had lost many crew members (nearly 900 had perished on the journey), but much had been accomplished. The travelers brought back a wealth of black pearls, diamonds and rubies, fine porcelain, incense, and valuable spices like cinnamon, ginger, and pepper. A new land in the Americas had been discovered and a trade route to India via the Atlantic and Indian oceans had been firmly established. Portugal's ships and weaponry had proven superior in battle, assuring future dominance at sea.

King Manuel planned a third expedition to India at once to strengthen the trade relations established by Cabral. This time led by Vasco da Gama, the fleet departed Lisbon in February of 1502. It is not known why Cabral was not chosen to head the voyage, or why he left the royal court at that time and never returned. He married in 1503, retired to a small estate near the Portuguese town of Santarém on the Tagus River, and had six children. He remained there until his death, around the year 1520.

Sources

Baker, Daniel B., ed. *Explorers and Discoverers of the World.* Detroit: Gale Research, 1993.

Bohlander, Richard E., ed. *World Explorers and Discoverers.* New York: Macmillan, 1992.

Marshall Cavendish Illustrated Encyclopedia of Discovery and Exploration, Volume 5: *Land of Spice and Treasure,* written by William Napier. Freeport, NY: Marshall Cavendish, 1990.

Waldman, Carl and Alan Wexler. *Who Was Who in World Exploration.* New York: Facts on File, 1992.

Eugenie Clark

Born May 4, 1922, New York, New York

Marine biologist Eugenie Clark has devoted much of her life to learning about tropical fish, particularly sharks. Her years of researching the misunderstood predators have led to surprising discoveries.

Ichthyologist (fish scientist) Eugenie Clark has devoted more than half a century to learning about the lives and behavior of the fish that inhabit the tropical waters of the world. As founder and director (between 1954 and 1967) of the Cape Haze Marine Laboratory in Florida, she conducted long-term studies of captive sharks, creatures long feared as vicious man-eaters at sea. Performing behavioral experiments, she found that these lower vertebrates are not the "stupid" predators that they were believed to be; they have surprising memory and learning capabilities, and can be taught to press underwater targets of different shapes and colors to obtain food. During the following decades, Clark would continue to study the shark—in its own habitat—using scuba gear and, later, deep-sea submersibles (underwater craft). She would learn that few of the 250 species of shark that exist are interested in attacking man. Furthermore, the creatures play a vital role in the ocean's cycle of life, keeping waters healthy by preying on sick and injured marine animals.

Passion for fish begins

Clark was born on May 4, 1922, in New York City. Her American father died when she was two, and her Japanese-born mother took a job in lower Manhattan. On Saturdays, Clark's mother would often drop her off at the old New York Aquarium at Battery Park while she worked. The young girl loved the time she spent there, peering into the fish tanks. She especially liked watching the sand tiger sharks, admiring their beauty and graceful movement. She decided to learn more about these and other fish and their wonderful undersea world.

For a Christmas gift, Clark received a fifteen-gallon aquarium and began her own—less exotic—collection of fish. It became a passionate hobby. She also began reading about the ocean's inhabitants and undersea exploration. William Beebe (1877–1962), an American adventurer and naturalist who made deep-sea dives and had made a record descent into the ocean in a bathysphere in 1934, was her hero. Clark loved the captivating way he wrote about sea creatures and she hoped to be like Beebe one day.

Clark went to Hunter College in New York and studied zoology, the science of animal life. During the summers of 1940 and 1941 she did field work at a biological station of the University of Michigan, located on Douglas Lake in northern Michigan. She graduated in 1942 and married a U.S. pilot, Hideo Umaki, who spent much of their seven-year marriage overseas. During World War II (1939–45), Clark worked as a chemist for the Celanese Corporation, headquartered in Newark, New Jersey. She intended to return to school after the war, and pursue her interest in marine animal life.

Encouraged to become ichthyologist

When trying to apply for admission to graduate school at New York's prestigious Columbia University, Clark was discouraged because she was a woman. She enrolled at New York University, where she met Professor Charles M. Breder Jr., who would become her mentor, encouraging her to pursue a scientific career studying fish. Curator of the Department of Fish at the American Museum of Natural History in New

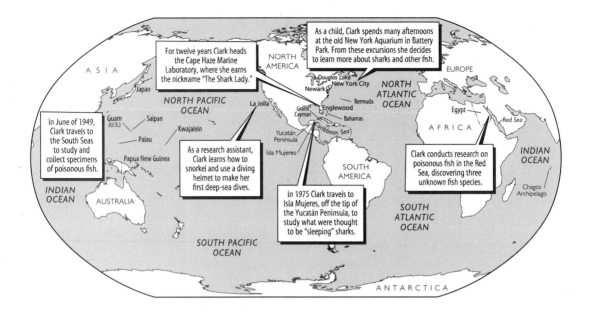

As a child, Clark spends many afternoons at the old New York Aquarium in Battery Park. From these excursions she decides to learn more about sharks and other fish.

For twelve years Clark heads the Cape Haze Marine Laboratory, where she earns the nickname "The Shark Lady."

In June of 1949, Clark travels to the South Seas to study and collect specimens of poisonous fish.

As a research assistant, Clark learns how to snorkel and use a diving helmet to make her first deep-sea dives.

In 1975 Clark travels to Isla Mujeres, off the tip of the Yucatán Peninsula, to study what were thought to be "sleeping" sharks.

Clark conducts research on poisonous fish in the Red Sea, discovering three unknown fish species.

York City, Breder had once been director of the public aquarium at Battery Park that had so captivated Clark as a child. Clark received her master's degree from New York University in 1946. Her thesis was about the puffing mechanism of blowfish—tropical, poisonous fish that inflate themselves into a globe shape up to three times their normal size.

Makes first research dives

In 1947 Professor Carl Hubbs, a scientist at the Scripps Institute of Oceanography at the University of California, La Jolla, invited Clark to join him as his research assistant. She made the move, and—along with her research work—took classes that required time at sea and the handling of oceanographic equipment. Clark learned how to snorkel and to use a diving helmet for deep-sea observation (scuba gear had just been invented, and was not yet in wide use), and she published the first study of the puffing mechanism of the swell shark.

Studies poisonous fish

Clark returned to New York City, becoming a research assistant at the American Museum of Natural History. She also began work on her doctorate (which she received in 1951) at New York University. In June of 1949 she traveled to the South Seas to conduct a study of poisonous fish, sponsored by the Office of Naval Research. Over the next four months she visited Kwajalein, Guam, Saipan, the Palaus, and other islands in the South Pacific Ocean. Native island fishermen taught her their age-old technique of spearing fish underwater; using this technique, she collected many specimens.

In 1950 Clark (who had divorced her first husband a year earlier) married Ilias Papakonstantinou, a Greek-American surgeon. She received one of the first Fulbright scholarships to study at the Ghardaqa Marine Biological Station of Egypt's Fuad University, located at the edge of the Red Sea. Again the focus of her research was poisonous fish. While there she collected over a hundred fish species, including three previously unknown species. Clark later wrote about her South Seas and Red Sea experiences in *Lady With a Spear*. Published in 1953, the book became a bestseller and parts of it were even published in school textbooks. Clark realized that like her childhood hero Beebe, she had a talent for writing about the natural world. She returned to New York City in 1952, giving birth to her first child that same year.

Heads own marine research laboratory

Clark became a biology instructor at Hunter College, a research associate of the American Museum of Natural History, and traveled widely as a guest speaker. Following a lecture in southern Florida, she met with millionaire William H. Vanderbilt, who had just bought a 36,000-acre tract of land on Florida's Cape Haze Peninsula. He wanted to establish a marine laboratory there—near the city of Englewood, and about an hour from Sarasota—and asked Clark to head it. The scientist was wildly excited about the rare opportunity to create her own research facility.

A local fisherman, Beryl Chadwick, constructed a small wooden building that served as a laboratory. He built a dock and they acquired a boat for Clark's use. A stockaded pen was built in the water alongside the dock that so that live sharks could be collected and maintained for research by Clark and visiting scientists. Among her first experiments was the training of captive sharks to visually discriminate between different targets, which they pressed to release food. Clark studied other local marine life as well; in one of her first dives offshore at the Cape Haze Marine Laboratory, she discovered a baffling fish, a small grouper—*Serranus subligarius*—which both produced eggs and fertilized them. It was a hermaphrodite fish: simultaneously male and female.

Becomes known as "the shark lady"

Clark served as director of the Cape Haze Marine Laboratory for twelve years. Her success at keeping various sharks in captivity and her behavioral experiments with them earned her the nickname "the shark lady." The reputation of the laboratory grew and, with the financial help of organizations like the National Science Foundation and the Office of Naval Research, its operations expanded. Staff was added, the number of visiting scientists—many from foreign countries—increased, and it became a popular field-trip destination for schoolchildren. Sometimes visiting scientists at the laboratory made important discoveries: For example, John Heller and his colleagues from the New England Institute for Medical Research found a substance in shark livers known as "restim," which stimulates the human immune system and has been used in cancer research.

By 1958 Clark and her husband, who had shortened his name to Konstantinou, had four children. Konstantinou's medical practice required that he be close to Florida's Sarasota Memorial Hospital, so the family moved to the area. This meant an hour's drive to and from the laboratory for Clark, and the long commute began to interfere with her life as a wife and mother. So in 1960, the Cape Haze Marine Laboratory was moved to a new site in Siesta Key, Sarasota. Still, Clark's marriage continued to deteriorate and she left Konstantinou a few years later. She married American writer Chandler Brossard—who had interviewed her for an article in *Look* magazine—in 1967. She moved north with her children, settling again in New York City.

Joins University of Maryland staff

Clark's marriage to Brossard was brief, and another, to Igor Klatzo of the National Institutes of Health, also ended quickly. But her professional life was full of successes. Clark wrote a second book, *The Lady and the Sharks* (1969), which was an account of her years at the Cape Haze Marine Laboratory, now renamed the Mote Marine Laboratory (MML). Several editions later, it is still in print at the greatly enlarged and respected MML in Sarasota. In 1968 the scientist joined the Department of Zoology at the University of Maryland in College Park. There, her ability to communicate about the natural world found another appreciative audience, and she became one of the most popular teachers on campus. Clark became a full professor in 1973, and developed a research program that conducted projects in more than twenty other countries. She and her projects were frequent subjects of articles in *National Geographic* magazine. In 1982 the National Geographic television special "The Sharks" attracted the largest audience of any program shown on the Public Broadcasting System (PBS); its record still stands.

Clark's research interests varied widely, from tropical sand-dwelling fish that live in the waters of Papua New Guinea, the Caribbean, and the Red Sea to garden eels, which live in massive underwater colonies. On a steep, sandy slope in the Red Sea, Clark observed one such group—comprised of some 10,000 eels. Also in the Red Sea—a favorite research destination of Clark's—was the moses sole, an intriguing fish that releases a fluid that repels sharks and other marine predators. Clark thought that the poison it releases might be reproduced in a laboratory and used to protect swimmers and divers in shark-inhabited waters. (The scientist later found that the peacock sole could similarly produce the repellent.)

Investigates mysterious "sleeping" sharks

One of Clark's most fascinating undersea investigations involved the "sleeping" sharks said to exist in the waters off Mexico's Yucatán Peninsula. Local divers had reported seeing these predators (reef sharks) lying motionless in a trance-like state on the bottom of underwater caves. This contradicted the scientific belief that sharks—because of their structure—must keep moving in order to breathe. In 1975 Clark traveled to Isla Mujeres off the Yucatán Peninsula to investigate this phenomenon, sponsored by the Research and Exploration Committee of the National Geographic Society.

Clark and her diving companions located such sharks in the caves of La Punta, El Puente, and La Cadena. They were able to closely examine and even handle the immobile beasts. The scientist found that the sharks seemed more drugged than asleep, and connected their state with fresh water seeping into the caves, mixing with salt water and creating a weak electromagnetic field that could be detected by sharks. Furthermore, rich oxygen content of the cave water could allow the sharks to breathe without the usual required motion needed to pass sea water over their gills (sharks have to pump sea water over their gills when they stop swimming). In addition, its lower salt content could weaken the parasites that ordinarily clung to the sharks, making their removal by the shark's remora—or sucker fish—much easier. Clark concluded that the sharks may visit the caves for a cleaning, a rest, or an electromagnetic "high." She later observed the same shark behavior in undersea caves near southern Japan.

Engages in deep-sea studies

Beginning in 1987, Clark became involved in the Beebe Project, a program using manned submersibles to study deep-sea life. She became the chief scientist on many expeditions and directed dozens of dives in waters off Grand Cayman, Bermuda, the Bahamas, California, and Japan. Like her childhood hero, William Beebe, who was the first scientist to see and describe deep-sea animals from his bathysphere (in 1934), Clark descended to depths ranging from 1,000 to 12,000 feet to observe ocean creatures in their natural habitat. Often the submersibles could be settled on the sea floor, where a bait cage would be set out, and photographs were taken of the deep-sea diners that appeared. Frequent visitors included several varieties of sharks.

Clark officially retired from the University of Maryland in 1992, although she still keeps an office and laboratory there and teaches special classes. She continues to conduct scientific expeditions in tropical waters around the world. She has received many awards throughout her lifetime. She has received three honorary doctor of science degrees and four species of fish have been named in her honor. Concerned about the preservation of healthy oceans, she has led conservation efforts that have included protecting the Red Sea's coral reefs. Eager to raise public awareness of the wonders of the sea, Clark has been involved in many television specials about marine life, and she contributed to the just-completed "Search for the Great Sharks," an IMAX film.

Sources

Balon, Eugene K. "An Interview with Eugenie Clark." *Environmental Biology of Fishes,* Volume 41: 121–125, 1994.

Balon, Eugene K. "The Life and Work of Eugenie Clark: Devoted to Diving and Science." *Environmental Biology of Fishes,* Volume 41: 89–114, 1994.

Current Biography, 1953. New York: H. W. Wilson, 1954.

McGovern, Ann. *Shark Lady.* New York: Scholastic Book Services, 1978.

University of Maryland, Department of Zoology—Dr. Eugenie Clark. [Online] Available http://www.inform.umd.edu/EdRes/Colleges/ LFSC/life_sciences/.WWW/zoology/clark.htm, October 9, 1998.

Unlocking Secrets of the Unknown With National Geographic. "Exploring Beneath the Sea," written by Richard M. Crum. Washington, D.C.: National Geographic Society, Book Division, 1993.

Luigi Maria D'Albertis

Born November 21, 1841, Voltri, Italy

Died September 2, 1901, Sassari, Sardinia, Italy

Luigi Maria D'Albertis was an Italian naturalist who made three expeditions up the Fly River into the interior of the island of New Guinea.

By the end of the nineteenth century most regions of the world had been explored—at least to some degree. One exception, however, was the vast tropical island of New Guinea, located in the western Pacific Ocean, north of Australia. Although the island's coast had become familiar to Spanish and Portuguese explorers since their earliest days in the East Indies, New Guinea's interior had remained a mystery. Dense tropical rainforests and hostile native tribes—some headhunters—had kept most adventurers away.

But as Europeans began to venture into even the most difficult locations, it was certain that New Guinea would not remain unexplored. The man who first traveled deep into its interior, Luigi Maria D'Albertis, was as dramatic as the wildly beautiful island—with its exotic blooms, brightly colored birds, and mysterious native people—that he had come to study. For although D'Albertis was a skilled naturalist (a person who specializes in natural history) who collected many plant and animal specimens unknown to the Western world during his New Guinea expeditions, he was more interested in being the first person to blaze a trail into the island's unknown territories and, most of all, to do it with great romantic style. As he traveled up New Guinea's Fly River, which was the gateway to the island's central interior, he would sing operatic arias and shoot off fireworks, rockets, and guns—terrifying the local inhabitants.

D'Albertis was born in the coastal town of Voltri, not far from the great Italian port of Genoa, on November 21, 1841. His parents died when he was young and he was raised by an uncle, who sent the boy to a Jesuit school. There he was inspired by a priest—who later became a missionary in Tibet—to study distant and unexplored places. Childhood visits to nearby mountains, the Alps and the Apennines, also developed D'Albertis's interest in plants and wildlife. After participating in the military invasion led by Giuseppe Garibaldi (1807–82) that unified Italy in the early 1860s, D'Albertis returned to Genoa and began studying at the Museum of Natural History.

Arrives in New Guinea

Accompanied by another Italian naturalist, Odouardo Beccari, D'Albertis left Genoa on November 25, 1871, and traveled to the Vogelkop ("bird's head") Peninsula in western New Guinea. Arriving on April 9, 1872, the scientists spent much of the next two years in the Arfak Mountains, at the far western end of the island. There D'Albertis collected specimens of exotic birds and insects, and from a native chief he even bought a number of preserved human heads, which the explorer later gave to a museum in Florence, Italy. Illness forced D'Albertis to move to Sydney, Australia, after which he returned to Europe in April of 1874. He went back to the Pacific, though, in March of 1875, settling on Yule Island, which is in the Torres Strait between Australia and New Guinea. This tiny bit of land had become the headquarters for Westerners trying to learn about the great island to the north.

D'Albertis used the small island as a base as he traveled along the New Guinea coast and collected specimens. After some of the local inhabitants took a few of his belongings, he

Headhunting

Headhunting is the practice of taking and preserving as a trophy the head of an enemy who has been killed in combat. It is a ritual that has a long history, beginning in ancient times and ending only in the nineteenth century. It was often done for spiritual reasons: headhunters frequently believed that a person's soul was located in his or her head. By taking the head of an enemy, the hunter added spiritual power to his own community and weakened the community of the victim.

In many tribes the taking of a human head was also a symbol of courage and manhood. In such communities a young man could not marry until he had captured his first head. Acquiring more heads earned him increased respect, and he might wear a special feather or tattoo for each one captured. In places like New Guinea, the practice was to preserve or mummify the skull and skin of heads. Among the Jivaro of South America, just the skin was preserved—which contracted, producing what was known as a "shrunken head."

also spent much of his time terrorizing the native population. Interested in explosives of all kinds, D'Albertis used rockets, dynamite, and gunpowder to keep the frightened natives at a distance from him and his quarters. Although he did not know their language, he often imagined that the locals insulted him when they spoke, which he felt gave him ample reason to fire his gun at them.

Makes first trip into island's interior

On one expedition to New Guinea, D'Albertis joined the crew of a riverboat called the *Ellengowan*. It headed up the Fly, one of the great rivers that empties along the south coast of the island. Despite encountering canoes filled with armed

natives, the expedition managed to sail 150 miles upstream. Unprepared for a longer journey, however, the travelers made their way back to the coast. D'Albertis was gravely disappointed, because he was certain that the Fly was the key to entering New Guinea's unknown interior. He promised himself that he would sail up the river again.

Luigi Maria D'Albertis ascends the Fly River aboard the Neva.

Leads expedition into unknown regions

The government of one of Australia's colonies, New South Wales, was especially interested in exploring the neighboring island of New Guinea. Because of the excellent scientific work he had done in the Arfak Mountains, D'Albertis was able to convince the government of New South Wales to provide him with a nine-ton steam vessel with which to further explore the Fly. The riverboat *Neva* was a long, narrow barge with a simple, metal canopy to protect D'Albertis, his two European companions, and a crew of nine from the elements. The eccentric naturalist brought so many provisions along that the boat barely rode above the water's surface. The baggage included plenty of fireworks and other explosives, D'Albertis's pet dog, a live sheep, and a seven-foot python that he kept among his personal belongings as a way of discouraging thieves.

Makes steady progress despite hardships

The *Neva* and its international crew, including a pilot who was a local headhunter, began traveling up the Fly on May 23, 1876. On their first night out, D'Albertis set off fireworks and rocket-borne dynamite to celebrate—and to warn the local inhabitants that he was on his way. Within eight short days he had passed the point reached on his earlier trip on the *Ellengowan*; he made steady progress despite food shortages, constant fighting among members of his crew, and dealing with hostile natives. D'Albertis happily spent the days collecting unknown plant and animal specimens—including exotic orchids and centipedes that glowed in the dark—and recording his observations. In deserted villages along the way he collected native artifacts, among them two human skeletons from a burial platform.

But as the expedition continued to travel into New Guinea's interior, the land became more mountainous, and the river narrower and shallower. Progress slowed, food was harder to find, and many of the crew members became sick with malaria. In the distance loomed the great mountain chain that runs through the center of the island, which D'Albertis named after King Victor Emmanuel of Italy (and which was later renamed the Star Mountain range). While D'Albertis longed to reach the mountain range, by June 27 he had to admit that he could go no farther on the Fly. The *Neva* was stuck in the muddy riverbed until heavy rains finally set it free. He and his crew began their return journey to the coast.

On June 30 the *Neva* turned up a northwest branch of the Fly, which D'Albertis named the Alice River in honor of the

On April 9, 1872, D'Albertis arrives from Genoa, Italy, and spends the next two years collecting biological specimens in the Arfak Mountains.

On June 27, D'Albertis admits that the expedition can go no further up the Fly River and turns around to begin the return journey to the coast.

The *Neva* returns to the mouth of the Fly on July 16, having penetrated 580 miles into New Guinea's interior. D'Albertis makes another trip up the river in 1877, but his second expedition is less successful.

On May 23, 1876, D'Albertis sets out on the riverboat *Neva* to explore the interior of New Guinea.

In March of 1875, D'Albertis settles on Yule Island, where he establishes a base of operations for traveling the New Guinea coast and collecting specimens.

wife of John Robertson, then the premier of New South Wales. But by July 4 the travelers again ran aground, and had to wait for rain to release them once more. Most of the crew were now sick with fever, including D'Albertis, and on July 6 they turned back. With the help of a swift downstream current, it took just ten days for the *Neva* to reach the mouth of the river.

Trip a great success

The *Neva* expedition was considered an outstanding success, both geographically and scientifically. D'Albertis had penetrated 580 miles into New Guinea's interior, and he had brought back a large number of valuable plant and animal specimens, as well as objects that gave intriguing glimpses into the island's tribal culture. But when reports of his exploratory methods reached Sydney, the capital of New South

Wales, he was also roundly criticized. It was suspected—despite D'Albertis's accounts to the contrary—that his unrestrained use of force had terrorized the natives into fleeing their villages so that he could steal their belongings for his collection. Worse still, it was believed that many locals died unnecessarily at his hands.

Subsequent expedition up Fly River plagued by troubles

Regardless of such criticism, D'Albertis managed to find backing for another expedition up the Fly in 1877. It was an ill-fated journey: he merely repeated the voyage of the previous year without opening up any new territory. In fact, D'Albertis ended up fifty miles short of the distance he had reached in 1876. Furthermore, traveling conditions were even more difficult on this journey.

After their previous experience with D'Albertis, the local tribes were openly hostile, and the expedition was forced to fight its way both up and down the river. At one point in the journey, after a skirmish onshore, D'Albertis and his companions cut off the head of a native they had killed, and preserved it in a jar of spirits (alcohol). River conditions were also much less favorable on this journey, and it took almost six months to accomplish what had been done in two months during 1876. In addition, the crew members of this second expedition were even more unmanageable than those of the first: they often returned empty-handed after a day of collecting onshore, and sometimes disappeared for several days, claiming to have become lost. When D'Albertis deprived some of them of their meals in order to force their cooperation, they deserted during the night and were never heard from again. Later in the journey, the remaining crew members of the *Neva* attempted a mutiny (revolt), ordering the engineer to turn the boat around. D'Albertis prevailed, then but by October 13 an alarming lack of supplies forced him to admit defeat and head for the coast. By the time he returned to the mouth of the Fly on November 18, 1877, only one crew member remained onboard. While D'Albertis had collected many interesting specimens—especially tropical birds—the difficult trip seemed to end his taste for exploration, and he returned home to Italy.

D'Albertis settled in Rome, where he wrote about his expeditions. Titled *New Guinea: What I Did and What I Saw,* the two-volume work was published in Italy and England in 1880. He also spent a great deal of time on the Italian island of Sardinia, where he built himself a New Guinea-style house of cane and reeds, standing above the ground on stilts. There he lived and hunted by himself. He died in the Sardinian town of Sassari on September 2, 1901, the victim of mouth cancer. He left the specimens and artifacts that he had collected on his New Guinea expeditions to museums in Florence and Rome.

Sources

Baker, Daniel B., ed. *Explorers and Discoverers of the World.* Detroit: Gale Research, 1993.

Souter, Gavin. *New Guinea: The Last Unknown.* New York: Taplinger, 1966.

Semyon Ivanovich Dezhnev

Born 1605, Veliki Ustyug, Russia

Died c. 1673, Moscow, Russia

Russian soldier Semyon Ivanovich Dezhnev was the first Westerner to sail through what we now call the Bering Strait, the passageway that separates northeastern Asia from North America.

From the time the Russian people formed a state in the ninth century, they steadily expanded their empire eastward, across the vast northern lands of Siberia, toward the Pacific Ocean. They established routes and forts along the rivers of Siberia, conquering the inhabitants of successive river valleys as they made their way toward the ocean. The new lands were steady sources of furs and mineral wealth (especially silver), and it was rumored that in some inlets of the northern Pacific lay walrus breeding grounds that were heaped with the animals' tusks, which are a source of precious ivory. Such promises of new wealth spurred the czars—the imperial rulers of Russia—to continue to launch expeditions farther east.

Explores Russian frontier

During the seventeenth century Semyon Ivanovich Dezhnev, a Russian Cossack (frontier soldier), participated in

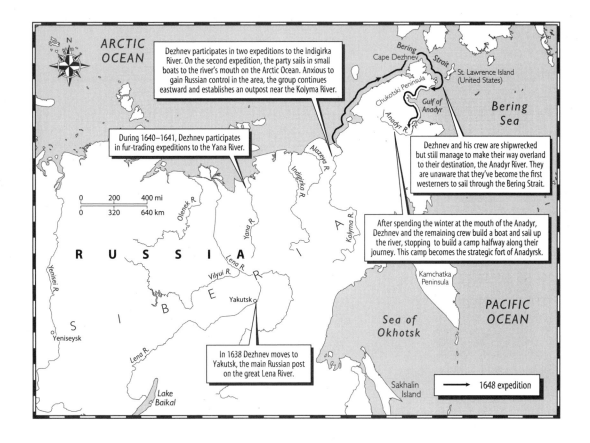

Dezhnev participates in two expeditions to the Indigirka River. On the second expedition, the party sails in small boats to the river's mouth on the Arctic Ocean. Anxious to gain Russian control in the area, the group continues eastward and establishes an outpost near the Kolyma River.

During 1640–1641, Dezhnev participates in fur-trading expeditions to the Yana River.

Dezhnev and his crew are shipwrecked but still manage to make their way overland to their destination, the Anadyr River. They are unaware that they've become the first westerners to sail through the Bering Strait.

After spending the winter at the mouth of the Anadyr, Dezhnev and the remaining crew build a boat and sail up the river, stopping to build a camp halfway along their journey. This camp becomes the strategic fort of Anadyrsk.

In 1638 Dezhnev moves to Yakutsk, the main Russian post on the great Lena River.

ARCTIC OCEAN

Bering Strait

Cape Dezhnev

St. Lawrence Island (United States)

Chukotski Peninsula

Bering Sea

Gulf of Anadyr

Anadyr R.

Alazeya R.

Indigirka R.

Olenek R.

Yana R.

Kolyma R.

Lena R.

Vilyui R.

Yakutsk

Lena R.

Yenisei R.

RUSSIA

SIBERIA

S

Yeniseysk

Kamchatka Peninsula

PACIFIC OCEAN

Sea of Okhotsk

Sakhalin Island

Lake Baikal

0   200   400 mi
0   320   640 km

→ 1648 expedition

several such expeditions. Born in 1605 in Veliki Ustyug, in the northern part of European Russia, he worked as a sailor before entering the czar's service. During the 1630s he lived in frontier settlements in Siberia, including Tobolsk and Yeniseysk, collecting tributes for the czar from the local inhabitants. In 1638 he moved to Yakutsk, the main Russian post on the great Lena River in eastern Siberia. During 1640–41 he participated in fur-trading expeditions to the Yana River, located farther east. In the winter of 1641–42 he was a member of Cossack leader Mikhail Stadukhin's expedition, which traveled east again, overland to the upper Indigirka River. The following year Dezhnev accompanied Stadukhin on a second expedition to the Indigirka, this time the party sailing in small boats to the river's mouth on the Arctic Ocean. The expedition sailed eastward along the northern Siberian coast to the mouth of the Alazeya River, and from there traveled overland to the Kolyma River, which also emptied into the Arctic Ocean even farther to the east. Stadukhin established an outpost there, anxious to assert Russian control in the area.

Embarks on Pacific expedition

In 1647 Dezhnev was asked to take part in another expedition, this time led by Cossack Fyodor Alekseyev Popov. The party's mission was a difficult one: to travel by sea from the mouth of the Kolyma, around the eastern tip of Siberia, and on to the Anadyr River, which empties into the Pacific Ocean. The Anadyr region was rumored to be heavily populated with walruses, which could provide a rich supply of ivory. But heavy Arctic ice forced the expedition to turn around well before they had reached their goal.

Second Pacific attempt marked by hardship

The next year, however, Dezhnev and Popov set out for the Anadyr again. They set sail with seven *koches,* ships built with very strong hulls meant to withstand the pounding of ice-filled waters. Popov had more than 100 men under his command: traders, explorers, and Cossacks like himself. The travelers departed the mouth of the Kolyma River on June 20, 1648, not suspecting how treacherous their journey would become.

By August, four of the ships and their crews had already been lost in the Arctic Ocean. But the remaining three vessels rounded the easternmost tip of Asia—what is now called Cape Dezhnev—on the Chukotski Peninsula. After one more boat was lost, the last two went ashore sometime around September 20; there the travelers were attacked by the local inhabitants. Popov was wounded, and Dezhnev became leader of the expedition.

Explorers unknowingly make landmark voyage

Not long after the ships resumed their journey, Popov's vessel was lost as well. Then Dezhnev and his crew were shipwrecked off the coast of northeastern Siberia, but managed—

over the course of ten weeks—to make their way overland to their destination. As the twenty-six survivors reached the Anadyr River, they were unaware of what they had achieved. Dezhnev and his men had become the first Westerners to sail through the narrow passageway that separates Asia and North America, answering a key geographical question of the time: Were the two continents joined? Seekers of the Northeast Passage—a northern water route from Europe to the Orient—were uncertain whether the two land masses were connected and if their quest to find an Arctic sailing route was hopeless. But because Dezhnev kept no records of his journey and word of his discovery did not make its way back to Europe, eighty years would pass before the nature of Siberia's coastline would at last be confirmed: In 1728 Vitus Bering (1681–1741), a Danish navigator in the service of Russian czar Peter the Great, would sail through the same passageway in which Dezhnev and his men had traveled, approaching it from the south, by way of Siberia's Pacific coast. The passageway would be called the Bering Strait in the Dane's honor.

Dezhnev claims unknown territories for czar

Dezhnev and his men were forced to spend the winter of 1648 at the mouth of the Anadyr. Some members of the party tried to travel up the river on foot, and perished in the bitter cold. Dezhnev and his remaining crew of twelve men built a boat, and when summer arrived, they sailed up the river, stopping halfway to build a camp. This became the fort of Anadyrsk, which would later serve as a major base for further Russian advances into eastern Siberia. In the river valley, Dezhnev and his men encountered the Anual people. Like many Cossack leaders before him, Dezhnev claimed the territory for the czar and forced the native inhabitants to give him goods, such as furs and ivory, as tributes to their new ruler. When some members of the Anual tribe refused Dezhnev's demands, he used the cruel Cossack methods of kidnapping and imprisonment to force their submission.

In 1652 Dezhnev and his men traveled to the Gulf of Anadyr, where they came upon several walrus rookeries

Walrus tusks were a bountiful source of ivory—precious goods sought after by Dezhnev and his men.

(breeding grounds). The animals provided them with a steady supply of ivory and hides. Dezhnev spent the next ten years exploring the area, and collecting more tributes for the czar. When Dezhnev was finally relieved of his command in 1662, he traveled overland to Yakutsk. With him was a treasure trove of silver, luxurious sables and other furs, and more than two tons of walrus tusks.

By 1664 Dezhnev had made his way to Moscow, bringing with him the riches he had collected during his travels. He presented most of the goods to the czar, but kept some for himself, which made him a wealthy man. He gave a detailed account of his various adventures in the Siberian wilderness, and he received payment for his nineteen years of service on the Russian frontier. He was also made an *ataman,* or Cossack leader. Dezhnev returned to Yakutsk with his nephew and remained in the area from 1665 to 1671, serving as a commander on the Olenek River for much of that time. Following a brief command on the Vilyui River, he was put in charge of a fur shipment, and accompanied it to Moscow. He remained in the city until his death, sometime during 1672 or 1673.

Sources

Baker, Daniel B., ed. *Explorers and Discoverers of the World.* Detroit: Gale Research, 1993.

Bohlander, Richard E., ed. *World Explorers and Discoverers.* New York: Macmillan, 1992.

Waldman, Carl and Alan Wexler. *Who Was Who in World Exploration.* New York: Facts on File, 1992.

Alice Eastwood

Born January 19, 1859, Toronto, Ontario, Canada

Died October 30, 1953, San Francisco, California

Scientist Alice Eastwood traveled throughout the western United States collecting wildflowers and other native plants, eventually building up a major botanical collection.

Alice Eastwood was a woman who had no formal schooling in botany, the passion to which she devoted her life. As a young adult roaming through the countryside near her Colorado home, she would gather wildflowers and other plant specimens, and carefully compare them to descriptions and illustrations in books—teaching herself scientific methods of identification and classification. In her determination to discover unknown species, Eastwood traveled into the frontier wilderness where she encountered mountaineers, Indians, wild animals, and other unfamiliar sights. But these did not keep her from building a major botanical collection, which would become the foundation of the University of Colorado's herbarium (a "museum" for plants—dried, mounted, and labeled for scientific study). When Eastwood's reputation as a scientist spread, she became curator of botany at the California Academy of Sciences in San Francisco, one of the most important scientific institutions in the country. Then she traveled throughout California as she had in Colorado, looking for plants to add to the academy's collection. Spending more than fifty years at the institution, she added 340,000 specimens to the herbarium, and helped raise public awareness of the need to save native American plants, especially California's majestic redwood trees. By her retirement in 1949, the contributions of this self-taught botanist were recognized around the world.

Uncle encourages early interest in plants

Eastwood's childhood was one of hardship and hard work. The eldest child of Irish immigrants, she was born January 19, 1859, in Toronto, Ontario. During her earliest years, the family lived on the grounds of the Toronto Asylum for the Insane, where her father, Colin Skinner Eastwood, worked as a superintendent. When Alice was six, her mother died and her father left her and her brother and sister in the care of an uncle while he went off to establish himself as a shopkeeper. The uncle, William Eastwood, was a physician who also enjoyed botany. After a day of wandering around her uncle's large estate or through the nearby countryside, Alice would discuss with her uncle the plants that she had seen. He would tell her their scientific, Latin names, and thus Alice's education as a botanist began.

Although Colin Eastwood was able to reunite with his children for a time, his store eventually failed, and he then moved to Colorado. He took his son with him, but left his daughters behind to be educated at a local convent. Alice lived at the Oshawa Convent, near Toronto, for six years. The religious education did little to stimulate her bright, scientific mind. She did, however, learn much from Father Pugh, a retired French priest who tended the gardens there. Alice spent a great deal of time following him about the grounds and observing his gardening practices.

Mountain vacation deepens enthusiasm

Living in Denver, Colorado, by 1873, Colin Eastwood sent for his daughters. He did not yet have a place for them to live, however, so Alice moved in with a wealthy French family,

While awaiting completion of the rebuilding of the California Academy of Sciences, destroyed in an earthquake, Eastwood travels to the town of Dawson in the Yukon Territory to gather plant specimens.

Alice Eastwood is born in Toronto on January 19, 1859, and spends her early years studying local plant life.

In 1873, Eastwood moves to Denver, Colorado, to be with her father. From here she takes numerous trips to the Rocky Mountains to collect plant specimens. As the years pass, her collection grows impressively and she gains a reputation as an expert on Colorado flora.

In 1890 Eastwood visits the California Academy of Sciences and is asked to write for the academy's natural history magazine. In 1892 she accepts a post there and spends the next several years building the academy's collection.

the Scherrers, and took care of their children. She was thrilled with the family's large library, for she loved to read. She enjoyed novels by writers like Charles Dickens (1812–70), but she also liked the works of Henry David Thoreau (1817–62) and John Burroughs (1837–1921), who wrote about nature. That summer the Scherrers went camping in the Rocky Mountains and Alice accompanied them. She was captivated by the wildflowers she saw there, and eagerly asked their names.

Local inhabitants told her the common names of many of the plants, but she knew from the teachings of her uncle and Father Pugh that all varieties also had scientific, Latin identities. If she was to continue her study of plants, Alice would need a book that contained this information.

In the fall of 1873, the shop that Alice's father was building, which had living quarters attached, was finished. The family was reunited at last. The Eastwood girls were finally able to attend public schools, but because of their haphazard education thus far, the girls were far behind their grade levels. As the oldest child, Alice did most of the cooking, cleaning, and clothing care in the new household. These tasks made keeping up with her schoolwork a challenge.

When Colin Eastwood remarried, it appeared that Alice would have more time to devote to school. But the family still struggled financially, and everyone had to help with expenses. When their father got a job as a custodian at the new East Denver High School, the family took up residence in its basement, and Alice and her sister helped clean the schoolrooms each day. On Saturdays Alice worked as a seamstress at a local department store. In 1878, during a particularly bad time for the family, she had to leave school altogether and went to work in a hat factory. Still, she continued to study on her own, and graduated from East Denver High in 1879, at the age of twenty. Despite the many disruptions in her education, she was class valedictorian (the student with the highest academic rank in a class).

Expands plant collection with yearly expeditions

Even before she graduated, Alice was offered a teaching position at the high school. During her first year as an instructor there she taught Latin, which forced her to become skilled in a language that would prove so important to her future work naming and identifying plants. Over the next ten years she taught other subjects as well, from writing to drawing. By living simply, Eastwood was able to save much of her small teacher's salary. She used her savings to buy botanical books, so that she could continue to educate herself. She took these along on her annual summer expeditions into the Rocky Mountains, to collect wildflowers and other plant specimens.

Passionate about her plant studies, Eastwood let nothing get in her way. If no lodgings were available where she wanted to go, she slept in an isolated cabin or out-of-doors. If a train or stagecoach could not take her to her destination, she traveled by horse or on foot. Fed up with riding sidesaddle, as women then were expected to do, she rode astride her horse. When her long, trailing skirts threatened to trip her as she tramped through the fields, she cut them off to ankle length, a solution no proper woman of the time would have chosen.

Each summer, Eastwood traveled farther into the wilderness, eager to find uncommon or even unknown species. She met some rough characters on the American frontier: woodsmen and miners, cowboys and Indians. She said that she was never afraid. As the years passed, her collection of native local plants grew impressively and she gained a reputation as an expert on Colorado's flora (plant life). Thus she acted as guide when famous English naturalist Alfred Russell Wallace (1823–1913) visited Denver in 1887 while touring the United States. He wanted to climb Grays Peak, the highest mountain in the Front Range of the Colorado Rockies, during the alpine (high altitude) flowering season. In July Eastwood and Wallace made their way up Grizzly Gultch to a miner's hut located some 13,000 feet above sea level. During the next three days the two scientists gathered specimens of the many wildflowers then in bloom—far above the treeline (the altitude at which trees can no longer grow).

Due to the financial success of some modest real estate investments that Eastwood and her father had made over the years, the botanist was able to leave her high school teaching position for a while and travel more extensively. In 1890 she journeyed throughout California, collecting wildflowers and other plant specimens. While in San Francisco she visited the California Academy of Sciences and met the curator of botany, Katharine Brandegee, and her husband, biologist Townsend Stith Brandegee. The Brandegees asked Eastwood to write for the academy's natural history magazine, *Zoe*. On her way back home, Eastwood made botanical side trips to remote places like Thompson Springs, Utah, and Mancos, Colorado. Back in Denver, she began work on her first book about local plant life, *A Popular Flora of Denver, Colorado*. She published the volume herself in 1893. It did not stir much interest.

Becomes head botanist at California Academy of Sciences

In 1892 Katharine Brandegee offered Eastwood the job of assistant curator of botany at the California Academy of Sciences. Eastwood accepted the post and, when the Brandegees retired a year later, she became curator of the herbarium and the temporary editor of *Zoe*. Eastwood was faced with the challenging job of organizing the large collection of plant specimens that her predecessors had left behind, piled here and there—unlabeled and casually stored. Eager to establish a first-rate herbarium at the academy, she applied the same enthusiasm and scientific care to these specimens as she had to her own in Denver (which she left to East Denver High School and which ended up at the University of Colorado at Boulder). Eastwood especially enjoyed her new instructing duties at the academy: for the first time in her life she was required to teach only about plants, her favorite subject, and to a group of advanced students who were as interested in plants as she was.

Travels throughout California on collecting expeditions

Just as she had in Colorado, Eastwood ventured into the California wilderness—from its mountains to its deserts—searching for wildflowers and other plant specimens to add to the academy herbarium. A favorite spot was the south Coast Ranges mountains that run along the Pacific coast, where in the interior a unique type of daisy (later named *Eastwoodia elegans* in the botanist's honor) flourished in the alpine land-

Alice Eastwood stands beside Eastwoodia elegans—the daisy that was named after her.

scape. (Another species, the desert flower *Aliciella,* would be named for her as well.) One expedition, which took place in 1903, included climbing the highest peak in the continental United States—Mount Whitney in the Sierra Nevadas. Over the next dozen years Eastwood added thousands of new plant samples to the herbarium. She also kept some 1,500 of the rarest specimens in a special collection; these were species that could no longer be replaced because they were believed to be extinct. Also during that time, Eastwood worked on a second botanical volume, *A Handbook of the Trees of California,* which was published in 1905.

Life shaken by Great San Francisco Earthquake

The following year would perhaps be the most challenging of Eastwood's life. On the morning of April 18, 1906, the city of San Francisco was rocked by a giant earthquake. The town was ablaze with fires that would—over the course of three days—destroy the heart of the city, kill as many as 3,000 people, and leave 250,000 to 300,000 residents homeless. Included in the wreckage would be the California Academy of Sciences building on Market Street, and the outstanding herbarium that Eastwood had so passionately helped build over the past twelve years.

But on the morning of that fateful day, Eastwood's quick thinking and bold actions helped save some of the academy's collection from destruction. After being shaken awake in her bed, she headed for the academy. When she saw the smoke from fires erupting all over the city (most from ruptured gas lines), fear gripped her. Was the academy already engulfed in flames or heaped in a pile of rubble?

To Eastwood's relief, when she reached Market Street, the academy building appeared undamaged. But it was locked, and fire was advancing toward it. With the help of a friend, Robert Porter, she broke through the front door and discovered that the interior was in ruins: the structure's glass-dome ceiling was shattered and its central marble staircase was in pieces. The academy's herbarium was located on the sixth floor. How could she possibly reach it?

Fortunately the stairway's handrail was still solidly attached to the wall in the center hall. So like mountain climbers, Eastwood and her friend pulled themselves all the way up to the sixth floor, using fragments of stairs for footing. Knowing that she could only save a small portion of the herbarium, Eastwood grabbed a large work apron and filled it with the rare specimens that she had earlier—and as it turned out, luckily—separated from the rest. Tying her treasures in a bundle, Eastwood and her companion descended in the same treacherous way that they had gone up. The pair escaped the academy building just before it was consumed by flames.

Sets out to rebuild academy's herbarium

At the age of forty-seven Eastwood found herself in the unsettling position of having to start all over again. It would take several years for the California Academy of Sciences to rebuild, and for Eastwood to resume her post as curator of botany there. Regardless, she set out to reestablish the collection at once, making field trips to the Coast Ranges and the Sierra Nevada Mountains. In preparation for the rebuilding task ahead of her, she also visited and studied famous botanical collections at places like the Gray Herbarium at Harvard University in Cambridge, Massachusetts, the National Herbarium at the Smithsonian Institution in Washington, D.C., and even overseas at locations including the British Museum in London and the Jardin des Plantes in Paris.

While awaiting completion of the California Academy of Sciences at its new site in Golden Gate Park, Eastwood went on an expedition to the town of Dawson in the Yukon Territory of northern Canada—just east of Alaska—to study the willows there and to gather plant specimens from the remote location. The difficult traveling conditions and crude surroundings reminded her of her earliest field expeditions, when she had braved the American western frontier. Eastwood traveled to Seattle by train, took a boat to the Alaskan city of Skagway, and then boarded a train to Whitehorse. From Whitehorse she traveled 300 miles in an open carriage, built on runners, over ice and snow to Dawson. There she stayed in a miner's cabin that was warmed by a woodburning stove; but the heater worked so poorly that a foot of ice covered the kitchen floor, and Eastwood cooked and ate in the living room. The scientist gathered countless plant specimens during her several months in the far north. On her return trip she found that spreading them out in the hot engine room of the boat on which she traveled was a fine way to dry them.

Efforts raise public appreciation of native plants

When the new California Academy of Sciences building was completed around 1912, Eastwood resumed her regular duties. She remained curator of botany there until her retirement in 1949, at the age of ninety (at eighty-one she was still doing field work, collecting plant specimens in Death Valley, California). During many years of service, she acquired more than 340,000 specimens for the academy herbarium and assembled an outstanding botanical library that included numerous rare books. She wrote countless scientific papers on botany, as well as articles for the general public on California gardening. In an effort to popularize botany and stir public appreciation of native American plants, Eastwood participated in many organizations, including the California Spring Blossom and Wildflowers Association and the Save the Redwoods League. For years the weekly display of freshly gathered flowers with which she decorated the main entry of the California Academy of Sciences was a popular San Francisco attraction.

Eastwood received many awards and honors during her long lifetime. In every volume of *American Men of Science* in which Alice Eastwood's name appeared, it was accompanied by a star of distinction. One of the greatest moments in her life occurred in 1950, when she was invited to serve as honorary president of the seventh International Botanical Congress. Meeting in Stockholm, Sweden, the congress convened in the garden of eighteenth-century Swedish botanist Carolus Linnaeus (also known as Carl von Linné, 1708–78), who had created the modern scientific system of plant and animal classification. Seated in the great man's chair, Eastwood was recognized by botanists from around the world for her years of careful field work and study, especially involving the flowering plants of the Rocky Mountains and the California coast. She remained active until shortly before her death from cancer on October 30, 1953.

Sources

Ogilvie, Marilyn Bailey. *Women in Science: Antiquity Through the Nineteenth Century*. Cambridge, MA: MIT Press, 1986.

Sicherman, Barbara and Carol Hurd Green, eds. *Notable American Women: The Modern Period.* Cambridge, MA: Belknap Press/Radcliffe College/Harvard University Press, 1980.

Stille, Darlene R. *Extraordinary Women Scientists.* Chicago: Children's Press, 1995.

Veglahn, Nancy J. *Women Scientists.* New York: Facts on File, 1991.

Linda Finch

Born 1951, U.S.A.

On March 17, 1937, American aviation pioneer Amelia Earhart (1897–1937) took off from an airfield in Oakland, California, in a twin-engine Lockheed Electra 10E, attempting to become the first woman to fly around the world at or near the equator. A crash at her first stop in Hawaii delayed the trip, which she resumed—accompanied by navigator Fredrick J. Noonan (1893–1937)—on May 21. This time, because of changes in the weather, she headed east, eventually departing from Miami, Florida, on June 1. All went well for 22,000 miles, until Earhart reached the most dangerous part of her journey—in the central Pacific. Scheduled to land on tiny and remote Howland Island, she and Noonan never arrived. Having departed from New Guinea on July 1, the fliers were not seen again and no traces of them or their aircraft have ever been found.

Sixty years later—on March 17, 1997—American businesswoman and aviator Linda Finch departed from Oakland International Airport in a Lockheed Electra 10E, one of only

In 1997 American businesswoman and aircraft pilot Linda Finch recreated the around-the-world flight that legendary aviator Amelia Earhart was attempting when she vanished in 1937.

two of the rare planes still in existence. It had been carefully restored to resemble Earhart's aircraft, right down to the rivet (bolt) patterns and paint scheme. Called World Flight 1997, Finch's mission was to recreate and complete Earhart's trip around the world, commemorating the courageous way the aviation pioneer had met challenges and set great personal goals. "She thought that if you have faith in yourself, anything is possible and you can accomplish your dreams," related Finch, who hoped to show this to the young people of the world as she realized her own dream of circling the globe like her longtime aviation idol.

Finch earns wings

Like Earhart, Finch is a determined and adventurous spirit. In her early twenties she decided that, not only did she want to learn how to fly, but she wanted to pilot vintage aircraft. A single mother living in San Antonio, Texas, she supported herself working as an accountant for as many as a dozen businesses. Saving the money she allowed herself for lunch each day, she used it for weekly one-hour flying lessons. By age twenty-nine Finch had earned her pilot's license.

One of the companies for which Finch did bookkeeping was a nursing home business. In 1979 she went into the business herself, and eventually founded four nursing home/retirement communities in Texas that made her a millionaire. With her financial future secure, Finch was better able to focus on her passion for flying and aviation history. Finch bought and restored six vintage aircraft and joined the Confederate Air Force, a group of veteran fliers who pilot World War II planes. By the time she undertook World Flight 1997, Finch had flown in air shows for more than ten years. She had logged more than 8,000 flying hours, with nearly 6,000 of them in vintage aircraft.

Considers restoration of Electra

In the early 1990s, Finch was looking for another aircraft restoration project. While at dinner with a friend, the conversation turned to Amelia Earhart and the Lockheed Electra 10E.

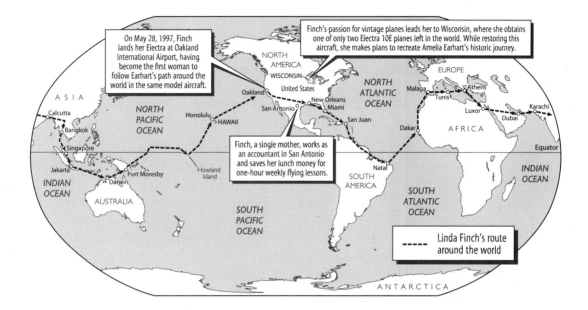

Finch's passion for vintage planes leads her to Wisconsin, where she obtains one of only two Electra 10E planes left in the world. While restoring this aircraft, she makes plans to recreate Amelia Earhart's historic journey.

On May 28, 1997, Finch lands her Electra at Oakland International Airport, having become the first woman to follow Earhart's path around the world in the same model aircraft.

Finch, a single mother, works as an accountant in San Antonio and saves her lunch money for one-hour weekly flying lessons.

Linda Finch's route around the world

Only fifteen of the planes, powered by massive Pratt & Whitney Wasp engines, had ever been made. The planes had been designed for long-distance flights to South America and Alaska. Earhart had chosen to use the Electra because it was the only existing aircraft that could carry the weight of the fuel she required for her trans-world flight; the plane also had the power to take off on the short runways she was forced to use as she made her way across the globe. By the time Finch thought of restoring an Electra, only two remained in the world.

Finch found her Electra in a hangar in Wisconsin. Its wings were off, its engines and instruments had been sold, and other parts were carelessly scattered about. She had the aircraft hauled back to Texas and contacted Pratt & Whitney, the manufacturer of the original Electra engine, in the hopes of securing another.

Decides to recreate Earhart's historic flight

One of only three plane engine manufacturers still in business from the early days of flying, Pratt & Whitney saw Finch's project as a wonderful way to celebrate the history of the aviation industry. They contributed more than $1 million to reconstruct the Electra. Pratt & Whitney also became the official sponsor of World Flight 1997, financing Finch's plan to recreate Earhart's historic journey—an idea that occurred to the Texas aviator during the restoration.

Finch began to prepare for her flight around the world in the vintage plane. It took some time for the aviator to get used to the bulky aircraft with its huge, hot engines; Finch called it "the loudest airplane I've ever been in." (Unlike Earhart, Finch would wear ear protection.) The ponderous Electra responded slowly to controls, and was somewhat unstable during landings and takeoffs because of the large amount of heavy fuel it was carrying (1,800 gallons). But this would enable the plane to travel 800 miles without refueling—crucial for a successful crossing of the Pacific Ocean.

Finch figured that the trip would take roughly ten weeks. It would include about thirty stops in eighteen different countries along the way. (She would not be able to follow Earhart's route exactly, because political problems would restrict Finch from the airspace of some nations.) She would fly a grueling eight to twelve hours at a time, and four mechanics would rotate shifts, serving as her navigators. Finch estimated that the flight would cover some 26,000 miles. But the exact duration and distance of the trip could only be estimated, because they would depend on the variable weather of the tropical region over which she would be flying. Because the tiny cockpit of the vintage aircraft was not pressurized, the aviator would be forced to fly at altitudes below 10,000 feet; unable to climb above bad weather as modern pilots do, she would have to fly around storms, or wait for them to pass.

Finch would have a decided advantage over Earhart, however, with the modern navigation, communications, and weather-tracking equipment that she would bring along to guide her. Earhart had found her way visually—directed by landmarks on the ground by day or the position of the stars at night (impossible when cloudy)—and her only means of contact with people on the ground had been a crackly radio. In contrast, Finch would be able to determine her position at all times using the Global Positioning System (GPS), a ring of orbiting satellites that constantly transmit radio signals to Earth (and to the receiver in the Electra's cockpit). In addition to radio contact with ground personnel, Finch would also receive regular weather reports by radar from U.S. naval stations around the world. And, as the ultimate precaution, another plane would trail her.

Mission unfolds before captivated young audience

With these careful preparations, Finch embarked on her around-the-world flight, which proceeded smoothly. Through the computer she brought with her and a satellite link, she was able to transmit her travel diary—along with digital "postcards" of the places she stopped—to a Web site on the Internet. She received e-mail messages from many schoolchildren, who were following the progress of her flight in the classroom. (Pratt & Whitney sold curriculum kits of World Flight 1997, with videos and workbooks, to schools.) When Finch finally landed her Electra at Oakland International Airport on the morning of May 28, she was greeted by hundreds of cheering fans.

Finch became the first woman to successfully follow Earhart's path in the same model aircraft. (In 1964, Geraldine Mock had flown a single-engine Cessna around the globe.) The Electra in which Finch made her historic flight now tours air shows throughout the United States. Pleased by the learning opportunity that World Flight 1997 had created for children, the aviator is currently at work on another such project. Hoping to make young people more aware of changing technology, Finch is planning a race between modern planes and vintage aircraft.

Linda Finch climbs out of the cockpit of her Lockheed Electra 10E after landing in Oakland on May 28, having successfully completed her flight around the world.

Sources

"Around the World in 73 Days: Pilot Linda Finch Finishes What Amelia Earhart Started." *People Weekly,* December 29, 1997: 170.

Holley, Joe. "Heirhart." *Texas Monthly,* March 1997: 30.

Plummer, William. "The Sky's the Limit: A Texas Pilot Retraces the Legendary Flight of Amelia Earhart." *People Weekly,* April 7, 1997: 153–154.

Vizard, Frank. "On Earhart's Wings." *Popular Science,* February 1997: 50–52.

"What Earhart Began, a Texan Finishes." *New York Times,* May 29, 1997: A16.

"World Flight." *Science World,* February 21, 1997: 6–7.

World Flight 1997. [Online] Available http://worldflight.org/, November 10, 1998.

Mel Fisher

Born August 21, 1922, Hobart, Indiana
Died December 20, 1998, Key West, Florida

In 1494 the great maritime powers of Spain and Portugal agreed to the terms of the Treaty of Tordesillas, which divided the non-Christian world into two spheres of influence. Africa and much of Asia fell under Portugal's dominion, while the Philippines and most of the Americas were added to Spain's empire in the sixteenth century. Gold and silver and other valuables from these colonial possessions poured into Spain in vast amounts, and it became the richest and most powerful nation in the world.

Fleets of treasure-laden ships would regularly cross the Atlantic on return trips to Spain. Their precious cargo was coveted by pirates and privateers (owners of privately owned warships sanctioned by their governments to capture foreign ships) and foreign navies. To protect against attacks at sea, treasure transport ships needed to be heavily armed or escorted by warships.

In 1985 American treasure hunter Mel Fisher made one of the greatest salvage finds of all time when he discovered the Nuestra Señora de Atocha, a sunken Spanish galleon, in the waters off Florida's Key West.

Final voyage of *Nuestra Señora de Atocha*

The *Nuestra Señora de Atocha* was one of these Spanish transport galleons. Records show that early in the summer of 1622 the vessel and its sister ship, the *Santa Margarita,* traveled to various ports in Central America and the West Indies and took aboard large quantities of precious goods and a number of wealthy passengers. In August the vessels traveled to Havana, Cuba, where they were to join a fleet of other treasure ships headed for Spain. It was important that they leave at once, for hurricane season in the Atlantic was fast approaching.

But an unfortunate calm delayed the fleets' departure until September 4. Although the day looked fair, disaster awaited the ships as they set off; a hurricane was approaching the Straits of Florida. Fierce winds drove the *Atocha* among sharp reefs and shoals, and it eventually went down. The *Margarita* sank soon after. Three hundred eighty-seven passengers and crew members perished, sharing their watery graves with a bounty of treasure.

Salvage attempts

An attempt to recover the ships' cargo was made a few years later. In 1626 a Cuban named Francisco Núñez Melian dragged the ocean floor with grappling (hooked) anchors and recovered some silver bars and coins from the *Margarita.* Still, most of the precious goods—carried primarily by the *Atocha*—remained irretrievable. After Núñez Melian filed a report about his salvage activities, the galleons and their treasures were eventually forgotten, becoming just two of countless legendary shipwrecks off Florida's coast.

Nearly 350 years later, American Mel Fisher, operator of a successful underwater salvage business in southern Florida, decided that he would devote himself to finding the *Atocha* and its sister ship. After searching for two years in Florida's Middle Keys, where the wrecks were thought to be located, he would have a stroke of luck that would make his dream come true. In 1970 an acquaintance of Fisher's, Eugene Lyon, was

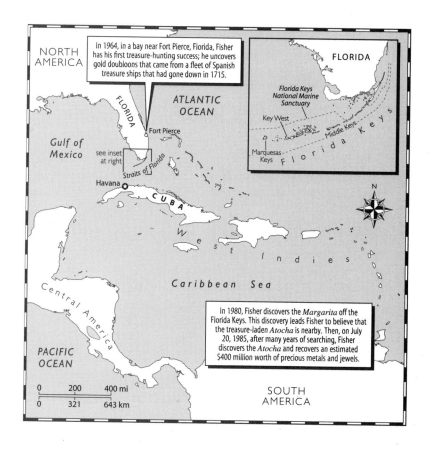

In 1964, in a bay near Fort Pierce, Florida, Fisher has his first treasure-hunting success; he uncovers gold doubloons that came from a fleet of Spanish treasure ships that had gone down in 1715.

In 1980, Fisher discovers the *Margarita* off the Florida Keys. This discovery leads Fisher to believe that the treasure-laden *Atocha* is nearby. Then, on July 20, 1985, after many years of searching, Fisher discovers the *Atocha* and recovers an estimated $400 million worth of precious metals and jewels.

doing research in Spain's Archives of the Indies, located in Seville. He came upon Núñez Melian's centuries-old report, which indicated that the *Margarita*—and most likely the *Atocha*—were located near Florida's Marquesas Keys, more than 100 miles west of the area that Fisher had been searching. With this new information, the salvager began his quest again, with thrilling results. Bit by bit, the ocean floor surrendered the ships' cargo, and in 1985 the hull of the *Atocha* itself was found. By 1986 Fisher and his team had retrieved an estimated $400 million worth of precious metals and jewels. What is more, the largely intact Spanish galleon and its artifacts proved historically and archaeologically invaluable.

There was no indication in Fisher's early life that he would become one of the world's most successful treasure hunters. He was born in 1922 in Hobart, Indiana, and one of his earliest jobs was working in a steel mill. Not caring for the hard, physical labor, he decided to study engineering. He attended Purdue University before joining the army during World War II (1939–45). He completed his engineering education while enlisted, and after the war returned home, where he worked in the mills again. A restless spirit, he moved to Chicago, Denver, and Tampa before settling in California in the mid-1950s to help his parents run a chicken farm.

Fisher takes to the sea

Fisher finally found an occupation that suited him when he began scuba diving, and he eventually opened a diving store. An excellent underwater cameraman, he became a small-time celebrity in California when he created his own local television program featuring his diving adventures. He wrote his own scripts, which sometimes included treasure hunting on the seafloor.

As an engineer, Fisher also enjoyed playing with and inventing gadgets. One creation, a portable dredge that sifted gold particles from streams, sold quite well. As a result, his financial future looked secure, and he retired in 1963. He decided to return to Florida—this time with his wife and five children—and spend the next year looking for sunken treasure.

Invention launches treasure-hunting success

Fisher had good luck with another device he had invented to uncover objects buried on the ocean floor. Called a prop wash deflector, it was a large metal machine that—when attached to the bottom of a boat—redirected the powerful wash of the vessel's propellers straight down, creating tremendous turbulence that removed tons of silt from the seabed. In 1964, in a bay near Fort Pierce, Florida, Fisher had his first success: he uncovered gold doubloons from a fleet of Spanish treasure ships that had gone down in 1715. The salvager recovered goods worth several hundred thousand dollars. The achievement made Fisher eager to find even greater treasures hidden in the sea. The *Atocha,* he knew, was one of them.

Dedicated to the search, Fisher used every means to find the legendary treasure ship. He employed magnetometers (instruments for measuring magnetic intensity), sonar (an apparatus that can detect the presence and location of an object underwater), and other devices (including, of course, his prop wash deflector). But during the two years that he searched miles and miles of ocean around the Middle Keys, he found nothing more than two musket balls and a fragment of a jar.

Relocation improves luck

With the news from Lyon about the *Margarita*'s true location, Fisher, his family, and his salvage company—Treasure Salvors, Inc.—moved to Florida's Key West. With that, the luck of the treasure hunter and his team changed at once. Their first find, in 1971, was an anchor and some gold coins. Two years later came the discovery of three silver bars, whose markings showed that they belonged to the *Atocha*. In 1975 bronze cannons from both ships were found. (That year, Fisher's son, daughter-in-law, and a crew man died in a boating accident, and the grief-stricken treasure hunter almost abandoned his mission.) Finally, in 1980, the *Margarita* was discovered. During the search process, other wrecks and artifacts were found. Many of these discoveries were sold to finance the continuing quest for the *Atocha*, with its legendary store of precious cargo.

Atocha and priceless cargo found at last

Having found the *Margarita*, Fisher and his team felt certain that the *Atocha* would be located nearby and easily found. But it would take another five years before the wreck was actually uncovered. On July 20, 1985, forty miles from Key West, ship magnetometers indicated the outline of a vessel located fifty-four feet below on the seabed, hidden under layers of silt. After the prop wash deflector did its work, the lower hull of the *Atocha* was revealed. The most complete remains of a Spanish galleon ever discovered, the find was so historically significant that the archaeologist employed by Treasure Salvors called in a team of experts from an independent ar-

Mel Fisher (holding a champagne bottle), his son Kane (lifting a bar of silver over his head), and crew members celebrate their sunken treasure find on July 21, 1985.

chaeological firm, Resource Analysts, to help document the wreck and the remarkable artifacts contained in and around it. Each discovery was photographed in place, plotted on a giant grid of the salvage area, raised to the surface, and then cataloged and analyzed. The hull itself would remain on the ocean floor because its timbers were too fragile—after centuries underwater—to be raised. Nevertheless, the hull did reveal important information about how such galleons were constructed.

By 1986, Fisher and his team had retrieved unimaginable riches from the *Atocha*. Included in the 400,000 items raised to the surface were more than 3,000 uncut emeralds, 78 gold coins and 160,000 silver coins, 32 tons of silver formed into more than 1,000 ingots, 115 gold bars and discs, and 78 gold chains. Also found were gold and ruby rosaries, daggers and swords, and other artifacts, including personal items belonging to the *Atocha*'s doomed passengers and crew. Fisher opened up a museum at his Treasure Salvors headquarters in Key West, casually displaying these wonders for public viewing as he continued to retrieve and catalog them. The story of Fisher's long search and final discovery of fabulous sunken treasure captured the public's imagination, and he became an instant celebrity. Four books, a documentary, and even a television movie profiled the treasure hunter and recounted his successful quest.

Fisher clashes with unhappy investors

The story of the *Atocha* did not have a fairytale ending, however. Not long after the cataloging of the sunken treasure was complete, trouble began. To finance his years of searching, Fisher had sold hundreds of shares in his enterprise to investors and now those stockholders expected to be paid. They were to receive allotments of treasure as compensation for their financial support.

More troubles for Mel Fisher

In 1992 the U.S. government brought suit against Mel Fisher, accusing him of causing environmental damage in the Florida Keys National Marine Sanctuary, an area of 2,000 square nautical miles surrounding the Florida Keys. The location had been a prime treasure-hunting spot for Fisher, who had found the sunken Spanish galleon, the *Atocha,* there. But it is also the site of coral reefs and surrounding beds of seagrass, which comprise a delicate ecosystem that supports a stunning variety of marine life.

The environmental culprit was Fisher's prop wash deflector, which redirects the force of a ship's propellers downward, stirring up layers of silt from the ocean floor. While prop wash deflectors can uncover buried archaeological treasures, they are often so forceful that they blast large craters into the seabed. Fisher, with his fleet of twenty salvage ships, admitted to making at least one hundred craters in the sanctuary, some measuring up to thirty feet in diameter and six to eight feet in depth. (Archaeologists also don't like the use of prop wash deflectors, because they can damage archeological sites and artifacts.)

Fisher was fined $500,000 for destroying beds of seagrass. The suit brought against him stopped the use of such invasive methods of treasure hunting in the Florida Keys National Marine Sanctuary and similar protected waters.

Investors complained that the goods they received were not valued anywhere near what Fisher claimed they were worth. Most of the silver coins that were distributed, for instance, were not in demand by collectors because they were not rare; they were also in terrible condition after centuries in the sea. Fisher was accused of keeping the most valuable pieces of treasure for himself and his company's directors, and for the museum and shop he ran in Key West. Stockholders filed multiple lawsuits, questioning the salvager's methods of bookkeeping and repayment distribution. (Many of the cases were settled out of court.) Another investigation regarding the way Fisher sold shares and ran his business was also undertaken by the Florida government.

Treasure hunter deals with new challenges

In 1998, a criminal probe into Fisher's activities involved accusations of counterfeiting. A Florida numismatist (coin expert) maintained that a number of gold coins sold through Fisher's museum were newly minted fakes; the good condition of the coins had aroused suspicion. Fisher, however, had dealt with such accusations before: a grand jury dismissed earlier charges involving silver coins when Fisher flew to Mexico City and searched colonial archives to recover the one-of-a-kind dies or molds—with the identical markings—from which the coins had originally been cast, thus proving the silver coins to be authentic. Fisher vowed to go to similar extremes to again prove the authenticity of the coins he sells at his museum.

In the meantime, Fisher moved his sunken treasure searches to the West Indies. He made the move when in 1987 the U.S. government passed the Abandoned Shipwreck Act, a law that returned ownership rights to foreign governments whose ships were downed in waters within three miles of American shores. Salvagers working in these areas must now get permission before removing wreckage and artifacts, and they must negotiate with government authorities over how much they can keep. In addition, Fisher made the move to escape U.S. environmentalists, who maintain that his salvage methods damage underwater ecosystems.

Fisher died of cancer at his home in Key West, Florida, at the age of seventy-six.

Sources

Elia, Ricardo J. "U.S. v. Mel Fisher." *Archaeology,* November/December, 1992: 26–27.

Fins, Antonio N. "A Passion for Rifling Davy Jones's Locker." *Business Week,* June 6, 1988: 71, 74.

Frankel, Bruce and Tim Roche. "Good as Gold?" *People,* June 15, 1998: 89–90.

Monroe, Sylvester. "The Trouble With Treasure." *Time,* May 11, 1998: 30.

Stall, Sam. "Treasures of the 'Atocha.'" *Saturday Evening Post,* November 1986: 50–55, 100.

Birute Galdikas

Born May 10, 1946, Wiesbaden, Germany

Canadian scientist Birute Galdikas is the world's leading authority on orangutans. Her years of field research have contributed greatly to a better understanding of the most elusive of the great apes.

For nearly three decades Birute Galdikas has been living in the jungles of the southeast Asian island of Borneo, studying orangutans—the most elusive of the great apes. She has gathered data on the behavior and lifestyle of these little-known, giant tree-dwellers, which she describes as our ancestral cousins "who we humans left behind in Eden." With their population decreasing alarmingly over the years, Galdikas has also been actively engaged in conservation efforts, her scientific studies frequently put aside for what she views as more pressing matters: protecting the orangutans' dwindling habitat, keeping them safe from poachers (those who hunt animals illegally), and rehabilitating animals who have been taken from the wild so that they can return to their rightful place among the trees. While many primatologists (those who study primates) have criticized her for neglecting her scientific work, Galdikas replies, "When a species is threatened with extinction, I don't understand how anyone can say it is more important to study than to save it."

Galdikas was born on May 10, 1946, in Wiesbaden, Germany, to Lithuanian parents who were in the process of immigrating to Canada. Her family settled in Toronto, and from an early age Galdikas showed a strong interest in nature. She loved to go to the nearby city park and search for salamanders and tadpoles around the pond. In the wilder sections of the park, she pretended she was an Indian slipping silently through the woods, and for hours she would secretly watch the small native creatures that lived there. Galdikas also liked to read books about animals. She was especially interested in stories about apes and jungles.

As she became older, Galdikas's interest in apes grew. She was intrigued by them because they shared the same ancient history as humans—the same common ancestors. By studying them, she thought, we might learn more about ourselves. When her family moved to Los Angeles, California, Galdikas attended the University of California (UCLA), studying anthropology. Familiar with the field work of Jane Goodall (b. 1934), who was living among chimpanzees in Tanzania's Gombe National Park, and Dian Fossey (1932–85), who had just begun a study of the mountain gorillas of east central Africa, Galdikas knew that she, too, wanted to conduct her own long-term investigation of the last of the great apes: the wild orangutans that lived in the Indonesian rainforests.

Becomes one of "Leakey's Angels"

In 1969, while Galdikas was a graduate student, Louis S. B. Leakey (1903–72)—famous for his amazing fossil finds of early man in Africa—visited UCLA to give a lecture. He was the chief sponsor of the studies of both Goodall and Fossey; like Galdikas, he believed that by investigating our closest living relatives—the great apes—we might learn more about human evolution. Galdikas asked him to sponsor her study of orangutans, and he eventually agreed, obtaining the necessary funding from organizations like the National Geographic Society. With Goodall and Fossey, she would become known as one of "Leakey's Angels," whose long-term field studies would provide groundbreaking information about the great apes.

An adult male orangutan. Male orangutans can reach five and a half feet in height and weigh 250 pounds.

Sets up research camp in southern Borneo

In 1971 Galdikas and her husband, Rod Brindamour, traveled by dugout canoe to their research site—which she named Camp Leakey—located deep in Tanjung Puting, a 1,200-square-mile swamp forest in southern Borneo (Kalimantan). Their shelter was a ruined hut filled with all sorts of pests; the swampy forest was far worse, with crocodiles and deadly snakes, leeches, and disease-carrying mosquitoes. Even some of the trees oozed caustic sap that burned the skin.

In studying the orangutan, Galdikas faced challenges that Goodall and Fossey did not encounter in their studies of other great apes. First, there was the grueling environment: many times Galdikas would be forced to observe her subjects while standing all day in waist-high swamp water. Second, orangutans are not social creatures like chimpanzees and gorillas; they are shy and solitary. Face-to-face meetings with them are rare, because they live in the treetops—some 100 feet up—traveling among the branches during the day and nesting there at night. Galdikas learned to detect the animals' presence by the sound of fruit peels and pits dropping to the forest floor. (At times orangutans discourage observers on the ground by throwing things on them: fruit, tree limbs, and even their own waste.)

And because they are not social animals, Galdikas often found that, even when she observed orangutans for days, "nothing happened." Most of the animal's time is spent swinging from tree to tree, foraging for food. An adult male's range is at least fifteen square miles and he can go weeks without encountering another orangutan. Furthermore, on those occasions when the animals do spend time together, they frequently seem unaware of each other's presence. Comparing her field research on chimpanzees with Galdikas's field re-

In 1971, Birute Galdikas and her husband travel by dugout canoe to their research site located deep in Tanjung Puting, a 1,200-square-mile swamp forest in southern Borneo. Here she devotes years to the study of orangutans, recording enormous amounts of new information about mating habits, reproductive cycles, and social interaction. In addition to her studies, Galdikas partakes in many conservation and rehabilitation efforts to protect the orangutan population.

search on orangutans, Goodall once said, "It might take her a year to see what I can observe in one lucky day."

Study reveals important new information

But Galdikas devoted years to the project, and learned much through patient observation. She recorded enormous amounts of new information about orangutan mating habits, reproductive cycles, and the way that females rear their young. (Young orangutans travel with their mothers for about eight years, while fathers are not involved in the parenting process.) She learned that the animal's life span in the wild is the same as in captivity, about fifty-five or sixty years. She marveled at the animals' complex foraging skills, which reflect high intelligence: with a diet consisting of more than 400 separate foods (fruits, nuts, insects, leaves, and bark), the orangutan seems to know the growing cycle and fruiting pattern of each plant in the forest. She also found that the animals are not entirely antisocial, with adolescent females often foraging together, and that all orangutans communicate with one another by vocalizing.

In 1978 Galdikas published her findings—the result of more than 5,000 hours of observation—in her doctoral thesis for UCLA (she had earned her master's degree there in 1969). Her efforts won the praise of the scientific community and captured the interest of the general public. *National Geographic* magazine did a cover story on her orangutan project and a television special followed. Some of the most compelling images in the program were those of Galdikas caring for the young orphaned orangutans who had been illegally captured by poachers who had killed the orangutans' mothers. Not long after she had established Camp Leakey, these rescued captives had been brought to her, and she had set about trying to rehabilitate them and reintroduce them into the wild. (Poachers sell the cute orangutan babies as exotic pets on a worldwide black market and local villagers often adopt the young animals, dressing them in children's clothing and training them to do chores. When the orangutans grow too big to handle, however, they are often inhumanely disposed of, sold to laboratories or to unauthorized zoos, or even eaten.)

Scientist expands conservation efforts

The rehabilitation program became just one of Galdikas's conservation efforts to protect the orangutan population, whose numbers and habitat had decreased alarmingly over the years. Once living all across southern Asia, these great apes are now found only on the islands of Borneo and Sumatra. And as a result of logging, mining, and increased farming on these islands, the rainforests in which the orangutans dwell have shrunk by 80 percent over the past two decades. Since 1987, in fact, a wild population of 180,000 has been reduced to just 27,000 animals. The captive orangutan trade has further threatened the species: A female orangutan spends many years raising a single offspring, and therefore gives birth perhaps just four times during her life. When adult

Why didn't the orangutan become "social"?

Scientists have speculated about why the orangutan did not develop the social skills and interdependence of the other great apes—the gorilla and the chimpanzee—or of humans. Orangutans possess the same degree of intelligence as their ape cousins: they can be taught how to use sign language and make simple tools. They are nearly identical to humans genetically, possessing 97 percent of our DNA (gorillas share 98 percent and chimpanzees, 99 percent).

It has been suggested that orangutans remained "unsocial" in order to survive. A solitary lifestyle suits a fruit-eater that lives in the rainforest; had the animal become sociable and gathered with others to feed off a single tree, the plant would have been stripped, and might not fruit again easily. A big animal (male orangutans can reach five and a half feet in height and weigh 250 pounds) needs a large foraging area, with few others around.

Galdikas believes that because these great apes never left the rainforest—a stable environment with no orangutan predators and few challenges—they never had to develop the interdependency and cooperative problem-solving skills that our own early ancestors were forced to evolve as they ventured beyond the shelter of the trees. In her book *Reflections of Eden: My Years with the Orangutans of Borneo*, Galdikas writes: "Orangutans reflect, to some degree, the innocence we humans left behind in Eden, before our social organization, bipedalism [walking on two feet], and toolmaking gave us dominion over the planet. Thus, understanding orangutans gives us a clouded, partial glimpse into what we were before we became fully human."

females are killed for their young, the population does not recover from such losses quickly.

Ensuring the survival of the wild orangutan soon became Galdikas's top priority. She patiently worked with the Indonesian government, whose economic interests—increasing agriculture and commerce to meet the needs of a growing human population—were in conflict with her conservation efforts. Still, she convinced government officials to move two villages from Tanjung Puting and declare it a national park, so that its forests and wild animal population would be protected; she also convinced them to put an end to the captive orangutan trade in her province. Galdikas made frequent trips to Canada, the United States, and other countries in an effort to raise money for her cause and to bring the plight of the orangutan to the attention of the world. She wrote magazine articles and books. Beginning in 1981 she traveled yearly to Simon Fraser University in Vancouver, British Columbia, to teach, becoming a highly popular visiting professor of anthropology there. In 1987 she established the Orangutan Foundation International, a nonprofit organization (headquartered in Los Angeles) that raises funds for orangutan conservation.

Not surprisingly, Galdikas's devotion to her work took its toll on her personal life. In the late 1970s Brindamour wanted to return to their home overseas, but Galdikas realized that her commitment to the orangutan project was going to be lifelong. Her husband returned to Canada and they divorced; not long afterward, their young son, Binti, joined his father. But in 1981 Galdikas married Dayak tribesman Pak Bohap bin Jalan, a native of Borneo who was once one of her head trackers and is now co-director of the orangutan project. The couple have two children, and live in the Dayak village of Pasir Panganj, close to Tanjung Puting National Park. Sponsored in its early years by important scientific organizations like the National Geographic Society, the L. S. B. Leakey Foundation, and the World Wildlife Fund, Galdikas's project now receives most of its financial support from Earthwatch, a Massachusetts-based environmental group that sends out teams of volunteers who help with field research. Orangutan rehabilitation continues at Camp Leakey, although crowded conditions have led to the establishment of other centers around Tanjung Puting National Park. All provide food, medical care, and "foster parenting" by humans, who take young orangutans on field trips into the forest to learn the skills they will need to survive in the wild—such as food gathering and nest building.

Sources

Current Biography. New York: H. W. Wilson, 1995.

Galdikas, Birute. *Reflections of Eden: My Years with the Orangutans of Borneo.* New York: Little, Brown & Co., 1995.

GCS: Profiles: Birute Galdikas. [Online] Available http://www.science.ca/scientists/Galdikas/galdikas.html, August 21, 1998.

Miller, Kenneth. "Saving the Last Orangutans." *Life,* May 1998: 66–68, 70.

Starowicz, Mark. "Leakey's Last Angel." *New York Times Magazine,* August 16, 1992: 29–31, 38–39, 44.

Unlocking Secrets of the Unknown with National Geographic. "Observing Animals in the Wild," written by Jennifer C. Urquhart. Washington, D.C.: National Geographic Society, Book Division, 1993.

Ernest Giles

Born July 20, 1835, Bristol, England

Died November 13, 1897, Coolgardie, Western Australia

Explorer Ernest Giles was the first person to make an interior crossing of the Australian continent from east to west, and then back.

By the time the Overland Telegraph Line was opened in Australia in 1872, most of the eastern part of the continent had been explored. The line reached from the port town of Darwin, on the north-central shore of Australia, to the city of Port Augusta, on the southeast coast. The vast stretch of land to the west of the Overland Telegraph Line was largely unknown, with settlements occurring only sparsely along the seacoast. It was to these interior western regions that explorers turned, not knowing that there they would face some of the most challenging deserts on Earth.

Ernest Giles was one of the first explorers to journey into the unknown regions west of the Overland Telegraph Line. After several unsuccessful attempts, he would manage, in 1875, to become the first person to make the east-to-west interior crossing of some 2,500 miles: from Port Augusta, across the Great Victoria Desert, and on to the west coast city of Perth. What is more, Giles would make a return west-to-east crossing by way of the even more grueling Gibson Desert.

While his achievement went unappreciated by his countrymen during his lifetime—for Giles had found no new land suitable for farming or grazing—he would later be recognized as one of Australia's most important explorers.

Giles was born on July 20, 1835, in Bristol, England. He was educated in London, and at the age of fifteen traveled to Adelaide in South Australia to join his parents, who had already emigrated there. He worked for a time as a clerk in the gold fields of Victoria in southeastern Australia and later in the city of Melbourne. In 1861, eager for adventure, he agreed to undertake a series of expeditions into the territory west of the Darling River, located in New South Wales. For the next four years he sought new pasture land for sheep-raising, which was fast becoming one of Australia's most important industries.

Leads first expedition into western territories

In 1872, sponsored by noted botanist Baron Ferdinand von Müller (1825–96) and several wealthy Victoria-based sheep farmers and businessmen, Giles planned a more ambitious expedition—to the lands west of the Overland Telegraph Line. Accompanied by five others, he left the frontier telegraph settlement of Charlotte Waters in the Northern Territory, and headed for the Murchison River, some 1,000 miles to the west. Setting off on August 11, Giles and his party traveled along the Finke River to the Macdonnell Mountain Ranges. From there they advanced to Lake Amadeus on the edge of desert country before lack of water forced them to turn back. While stopping well short of their destination, Giles and his group did discover one of Australia's great natural wonders on the trip: the monoliths (great stones) known as the Olgas.

The following year, Giles attempted a second expedition across Australia's western territories; his companions were Alfred Gibson, William Tietkins, and Jimmy Andrews. Hoping for better luck this time, Giles and his group departed on August 4, 1873, from Lake Eyre, several hundred miles south of the starting point of the last expedition. The travelers headed northwestward, across the Alberga River, then made

Dawn breaks over the Olgas, the great monoliths that Ernest Giles came across as he set off to explore Australia's western territories.

their way around the Musgrave Ranges in the hope of avoiding the Great Victoria Desert. But the land they traveled became more and more arid and, after journeying beyond the Petermann Mountain Ranges, they were faced with what appeared to be another vast desert.

Setting up a base camp, Giles and his men tried to continue west, making short trips in an effort to find a route that might continue to supply them with water. Veteran bushman Tietkins was Giles's usual companion on these excursions, but when the inexperienced Gibson complained about always being left behind, he was asked along instead. Carrying a week's worth of supplies, Giles and Gibson set out on horseback on April 20, 1874. After three days, disaster struck when Gibson's horse collapsed and died. The men were 110 miles from base camp, 90 miles from the last water hole, and 30 miles away from where they had stashed a small supply of food and water. They would have to turn back at once—but would they make it?

Second trip ends in disaster

The men took turns riding the horse, but Giles soon realized that their progress was too slow. He gave Gibson some of the meager food and water that was left, put him on horseback, and told him to ride back to the base camp for help. Gibson rode off—and was never heard from again. (Giles would later name the great desert that they had traveled together after his lost companion.) As Giles walked on alone through the arid land, he came upon the supply stash, with its keg of water that weighed forty-five pounds. Knowing that he would need every bit of the water to survive, he hoisted it to his shoulders. Resting in what shade he could find during the scorching days and traveling by night, he made his way to the distant water hole. Out of food, he grew so weak that he often hallucinated and even, at times, lost consciousness. In a book that he later wrote about the nightmarish expedition, Giles recalled a gruesome incident that showed just how desperate he was: as he stumbled upon a baby wallaby (kangaroo) that had fallen from its mother's pouch, he "pounced upon it and ate it, living, raw, dying—fur, skin, bones, skull and all."

Completes first east-to-west crossing of interior

Giles somehow made his way back to base camp, and then returned to the frontier settlement of Charlotte Waters. When he arrived there he was greeted with discouraging news: Western Australian surveyor John Forrest (1847–1918) had just made a west-to-east crossing of the continental interior (in November of 1874). But Giles still planned another expedition, for no one had yet made the journey from east to west. On May 6, 1875, he set out from Port Augusta at the head of Spencer Gulf in South Australia. He and his party of five men (including Tietkins) traveled this time with twenty-two camels. While not the first explorer to use the animals in

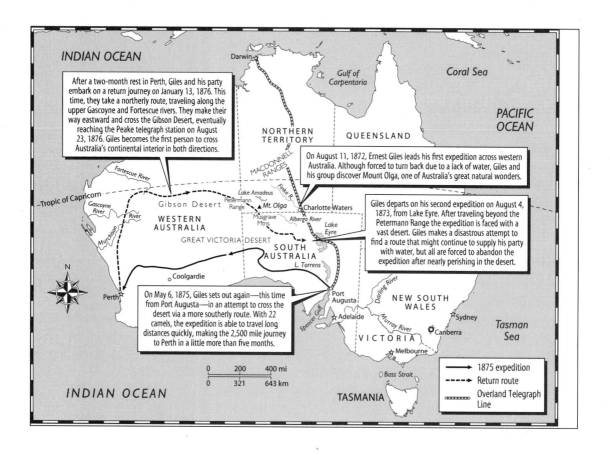

After a two-month rest in Perth, Giles and his party embark on a return journey on January 13, 1876. This time, they take a northerly route, traveling along the upper Gascoyne and Fortescue rivers. They make their way eastward and cross the Gibson Desert, eventually reaching the Peake telegraph station on August 23, 1876. Giles becomes the first person to cross Australia's continental interior in both directions.

On August 11, 1872, Ernest Giles leads his first expedition across western Australia. Although forced to turn back due to a lack of water, Giles and his group discover Mount Olga, one of Australia's great natural wonders.

Giles departs on his second expedition on August 4, 1873, from Lake Eyre. After traveling beyond the Petermann Range the expedition is faced with a vast desert. Giles makes a disastrous attempt to find a route that might continue to supply his party with water, but all are forced to abandon the expedition after nearly perishing in the desert.

On May 6, 1875, Giles sets out again—this time from Port Augusta—in an attempt to cross the desert via a more southerly route. With 22 camels, the expedition is able to travel long distances quickly, making the 2,500 mile journey to Perth in a little more than five months.

	1875 expedition
	Return route
	Overland Telegraph Line

the Australian interior, Giles was confident that they were key to successful desert travel. He and his party took a southerly route, passing Lake Torrens before crossing the Great Victoria Desert. As he suspected, the camels performed wonderfully: they could carry a large amount of supplies, travel long distances quickly, and needed very little water. In little more than five months the expedition had made the 2,500-mile journey to Perth, arriving in mid-November. At one point during the trip, the men had passed a 330-mile stretch of desert that held no trace of water.

Makes grueling return journey

After a two-month rest in Perth, Giles and his party of men and camels embarked on the return journey. Irresistibly drawn back to the Gibson Desert, which had earlier presented him with his greatest challenge as an explorer, Giles set out from Perth on January 13, 1876, taking a more northerly route than the one he had successfully traveled from east to west. Traveling along the upper Gascoyne and Fortescue rivers, he made his way eastward through the harsh country just south of the tropic of Capricorn (the edge of the Tropics in the Southern Hemisphere), and reached the Gibson Desert. The trip was grueling, with temperatures reaching 100°F during the day and dropping to 15°F at night. The travelers experienced violent windstorms and attacks by swarming flies and ants. Reaching the area where fellow explorer Alfred Gibson had disappeared two years before, Giles would go out alone to search for his lost companion's remains while the other expedition members rested. No traces of Gibson were found.

Giles suffered from periodic attacks of blindness during the journey, but the expedition had no choice but to press on. After traveling south into Australia's Northern Territory, the travelers reached Lake Amadeus and the Finke River. They arrived at the Peake telegraph station on August 23, 1876. Giles had become the first person to cross the continental interior in both directions. Later, he would write about his hard-won accomplishment: "Exploration of a thousand miles of Australia is equal to ten thousand miles in any other part of the earth's surface, always excepting Arctic and Antarctic travel."

Achievement goes unappreciated by countrymen

Giles soon returned to Adelaide. His crossing back and forth of Australia's interior was appreciated around the world, and he was honored by the Royal Geographical Society in London. His successful use of camels was adopted by future travelers, and the animals became the accepted form of transportation into Australia's arid interior. Still, Giles's achievement earned him little recognition in his Australian homeland, for he had failed to discover the new farming and grazing lands that his sponsors had hoped he would find. He was turned down for an official position with the South Australian government because it was said that he gambled and drank too much. He participated in explorations of southwestern Australia in 1882, and worked as a land surveyor and a prospector. In the 1890s he joined the gold rush to Coolgardie in western Australia. There he remained, working as a clerk in the gold fields. Suffering from pneumonia, Giles died on November 13, 1897.

Sources

Baker, Daniel B., ed. *Explorers and Discoverers of the World.* Detroit: Gale Research, 1993.

Bohlander, Richard E., ed. *World Explorers and Discoverers.* New York: Macmillan, 1992.

Marshall Cavendish Illustrated Encyclopedia of Discovery and Exploration, Volume 9: *Lands of the Southern Cross,* written by Julian Holland. Freeport, NY: Marshall Cavendish, 1990.

Waldman, Carl and Alan Wexler. *Who Was Who in World Exploration.* New York: Facts on File, 1992.

Hanno

Born c. 500 B.C.
Died ?

Hanno was a
Carthaginian navigator
who around 470 B.C. led
an expedition down the
west coast of Africa.

Phoenicia was an ancient civilization that dominated the Mediterranean world around 1250 B.C. The Phoenicians were great navigators and traders, and as they roamed the coasts of the Mediterranean Sea they founded ports and colonies along its shores. One of the most important of these was Carthage, an independent city-state (a self-ruling area made up of a city and its surrounding territory) located on the north coast of Africa, near present-day Tunis.

It is believed that Hanno was a leading statesman and admiral of Carthage during the fifth century B.C. By that time, other peoples had challenged the dominance of Phoenicia in the Mediterranean. The Carthaginians had recently suffered defeats in war against the Greeks of Sicily, and were anxious to maintain their control over western Mediterranean shores. This spurred an enormous exploring and colonizing expedition from Carthage along the west coast of Africa, led by Hanno.

When his journey was complete, Hanno wrote an account of it on a bronze tablet, which was placed in a temple in

Carthage as a commemoration; his is the only ancient voyage of exploration for which an eyewitness narrative, in effect, survives. The tablet was later destroyed, but a Greek copy, known as the "Periplus of Hannon" (from the tenth century A.D.), recounts his journey. While this translation contains many inaccuracies, including factual errors about the areas explored (leaving scholars with numerous questions), it still includes enough information to indicate that Hanno and his people made a significant journey along the west coast of Africa. Furthermore, the undertaking is mentioned by other ancient writers. (One difficulty faced by historians is the fact that the Carthaginians, in an effort to stop their competitors, often recorded misleading information about trade and exploration.)

Giant expedition sets sail

According to the Greek account, Hanno set out from Carthage sometime around 470 B.C. He commanded a fleet of sixty galley ships, each one rowed by fifty oarsmen. He carried 30,000 men and women who would inhabit the new African settlements, along with enough materials to build the settlements.

Founds coastal colonies

Sailing through the Strait of Gibraltar (between present-day Spain and northern Africa), Hanno continued along what is now the Moroccan coast. He founded the first of seven colonies at Thymiaterium, on the site of the present-day seaport of Mehdia. Other coastal settlements followed, including one built on the site of the modern city of Essaouira—indicated by archaeological artifacts that have been discovered there. Near the southern border of present-day Morocco, the Carthaginians befriended a nomadic people who were tending their flocks along a large river, probably the Wad Dra. The travelers took some of these natives with them to serve as interpreters as they continued to sail south along the coast of the western Sahara.

Hanno and his fleet then came to a small island situated at the top of a gulf. The commander liked its strategic location so much that he made it their final settlement, and the remaining colonists disembarked there. He named the island Cerne, which is thought to be present-day Herne Island, located at the mouth of the Río de Oro. With a small but active gold trade, Cerne would become West Africa's most important colony for a number of years before the Carthaginians would fall in defeat to the Romans in 146 B.C.

Investigates inland river

With his mission of colonizing the western coast of Africa complete, Hanno and his fleet undertook two southern voyages of exploration. The first proceeded along the coast to the delta of a large river, where Hanno decided to sail inland. There he reported seeing great mountains that were inhabited by forest-dwellers wearing animal skins; these unfriendly natives tried to stop the travelers from coming ashore by throwing stones at them. Hanno and his men next came upon a second deep, wide river that was full of crocodiles and hippopotamuses. Historians believe that the rivers Hanno traveled were branches of the Senegal River, which forms the western border between present-day Mauritania and Senegal, and is the home to both aquatic animals described by Hanno. Following these sights, the explorers retraced their river route and returned to Cerne.

Hippopotamuses and crocodiles were plentiful in the inland river that Hanno and his expedition explored. It is believed that the men traversed branches of the Senegal River, known to be a home to both animals.

Continues explorations down coast

A short time later, Hanno and his men embarked on their second voyage of exploration, during which they encountered more unusual sights. After a journey of fourteen days, the explorers arrived at what is believed to be the mouth of the Gambia River, where they stopped to replenish their supply of water. Five days later they landed on an island (probably one

Sailing through the Strait of Gibraltar, Hanno continues along the Moroccan coast, establishing the first of seven colonies at Thymiaterium, on the site of present-day Mahdia.

Hanno establishes another colony at the site of the modern city of Essaouira.

Hanno and his expedition set sail from Carthage around 470 B.C. to colonize the west coast of Africa.

Hanno establishes the final settlement on Cerne Island. Cerne would become West Africa's most important colony for a number of years.

After completing his mission of colonizing the western coast of Africa, Hanno and his fleet undertake two southern voyages of exploration. The first proceeds along the coast, probably to the delta of the Senegal River.

Hanno's second expedition continues south, where the men witness burning lands and a mountain on fire. This could possibly have been the active volcano Mount Cameroon, but it's doubtful Hanno's expedition reached that far south in the time period he describes.

of the Bijagós Islands, off the coast of present-day Guinea-Bissau). It was so heavily forested that during the day the explorers could not see any inhabitants. At night, however, they were made vividly aware of the presence of natives: the explorers saw many fires, and heard pipes and cymbals and the beating of drums, along with human cries. All of this frightened Hanno and his men so much that they fled the island at once.

Travels past frightening lands of fire

More disturbing experiences followed. Hanno reported that the fleet sailed along a country that was burning, the air heavy with smoke. The heat was so intense that the men could not go ashore. Streams of fire actually appeared to be running out to the sea. Again filled with fear, the explorers quickly sailed away. Scholars think that Hanno and his men may have witnessed a common practice among Guinea coast farmers, who burn the their fields after the harvest each year in order to prepare the ground for the next planting.

As they continued to sail south, Hanno and his men encountered more burning lands. One night they saw a mountain that was on fire; their interpreters told them it was called the "Chariot of the Gods." The explorers may have witnessed an active volcano, perhaps Mount Cameroon. It is West Africa's highest mountain, located in what is now the Republic of Cameroon. But most historians believe that Hanno could not have reached a location that far south along the West African coast in the time period he describes. Instead, the Chariot of the Gods may have been Mount Kakulima, on the Guinea-Sierra Leone border, with its slopes mysteriously in flames.

Hairy natives resist capture

Frequently during their expeditions Hanno and his men had gone ashore to investigate trade opportunities with coastal natives. Near the end of their second journey, the explorers landed once more, on another island (possibly Sherbro Island, off the coast of Sierra Leone). Like before, unfriendly forest-dwellers pelted them with stones. These natives were particularly odd, however, because their small bodies were covered with hair. Called "gorillas" by the expedition interpreters, the agile creatures were pursued over steep rocks by Hanno's men, who captured three females. The captives behaved so violently—biting and scratching—that they were killed and later skinned; their hides were taken back to Carthage. Because they were small and so easily captured, it is likely that the gorillas Hanno and his men encountered were actually chimpanzees.

After recording that the expedition could travel no farther because of dwindling supplies and unfavorable winds, Hanno's account of his voyage stops; he does not describe his journey back to Carthage. Although the extent of his expedition remains uncertain, it is likely that he traveled some 3,000 miles south along the west coast of Africa, a remarkable achievement. The colonies he founded, however—with the modest exception of Cerne—did not attain much importance.

Commerce must have been difficult in West Africa, for when the Romans subsequently took control of the western Mediterranean they did not pursue trade there. In fact, nearly 2,000 years would pass before another people, the Portuguese, would again explore Africa's western shores.

Sources

Baker, Daniel B., ed. *Explorers and Discoverers of the World.* Detroit: Gale Research, 1993.

Bohlander, Richard E., ed. *World Explorers and Discoverers.* New York: Macmillan, 1992.

Delpar, Helen, ed. *The Discoverers: An Encyclopedia of Explorers and Exploration.* New York: McGraw-Hill, 1980.

Marshall Cavendish Illustrated Encyclopedia of Discovery and Exploration, Volume 1: *The First Explorers,* written by Felix Barker and Anthea Barker. Freeport, NY: Marshall Cavendish, 1990.

Waldman, Carl and Alan Wexler. *Who Was Who in World Exploration.* New York: Facts on File, 1992.

Thor Heyerdahl

Born October 6, 1914, Larvik, Norway

S cientist and adventurer Thor Heyerdahl has spent much of his life trying to understand the history of people before they left written records. One question he has pondered is why certain native inhabitants of the islands of the Pacific, specifically the Polynesians, speak a single, separate language and differ so greatly in appearance from their neighbors in Micronesia and Melanesia. Did the Polynesians' ancestors reach the Pacific by a different migratory route? Did they arrive not from the Asian mainland—as was traditionally thought—but by way of a long western journey across the ocean?

Heyerdahl has also tried to find a reason for the many shared cultural practices and beliefs of the great Indian civilizations of the Americas (such as the Aztec, Maya, and Inca) and the ancient peoples of the Middle East (such as the Egyptians). The Indians wrote in hieroglyphs or pictures, just as the Egyptians did. Their calendars were similar. And all worshipped a sun god, to whom they built great altars, temples, and pyramids. While traditional anthropological theories

Norwegian anthropologist and adventurer Thor Heyerdahl undertook sea voyages in replicas of primitive sailing craft to prove his theory that ancient peoples made migratory trips across the oceans.

maintained that no ocean crossings were possible in ancient times—before the use of wooden boats—Heyerdahl wondered if such thinking was flawed. Had ancient Egyptians or their neighbors sailed to South America in reed ships, taking their culture with them?

The scientist knew that if he could recreate successful sea voyages using primitive vessels, he would be closer to solving the anthropological questions that puzzled him. He felt certain that ancient peoples were capable of migrating across the oceans.

Heyerdahl was born on October 6, 1914, in the Norwegian seaport of Larvik. It was the second marriage for both his parents and, although Heyerdahl had older step- and half-brothers and sisters, he spent much of his time playing alone. He liked to daydream about adventure, and sometimes wrote stories about children who ran off to tropical islands.

Heyerdahl also had a keen interest in nature, and gradually gathered impressive specimens that included shells, starfish, insects, and snakes. He built a little museum in the courtyard of his house to share his treasures with the neighborhood. He eventually constructed a freshwater aquarium to add to his collection.

Fascination with Polynesia begins

Not surprisingly, Heyerdahl studied zoology at the university he attended in the Norwegian capital of Oslo, beginning in 1933. He was always happy to leave the classroom to engage in field studies, and soon developed a strong interest in geography. He was particularly intrigued by Polynesia—the islands of the central Pacific Ocean—and read all he could about them. After his marriage to Liv Coucheron Torp on December 24, 1936, the couple embarked by ocean liner on a romantic quest to the Polynesian island of Tahiti, where they planned to lead a simple life in a natural paradise.

A local Tahitian leader, Chief Teriieroo, soon adopted the Heyerdahls and taught them island ways. The couple then headed by schooner for the more remote island of Fatu Hiva (one of the Marquesas), where they lived for a year. Their island paradise was not what they had hoped for: poisonous insects and disease-carrying mosquitoes plagued them, and bugs even began to eat their house. Also, the native diet of raw fish, sea snails, and sea urchins was unappealing. When a schooner came to retrieve the Heyerdahls after their trial year, they were more than happy to leave, and returned to Norway in March of 1938.

Puzzles over islanders' ancient past

Thor Heyerdahl had collected biological specimens on Fatu Hiva. But while there, his scientific interest had shifted from animals to people. He became engrossed in the ancestral past of the people of Polynesia. Traditional anthropological theories claimed that Polynesia had been the last of the Pacific islands to be settled, and that its inhabitants had come from the west—from the Asian mainland—just like the peoples of nearby Micronesia and Melanesia. But differences in language and appearance set the Polynesians apart from their neighbors.

Heyerdahl developed the controversial theory that Polynesia had been settled by people sailing out of the east, from the Americas, and across the Pacific Ocean about 1,500 years ago. Migrations from the west were contrary to prevailing systems of winds and currents, while Heyerdahl's theory—with ancient sailors following the trade winds and equatorial currents that come out of the east—made greater practical sense. Furthermore, Heyerdahl couldn't dismiss the legend of Tiki, the ancestor-chief of the Polynesians, who had come to them from the east. Indians of Peru (before the Inca) had also had a legend about Kon-Tiki, a high priest and sun-king who had sailed west with his people from the Peruvian coast to seek new lands and who was never seen again. Heyerdahl wondered if these legendary figures weren't the same ancient sailor. To prove his theory, he would have to ride the winds and currents of the Pacific Ocean, from Peru to Polynesia, aboard a primitive craft. (After seeing ancient carvings from British Columbia that also resembled Tiki, Heyerdahl theorized that sailors from North America—as well as South America—journeyed to Polynesia long ago).

Undertakes sea voyage to prove theory

Heyerdahl and a crew of five other adventurers built a raft from balsa wood, just like those used by South American Indians hundreds of years ago. The logs were harvested in the jungles of the Andes Mountains, and lashed together with tropical vines before they were floated down the river toward the sea. There, on the Peruvian coast, the forty-five-foot-long raft was constructed. Split bamboo canes were laid over the rope-tied logs for a deck. The canes also formed the small cabin, which had a roof of bamboo leaves. Two strong mangrove wood masts held a square sail, and there was a single large back oar for crude steering. The vessel was named *Kon-Tiki,* after the legendary chief/king.

Carrying food and drinking water to last four months, *Kon-Tiki* was towed out of the harbor at Callao, Peru, and set adrift on April 28, 1947, before a large crowd of well-wishers. The winds and currents carried it north along the South American coast, then west just below the equator. Heyerdahl and his companions clung to the raft when they experienced heavy seas. If they lost a man overboard, rescue would be unlikely, because the simple raft could not be turned around. Sharks visited the vessel daily, and flying fish often fell into the raft and were eaten by the crew or used as bait to catch other fish.

Ocean crossing a success

A few months into their quest, Heyerdahl and his companions worried they were not going to make it. By then the raft's soft balsa logs had soaked up loads of water and the vessel rode dangerously low in the water. The ropes that held the logs together were becoming loose with wear. Provisions and drinking water were running low. But soon the sailors sighted land, and on the ninety-seventh day of their journey, two Polynesian islanders canoed out to greet them.

Heyerdahl and his companions remained on *Kon-Tiki* as it continued to drift. As it was propelled toward a coral reef (Roroia Reef) by pounding waves, the men prepared for a wreck landing. Within seconds, the raft was shattered, but no

one was hurt. The crew radioed to nearby islands for help, and were rescued on August 6 by canoeists, who took them to one of the Tuamotu Islands. *Kon-Tiki* and its crew had crossed some 4,000 miles of open ocean in 101 days. They had proved that Heyerdahl's theory of an east-to-west ocean migration to Polynesia was possible.

Heyerdahl wrote a bestselling book about the voyage, titled *Kon-Tiki,* which was published in 1948. His documentary of the same name won an Academy Award in 1951. Two years later he formally presented his controversial anthropological theories in *American Indians in the Pacific.*

Having succeeded so well in illuminating one anthropological puzzle, Heyerdahl turned his attention to another. Heyerdahl wondered why so much of ancient North African culture—from places like Egypt and Phoenicia—was also seen in the great Indian civilizations of the Americas. He theorized

The Kon-Tiki *under sail in the Pacific Ocean. Though not without its perils, Heyerdahl's trip proved that an early east-to-west ocean migration to Polynesia was possible.*

that North Africans had crossed the Atlantic to the New World more than twenty centuries before European sailors, contributing to the population and culture there.

This was again a controversial theory, because wooden boats were not yet in use during these ancient times. Boats and barges made of papyrus reeds were used to travel rivers like the Nile, but were traditionally thought not to be seaworthy. Heyerdahl would need to disprove this claim—by sailing across the Atlantic in a reed boat.

Plans second theory-proving voyage

Heyerdahl studied pictorial records and models of reed boats left by ancient Egyptians. He also visited places where reed boats were still in use: locations in Bolivia and Mexico, and on Lake Chad in north-central Africa. While papyrus no longer grew in Egypt, Heyerdahl found the reed in Ethiopia. He bought twelve tons of it, and had it delivered to his building camp in the Egyptian desert near the Great Pyramids. Buduma tribesmen from Chad traveled there and began construction of an ocean-worthy papyrus boat.

First, the papyrus reeds were soaked in water to soften them. Then they were gathered in bundles and tied together with ropes. The bundles were shaped into a boat fifty feet long and sixteen feet wide, resembling a giant curved basket. The boat's cabin was made of wicker. Completed in April of 1969, the vessel was named *Ra,* in honor of the Egyptian sun god. It was pulled across the desert on log rollers, then transported to the Moroccan city of Safi, located on Africa's northwest coast. There the ship received a mast and sail (picturing a giant sun), and a pair of wooden rear oar rudders for steering. As *Ra* sat in the harbor, its reeds began to swell as they absorbed salt water, and the boat sat lower in the water. Would the papyrus vessel be able to withstand the rigors of a long ocean voyage?

Sea journey begins

Ra set out on May 27, 1969. Heyerdahl expected the journey to take less than two months. He was accompanied by

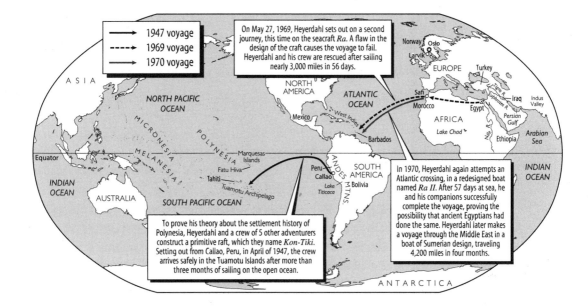

On May 27, 1969, Heyerdahl sets out on a second journey, this time on the seacraft *Ra*. A flaw in the design of the craft causes the voyage to fail. Heyerdahl and his crew are rescued after sailing nearly 3,000 miles in 56 days.

1947 voyage
1969 voyage
1970 voyage

In 1970, Heyerdahl again attempts an Atlantic crossing, in a redesigned boat named *Ra II*. After 57 days at sea, he and his companions successfully complete the voyage, proving the possibility that ancient Egyptians had done the same. Heyerdahl later makes a voyage through the Middle East in a boat of Sumerian design, traveling 4,200 miles in four months.

To prove his theory about the settlement history of Polynesia, Heyerdahl and a crew of 5 other adventurers construct a primitive raft, which they name *Kon-Tiki*. Setting out from Callao, Peru, in April of 1947, the crew arrives safely in the Tuamotu Islands after more than three months of sailing on the open ocean.

six other adventurers from different countries (including navigator Norman Baker of the United States), and flew the flag of the United Nations to show the unity of the crew. Trade winds and ocean currents carried the boat westward, toward the Americas. On the first day of the voyage, the rudder oars—too weak to withstand the ocean's pounding—broke. Even after they were repaired, the men struggled to control *Ra* in rough seas. Nonetheless, they managed to sail about 70 miles each day. And the papyrus reeds from which *Ra* was constructed did not disintegrate—as doubters had feared—but swelled with the salt water and became as strong and as pliable as rubber.

Vessel's flaw stops mission

As time went on, however, Heyerdahl detected a flaw in the design of *Ra* that would ultimately bring disaster. He had failed to include a special rope on the stern (its purpose unknown), which he had observed in ancient pictures. Too late, Heyerdahl realized that the rope was meant to keep the tail of the boat in a high and firm position against rough seas. Without it the soggy vessel's back end was flattening out and riding dangerously low in the water. Although the men cut up their plastic foam life raft (a risky measure) and attached it to *Ra*'s stern to help it float, their efforts eventually failed. The boat and its crew were in danger of sinking in shark-infested waters. Just 500 miles from Barbados, a West Indies island close to the South American mainland, Heyerdahl called off the journey. A rescue boat retrieved the men and *Ra* was abandoned, after sailing nearly 3,000 miles in fifty-six days.

So tantalizingly close to proving his theory, Heyerdahl attempted the voyage again. This time he convinced Aymara Indians from the Lake Titicaca region of Bolivia to come to Egypt and build the boat, because they used a different method of working with reeds that produced a stronger vessel. This time the rudder oars were made of thick tree trunks, to withstand the force of ocean waves. The same team of adventurers (with the addition of another man) would repeat the journey.

Redesigned boat makes successful crossing

Ra II set out from Safi, on Africa's northwest coast, on May 17, 1970. The boat made steady progress, although at one point the crew had to throw every nonessential supply overboard: the vessel, which had soaked up tons of seawater, was riding dangerously low in the water. This made *Ra II* travel more slowly and become even more difficult to control. As time wore on the men grew weary of their adventure and longed for home. Their provisions and water supply were low and they got salt-water sores from always being wet. The Caribbean island of Barbados was spotted not a moment too soon.

On July 12, 1970, *Ra II* reached Barbados after fifty-seven days at sea. Heyerdahl and his companions had at last completed their ocean voyage, and proved the possibility that ancient Egyptians had done the same. The *Ra II* crew received messages of congratulations from all over the world.

Heyerdahl made yet another voyage to further prove that great bodies of water and primitive sailing craft did not keep ancient civilizations isolated from one another. He built a sixty-foot boat based on a Sumerian design (Sumer was a southern region of ancient Babylonia, located in present-day

Iraq) with reeds grown in the Tigris-Euphrates Valley in what was once Asia Minor (now Turkey). With a crew of eleven he traveled 4,200 miles in four months, sailing through the Persian Gulf and around the Arabian Sea to Pakistan's Indus Valley. In 1979 Heyerdahl stopped making voyages of adventure, confident that he had proved his theories. He is the recipient of many important anthropological and geographical awards, although his ideas still remain controversial, because more evidence is needed to confirm them.

Sources

Bohlander, Richard E., ed. *World Explorers and Discoverers.* New York: Macmillan, 1992.

Engel, Dolores. *Voyage of the* Kon-Tiki. Milwaukee: Raintree Publishers, 1979.

Marshall Cavendish Illustrated Encyclopedia of Discovery and Exploration, Volume 7: *Charting the Vast Pacific,* written by John Gilbert. Freeport, NY: Marshall Cavendish, 1990.

Murphy, Barbara Beasley and Norman Baker. *Thor Heyerdahl and the Reed Boat* Ra. Philadelphia: Lippincott, 1974.

Abu Abd-Allah Muhammed al-Sharif al-Idrisi

Born 1100, Ceuta, Morocco

Died 1166, Sicily

Idrisi was an Arab traveler and geographer who produced what is largely considered the most important geographical work of the Middle Ages.

Abu Abd-Allah Muhammed al-Sharif al-Idrisi was born in the North African city of Ceuta, once a part of Morocco (now ruled by Spain). He was a member of a noble Arab family that claimed descent from the Prophet Muhammad (c. 570–632), the founder of the Islamic religion. Idrisi's ancestors had once ruled parts of southern Spain (around Malaga) and North Africa (the Fez region) until 1057, when they lost their power and fled to Morocco.

Begins life of travel

Information about Idrisi's early life is brief. It is known that he lived in Marrakesh, Morocco, and Qustantinah, Algeria. He also lived and studied in the great Muslim center of Cordoba in southern Spain. In addition, he began—at around age sixteen—to travel throughout the Middle East between North Africa and Asia Minor (what is now Turkey), and may even have journeyed well into Europe to places like Portugal,

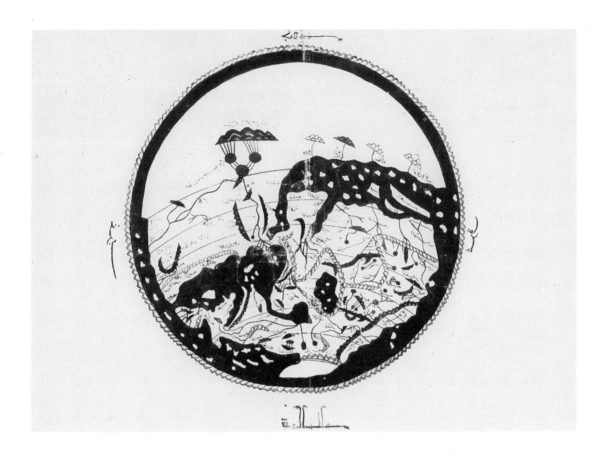

the west coast of France, and even as far north as England and Denmark.

Idrisi's great map of the world, drawn with the south at the top.

Becomes member of Sicily's royal court

The well-traveled Idrisi was invited to the court of the Christian king Roger II (1095–1154) of Sicily, the descendent of the Norman conquerors who had taken the Mediterranean island of Sicily from the Arabs. In 1145 Idrisi journeyed to the Sicilian capital city of Palermo, and became the royal geographer and cartographer (mapmaker). Why an Arab like Idrisi—with such a distinguished Islamic heritage—would accept the appointment of a Christian king has been the source of much speculation. Idrisi's choice was considered a dishonorable one by the Islamic leaders of his time.

Greek astronomer and mathematician Ptolemy. Idrisi used Ptolemy's work as one of the sources for his own maps and writings.

Regardless, Idrisi set to work on several projects for the king. These included the construction of a large planisphere—an engraved silver globe—that projected an image of the sphere of the heavens on a flat surface. He also began work on a map of the world; the map measured five feet by twelve feet and was engraved in silver. This was accompanied by a book, the *Nuzhat al-Mushtak fi Khtirak al-Nafs,* translated as *The Would-Be Traveler's Stroll Across the Horizons of the Globe.* Also referred to as *The Book of Roger* after its royal sponsor, the volume was meant to explain the globe and map, and to give a description of the known parts of the world—in Asia, Africa, and Europe.

Idrisi used a number of sources as he drew his map and wrote his book on geography. As a traveler who had seen much of the world, he knew the value of personal observation. He included his own travel experiences in the book, and he sent out others—including artists—to visit different countries and bring back firsthand accounts and sketches of geographical features. He used information from the works of earlier geographers and cartographers as well, including the books *Megiste,* written by the second-century Greek astronomer and mathematician Ptolemy.

Important geographical projects completed

Shortly before Roger's death in 1154, Idrisi presented his completed works to the king. While the engraved map was destroyed a few years later by invading enemy forces, copies of the book—with its series of seventy-one maps of the known world—were spared, and are in existence today. Largely considered to be the finest made in the Middle Ages, both in accuracy and scope, the maps (some of them in color) show the earth divided into seven climate zones, according to Islamic beliefs. They are plotted on a grid system of horizontal and vertical lines, to show how geographic locations correspond with coordinates in the heavens. (But they do not yet allow for the curvature of the earth, as does our modern system of longitude and latitude.) Grid maps had originated in China, and were brought back to the Middle East and Europe by Arab navigators. Idrisi was the first cartographer to introduce the system into European mapmaking. Along with geographic data about the areas, the cartographer included detailed information about the peoples who lived there and their cultural and economic practices. *The Book of Roger* gives a comprehensive picture of Europe and the Middle East during the twelfth century.

It appears that Idrisi subsequently produced an even larger geographical work for Roger's successor, William I (1120–66). But this project is only known through an extract that has survived and is preserved in a library in Istanbul, Turkey. A man of many talents and interests, Idrisi also wrote about the common drugs of his day, in several different languages, in the *Book of Simple Drugs*. He studied Arabic literature as well, and was a gifted poet; some of his verse still survives today. The circumstances of Idrisi's death are not known, although it is assumed that he lived out his life in the royal court at Sicily.

Sources

Baker, Daniel B., ed. *Explorers and Discoverers of the World.* Detroit: Gale Research, 1993.

Bohlander, Richard E., ed. *World Explorers and Discoverers.* New York: Macmillan, 1992.

Delpar, Helen, ed. *The Discoverers: An Encyclopedia of Explorers and Exploration.* New York: McGraw-Hill, 1980.

Waldman, Carl and Alan Wexler. *Who Was Who in World Exploration.* New York: Facts on File, 1992.

Gonzalo Jiménez de Quesada

Born c. 1501, Córdoba or Granada, Spain

Died c. 1579, Bogotá, Colombia

Gonzalo Jiménez de Quesada traveled into the interior of Colombia, where he conquered the Chibcha, the last of the great Andean civilizations to be subdued by the Spanish.

Between 1518 and 1521, Spanish conquistador Hernán Cortés (1485–1547) subdued the Aztecs in Mexico. The territories and treasures (including precious metals and finely crafted objects and jewelry) of the advanced Indian civilization became the possessions of Spain. During the 1530s Spanish conquistador Francisco Pizarro (c. 1475–1541) similarly subdued the Incas of Peru, also claiming their extended realm and fabulous wealth for Spain. Convinced that more rich kingdoms existed in South America, other conquistadors followed, traveling through the continent's densest jungles and most remote mountains to find them. While they did not discover empires equal in grandeur to those of the Aztecs or the Incas, these men essentially opened up all of South America to European colonization. Gonzalo Jiménez de Quesada was one explorer who followed in the footsteps of Cortés and Pizarro: he found and conquered the Chibcha, an advanced Indian civilization located in the high plains of the central Colombian Andes.

Arrives in South America

Jiménez de Quesada was born sometime around the year 1501 in either the city of Córdoba or Granada in southern Spain. He studied law at the Spanish University of Salamanca, and set up a legal practice in Granada by 1533. Two years later, however, he was headed for South America after becoming a member of the staff of Pedro Fernández de Lugo, the newly appointed governor of the Spanish colony of Santa Marta on the northern coast of present-day Colombia. Jiménez de Quesada sailed with a large expedition to the colony, arriving in 1536.

Soon after reaching Santa Marta, rumors of a fabulously rich South American city and its Indian ruler reached Lugo. Known as El Dorado, or "the gilded one," this legendary native king possessed such wealth that he reportedly powdered his body with gold dust each morning and washed it off every evening in a sacred lake into which emeralds and gold objects were thrown. Hoping to find the legendary city, Lugo chose Jiménez de Quesada to lead an expedition to explore the province of Santa Marta and the Magdalena River, the great waterway that rises in the Andes of southern Colombia and flows into the Caribbean Sea. He also wanted Jiménez de Quesada to find a route from Santa Marta to Peru, the center of Spanish colonial activity in South America.

Leads expedition into Colombian interior

Jiménez de Quesada left Santa Marta on April 5, 1536, with some 600 men, proceeding by horseback and on foot. They avoided traveling along the lower reaches of the Magdalena River, where hostile Indian tribes were known to dwell. They headed east instead, around the Sierra Nevada de Santa Marta Mountains, and journeyed into what is now Venezuela. From there they trekked to the Magdalena River farther south, at the place where it meets the Cesar River. Along the way they stopped at Chiriguaná in the Cesar River valley.

Presses on despite terrible hardships

Traveling along the Magdalena River was miserable. It was the rainy season, the riverbanks were flooded, and the air was heavy with steamy heat. Jiménez de Quesada and his men were attacked by swarms of insects, hungry crocodiles, and other wild animals. Still, the expedition members managed to make their way to Tamalameque, a rendezvous point on the Magdalena River where they were to be met by five supply ships sent from Santa Marta. After days of waiting, Jiménez de Quesada received word that the vessels had been unable to ascend the river: a storm had wrecked three of them and the other two had turned back. In spite of this disaster—and the protests of his men—the expedition leader refused to abandon his mission.

By now supplies where dangerously low and many of Jiménez de Quesada's men were sick or dying. A second group of supply ships did manage to make its way to them, but not before the explorers had been forced to eat anything they could find in the swampy jungle—bats, snakes, and lizards. Hacking their way through the thick vegetation that bordered the Magdalena, their progress was painstaking. It took the expedition eight months to reach the Indian village of Tora (what is now Barrancabermeja, Colombia), only 300 miles from their starting point on the river.

Searches for legendary mountain kingdom

It was here that Jiménez de Quesada heard rumors about an advanced Indian civilization that lived on the eastern slopes of the Andes. He had already seen signs that the tales might be true: the natives he now encountered sometimes possessed things like woven fabrics and well-crafted objects. In October of 1536 he decided to leave the Magdalena and travel into the mountains to look for the hidden kingdom.

By spring of 1537, Jiménez de Quesada and his expedition had reached the large mountain valleys where the Chibcha Indians were thought to dwell. At this point only 166 members of his force of several hundred men, and only 60

Jiménez de Quesada leaves Santa Marta on April 5, 1536, to find the kingdom of El Dorado and a route to Peru, the center of Spanish colonial activity in South America.

After 8 months of difficult travel, the expedition reaches the Indian village of Tora, only 300 miles from its starting point on the river.

In October of 1536 Jiménez de Quesada decides to leave the Magdalena and travel into the mountains to look for the hidden kingdom of the Chibcha Indians.

In 1569 Jiménez de Quesada leads a final expedition in search of the legendary land of El Dorado. The expedition gets as far as the point where the Orinoco and Guaviare rivers meet. After three years of great hardship, he and his men return to Santa Fé de Bogotá, unsuccessful in their mission.

After finding the kingdom on the plateau of Bogotá, Jiménez de Quesada subdues the Chibcha Indians and names the conquered land New Granada.

Modern-day political border

horses, were still alive. In August the conquistador and his small army defeated the leaders of Tunja, a kingdom in the mountains north of the present-day Colombian capital of Bogotá. The king was imprisoned in his own palace and forced to turn over all his gold and other precious metals to the Spanish. At the end of 1537 and the beginning of 1538, Jiménez de Quesada conquered the minor rulers of Cundinamarca, located in the region surrounding present-day Bogotá.

Locates and subdues the Chibcha

On the plateau of Bogotá, Jiménez de Quesada and his men at last reached the kingdom of the Chibcha Indians. Like the Aztecs and Incas, these native Americans had developed an advanced civilization. They built temples in which to perform their religious ceremonies, practiced agriculture, and had developed a system of currency. They made gold and copper ornaments, mined emeralds, wove textiles, and made pottery and baskets. They possessed the wealth that Jiménez de Quesada had been seeking. (Although he, and subsequent conquistadors, still believed that El Dorado remained to be found.)

For the next several months Jiménez de Quesada and his men subdued the Chibcha. The tribe was politically divided, and the lawyer/conquistador formed alliances and negotiated deals that helped him avoid the wide-scale brutality and bloodshed that usually accompanied such Spanish takeovers in the Americas. He lost just four of his men during the conquest. Still, unscrupulous incidents did occur. During an early encounter, for example, the reigning king was killed, and Jiménez de Quesada appointed the dead ruler's cousin to the throne with the understanding that he turn over all royal treasures to the Spanish (some were believed to be hidden). Once the new king obeyed the order, he was also killed.

Jiménez de Quesada named the land he had conquered New Granada. On August 6, 1538, he founded the town of Santa Fé de Bogotá (now Bogotá) on the site of the old Chibcha capital. Early in 1539 two other conquistadors and their forces reached the plateau of Bogotá: Spaniard Sebastián de Belalcázar arrived from Quito, Ecuador, to the south, and German Nikolaus Federmann came west from Venezuela. Both men were looking for the land of El Dorado. And both were dismayed to find that Jiménez de Quesada had beaten them to the wealth of the Chibcha empire.

Other conquistadors claim conquered territory

But Federmann maintained that the newly conquered region was in territory under German rule, and Belalcázar felt that the land belonged to Ecuador. Would the dispute force a bloody war among the conquistadors? On March 17, 1539, Jiménez de Quesada negotiated an agreement to avoid that: the three expeditionary forces consented to leave together and present their claims to the Council of the Indies in Spain. They embarked from Santa Marta sometime in late 1539 or early 1540.

While awaiting the Spanish government's decision regarding New Granada, Jiménez de Quesada traveled in France and Portugal, returning to Spain in 1545. He was quite confident that he would be named governor of the new territory. But control of the region went to Alonso Luis de Lugo, who had become governor of Santa Marta following the death of his father. Still, the efforts of Jiménez de Quesada did not go unrecognized. He was made marshal of the new province and, in 1565, royal councilor of Santa Fé de Bogotá.

Leads final search for El Dorado

Jiménez de Quesada returned to New Granada in 1551 and for the next two decades served as a colonial administrator in Santa Fé de Bogotá. In 1569—when he was almost seventy years old—he led a final expedition, which he financed himself, in search of El Dorado. (It is likely that the Chibcha kingdom he had already discovered was that legendary land of wealth.) His large exploring party traveled across the Andes to the *llanos,* or plains region, of eastern New Granada. The expedition got as far as the point where the Orinoco and Guaviare rivers meet, on the border between present-day Colombia and Venezuela. After three years of great hardship, Jiménez de Quesada and his remaining men returned to Santa Fé de Bogotá, unsuccessful in their mission.

Jiménez de Quesada spent his remaining years in Santa Fé de Bogotá. He was one of the few Spanish conquistadors who was well-educated, and he wrote several works, including a valuable personal account of his conquest of New Granada. Some scholars believe that the Spanish writer Miguel de Cervantes (1547–1616)—who lived during Jiménez de Quesada's time—may have modeled the hero of his great novel, *Don Quixote de la Mancha,* after the conquistador. A country gentleman who embarks on grand adventures and impossible quests, Don Quixote resembles the refined explorer Jiménez de Quesada, who restlessly searched for the legendary El Dorado.

Sources

Baker, Daniel B., ed. *Explorers and Discoverers of the World.* Detroit: Gale Research, 1993.

Bohlander, Richard E., ed. *World Explorers and Discoverers.* New York: Macmillan, 1992.

Delpar, Helen, ed. *The Discoverers: An Encyclopedia of Explorers and Exploration.* New York: McGraw-Hill, 1980.

Marshall Cavendish Illustrated Encyclopedia of Discovery and Exploration, Volume 4: *God, Gold, and Glory,* written by Nicholas Hordern. Freeport, NY: Marshall Cavendish, 1990.

Waldman, Carl and Alan Wexler. *Who Was Who in World Exploration.* New York: Facts on File, 1992.

Wilhelm Junker

Born 1840, Moscow, Russia

Died 1892

By the last decades of the nineteenth century, much of the interior of the continent of Africa had been explored and mapped. Still, there were some areas that had not yet been investigated or where geographical questions remained. One such region was located between the upper reaches of the Nile and the Congo, the continent's two great rivers. Mapping the Congo River—which extends through much of central Africa—was especially difficult because of its numerous large and small tributaries. The Congo and its branches form a system of navigable waterways some 9,000 miles long.

One explorer who helped add some geographical answers to the puzzle of Africa's complex waterways was Wilhelm Junker. He was born in Moscow, Russia, in 1840, to German parents. At the age of twenty-nine he sailed to Iceland, beginning a life of travel to distant places. In 1873 he decided to explore Africa, and traveled to Tunisia on its northern coast, where he remained for almost a year. He then made his way to Egypt, and to the Sudan to its south.

German explorer Wilhelm Junker traveled through northern and east-central Africa, and discovered important information about an upper branch of the Congo River.

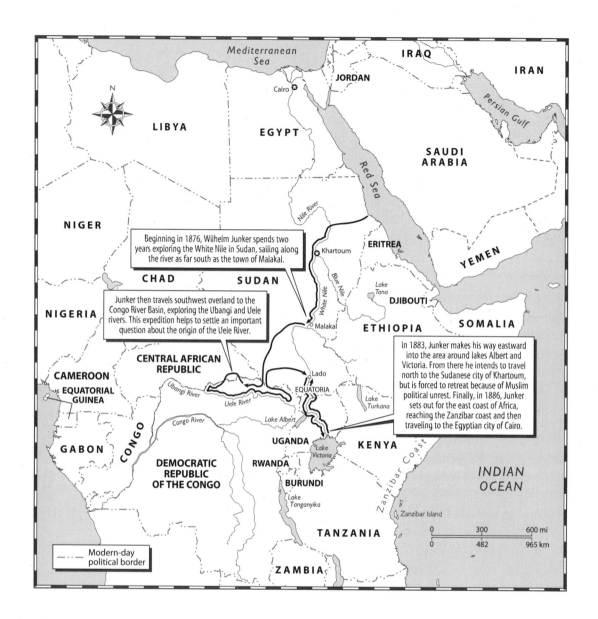

Beginning in 1876, Wilhelm Junker spends two years exploring the White Nile in Sudan, sailing along the river as far south as the town of Malakal.

Junker then travels southwest overland to the Congo River Basin, exploring the Ubangi and Uele rivers. This expedition helps to settle an important question about the origin of the Uele River.

In 1883, Junker makes his way eastward into the area around lakes Albert and Victoria. From there he intends to travel north to the Sudanese city of Khartoum, but is forced to retreat because of Muslim political unrest. Finally, in 1886, Junker sets out for the east coast of Africa, reaching the Zanzibar coast and then traveling to the Egyptian city of Cairo.

Modern-day political border

Investigates Africa's waterways

Beginning in 1876, Junker spent two years exploring Sudan's White Nile, sailing along the river as far as the town of Malakal. He then traveled overland to the southwest, entering the Congo River basin. He explored the Ubangi and Uele rivers, both important navigable northern branches of the Congo. His investigation of the Uele, located in what is now the Democratic Republic of the Congo, settled an important question about that river's origin. Up until Junker's investigation it had been wrongly believed that the Uele was connected with the Niger, a great river in western Africa with a large eastern tributary that extends near the Congo River region.

Muslim revolt stops travel plans

In 1883, Junker made his way eastward into the area around lakes Albert and Victoria, which are part of the Nile River system and are located in present-day Uganda and Tanzania. From there he intended to travel north, rejoining the White Nile and then making his way to the great Sudanese city of Khartoum. But that would take him through an area that was undergoing great political unrest: led by Muslim religious leader Muhammad Ahmad (1844–85), who called himself the Mahdi, Muslims in the Sudan had risen in violent revolt against their Egyptian rulers. In 1885 they had even managed to overtake the capital city of Khartoum, where, after a lengthy siege, they had killed British General Charles Gordon (1833–85) and his Egyptian forces.

Serving under Gordon in Africa was a German explorer and surgeon named Eduard Schnitzer (1840–92). In 1876 Schnitzer had been assigned to a post at Lado on the Nile River in southern Sudan. Performing his duties well, he was appointed governor of Equatoria—as that part of Sudan was then called—and he took the name Emin Pasha. The Muslim revolt to the north then cut him off from all contact with the outside world.

Journey leads to rescue of besieged governor

Junker joined Emin Pasha and his band of Egyptian and Sudanese soldiers at Lado. (Also present was Emin Pasha's European companion, Gaetano Casati.) As the Mahdi threat spread, the group retreated bit by bit to Wadelai, just north of Lake Albert. Time passed, and Junker, Emin Pasha, and their men feared they had been forgotten. Finally, in 1886, Junker set out for the east coast of Africa, hoping to bring news of

Who Is the Mahdi?

In Arabic, Mahdi means "he who is divinely guided." Many Muslims believe that near the end of time a holy figure—the Mahdi—will appear on Earth, and establish a universal Islam. Throughout Islamic history, many men have arisen claiming to be the Mahdi. They have usually been reformers whose ideas have gone against those held by ruling religious authorities.

The most famous Mahdi known to the Western world was Muhammad Ahmad (1844–85), a Muslim religious leader in Anglo-Egyptian Sudan, that extensive area of the Sudan ruled by Egypt and under the protection of Great Britain during the nineteenth century. Muhammad Ahmad declared himself to be the Mahdi in 1881 and led a war to free Sudanese Muslims from Egyptian military rule. His followers—called Mahdists—rose up and took the Sudanese capital of Khartoum in 1885, and for a brief time controlled the Sudan. Muhammad Ahmad died soon after the taking of the city and was succeeded by the caliph—the Muslim civil and religious leader—Abdullahi (or Abd Allah, 1846–99). In his reform of Islam, the Mahdi had forbidden the pilgrimage to Mecca—the birthplace of the Prophet Muhammad (c. 570–632), the founder of the Islamic religion—and instead ordered devout Muslims to join the holy war against unbelievers.

An Anglo-Egyptian army led by British General Horatio Herbert Kitchener (1850–1916) conducted a two-year military campaign to defeat the Mahdists. The revolutionaries were dealt a final blow in 1898 at the city of Omdurman, located across the Nile River from Khartoum.

Emin Pasha's plight. The explorer reached the Zanzibar coast and then traveled to Egypt's capital city of Cairo, where he shared the bad news of the Egyptian governor's situation. An alarmed British public raised more than 20,000 pounds (British currency) to finance a relief expedition and chose veteran African explorer Henry Morton Stanley (1841–1904) to lead it. Enduring countless hardships and suffering a great loss of lives, Stanley's expedition through the Congo at last reached Emin Pasha on April 29, 1888. Surprisingly, the governor of Equatoria did not want to be rescued, as he was under the impression that Stanley's men would furnish him with enough weaponry and reinforcements to reassert his control of the area. Stanley had to force him to join the expedition as it proceeded to Zanzibar.

Emin Pasha, governor of Equatoria. He was murdered in 1892 by Arab slave raiders.

After his ordeal in the Sudan, Junker soon returned to Europe. He wrote a three-volume account of his time in Africa, titled *Reisen in Afrika 1875–86* (*Travels in Africa 1875–86*), which was published in 1889–91.

Sources

Explorers and Exploration, Volume 8: *Africa and Arabia,* written by Geoffrey Nowell-Smith. Danbury, CT: Grolier Educational, 1998.

Marshall Cavendish Illustrated Encyclopedia of Discovery and Exploration, Volume 11: *The Challenge of Africa,* written by Elspeth Huxley. Freeport, NY: Marshall Cavendish, 1990.

Saari, Peggy and Daniel B. Baker. "Henry Morton Stanley." *Explorers and Discoverers.* Detroit: U•X•L, 1995.

Waldman, Carl and Alan Wexler. *Who Was Who in World Exploration.* New York: Facts on File, 1992.

Elisha Kent Kane

Born February 3, 1820, Philadelphia, Pennsylvania

Died February 16, 1857, Havana, Cuba

American naval officer and physician Elisha Kent Kane made two expeditions into the Arctic in search of lost British explorer Sir John Franklin. Along the way he explored unknown territories and set a northern distance record in the Western Hemisphere.

In 1845 British naval officer Sir John Franklin (1786–1847) led an expedition into the Canadian Arctic in search of the Northwest Passage, a northern sailing route between the Atlantic and Pacific oceans in the Western Hemisphere. When he and his party of 129 men were never heard from again, several rescue expeditions were launched over the next decade, to find survivors or to discover the travelers' fate. Leaders of British expeditions included Sir James Clark Ross (1800–62) and Sir Robert McClure (1807–73). American search efforts were also undertaken, sponsored by wealthy New York businessman Henry Grinnell (1799–1874). American naval officer and physician Elisha Kent Kane commanded one of these expeditions into the Arctic.

Kane was born February 3, 1820, in Philadelphia, Pennsylvania, the son of a prominent attorney. In 1838 he attended the University of Virginia, hoping to become an engineer. A bad bout of rheumatic fever, however, weakened his health, and he decided to change his career path and become a physician instead. He went on to attend the University of Pennsylvania, graduating as a medical doctor in 1842.

Joins U.S. Navy to see world

After working a short time as a medical researcher, Kane joined the U.S. Navy as an assistant surgeon in 1843. Despite his frail health, he craved adventure and longed to see the world. As a navy medical officer he visited many exotic places, such as Brazil and India. When he accompanied a U.S. diplomatic mission to China, he toured much of Asia. As he traveled from place to place, Kane often asked for extended leave so that he could go off and explore. While stationed on the island of Macao near Hong Kong, for instance, he traveled to the Philippines, where he descended into the crater of an active volcano.

While serving with a U.S. naval squadron off the coast of Africa, Kane was stricken with tropical fever, and was sent home. In 1846 he was stationed in Mexico during the Mexican-American War (1846–48), where he was wounded and contracted typhus. After more than a year's recovery, he returned to active duty aboard a ship conducting a government survey of the Gulf of Mexico. It was then that Kane learned of the American polar expedition proposed by Grinnell to look for Franklin's lost expedition. Anxious to be a part of the great adventure, he applied to become the mission's chief medical officer. He received the post.

Ice defeats polar search for missing explorer

The First U.S. Grinnell Expedition to the Arctic was led by Lieutenant Edwin Jesse De Haven. Setting sail in May of 1850, the mission had very little success. Reaching Smith Sound—the southern end of the strait separating northern Greenland from the east shore of Canada's Ellesmere Island—the ship spent most of the year drifting, trapped in pack ice. The expedition members did manage to do some exploring, though, investigating the northern part of Devon Island (which De Haven named Grinnell Land, in honor of his sponsor).

Elisha Kent Kane searches for the missing Sir John Franklin and his party.

Forced to abandon its search mission, the expedition returned to New York. Kane had been the ship's historian as well as its doctor, and he wrote an account of the voyage, *The U.S. Grinnell Expedition in Search of Sir John Franklin,* which was published in early 1853. The book was an instant success: Kane had a gift for making those long months stranded in the forbidding Arctic sound like a grand adventure in majestic surroundings. Despite his brief experience, he became known as America's leading polar explorer and a popular lecturer.

Like many Arctic explorers of his day, Kane believed in an open polar sea. It was thought that once a ship made its way through a thick belt of Arctic ice, the climate grew warmer approaching the North Pole and the ocean became ice-free. Because no traces had yet been found of Franklin and his party, it was Kane's theory that the British officer might have found a way northward through Smith Sound and had reached the shores of that polar sea, leaving clues to his fate there. Kane wanted to launch his own expedition to test the theory.

Leads own search team into Arctic

It did not take long for the widely admired Kane to gather the support he needed to fulfill his ambition. With money raised by public contributions and a ship—the *Advance*—donated by Grinnell, Kane led what would become known as the Second U.S. Grinnell Expedition. Embarking from New York on May 31, 1853, the *Advance* had a small but expert crew of sixteen scientists and U.S. Navy members. Despite arriving in Smith Sound in the summer, Kane found its northern reaches still frozen and unnavigable, and he looked for a better way to proceed. He decided to travel along the coast of northwestern Greenland, hoping to find a clear sailing route to the polar sea. Kane was also interested in discovering how far north the land mass of Greenland extended, and if it could be used in an over-land crossing to the North Pole.

Ice-locked explorers reach new territories by sled

The *Advance* was able to travel as far north as Rensselaer Bay along Greenland's coast before becoming trapped in heavy ice. From there the expedition members made several exploratory trips in sledges (heavy sleds). They investigated the mainland of Greenland, where one group discovered Humboldt Glacier, the largest known glacier in the world. Another team, led by William Morton, traveled to the east coast of Greenland, reaching the northern latitude of 80°10'. That was a distance record for non-natives in the Western Hemisphere at that time.

In May of 1854, *Advance* officer Isaac Israel Hayes crossed a large frozen expanse of water to Ellesmere Island; that passage would become known as Kane Basin. He also observed that open water lay to its north. Kane was excited when he learned the news: surely here was the edge of the polar sea he had been seeking. In fact, it was an open stretch of water (today called Kennedy Channel), which runs between northern Greenland and Ellesmere Island. But Kane would bring back the misleading information, and for quite some time future expeditions would follow this route, attempting to reach the open polar sea and the North Pole. Only when explorers learned how truly vast and permanent the Arctic Ocean's ice cover is would they be able to reach the pole—by dogsled, not by sea.

Nonetheless, Kane and his team of scientists gathered much valuable information during the nearly two years they were stranded in Rensselaer Bay. They examined Arctic tides, the way glaciers are formed, and the earth's magnetism, which increases near the poles. They observed Inuit (Eskimo) culture and native animal life. But they did not find the information that had sent them to the Arctic in the first place: traces of the missing explorer Franklin and his expedition.

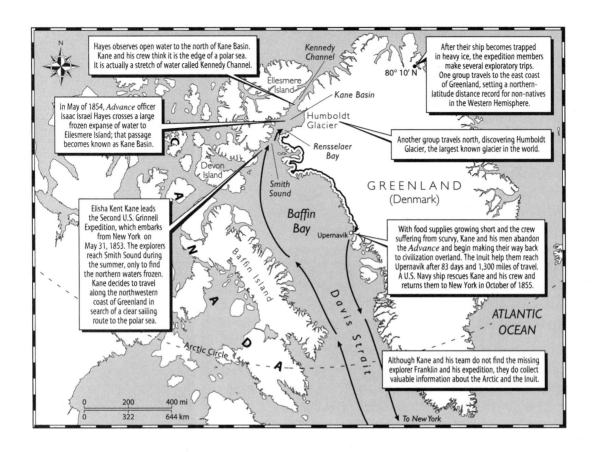

Hayes observes open water to the north of Kane Basin. Kane and his crew think it is the edge of a polar sea. It is actually a stretch of water called Kennedy Channel.

In May of 1854, *Advance* officer Isaac Israel Hayes crosses a large frozen expanse of water to Ellesmere Island; that passage becomes known as Kane Basin.

Elisha Kent Kane leads the Second U.S. Grinnell Expedition, which embarks from New York on May 31, 1853. The explorers reach Smith Sound during the summer, only to find the northern waters frozen. Kane decides to travel along the northwestern coast of Greenland in search of a clear sailing route to the polar sea.

After their ship becomes trapped in heavy ice, the expedition members make several exploratory trips. One group travels to the east coast of Greenland, setting a northern-latitude distance record for non-natives in the Western Hemisphere.

Another group travels north, discovering Humboldt Glacier, the largest known glacier in the world.

With food supplies growing short and the crew suffering from scurvy, Kane and his men abandon the *Advance* and begin making their way back to civilization overland. The Inuit help them reach Upernavik after 83 days and 1,300 miles of travel. A U.S. Navy ship rescues Kane and his crew and returns them to New York in October of 1855.

Although Kane and his team do not find the missing explorer Franklin and his expedition, they do collect valuable information about the Arctic and the Inuit.

Kennedy Channel

80° 10′ N

Ellesmere Island

Kane Basin

Humboldt Glacier

Rensselaer Bay

Devon Island

Smith Sound

GREENLAND (Denmark)

Baffin Bay

Upernavik

Baffin Island

Davis Strait

ATLANTIC OCEAN

Arctic Circle

CANADA

0   200   400 mi
0   322   644 km

To New York

Arctic captivity produces hardships

Their unexpected polar captivity took a toll on the crew of the *Advance*. Food supplies grew short and the men suffered from scurvy. In the early winter of 1854, eight members of the expedition—led by *Advance* officer Hayes—attempted to travel overland to Danish colonial settlements located farther south in Greenland. Bad weather and inexperience defeated their efforts, however, and the travelers returned to the *Advance* in December 1854 in terrible shape. It was fortunate that their commander was a physician; Kane used his medical skills to bring them back to health.

Crew finally abandons trapped ship

Realizing how desperate their situation was becoming, Kane decided to abandon the *Advance* altogether in May of

1855. It was clear that a thaw would never release the ship, and that he and his men would have to make their way back to civilization overland. Kane and his men traveled south along the coast of Greenland, heading for Danish settlements. Had it not been for the help of Inuit along the way, it is unlikely that they would have survived the journey. After an eighty-three-day trek of more than 1,300 miles, the expedition at last reached Upernavik—on Greenland's west coast—on August 6. Shortly thereafter, a U.S. Navy rescue ship, commanded by Lieutenant H. J. Hartstene, arrived, and Kane and his crew were taken aboard. They arrived in New York in October of 1855.

Kane wrote an account of the expedition soon after his return, and it was published a year later. Like his earlier book, *Arctic Explorations: The Second Grinnell Expedition in Search of Sir John Franklin in the Years 1853, '54, '55* was an immediate success. Kane became a national celebrity, and traveled to England to meet with Lady Jane Franklin, the wife of Sir John Franklin. (In 1859 she would sponsor a private search led by Francis McClintock that would at last uncover the remains of her husband's lost expedition.)

Arctic adventures inspire others

Kane was in ill health following his grueling two years in the Arctic. He traveled to Cuba, hoping that the warm climate would improve his condition. He died in Havana, its capital city, on February 16, 1857. He was buried in Philadelphia, his grand funeral reflecting his standing as a national hero. America's first well-known Arctic explorer, Kane would fire the imaginations and inspire the efforts of future U.S. polar adventurers like Charles Francis Hall (1821–71) and Adolphus Washington Greely (1844–1935). In 1909 an American naval officer, Robert Edwin Peary (1856–1920), would lead the first expedition to successfully reach the North Pole.

Sources

Bohlander, Richard E., ed. *World Explorers and Discoverers.* New York: Macmillan, 1992.

Delpar, Helen, ed. *The Discoverers: An Encyclopedia of Explorers and Explorations.* New York: McGraw-Hill, 1980.

Explorers and Exploration, Volume 4: *Scientists and Explorers,* written by Michael Sullivan. Danbury, CT: Grolier Educational, 1998.

Waldman, Carl and Alan Wexler. *Who Was Who in World Exploration.* New York: Facts on File, 1992.

Kintup

Born c. 1849, Sikkim
Died ?

In the middle of the eighteenth century Great Britain took possession of much of the Indian subcontinent. During the next several decades British surveyors set about making accurate maps of India and the regions to its north, including the Himalayas. (By 1818 the project would be known as "The Great Trigonometrical Survey.") The British felt that in order to keep their Indian holdings safe from the powerful nearby empires of Russia and China, they needed to expand their geographic knowledge, especially of the remote mountain kingdoms of Nepal and Tibet.

Getting that information was difficult, for the mountainous terrain made traveling treacherous. The surveyors also encountered hostile native inhabitants and, after a while, some countries closed their borders to them. In order to continue their mapmaking, the British began training Indians, disguised as merchants or pilgrims in order to enter forbidden areas, to secretly carry out their surveys for them. These Indians were usually well-educated men who received extensive training

Kintup was an Indian pundit-explorer who investigated the Tsangpo River in Tibet, and proved its connection with India's Brahmaputra River.

for their new lives as surveyors and spies. Thus they were called "pundit-explorers," because "pundit" means "learned man" in Hindi (the language spoken in India).

Indian explorer Kintup, however, did not fit the profile of the usual pundit. An illiterate native of Sikkim, a kingdom bordering India in the Himalayas, he was untrained in the skills of surveying and spying. Still, after four long years and despite many obstacles—including being sold into servitude—he managed to complete the task assigned to him by the British Survey Department. He succeeded in investigating more of the Tsangpo, Tibet's main navigable river, than had any previous explorer. He also proved that it was connected to the Brahmaputra River of northeastern India.

Receives important survey assignment

Given the code name K. P., Kintup made his first expedition into Tibet as the assistant to pundit-explorer Nem Singh. On the mission Kintup proved to be a hard worker and very reliable, and it was clear that he was ready to take on greater responsibilities. Unfortunately, his illiteracy kept him from traveling alone, for he could not record his observations. Therefore, on his second assignment he was paired with a Mongolian lama (Buddhist monk), and posed as his servant. Their mission was to travel to the Tsangpo River, which runs from west to east in southern Tibet. They were to find out if it was, in fact, the same river as the Brahmaputra, which flows through the Assam region of India.

Previous explorations of the Tsangpo, including one by pundit-explorer Nain Singh (c. 1832–c. 1882), had suggested that it was the only river in Tibet that was large enough to be the Brahmaputra. Still, the connection was not certain, for some 120 miles of the Tsangpo remained unexplored. Also unknown was how the river dropped from 10,000 feet to 500 feet in altitude in that short 120 miles. Did the Tsangpo descend sharply in what could be the world's greatest waterfall (it does not), or did it move along in a series of rapids?

Efforts had been made to investigate the Tsangpo by traveling from the south—from Assam—but explorers had

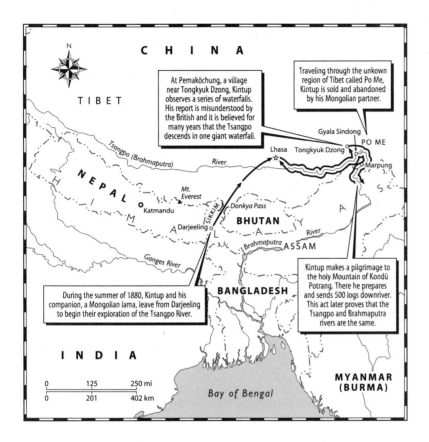

At Pemaköchung, a village near Tongkyuk Dzong, Kintup observes a series of waterfalls. His report is misunderstood by the British and it is believed for many years that the Tsangpo descends in one giant waterfall.

Traveling through the unkown region of Tibet called Po Me, Kintup is sold and abandoned by his Mongolian partner.

During the summer of 1880, Kintup and his companion, a Mongolian lama, leave from Darjeeling to begin their exploration of the Tsangpo River.

Kintup makes a pilgrimage to the holy Mountain of Kondü Potrang. There he prepares and sends 500 logs downriver. This act later proves that the Tsangpo and Brahmaputra rivers are the same.

been stopped by hostile hill tribes. So Kintup and his companion were instructed to make their way to the Tsangpo by starting in Tibet (to the north) and attempting to follow it downstream instead. If that were physically impossible, Kintup was to relay a message to the British Survey Department. The pundit-explorer was instructed to send specially marked logs down the Tsangpo, and if they reached alerted workers on the Brahmaputra River in Assam, the connection between the two rivers could be made.

Kintup and the Mongolian lama left the city of Darjeeling in northern India near the Sikkim border in the summer of 1880. They crossed into Tibet by way of the Donkya Pass and traveled to a monastery near Lhasa, Tibet's capital city. By March of 1881, after many delays, they reached Gyala Sindong, the farthest known point on the Tsangpo River. At the small village of Pemakîchung, Kintup observed a series of waterfalls. While he reported this to the Survey Department, the message was misunderstood, and for many years it was believed that the waters of the Tsangpo descended in one giant waterfall.

Abandoned and sold into slavery

Unable to proceed any farther along the river there, Kintup and his companion were forced to travel through an unknown region of Tibet called Po Me. On May 24, 1881, at a town named Tongkyuk Dzong, the lama announced that he had to leave to take care of some business, and that he would return in two or three days. But he really traveled back to his home in Mongolia and was never seen again. Before leaving, however, he had sold Kintup to the head man of the village. The pundit-explorer was forced to work as a house servant for nearly a year, until he escaped on March 7, 1882.

Serves in Tibetan monastery

His determination to complete his mission unshaken by the ordeal, Kintup headed back to the Tsangpo River. But in the town of Marpung, Tibet, he was captured by agents sent out by his former master; things again looked bleak for the pundit-explorer. Kintup begged assistance from the head lama of the local monastery, who agreed to rescue the explorer from his enslavement if Kintup would work for him. So Kintup became a servant in the monastery.

After four and a half months there, Kintup was given permission to make a pilgrimage downriver to the holy mountain of Kondü Potrang. He instead used the time to prepare some 500 logs that he intended to send down the Tsangpo River. Returning to the monastery at Marpung, Kintup then had to find a way to alert the Survey of India staff in Assam to look for the logs. The opportunity came— probably in December of 1882—when he was given two months' leave to make another religious pilgrimage. This time he traveled to Lhasa, where he managed to find someone to carry a message back to India.

Relays information by floating logs downstream

Kintup returned to Marpung and his life of servitude once more. He stayed in the monastery for nine more months, until the head lama—impressed by Kintup's religious devotion—gave him his freedom. The pundit-explorer traveled to the place where he had hidden his logs. He was supposed to mark them by inserting metal tubes inside, but because he lost the drill he needed to do this, he tied the tubes to the surface of the logs with bamboo strips instead. He then released them down the river, at the rate of fifty a day.

Kintup also tried to follow the river downstream himself. He was able to get to within forty miles of the border of British territory before hostile native tribes stopped him. So he embarked on a return trip the same way he had come: back to Sikkim by way of Lhasa. He finally reached the offices of the Survey in Assam on November 17, 1884, four years after he had left.

Geographical findings at last recognized

On his return, Kintup learned that nobody had followed up on his message from Tibet, and that the logs that he had so painstakingly prepared had floated down the river unnoticed in Assam. His efforts went unappreciated; two years passed before anyone even bothered to take down his story. When an account of Kintup's explorations was published, it was revealed that he had investigated more of the Tsangpo than had any previous explorer. What is more, some of the logs that he sent down the Tsangpo had later been discovered in the great river delta where the Brahmaputra and Ganges rivers meet to empty into the Bay of Bengal. Thus Kintup's efforts had proved that the Tsangpo and the Brahmaputra were, indeed, the same river.

Kintup was finally given a reward for his work. He served in a minor role in one further expedition for the British Survey Department. He then returned to his native village, and resumed his work as a tailor. The date of his death is unknown.

Sources

Baker, Daniel B., ed. *Explorers and Discoverers of the World.* Detroit: Gale Research, 1993.

Marshall Cavendish Illustrated Encyclopedia of Discovery and Exploration, Volume 12: *The Heartland of Asia,* written by Nathalie Ettinger. Freeport, NY: Marshall Cavendish, 1990.

Pear, Nancy and Daniel B. Baker. "Hari Ram." *Explorers and Discoverers.* Detroit: U•X•L, 1998.

Waldman, Carl and Alan Wexler. *Who Was Who in World Exploration.* New York: Facts on File, 1992.

Jacob Le Maire

Born 1585, the Netherlands

Died 1616

Since the 1494 Treaty of Tordesillas, Portugal had controlled European commerce in the Far East, including the rich spice trade of the East Indies. But after the Netherlands declared its independence from Spain in 1581, the rising young nation—with its large population of merchants and seamen—decided to challenge Portugal's declining position in the Orient. By the beginning of the seventeenth century, the Netherlands had displaced Portugal as the major maritime and trading power in Southeast Asia. In 1602 the Dutch East India Company was formed to establish trade policy and control in the area. The Dutch government granted the company exclusive rights to trade in the Indies. The company was allowed its own armed forces on land and sea, and could wage war against Spain and Portugal. It could also establish trading posts and colonies, make treaties, and had legal authority over the territories it managed.

Independent Dutch businessmen did not think that the trade monopoly of the Dutch East India Company was fair.

Jacob Le Maire was a Dutch navigator who discovered a new route between the Atlantic and Pacific oceans near the tip of South America.

The firm had control of trade to and from the Orient, either around Africa's Cape of Good Hope or through the Strait of Magellan at the southern end of South America—the only two routes known and used by European traders. One merchant from Amsterdam, Isaac Le Maire, set out in 1610 to end the company's eastern monopoly.

Australian company founded

Le Maire was a Jew who had been forced to leave Tournai, the city of his birth (now in western Belgium), because of religious persecution. He had settled in the growing commercial center of Amsterdam, where he had prospered in the overseas trade business, and had become the largest shareholder of the Dutch East India Company the year it was established. But it did not take long for him to become unhappy with the company's absolute control over Dutch trade in the Far East. In 1610 Le Maire went before the Dutch legislature, or States-General, hoping to form a new trading firm that would put an end to the Dutch East India Company's monopoly. He succeeded in establishing the Australian Company, which was granted the right to trade with China, Tartary (northeastern Asia), Japan, New Holland (Australia), and the islands of the South Pacific. The only restriction—and it seemed an impossible one to overcome—was that the Australian Company not use established trade routes around the Cape of Good Hope or through the Strait of Magellan.

Le Maire consulted well-known Dutch navigator Willem Corneliszoon Schouten (1567–1625), who had already made three successful voyages to the East Indies while in the employment of the Dutch East India Company. From his own experience and from studying the reports made during the 1577–80 journey of English seaman Francis Drake (c. 1540–1596) as he traveled through the Strait of Magellan, Schouten suspected that another passage between the Atlantic and Pacific oceans lay farther south. While many Europeans at that time believed that Tierra del Fuego—the land south of the Strait of Magellan—was the northernmost tip of a great southern continent, Schouten thought that it was a

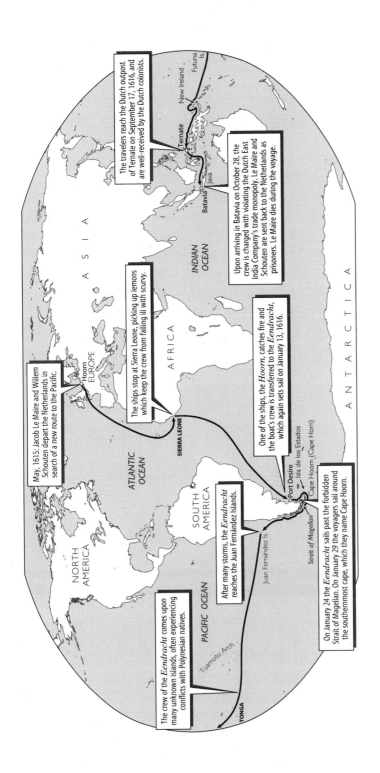

The travelers reach the Dutch outpost of Ternate on September 17, 1616, and are well-received by the Dutch colonists.

Upon arriving in Batavia on October 28, the crew is charged with violating the Dutch East India Company's trade monopoly. Le Maire and Schouten are sent back to the Netherlands as prisoners. Le Maire dies during the voyage.

The ships stop at Sierra Leone, picking up lemons which keep the crew from falling ill with scurvy.

One of the ships, the *Hoorn*, catches fire and the boat's crew is transferred to the *Eendracht*, which again sets sail on January 13, 1616.

May, 1615: Jacob Le Maire and Willem Schouten depart the Netherlands in search of a new route to the Pacific.

After many storms, the *Eendracht* reaches the Juan Fernández Islands.

On January 24 the *Eendracht* sails past the forbidden Strait of Magellan. On January 29 the voyagers sail around the southernmost cape, which they name Cape Hoorn.

The crew of the *Eendracht* comes upon many unknown islands, often experiencing conflicts with Polynesian natives.

Futuna Is.
New Ireland
Ternate
NEW GUINEA
Java
Batavia

ASIA

EUROPE
Hoorn

AFRICA

INDIAN OCEAN

SIERRA LEONE

ATLANTIC OCEAN

NORTH AMERICA

SOUTH AMERICA

PACIFIC OCEAN

Juan Fernández Is.

Tuamotu Arch.

TONGA

Port Desire
Isla de los Estados
Cape Hoorn (Cape Horn)
Strait of Magellan

ANTARCTICA

large island. He believed that a clear sailing route could be found around it.

Jacob Le Maire chosen expedition commander

With Schouten signed on as master pilot, Isaac Le Maire launched an expedition to find a new southern route between the oceans. He convinced the wealthy businessmen of the Dutch seaport of Hoorn, where Schouten was born, to invest in the venture; if the navigator's theory was correct, the merchants might again enjoy free trade in the Far East. Isaac Le Maire's son, Jacob, was named commander of the expedition, and another son, Daniel, also joined the voyage. At the end of May in 1615, two ships set sail from Hoorn: the *Eendracht* was piloted by Willem Schouten, and the smaller *Hoorn* was directed by Jan Schouten, Willem's brother.

Before crossing the Atlantic, the ships stopped at Sierra Leone on the west coast of Africa. Commander Le Maire had his men exchange some of their trade goods for 25,000 lemons, which would keep them—with their diet of dried meat and fish—from falling ill with scurvy. (All but three of the eighty-seven-man crew would survive the fifteen-month journey.) On December 8 the ships reached the southeast coast of South America, and anchored to make repairs at Puerto Deseado in Patagonia, now part of Argentina. There the men saw many curious sights, including ostriches and llamas. But while in port, the *Hoorn* caught fire and was destroyed. The boat's crew and what supplies could be saved were transferred to the *Eendracht*. The expedition again set sail on January 13, 1616, heading farther south along the coast.

Travelers pass through unknown strait and reach continent's southern tip

On January 24 the *Eendracht* sailed past the forbidden Strait of Magellan. But not long after that, Le Maire and his men came upon another passage to the west and were able to head toward the Pacific. Tierra del Fuego lay to their north and a small island (now called Isla de los Estados, or Staten

Island) lay to their south. The commander named the south-ernmost point of land they passed—on January 29—Cape Hoorn (Cape Horn) after the town that had sponsored their voyage. Beyond that, as far as the eye could see, rolled deep blue ocean.

During the following month Le Maire and his crew endured violent storms as they made their way through the rough waters where the Atlantic and Pacific oceans and Antarctic seas come together; they were the first Europeans to successfully navigate the route. By March the expedition had come upon a group of islands (the Juan Fernández Islands) about 400 miles off the coast of present-day Chile, and stopped to gather a fresh supply of food and water. After the months of hard travel, many of the *Eendracht* crew had become sick. On March 9 Jan Schouten died.

Expedition discovers numerous South Sea islands

Because of unfavorable winds, the *Eendracht* was not able to continue its northerly course across the Pacific Ocean. Le Maire and his crew headed west, hoping to reach the Orient. They eventually came upon the present-day island groups of the Tuamotu Archipelago and the Tonga. The expedition members and the island natives often had difficulty understanding each other, which eventually led to conflicts and bloodshed. Many of the Polynesians fell victim to the superior weaponry of the Europeans.

In May the Dutchmen came upon more unknown islands. They named one group the Hoorns (later known as the Futuna Islands), again to honor their sponsors. There they enjoyed better relations with the natives, and were invited to participate in a feast held by a local king. The men so enjoyed themselves that they remained in the islands for more than two weeks—observing Polynesian culture. But they were still far from their destination.

At this point in the journey, Le Maire and Schouten argued about which course to take next. Le Maire wanted to continue to search for and claim new trading lands not yet under the control of the Dutch East India Company. Perhaps the travelers might even look for the Solomon Islands (which had not been visited by Europeans since the islands were first discovered by the Spanish in 1568) or they might find the legendary Great Southern Continent, a land mass that most geographers of the time were certain existed somewhere in the extreme southern regions of the world. Schouten, on the other hand, did not wish to continue to sail into unknown waters. He wanted to head northwest, toward the north coast of New Guinea, which was an established route that would lead to Batavia (now Jakarta, Indonesia)—the capital of the Dutch East Indies, located on the island of Java. Le Maire listened to the advice of his experienced master pilot, and the expedition headed toward Dutch territories.

On the way, the expedition discovered more Pacific islands. Le Maire and his crew sailed along the coast of what would later be known as New Ireland, sighted present-day New Hanover, and came upon several islands in the Admiralty group. During July and August they sailed along the northern coast of New Guinea, mapping it and stopping occasionally to get fresh water and food. They also named an island group off its northeast coast after Jan Schouten. The men reached the Dutch outpost of Ternate in the Moluccas—or Spice Islands—on September 17, 1616. There they were well-received by the Dutch colonists. But when the travelers landed in Batavia on October 28, their reception was anything but friendly.

Dutch authorities arrest *Eendracht* commander and crew

In Batavia the governor general of the Dutch East India Company, Jan Pieterszoon Coen (1587–1629), refused to believe that Le Maire and Schouten had found a new passage connecting the Atlantic and Pacific oceans. He charged them with sailing through the Strait of Magellan without permission—violating the company's trade monopoly. On these grounds Coen seized the *Eendracht* and its cargo. Le Maire and Schouten and ten members of the crew were placed under arrest and sent back to the Netherlands on a company ship. Le Maire, just thirty-one years old, died on the return trip. But Schouten lived to tell the story of their discoveries. His account of the expedition was published in Amsterdam in 1619. Jacob Le Maire's journal was published later that same year.

Expedition discovery breaks trade monopoly

In the Netherlands Daniel Le Maire (Jacob's brother) and Willem Schouten went before the Dutch legislature, defending their actions and insisting that they and their commander had done nothing wrong—that they had, in fact, found a new southern sailing route between the oceans. Joined by Isaac Le Maire, they demanded that the Dutch East India Company release the illegally taken *Eendracht* and its goods. When the firm refused, the elder Le Maire sued the company. Following two years of litigation, the Dutch courts at last accepted the claim that a passage existed south of the Strait of Magellan. The *Eendracht* and its cargo were finally returned to Isaac Le Maire and the expedition's sponsors.

The elder Le Maire also made sure that the new southern waterway that Jacob and his expedition had discovered was named Le Maire Strait in his deceased son's honor. It would provide future sailors with an alternate passage between the oceans, which was important since travel along the 370-mile-long Strait of Magellan, winding and heavy with fog, was at times dangerous. By journeying south of Tierra del Fuego and discovering Cape Horn, the Le Maire-Schouten expedition had proved that the continent of South America was not connected to a second land mass farther to its south. Later explorers would confirm the discovery, sailing around Tierra del Fuego to show that it was, indeed, an island.

Sources

Baker, Daniel B., ed. *Explorers and Discoverers of the World.* Detroit: Gale Research, 1993.

Bohlander, Richard E., ed. *World Explorers and Discoverers.* New York: Macmillan, 1992.

Marshall Cavendish Illustrated Encyclopedia of Discovery and Exploration, Volume 7: *Charting the Vast Pacific,* written by John Gilbert. Freeport, NY: Marshall Cavendish, 1990.

Pear, Nancy and Daniel B. Baker. "Willem Corneliszoon Schouten." *Explorers and Discoverers.* Detroit: U•X•L, 1998.

Waldman, Carl and Alan Wexler. *Who Was Who in World Exploration.* New York: Facts on File, 1992.

S.S. Manhattan

Departed from Chester Harbor, Pennsylvania,
August 24, 1969

Returned to New York Harbor, New York,
November 12, 1969

In 1968 at Prudhoe Bay on the North Slope of Alaska—located along the Arctic coast—oil fields were discovered by the Humble Oil & Refining Company and the Atlantic Richfield Company. With an estimated yield of 25 billion barrels, the discovery was by far the largest oil strike ever made in North America. Besides the enormous problems involved in drilling for petroleum in the harsh environment, there was also the huge puzzle of how to get the petroleum to refineries and markets thousands of miles away. Because overland transport seemed a costly solution, the possibility of shipping the oil along an Arctic route to the East Coast of the United States was investigated. The route would be through the waterway known for centuries as the Northwest Passage, made famous by fearless navigators who risked their lives attempting to find a northern sailing route between the Atlantic and Pacific oceans in the Western Hemisphere. (Norwegian explorer Roald Amundsen [1872–1928] finally traversed the passage in 1903–06).

The Manhattan was a large U. S. oil tanker that was converted into an icebreaker and sent on a voyage through the Northwest Passage to see if such a route could be used to transport oil from Alaska to North America's East Coast.

It was thought that giant, icebreaking oil tankers might be able to make the transcontinental Arctic voyage. In order to test this theory, the Humble Oil & Refining Company paid $36 million to convert the largest American oil tanker then in existence—the S.S. *Manhattan*—into an icebreaking oceanographic research vessel, and to finance its polar journey. (The Atlantic Richfield Company and BP Oil also contributed money to the project.) The crew of the *Manhattan* would include marine and ice scientists, who would be able to study polar areas never before visited by man. The only Arctic route possible for a vessel of its size would be a westward one—past the west coast of Greenland, across Baffin Bay, and through the main channels that separate the many islands that comprise the Canadian Arctic Archipelago, before finally reaching Alaska. Unlike smaller vessels that could travel closer to the North American mainland in more sheltered waters, the *Manhattan* would have to face the full fury of Arctic weather and ice.

Transformation takes place for Arctic journey

The *Manhattan* was so large that it had to be separated into four pieces during its transformation into an icebreaker. From its dock in the port city of Chester, Pennsylvania, two sections were towed to shipyards in Virginia and Alabama, where extra rudder guards were installed, a heavy "girdle" was placed around the midsection, and the forward section received additional beams. The specially designed armored prow (front)—jutting out like a shark's snout in order to cut through Arctic ice—was manufactured in Bath, Maine. After the *Manhattan* was reassembled, nine-foot-high armored "blisters," made of two-inch-thick steel, were attached at the waterline in order to protect the inner hull. When complete, the ship weighed 150,000 tons and was more than 1,005 feet long, its deck the size of three football fields. It was nine times larger than any existing icebreaker. The *Manhattan* was driven by 43,000 horsepower, twice as much as any other tanker then afloat.

First encounter with polar ice a success

The ship left Chester, Pennsylvania, on August 24, 1969, heading for the Arctic Ocean. The 126 people onboard included a volunteer crew, a number of scientists, and several journalists ready to record what they hoped would be an historic journey. The first icebergs were sighted on September 1, off the west coast of Greenland. That same night the *Manhattan* was met by a Canadian icebreaker escort, the *John A. Macdonald.* The following day a vast field of ice was sighted along the shores of Baffin Island to the west. The ice that gathered in Baffin Bay was notorious: during the nineteenth century it had crushed more than 500 whaling ships and had taken the lives of most of their crews. Roger Steward, the *Manhattan*'s master captain, thought it a fitting place to test his vessel's icebreaking capabilities. On September 2 the ship plowed into a sheet of ice sixty feet thick and a mile wide. Though sea water shot sixty feet over its bow, the *Manhattan*

S.S. Manhattan *master captain Roger Steward, a veteran seafarer.*

remained steady and shattered the giant floe, which was the largest piece of ice ever torn apart by a ship. The crew members heard giant pieces of ice popping against the propellers below and the captain slowed the ship for fear of breaking them. But later inspection by scuba divers from the *Macdonald* revealed that the *Manhattan*'s propellers showed no damage from the battering.

The *Manhattan* sailed into Lancaster Sound north of Baffin Island, at the eastern end of the Canadian Archipelago. The Sound was largely free of ice that year. But off Bathurst Island the ship's crew had an unusual experience: the *Manhattan* passed near the North Magnetic Pole, which was far from its usual position because of a giant storm in progress on the sun's surface. The subatomic particles generated by the solar activity affected the earth's magnetic field. The nearness of the magnetic pole interfered with the *Manhattan*'s powerful radios and made its magnetic compasses spin uselessly; it even affected the gyroscopic compasses. For a time the *Manhattan*'s crew

What are the magnetic poles?

Earth possesses a magnetic field. While the cause of this phenomenon is unclear, it is believed to be caused by the motion and electrical currents in Earth's liquid outer core. External forces, like sunspot activity and solar storms, can also affect Earth's magnetism.

There are two regions on the surface of Earth, one in the Northern Hemisphere and one in the Southern Hemisphere, that attract one end of a compass needle and repel the opposite end. The two places where Earth's magnetic force is vertical are called magnetic poles, and it is to these spots, and not to the geographical North and South Poles—which lie at the extremes of Earth's axis—that the needle of a compass points. (Because magnetic forces *are* vertical at the true poles, magnetic compasses cannot show direction when used nearby; their needles would point down if they were free to do so.) Unlike the geographical North and South Poles, the North and South Magnetic Poles constantly change position. When first discovered in 1831 by English explorer James Clark Ross (1800–62), the North Magnetic Pole was located at latitude 70°51'N and longitude 96°46'W. In 1970 it was found at approximately 76°N and 101°W. Australian geologists T. W. E. David (1858–1934) and Douglas Mawson (1882–1958) first charted the South Magnetic Pole in Antarctica in 1909.

had to guide the vessel using the position of the sun and stars—just as crews in ancient times had navigated their ships.

Serious flaws come to light

When the *Manhattan* reached Viscount Melville Sound, its progress came to a halt. The ship had run into a jumble of

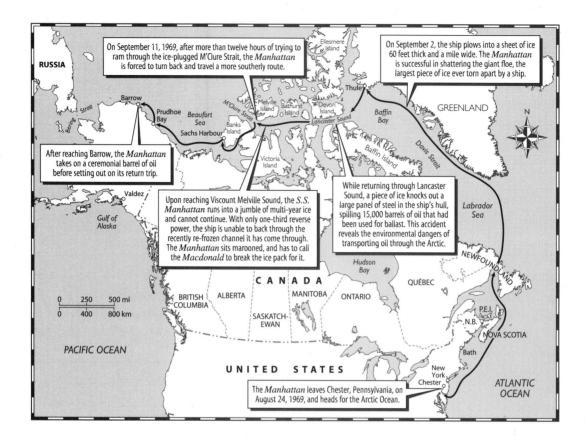

On September 11, 1969, after more than twelve hours of trying to ram through the ice-plugged M'Clure Strait, the *Manhattan* is forced to turn back and travel a more southerly route.

On September 2, the ship plows into a sheet of ice 60 feet thick and a mile wide. The *Manhattan* is successful in shattering the giant floe, the largest piece of ice ever torn apart by a ship.

After reaching Barrow, the *Manhattan* takes on a ceremonial barrel of oil before setting out on its return trip.

Upon reaching Viscount Melville Sound, the *S.S. Manhattan* runs into a jumble of multi-year ice and cannot continue. With only one-third reverse power, the ship is unable to back through the recently re-frozen channel it has come through. The *Manhattan* sits marooned, and has to call the *Macdonald* to break the ice pack for it.

While returning through Lancaster Sound, a piece of ice knocks out a large panel of steel in the ship's hull, spilling 15,000 barrels of oil that had been used for ballast. This accident reveals the environmental dangers of transporting oil through the Arctic.

The *Manhattan* leaves Chester, Pennsylvania, on August 24, 1969, and heads for the Arctic Ocean.

multi-year ice—ice that had been broken and tossed about by storms, had lost its salt content during summer melts, and had been refrozen again, year after year. The result was bright blue freshwater ice that was as hard as steel. The ship was forced to stop, and the scientists onboard traveled over the pack ice to study its characteristics and gather core samples.

It was during this time that the *Manhattan*'s most serious flaw as an icebreaker was revealed. It was constructed so that its engines could produce only one-third of their power in reverse (a characteristic of all turbine-driven ships). Because the channel cut in pack ice behind an icebreaker refreezes almost immediately after the vessel passes through, such a ship needs full reverse power to make enough room for subsequent ramming charges as it propels its way forward. Lacking that capability, the *Manhattan* sat marooned, and its captain had to call upon the *Macdonald* to break the ice pack for it.

Once it had cleared the multi-year ice, the *Manhattan* proceeded toward M'Clure Strait, a notorious 220-mile-long, ice-plugged channel that had stopped all vessels that had ever tried to pass through it from east to west. Winds from the west drove the ice in the Sound into jumbled ridges that sometimes reached 20 feet high and 100 feet deep. Stopped by a broken and refrozen floe three miles wide, the *Manhattan* tried to ram its way through for more than twelve hours. But on September 11, 1969, the captain decided that the strait had defeated them. While the *Manhattan* had made more progress into the channel than any vessel before it, it was forced to turn back and travel a more southerly route through Prince of Wales Sound and across Amundsen Gulf, off the Canadian mainland.

On September 14 the helicopter scouting team that had accompanied the *Manhattan* throughout its voyage reported that the vessel was close to open water. After nearly a month of traveling through ice-filled seas, the ship was just ten miles away from clear sailing. The following day, at 2:34 in the morning, the *Manhattan* broke free of polar ice at last.

Reaches Alaskan destination

The ship then sailed through 1,000 miles of open sea to its destination: Barrow, Alaska. The city sits at Barrow Point, Alaska's most northerly location. There the *Manhattan* took a ceremonial barrel of oil onboard, perhaps the first of many millions. The ship and its crew then headed back toward the East Coast of the United States by the same route it had come. With winter approaching, the travelers had to deal with shorter days and colder temperatures; many of the channels that were open on their westward trip were now frozen over. It took the *Manhattan* four weeks to recross Viscount Melville Sound, and when returning through Lancaster Sound, a piece of ice knocked out a large panel of steel in the ship's hull, spilling 15,000 barrels of oil, which had been used for ballast (to increase the boat's stability), into the sea. This accident revealed the environmental dangers of transporting oil through the Arctic. The *Manhattan* sailed into New York Harbor on November 12, 1969.

The voyage of the *Manhattan* had shown that it was physically possible for large tankers to travel through the Northwest Passage. It also revealed that it was too risky, however, both economically and environmentally. The oil companies decided to build an oil pipeline from the fields of the North Slope to the port city of Valdez, located on the south coast of Alaska. From that point, they would ship petroleum by tanker. The *Manhattan*'s pioneering route through the Arctic has never been used for transport.

Sources

Baker, Daniel B., ed. *Explorers and Discoverers of the World.* Detroit: Gale Research, 1993.

Keating, Bern. *The Northwest Passage: From the* Mathew *to the* Manhattan, *1497 to 1969.* Chicago: Rand McNally, 1970.

Dervla Murphy

Born November 28, 1931, Lismore, Ireland

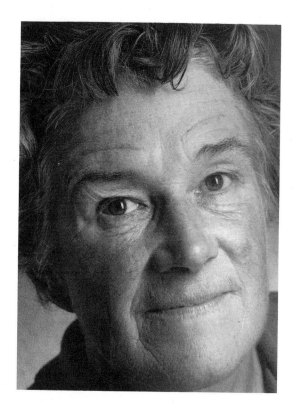

Dervla Murphy was born on November 28, 1931, in the town of Lismore, located in the southern Irish county of Waterford. On her tenth birthday she received a bicycle and an atlas; this happy coincidence would provide the spark that would later ignite her life of travel. As a young girl, she would pore over the atlas's maps and descriptions of faraway places. India, she decided, would be her first travel destination. By her calculation, the way to India had fewer watery obstacles than the routes to other exotic places. This was important because Murphy intended to make her journey by bicycle.

When Murphy was fourteen, her mother developed crippling arthritis. An only child, Murphy was obliged to leave the local convent school to care for her mother and keep house for her father. Done with formal schooling, she continued to educate herself by reading great literature. She began to write stories of her own, filled with the adventure that she longed for as she dutifully stayed home and cared for her parents. She became a pen pal to a girl who lived in Kuala

Dervla Murphy is an Irish adventurer and travel writer whose trips have taken her to remote parts of Asia, South America, and Africa.

Lumpur, Malaysia. This increased Murphy's desire to visit foreign places.

Becomes long-distance bicyclist

On the rare occasions Murphy could leave her caretaking duties, she went bicycling through the Irish countryside. Sometimes she would ride as much as 70 miles a day. She once went on a three-week tour through Wales and southern England, and was able to sell the articles she wrote about it. She also made a five-week tour of Belgium and traveled twice to Spain.

In 1962, Murphy's mother died. Since her father had died a short time earlier, Murphy was now able to make her ambitious dreams a reality. She would travel from Dunkerque (Dunkirk), France, to Delhi, India. Her vehicle would be a sturdy, nearly new, man's bicycle which she called Rozinante—after the horse ridden by the fictional adventurer Don Quixote—or "Roz" for short. Murphy carefully planned her route, and sent four spare tires to various British embassies she hoped to visit along the way. She assembled her supplies—clothes, medicine, personal care items, and bicycle parts and maintenance equipment—to be carried in pannier bags (which resemble wicker baskets) that hung on either side of Roz's back wheels. Because Murphy intended to stay in tourist hostels, she brought no sleeping bag or tent. She did buy a .25 caliber gun, however, and learned how to use it.

Embarks on first foreign adventure

Vaccinated, inoculated, and carrying the proper visas, Murphy set out from Dunkerque on January 14, 1963. Unknowingly, she had begun her adventure during the coldest winter Europe had experienced in eighty years. Nonetheless, she bicycled her way across France and Italy, through ice storms and along slippery roads. Crossing the Alps by train, Murphy proceeded through Eastern Europe. Near Belgrade, Yugoslavia, she had a frightening encounter with starving wolves, which were entering the city to look for food. As one sprang to her shoulder, she shot it with her revolver. Murphy would use her gun twice more during her journey, but on these occasions it would be to warn away threatening men.

During the first two months of her trip, Murphy tried to write frequent letters home to keep four close friends informed of her progress. This practice became too difficult to continue, however, and Murphy started to write about the day's events in a diary. She sent pages to her friends at intervals, and would later write a popular book about her journey—*Full Tilt: Ireland to India With a Bicycle* (1965)—using this diary format. She continued the habit of keeping a diary on all subsequent trips.

Murphy made her way to the Middle East. The sight of a woman traveling alone there—and on a bicycle—was quite an unusual sight. While authorities in countries like Persia (present-day Iran) and Afghanistan didn't like the idea, they still treated Murphy with courtesy and even watched out for her safety. Murphy's adventurous spirit took her far from the usual tourist sites. In Afghanistan she journeyed through the Hindu Kush Mountains to Bamian—once a center of the Buddhist religion—where she explored the giant carved Buddhas there.

One of the giant Buddhas in Bamian, Afghanistan, visited by Dervla Murphy. This Buddha, 173 feet tall, was disfigured by Genghis Khan's invading forces in the eleventh century.

Travel challenges plentiful

Murphy proceeded to Pakistan, where she stayed for a time at a prince's palace and also at the luxurious estate of a raja (Hindu nobleman). The raja offered her a farm where she could settle down for life, but she refused his generous gift, eager to return to the road. One of her greatest travel challenges lay just ahead, in the Himalaya Mountains. Crossing the Babusar Pass out of Gilgit (in Pakistan), Murphy found that she could not ride, but had to push or carry her bicycle amid slippery glaciers and sheer drops. At one desperate point Murphy pushed Roz down a glacier and rolled down herself. Another time in the mountains, when confronted with a damaged, useless bridge spanning a swift, icy river, Murphy entered the stream and carried her bicycle across, hanging onto the back of an agreeable cow that was making the crossing too.

Murphy encountered other hardships during her extraordinary bicycle journey. Besides dealing with frostbite, sunburn, and heatstroke, Murphy was bitten by a scorpion along the way. She also had three ribs broken when she was accidentally hit by a rifle butt during a riot on a crowded bus. She drank contaminated water and had to be treated for dysentery. Still, Murphy felt that the primitive way she traveled had its rewards. She was able to go to remote locations, and share in the lives of the simplest native inhabitants. She was always deeply touched by the generosity of the people she met during her travels. Murphy cheerfully slept on the floors of mud huts or on humble outdoor beds that were kindly offered to her.

Reaches destination

Murphy finally reached India, the travel destination of her childhood. She arrived at its capital city of Delhi on July 18, 1963, almost six months after leaving Ireland. Once there, she had to stop bicycling, though, for the summer months in India were simply too hot for such an activity. Murphy spent the next six months working with Tibetan refugees in northern India until the weather cooled. (Communist China had invaded Tibet in 1950, and nearly obliterated its Buddhist culture. Many Tibetans fled the country, and some of them sought refuge in northern India as well as in Nepal.) Murphy then made a few trips into the Himalayas and southwest Nepal before flying home on February 23, 1964. She had bicycled some 3,000 miles.

While she was in India, a newspaper there had written an article about Murphy and her incredible journey. London publishers learned of the report and contacted her, hoping to print her story. When she completed a manuscript it was accepted by the prestigious publishing firm of John Murray. Murphy

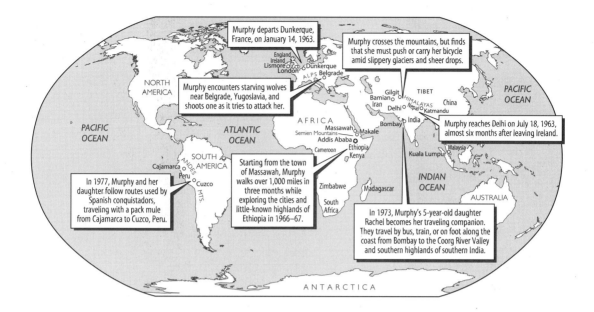

Murphy departs Dunkerque, France, on January 14, 1963.

Murphy crosses the mountains, but finds that she must push or carry her bicycle amid slippery glaciers and sheer drops.

Murphy encounters starving wolves near Belgrade, Yugoslavia, and shoots one as it tries to attack her.

Murphy reaches Delhi on July 18, 1963, almost six months after leaving Ireland.

Starting from the town of Massawah, Murphy walks over 1,000 miles in three months while exploring the cities and little-known highlands of Ethiopia in 1966–67.

In 1977, Murphy and her daughter follow routes used by Spanish conquistadors, traveling with a pack mule from Cajamarca to Cuzco, Peru.

In 1973, Murphy's 5-year-old daughter Rachel becomes her traveling companion. They travel by bus, train, or on foot along the coast from Bombay to the Coorg River Valley and southern highlands of southern India.

was overjoyed. The book sold very well, and Murphy realized that she could earn a living writing about what she loved best: foreign adventure. (Murray would publish the author's many subsequent travel books, produced after each new trip.)

Murphy was so moved by the plight of the Tibetans that she returned to work among them in 1965. She settled near a refugee camp in Nepal, and came to love the country, its inhabitants, and their way of life. For adventure, she journeyed into the Langtang area north of the Nepalese capital of Katmandu, led by a native Sherpa guide.

Looks for more adventure in Ethiopia

In late December of 1966 Murphy took her restless spirit to another continent: Africa. Since childhood she had been intrigued by tales of the ancient kingdoms of Abyssinia—now Ethiopia—located in eastern Africa. Because of its mountainous terrain, Ethiopia had always been difficult to explore, with much of the country nearly inaccessible. This kind of challenge appealed to the fearless Murphy. Because of the mountainous travel, she left Roz at home and prepared herself for hiking. She carried her supplies in a backpack, which weighed about fifty pounds. Starting out from the town of Massawa, Murphy soon wished that she could travel by bicycle. Foot blisters and her heavy pack nearly stopped her. In the northern Ethiopian city of Makale, she bought a mule (which she named Jock) to carry her provisions.

Murphy then proceeded to explore the little-known highlands of Ethiopia. Her greatest problem was not having reliable maps. Nonetheless, she managed to make her way to such places as Aksum, capital of the ancient Axumite empire, where the Ark of the Covenant (which held the tablets of the Ten Commandments) was once reportedly kept; Gondar, the one-time capital of Ethiopia, filled with architectural ruins; and Addis Ababa, the current capital of the country. She also trekked through the Semien Mountains—which rise to more than 15,000 feet—and across the grueling Plateau of Manz. At the end of a difficult but exhilarating three months, Murphy had walked more than 1,000 miles, and had developed a real affection for the Ethiopian highlanders. (Jock did not survive the rigors of the trip.) Her adventures were recounted in *In Ethiopia With a Mule,* published in 1968.

Young daughter becomes traveling companion

In 1968 Murphy gave birth to a daughter, Rachel, and several years passed before she undertook her next travel adventure. In 1973 she returned to India, accompanied by her five-year-old daughter, who would serve as her traveling companion for the next several years. She and Rachel traveled by bus, train, or on foot, beginning their journey in Bombay and proceeding down India's western coast before turning inland to the remote and rugged highlands of the south. Along the way they stayed in hostels, hotels, and the homes of friends and strangers. They settled for a while in Coorg, a valley in southern India that was not afflicted by either the overpopulation or the poverty they had seen in most of India. Murphy enjoyed the challenge of being both a traveler and a mother. *On a Shoestring to Coorg: An Experience of Southern India* (1976), chronicles the pair's trip.

Following in footsteps of conquistadors

Murphy and Rachel returned to India in 1974, visiting Baltistan (Little Tibet) in the western Himalayas and spending the winter in the Karakorum Mountains. Then Murphy turned her sights to a new destination: South America. She and her daughter, now nine years old, traveled with a pack mule from the town of Cajamarca in northern Peru to the southeast Peruvian city of Cuzco—once the capital of the great Indian empire of the Inca. Making their way through the Andes, Murphy and Rachel traveled routes that had been used by Spanish conquistadors long ago. *Eight Feet in the Andes,* published in 1983, describes the adventures of mother, daughter, and mule as it simultaneously relates the story of the Inca conquest.

More exotic travel followed for Murphy and her daughter. They journeyed through Madagascar, the large island off the southeast coast of Africa. In 1987, when Rachel was eighteen, they visited West Africa, trekking into the highlands of Cameroon. Then, with her daughter grown, Murphy again traveled alone. In her sixties, the travel writer undertook a 3,000-mile, four-month bicycle ride through southern Africa, traveling from Kenya to Zimbabwe. She later visited the country of South Africa, anxious to see if the abolition of apartheid (racial segregation) had improved the life of the average black citizen there.

Perhaps one of Murphy's most unusual travel books is the award-winning *A Place Apart,* published in 1978. Frequently asked by the inhabitants of distant lands why the Irish fought one another, Murphy had set out to find the answer by making a bicycle tour of Northern Ireland in 1976, viewing the country and its problems with the impartial eyes of a foreign visitor.

Sources

Contemporary Authors, New Revision Series, Volume 21. Detroit: Gale Research, 1987.

The Irish Times on the Web. "Dervla Murphy Talks to Eileen Battersby." [Online] Available http://www.irish-times.com/irish-times/paper/1997/0911/fea1.html, September 11, 1997.

Murphy, Dervla. *Full Tilt: Ireland to India With a Bicycle.* London: J. Murray, 1965.

Murphy, Dervla. *In Ethiopia With a Mule.* London: J. Murray, 1968.

Tinling, Marion. *Women Into the Unknown: A Sourcebook on Women Explorers and Travelers.* Westport, CT: Greenwood Press, 1989.

National Air
and Space Museum

Opened on July 1, 1976

I n 1946 the Congress of the United States called for the creation of a National Air Museum. Its purpose was to memorialize the development of aviation by collecting, preserving, and displaying important aeronautical vehicles and equipment. The museum was established and for many years displayed its artifacts in the Arts and Industries Building of the Smithsonian Institution, located in Washington, D.C.

By the 1960s space travel had become an important facet of human flight. In 1966 Congress passed a new law changing the museum's name to the National Air and Space Museum (NASM) and adding the commemoration of space flight to its mission. Congress also authorized the construction of a new building to house the expanded museum. Built on a three-block section of the National Mall in Washington, D.C., it was to be completed in July of 1976, as a bicentennial gift to the nation.

With the largest collection of aeronautic and space artifacts ever assembled, the Smithsonian Institution's National Air and Space Museum is the most-visited museum in the world.

New museum an enormous success

With 161,145 square feet of exhibition floor space, the steel structure, faced with Tennessee pink cedar marble, was opened on the morning of July 1, 1976. U.S. president Gerald Ford (b. 1913) dedicated the new museum in a dramatic ceremony in which a ten-foot mechanical arm—identical to the one on the *Viking* probe that would soon be used to scoop soil samples when the spacecraft landed on Mars—cut the symbolic ribbon (responding to a signal from the real *Viking 1* Lander in space). Just twenty-five days after the museum's opening, more than 1 million visitors had walked through its doors. In the twenty-five days after that, another million people had visited. Within a year, the National Air and Space Museum had become the biggest tourist attraction in Washington, D.C. Today, with more than 8 million visitors a year, it is the

Planning a trip to the National Air and Space Museum

The National Air and Space Museum is located in Washington, D.C., on the National Mall at Seventh and Independence Avenue, S.W.—just west of the Capitol building. It is open every day of the year except December 25. Admission is free.

Tours are given throughout the day. Advance reservations are available for groups of twenty or more. The museum conducts daily science demonstrations; one such program teaches visitors about the principles of flight and aircraft design by inviting them to make their own paper airplanes. Special tours and educational programs are also available. The National Air and Space Museum Archives, which preserves documents, films, and photographs relating to the history and technology of aviation and spaceflight, may be used by researchers by appointment.

The National Air and Space Museum has twenty-three main exhibition galleries, each displaying major artifacts from the museum's collection. Smaller, temporary exhibitions supplement the permanent displays. The museum also presents daily shows in its planetarium and theater. In the Albert Einstein Planetarium visitors can experience simulated astronomical phenomena and other visual effects under a dome that measures seventy feet across. In the Samuel P. Langley IMAX Theater, visitors can watch a variety of films on a movie screen as tall as a five-story building. The museum's most popular film, *To Fly!* takes viewers on an aerial adventure that includes ballooning, airplane stunt-flying, and rocketing into space.

most popular museum in the world. Its planners had underestimated how the wondrous history and ingenious tools of human flight—within Earth's atmosphere and beyond—would seize the public's imagination.

Historical treasures

The first artifact that a visitor sees as he or she enters the National Air and Space Museum is the *Wright 1903 Flyer.* Constructed by American brothers Orville (1871–1948) and Wilbur (1867–1912) Wright, it became the first machine-powered aircraft to successfully fly with a passenger—on December 17, 1903, at Kitty Hawk, North Carolina. From that day forward, the development of human flight progressed with astonishing speed. The museum follows this amazing trail of human discovery, conveying the evolving history, science, and technology of aviation and spaceflight through its displayed collections and themed exhibitions.

Aerial balloons, gliders, airplanes, and rockets are among the hundreds of artifacts on display at the museum. One of the world's most famous planes, the *Spirit of St. Louis,* is housed there; it was used by American aviator Charles A. Lindbergh (1902–74) as he made the first solo, nonstop flight across the Atlantic Ocean in 1927, from New York to Paris. The historic *Apollo 11* command module—which carried U.S. astronauts to and from the first moon landing—is also on display, as are lunar rock samples (which visitors can touch). Themed exhibits at the museum include examinations of the cultural, political, and military factors that have influenced the development of aviation and spaceflight, and, conversely, of the impact that air and space technology has had on science and society. In the World War I gallery, for instance, the exhibit "Legend, Memory, and the Great War in the Air" compares popular myths about aerial combat during World War I (1914–18) with real, historical information. The exhibition "Space Race" looks at U.S.-Soviet competition and cooperation in space, from the beginning of the Space Age to the current construction of the International Space Station.

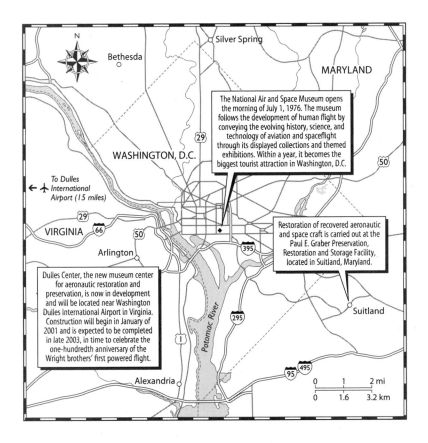

The National Air and Space Museum opens the morning of July 1, 1976. The museum follows the development of human flight by conveying the evolving history, science, and technology of aviation and spaceflight through its displayed collections and themed exhibitions. Within a year, it becomes the biggest tourist attraction in Washington, D.C.

Restoration of recovered aeronautic and space craft is carried out at the Paul E. Graber Preservation, Restoration and Storage Facility, located in Suitland, Maryland.

Dulles Center, the new museum center for aeronautic restoration and preservation, is now in development and will be located near Washington Dulles International Airport in Virginia. Construction will begin in January of 2001 and is expected to be completed in late 2003, in time to celebrate the one-hundredth anniversary of the Wright brothers' first powered flight.

Maintaining the largest collection of flight artifacts in the world is a difficult task. Restoration of a recovered aircraft or spacecraft can take a team of workers from 2,000 to 30,000 hours to complete. Since the mid-1950s this kind of work has been carried out at the Paul E. Garber Preservation, Restoration and Storage Facility, located in Suitland, Maryland. Because the facility also houses museum artifacts when not on display, it is open for informal tours.

Vast museum extension planned

A new museum center for state-of-the-art restoration and preservation is now in development. Called the Dulles Center, the facility will be located near Dulles International Airport in Virginia, just outside the nation's capital. Many artifacts of the National Air and Space Museum that have not been publicly viewed before—because of their great size—will also be featured there. The building will be more than 700,000 square feet and will sit on 185 acres. This capacity will allow for the display of more than 180 aircraft and 100 spacecraft, including the space shuttle *Enterprise.* Donations from individuals, corporations, and foundations will fund the enormous project. Construction is scheduled to begin in January of 2001. Completion is expected in late 2003, in time to celebrate the one-hundredth anniversary of the Wright brothers' first powered flight.

Sources

Airpower's Struggle on the Mall. [Online] Available http://www. afa.org/enolagay/sson2.html, December 10, 1998.

Smithsonian National Air and Space Museum Home Page. [Online] Available http://www.nasm.edu/NASMhome.html, December 11, 1998.

Nearchus

Born c. 360 B.C., Crete

Died 312 B.C.

By the sixth century B.C., Persia had become the largest and strongest empire in the known world, presiding over Egypt and all of western Asia. Persian ruler Darius I (reigned 521–486 B.C.) decided to add Greece to his vast holdings, and a series of conflicts known as the Persian Wars took place in 500–449 B.C. between the Persian empire and the Greek city-states (self-ruling areas, each made up of a city and its surrounding territory). By the fourth century B.C., however, the Greeks had grown in military strength and Persia had weakened. The Greeks looked to avenge the earlier invasions and conquer the huge Persian empire.

Philip II of Macedon (reigned 359–336 B.C.), ruler of a kingdom in northern Greece, united the Greek city-states and prepared to attack Persia, now led by Darius III (reigned 336–330 B.C.). But Philip was assassinated, and was replaced by his twenty-year-old son, Alexander, whose military genius and far-reaching conquests over the next several years would earn him the name Alexander the Great (356–323 B.C.).

Nearchus was a Greek military officer under Alexander the Great. He explored the waters along the coast of present-day Pakistan and Iran, looking for a sea route between the Near East and India.

Alexander the Great, who was both Nearchus's friend and military commander.

Alexander and his army vanquished Persian forces and overtook Asia Minor—the west Asian peninsula that is now Turkey—and proceeded through Syria, Egypt, and Persia's homeland (present-day Iran). Continuing east across Asia, Alexander pushed beyond the borders of the Persian empire.

Joins Alexander's forces

Nearchus was a native of the Greek island of Crete. As a boy he moved to Amphipolis in Macedon (present-day Macedonia), and became Alexander's friend. Beginning in 334 B.C., he participated in Alexander's military campaigns against Persia; that same year—following a victory over Darius III at Granicus—he was appointed governor of Lycia (now southwest Turkey).

By 327 B.C. Alexander and his army were camped in Bactria (present-day Afghanistan) as he planned his invasion of India. Nearchus traveled there, taking supplies and more soldiers to his commander. In midsummer the massive army proceeded through the Khyber Pass (on the present-day border between Afghanistan and Pakistan) and then headed south, where it met strong resistance from Indian rulers. Alexander and his forces prevailed, however, even though their opponents used large Indian elephants in battle. He crossed the Indus River and planned to continue east to the Ganges River, eager to explore and conquer the vast Indian subcontinent.

By 325 B.C. Alexander and his army had reached what is now the Jhelum River, located in western India. Here his men—weary after nearly eight long years of military campaigns—refused to continue into unknown regions. Alexander reluctantly agreed to turn back, but along a different route. Almost as interested in exploration as he was in conquest, Alexander wanted to travel through as much unknown territory as possible on the homeward journey.

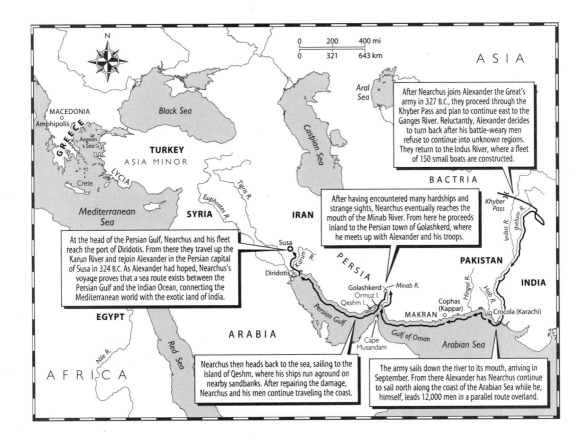

At the head of the Persian Gulf, Nearchus and his fleet reach the port of Diridotis. From there they travel up the Karun River and rejoin Alexander in the Persian capital of Susa in 324 B.C. As Alexander had hoped, Nearchus's voyage proves that a sea route exists between the Persian Gulf and the Indian Ocean, connecting the Mediterranean world with the exotic land of India.

After Nearchus joins Alexander the Great's army in 327 B.C., they proceed through the Khyber Pass and plan to continue east to the Ganges River. Reluctantly, Alexander decides to turn back after his battle-weary men refuse to continue into unknown regions. They return to the Indus River, where a fleet of 150 small boats are constructed.

After having encountered many hardships and strange sights, Nearchus eventually reaches the mouth of the Minab River. From here he proceeds inland to the Persian town of Golashkerd, where he meets up with Alexander and his troops.

Nearchus then heads back to the sea, sailing to the Island of Qeshm, where his ships run aground on nearby sandbanks. After repairing the damage, Nearchus and his men continue traveling the coast.

The army sails down the river to its mouth, arriving in September. From there Alexander has Nearchus continue to sail north along the coast of the Arabian Sea while he, himself, leads 12,000 men in a parallel route overland.

Nearchus heads return voyage

Alexander and his men returned to the Indus River, where a fleet of 150 small boats were constructed. Then the army sailed down the river, arriving at its mouth (which empties into the Arabian Sea) in September. From there Alexander sent many of his men home by an overland route that would take them north of Persia's deserts. But Nearchus, leading a force of 5,000 men, would continue to sail north along the coast of the Arabian Sea toward the Persian Gulf, keeping detailed notes of good harbors, land features, and other discoveries. Alexander hoped that Nearchus would chart a new water route that would connect recent conquests in the Near East with India. As for himself, Alexander would lead a force of 12,000 men in a parallel route overland, along the coast. They would frequently rendezvous with the fleet, and provide its voyagers with food and water.

Sailors encounter hardships and strange sights

For twenty-four days, Nearchus's expedition was delayed at Crocola (now Karachi, Pakistan), near the Indus delta, by unfavorable monsoon winds. He then headed westward along the coast of what is now Pakistan. During his five-month voyage, Nearchus was rarely in contact with Alexander and his troops, and he and his men had to deal with supply shortages, hostile natives, and other challenges on their own. Not long after their departure, near the mouth of the Hab River, three of the expedition's ships capsized in a storm, but all crew members were saved.

Nearchus and his men frequently encountered many primitive peoples as they went ashore to replenish their supplies. Near the mouth of the Hingol River (in present-day Pakistan), they were attacked by 600 native inhabitants, whom Nearchus described as "hairy" from head to toe. These people possessed "nails like wild beasts," which they used as tools. Nearchus and his forces defeated them and took several captive.

The expedition proceeded up the coast. Along one desolate stretch of land—in present-day Makran (which lies both in Pakistan and Iran)—the travelers could find no fresh water for twenty days. It was here that Nearchus and his men encountered "savage" native inhabitants whom they called "fish-eaters," for the people subsisted on a diet of fish and lived in dwellings built of whale bones. As the voyagers sailed along the barren coast, their food supplies dwindled and they were forced to hunt wild goats on the shore.

As the land they passed became more fertile, Nearchus and his men encountered more ports, where they were able to restock their boats. While stopped at Cophas (Kappar in present-day Pakistan) Nearchus observed that the people there paddled canoes rather than rowing their vessels, as the Greeks did. Nearby, the voyagers were surprised to see great towers of water rising up in the air. When they asked their guides about it, they were told that they were viewing a group of whales, creatures altogether unfamiliar to Mediterranean sailors.

A fleet of sperm whales spouting water through their blowholes. Nearchus and his men saw whales for the first time near Cophas around 325 B.C.

Nearchus and his fleet reached the coast of Persia, where it was easier to get provisions. As the voyagers traveled north, they sighted Cape Musandam (in the present-day United Arab Emirates), the tip of the Arabian Peninsula that divides the Gulf of Oman from the Persian Gulf. Nearchus rejected the suggestion of his second-in-command that they cross over and explore the other coast. Instead, he continued to follow the directive given by Alexander: to investigate the eastern shores of the Arabian Sea and Persian Gulf.

Reunites with commander

When Nearchus reached the mouth of the Minab River (in present-day Iran), he traveled inland. Proceeding to the Persian town of Golashkerd, he at last met up with Alexander and his troops. There was much rejoicing on both sides, for the great commander and his men had also had a hard journey; the difficult march through dry and mountainous terrain had taken many lives. After the visit, Nearchus headed back to sea, sailing past Ormuz Island (in the Strait of Ormuz)—which would become the main port of the Persian Gulf for many centuries. Then Nearchus sailed on to the larger island of Qeshm (also in the Strait of Ormuz). There his ships ran aground on sandbanks; the damage took three weeks to repair. Afterward, Nearchus and his men continued traveling northwest along the coast of Persia. At the head of the Persian Gulf they came upon the port of Diridotis, located at the mouth of the Euphrates River (which runs through present-day Iraq).

Completes voyage of exploration

Nearchus and his fleet then traveled up the Karun River to rejoin Alexander in the Persian capital of Susa (situated in southwest Iran) in 324 B.C. As Alexander had hoped, Nearchus's voyage had proven that a sea route did exist between the Persian Gulf and the Indian Ocean, connecting the Mediterranean world with the exotic and intriguing land of India. Perhaps with conquest in mind, Alexander planned more voyages of exploration led by Nearchus, which included a trip around the Arabian Peninsula and one circling the African continent. These voyages never took place, however, because Alexander died in 323 B.C. and his great empire soon broke apart. Nearchus returned to his post as governor of Lycia.

Nearchus published a full account of his sea journey, which became well known by ancient writers. In the second century A.D. Greek historian Arrian—in his work *Indica,* which still survives—published full extracts from the military officer's narrative. Still, Nearchus's report probably had very little geographical or navigational impact. His descriptions of the bleak northeastern coast of the Arabian Sea and its primitive inhabitants discouraged Greeks from revisiting there. Furthermore, a better sailing route from the Mediterranean world to India by way of the Red Sea—employing the variable monsoon winds of the Indian Ocean—would subsequently be found.

Sources

Baker, Daniel B., ed. *Explorers and Discoverers of the World.* Detroit: Gale Research, 1993.

Delpar, Helen, ed. *The Discoverers: An Encyclopedia of Explorers and Exploration.* New York: McGraw-Hill, 1980.

Explorers and Exploration, Volume 1: *The Earliest Explorers,* written by Nathaniel Harris. Danbury, CT: Grolier Educational, 1998.

Marshall Cavendish Illustrated Encyclopedia of Discovery and Exploration, Volume 5: *Lands of Spice and Treasure,* written by William Napier. Freeport, NY: Marshall Cavendish, 1990.

Waldman, Carl and Alan Wexler. *Who Was Who in World Exploration.* New York: Facts on File, 1992.

Helen Thayer

Born 1938, Whangarei, New Zealand

In 1988 adventurer Helen Thayer became the first woman to travel to the North Magnetic Pole alone.

Modern polar exploration is usually a sophisticated undertaking. Adventurers travel by dogsleds or—more commonly—snowmobiles, and are often resupplied by airplanes throughout their journeys. Helen Thayer, an athlete and veteran outdoorswoman, developed a different sort of plan for traveling in the Arctic. In 1988 she journeyed to the North Magnetic Pole on foot and skis, taking only what provisions she could pull behind her on a sled. And the fifty-year-old adventurer traveled alone, except for a black husky dog named Charlie, whose sole purpose was to protect her from hungry polar bears. After a trying twenty-seven-day, 364-mile Arctic journey, Thayer succeeded in becoming the first woman to travel alone to either of the world's magnetic poles.

Thayer began her life of high adventure early. She grew up on a large, hilly New Zealand farm where sheep and cattle were raised, and her parents were avid mountain climbers. At age nine, Thayer made her first ascent, climbing New Zealand's 8,258-foot Mount Egmont. Mountain climbing became a passion after that, and in later years she would scale some of the world's highest peaks—Mount Cook in New Zealand, Mount McKinley in Alaska, peaks Lenin and Communism in the former Soviet Union—as well other mountains in China, South America, Mexico, and the western United States.

Thayer was a gifted athlete. She competed in international track-and-field events, and became a prizewinning discus thrower. Drawn to winter sports, she enjoyed skiing, and—after moving to America—took up luging, becoming the U.S. National Champion in 1975. But Thayer found that competing against others was not as rewarding as competing against herself; she most enjoyed setting dramatic goals and meeting them. She began to think about traveling to polar regions, areas of the world that had fascinated her since childhood.

Plans expedition to North Magnetic Pole

Thayer decided to travel to the North Magnetic Pole. She reasoned that during all her mountain excursions, the magnetic pole had guided her—via her compass needle—through unknown valleys and across unfamiliar ridges. Unlike the geographical North Pole, with a fixed position at the northern extreme of the earth's axis, the North Magnetic Pole changes location constantly, in response to solar activity interacting with the earth's magnetic field. In 1988, the year that Thayer planned to make her polar journey, scientists estimated that the North Magnetic Pole would lie about 800 miles north of the Arctic Circle, in the Northwest Territories of Canada, south of King Christian Island.

In Snohomish, Washington, where Helen lived with her husband Bill Thayer (a commercial helicopter pilot), she began preparing for her polar trek. She and her husband worked hard to put aside the $10,000 they thought the trip (and the specialized survival equipment it would require) would cost. To increase her strength and endurance, which she would need to pull a heavy sled, Helen undertook a strenuous regime that included lifting weights, a daily ten-mile run, climbing and skiing in the nearby Cascade Mountains, and kayaking on a local lake. She also practiced shooting a gun, in case she met up with polar bears, who were known to hunt and kill humans for food.

In November of 1987, Thayer traveled to Resolute Bay on Cornwallis Island in the Northwest Territories to make a short trial trip to test her equipment—deciding on the best clothing, tent, stove, and other items. She took along a shotgun in case she ran into bears, but encountered none on the five-day trek. Instead, she found the desolation and loneliness of the Arctic surprisingly disturbing. Would she be able to endure it?

Joined by Inuit dog

Returning to Resolute Bay in March of 1988, Thayer trained for another two weeks with the Inuit, native inhabitants of the area who taught her about the Arctic and polar survival skills. One man, a polar bear hunter, was particularly concerned about her safety without a dog team, for Inuit dogs and polar bears are natural enemies. He insisted that Thayer take along a four-year-old, ninety-three-pound husky-Newfoundland dog—Charlie—for protection. Many times during her difficult journey, Thayer would be glad that she did.

Charlie becomes lifesaving companion

Thayer set out from Little Cornwallis Island on March 30, heading over frozen, barren islands and vast stretches of sea ice as she made her way to the North Magnetic Pole. She pulled a loaded 160-pound sled behind her, and Charlie—attached to a harness around her waist—pulled his 85 pounds of dry dog food. Thayer's first encounter with polar bears ended quickly, when she frightened three of them away with her flare gun. In her next meeting she was not so fortunate: a bear charged to within feet of her before Charlie attacked it, fighting the huge beast until it ran off. Thayer would survive two more polar bear attacks, thanks to Charlie. After one such episode, she cried with relief, and her eyelids instantly froze shut in the bitter cold.

Charlie did more than protect Thayer from polar bears. He became a close companion that helped her endure the iso-

During the summer of 1994, the Thayers make a 600-mile trek from Dawson to Inuvik, studying the Arctic wolf. They return to the far north in 1998 to observe the migration of the Arctic caribou; however, they are forced to postpone the second leg of their trip because of heavy summer rains in the area.

On April 21, 1988, Thayer's charts and instruments indicate that she has arrived at the North Magnetic Pole, making her the first woman to travel alone to either of the world's magnetic poles. In 1992, she makes the same trip with her husband. The Thayers become the only married couple to walk and ski to the destination.

Thayer prepares for her first polar trek by lifting weights, running ten miles daily, climbing and skiing in the Cascade Mountains, and kayaking on a local lake. She also practices shooting a gun for protection from bears.

lation of the Arctic. He became a partner with which to share her daily trials: temperatures that fell to -45°F, fierce winds and storms that kept her in her tent for days, and shifting sea ice that could split at any moment, plunging her into frigid waters. Just seven days before the end of her journey, a storm blew away most of Thayer's supplies, and she subsisted on so little food and water that she became dehydrated and weak. But in her nightly radio calls to base camp at Resolute Bay, she reported none of this, for she knew her support team would force her to return before she reached her destination.

Achieves historic goal

Finally, on April 21, 1988, Thayer's charts and instruments indicated that she had arrived at the North Magnetic Pole. She traveled throughout the area, walking and skiing many more miles because the exact location of the pole is never certain. She photographed the region, and collected snow samples and temperature data, which Canadian scientists had asked her to do. Making her way to a designated pickup point on Helena Island, she radioed for a return flight. She had completed her historic journey.

Charlie returned with Thayer to her home in Washington. The adventurer wrote a bestselling book about her Arctic trip, *Polar Dream,* which was published in the United States in 1993, and subsequently appeared in many other languages. Thayer also gathered together the photographs and notes she had taken during her journey, and created an educational program for schoolchildren, which taught about the little-known and fragile Arctic environment and emphasized the need to protect it. Students in thirty-eight countries have used the program and Thayer has traveled extensively to deliver her message, speaking to more than 450,000 schoolchildren.

Since Thayer's historic journey to the North Magnetic Pole, she has engaged in many other exciting adventures, using the opportunities to teach schoolchildren more about different parts of the world; her husband has joined her in most of these expeditions. In the spring of 1992 she returned to the North Magnetic Pole with Bill, traveling the same route she had taken in 1988. The couple recorded scientific data and noted changes in the environment. They traveled on foot and skis, but this time the trip took longer, because ice conditions were rougher. This was because the previous fall had been stormy, moving ice around before the winter freeze. It took the Thayers more than a month to reach the pole, as they pulled their sleds through ridges of ice that seemed to go on forever. The pair persevered, however, reaching their goal on May 3. The Thayers became the only married couple to walk and ski to the North Magnetic Pole, and Bill—at age sixty-five—became the oldest individual to make the trip.

Thayers study Arctic wolves

In the summer of 1994 the Thayers returned to the Far North, this time to study Arctic wolves. They made a 600-mile trek across the Arctic tundra (treeless plains) located in the Yukon and Northwest Territories of Canada. Beginning their journey in Dawson—a frontier town that became the center of the Klondike Gold Rush at the end of the nineteenth century—they headed north along an historic Canadian Mounties trail, ending their journey in the town of Inuvik, just south of the Beaufort Sea on the edge of the Arctic Ocean. Accompanied by Charlie, the Thayers had encounters with wolves as they traveled, and the dog's presence seemed to calm the wild animals. When the travelers located a wolves den, they set up camp, and patiently moved closer and closer until their presence was accepted by the pack (eight adults and four pups). After a month of observing Arctic wolf behavior, the Thayers moved on, but decided to return for a visit the following year. They kept the location of their special wolf pack a secret, though, because in Alaska and parts of Canada these beautiful, intelligent, and gentle carnivores are often senselessly destroyed.

Couple visits Amazon

In sharp contrast to the Arctic, the Thayers's next expedition—in 1995—took place in the steamy Amazon jungle. Flying to the western Brazilian city of Manaus, the couple took a riverboat up the Rio Negro (the Amazon River's largest tributary) to a remote area in which the Jaquare and Irixana rivers are located. The pair kayaked up the Jaquare and down the Irixana, crossing on foot the dense rainforest that separates the rivers. During their 1,200-mile trip, the Thayers encountered a breathtaking variety of animals and plants. (Some of them were unpleasant: the swarms of stinging and biting insects, and the toxin-producing trees and shrubs that left painful rashes when touched.) The travelers also visited with the Yanomami Indians, native jungle dwellers who are protected by the Brazilian government. Noting that the rainforest was being burned to clear land for grazing and farming (which would ultimately bring disappointing results, since the soil is very poor), the Thayers left the Amazon with concern for the safety of the unique environment and its diverse array of inhabitants.

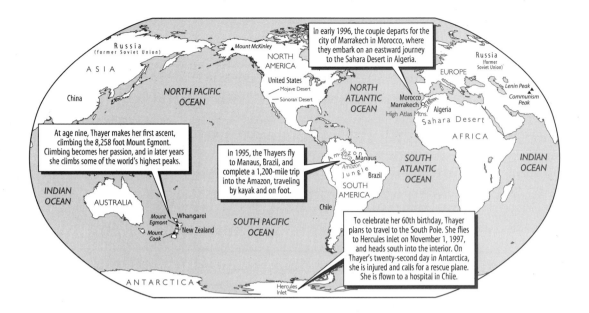

In early 1996, the couple departs for the city of Marrakech in Morocco, where they embark on an eastward journey to the Sahara Desert in Algeria.

At age nine, Thayer makes her first ascent, climbing the 8,258 foot Mount Egmont. Climbing becomes her passion, and in later years she climbs some of the world's highest peaks.

In 1995, the Thayers fly to Manaus, Brazil, and complete a 1,200-mile trip into the Amazon, traveling by kayak and on foot.

To celebrate her 60th birthday, Thayer plans to travel to the South Pole. She flies to Hercules Inlet on November 1, 1997, and heads south into the interior. On Thayer's twenty-second day in Antarctica, she is injured and calls for a rescue plane. She is flown to a hospital in Chile.

Undertake desert travels

Later in 1995, the Thayers traveled to New Zealand—Helen's homeland—and journeyed through its most northerly province, Northland. Then, in early 1996, the couple departed for the city of Marrakech in Morocco, a country located on Africa's northwest shore. From there they embarked on an eastward journey of 1,400 miles, across the snow-covered High Atlas Mountains, through the Draa River Valley, and on to the Sahara Desert across the Algerian border. Hiking alone through the windswept, icy mountains, the couple were joined by a pair of camels and interpreters in the desert, where they exchanged their cold-weather gear for lightweight survival equipment. The camels carried provisions, including a precious supply of water—long distances separated oases and wells in the brutal desert.

After that grueling trek, the Thayers made a 1,500-mile journey through North American deserts like the Mojave and Sonoran. Helen then began preparations for another solo polar expedition to take place roughly a decade after her historic trip to the North Magnetic Pole: to celebrate her sixtieth birthday, she planned to travel to the South Pole in Antarctica.

Helen tackles Antarctic

Like before, Thayer would journey alone, pulling her 260-pound sled behind her. On November 1, 1997, she was taken by plane to her starting point, Hercules Inlet (80°S, 80°W) on the edge of the Antarctic continent. She made her way across the low mountains of the coast and headed south, into the desolate interior. Before her lay *sastrugi*—hard mounds and ridges of slippery ice—that had been caused by an unusually windy winter. These made traveling frustrating, and the furious winds continued. At one point Thayer had to tie a rope around her waist and screw it into the ice to keep from blowing away in a screaming wind storm that produced gusts of 100 miles per hour.

While not threatened by hungry polar bears or shifting sea ice in Antarctica, Thayer had other things to worry about. She had to be wary of deep crevasses—some as wide as twenty feet, some narrow and deceptively hidden by snow— that occurred in the thick icecap that covered the continent. In one terrifying moment Thayer dropped into such a crevasse, with her only lifeline to the surface a rope attached to her heavy sled; the deep blue chasm in which she hung—upside down—extended hundreds of feet below her. Because she had practiced crevasse self-rescue many times in the Cascade Mountains near her home, Thayer was able to inch her way out of the chasm using two ice screws, proceeding up the walls of the crevasse in the same way that a climber proceeds up rock.

Despite such heart-stopping incidents, Thayer made good progress, traveling almost 200 miles. But on the twenty-second day of her journey, her luck changed. Her sled slid off an ice ridge and slammed into her, leaving her with leg and hip injuries and a concussion. After a period of recuperation, the tough adventurer couldn't decide whether to go on or to discontinue the trip. Finally she did the responsible thing: she sent an emergency signal to her base camp. A rescue plane soon arrived, and she was later flown to a hospital in Chile. Thayer eventually made a complete recovery.

Thayers follow Arctic caribou migration

In early 1998, Helen and Bill Thayer journeyed to the Far North yet again. This time they traveled alongside a herd of almost 500,000 Arctic caribou as the animals made their annual 600-mile migration across northern Alaska—from their winter feeding grounds in the Unalakleet River Basin, across the Brooks Mountain Range, and on to their summer calving grounds on the tundra of the North Slope. The migration had taken place for centuries, and the Thayers hoped to gain a better understanding of the awe-inspiring natural phenomenon by observing it firsthand. They followed the herd along weblike trails, which generations of caribou had permanently etched into mountainsides, hills, and plains. Traveling north with the animals in March and April, the Thayers planned to return south with them—the herd greatly expanded by the new calves that had been born in early summer—in August and September.

The Thayers's return trip had to be postponed, however, because a rainy summer had flooded the two rivers they needed to cross to follow the southern migration. While this did not stop the caribou (they are strong swimmers), the Thayers could not proceed safely. Nevertheless, the couple hopes to complete their study in August and September of 1999, and they continue to plan other world adventures.

Sources

Bill and Helen Thayer Expeditions: A GOALS Adventure. [Online] Available http://www.goals.com/thayer/expfrm.htm, December 10, 1998.

Hubbard, Kim. "Travels With Charlie." *People Weekly,* February 22, 1993: 41–42.

McLoone, Margo. *Women Explorers in Polar Regions.* Mankato, MN: Capstone Press, 1997.

Thayer, Helen. *Polar Dream.* New York: Simon & Schuster, 1993.

Karen Thorndike

Born c. 1942, U.S.A.

On August 18, 1998, American sailor Karen Thorndike arrived in San Diego, California, aboard her thirty-six-foot yacht *Amelia.* She had just completed a 33,000-mile solo trip around the world, which she had begun on August 4, 1996. During her two years at sea, she encountered bad weather and rough waters, illness, exhaustion, and loneliness. But from friends and strangers alike she also experienced incredible support for her quest, and she discovered an inner strength that kept her going despite daunting obstacles—allowing her to fulfill her dream.

Up until Thorndike's successful solo circumnavigation (circling) of the world, only six other women had achieved the feat. In 1977–78, England's Naomi James, Poland's Krystyna Chojnowska-Liskiewicz, and France's Brigitte Oudry had all sailed solo around the world south of the five great capes of the Southern Hemisphere: South America's Cape Horn, Africa's Cape of Good Hope, Australia's Cape Leeuwin (south of Perth), Tasmania's South East Cape, and New

Karen Thorndike is the first and only American woman to have successfully sailed solo around the world.

Zealand's Southwest Cape. In 1988 Australian Kay Cotee became the first woman to make a solo circumnavigation nonstop, embarking from the city of Sydney. In 1990–91, Isabelle Autissier of France completed her first circumnavigation of the globe. And in 1995–96, Samantha Brewster made a swift world crossing, departing from Southampton, England, and returning in 161 days.

Thorndike is a resident of Snohomish, Washington, which is located north of Seattle. She learned to sail along the Washington coast and developed a passion for blue water (open sea) sailing. She also took part in major offshore races. In 1988, for example, she was a member of the first American all-woman team to participate in the Victoria-Maui International Yacht Race. As her boating skills and experience grew, she began to dream of sailing alone around the world.

Acquires *Amelia* for world voyage

By the time Thorndike made her first try at circumnavigation in 1995, she had been sailing for twenty years and had covered 40,000 blue water miles. In order to purchase a new vessel for her mission, she sold some real estate she owned. Her "new" boat was a sturdy fiberglass, cutter-rigged Rival built in 1985 and was well-suited for single handling. *Amelia*'s former English owner had also been a well-traveled mariner, sailing the yacht to Scotland, Ireland, France, the Mediterranean, Russia, Iceland, and across the Atlantic Ocean to the United States. With such a boat, Thorndike felt confident she could achieve her goal.

Journey begins

In 1995 Thorndike set out from Washington's Neah Bay as she began her world voyage. Her friends and family gathered at Port Angeles to watch her as she passed by to the sea. She did not get far before rigging problems and damage from a lightning storm caused her to abandon her mission and head to San Diego for repairs. She made a second attempt the following year, this time departing from San Diego. Her plan

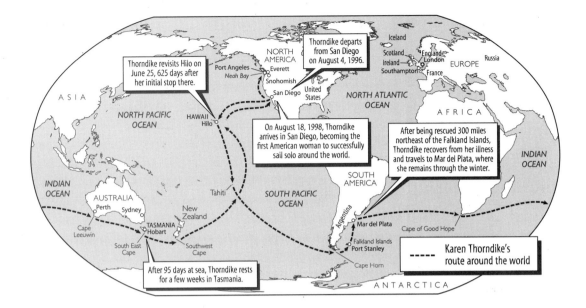

Thorndike revisits Hilo on June 25, 625 days after her initial stop there.

Thorndike departs from San Diego on August 4, 1996.

On August 18, 1998, Thorndike arrives in San Diego, becoming the first American woman to successfully sail solo around the world.

After being rescued 300 miles northeast of the Falkland Islands, Thorndike recovers from her illness and travels to Mar del Plata, where she remains through the winter.

After 95 days at sea, Thorndike rests for a few weeks in Tasmania.

----- Karen Thorndike's route around the world

was to first sail to Hawaii and Tahiti, making a wide westward arc in the Pacific to take advantage of ocean currents and trade winds. Then she would sweep south around the first of the great capes—South America's Cape Horn—as she made her way across the Southern Hemisphere.

The southern Pacific Ocean near South America's cape proved as challenging as its reputation. Thorndike, always tethered to *Amelia* with a safety harness when on deck, encountered forty-knot (nautical miles per hour) winds and twenty-foot waves. Still, the veteran sailor managed to round Cape Horn on January 9, and, a few days later, to reach the Falkland Islands. There she stopped at Port Stanley to rest and to make repairs to her battered yacht. It was Thorndike's bad luck to be in the town while it was experiencing a flu epidemic.

Signals for help at sea

Thorndike was feeling well when she left Port Stanley on January 29. But a day later the flu caught up with her. The weather also turned foul, with a fierce storm hitting February 1. Weakened, dehydrated, and exhausted from trying to steer *Amelia* through the driving wind and rain, lightning, and sweeping waves, Thorndike sent out a distress signal the following day. About 300 miles northeast of the Falkland Islands, she knew she needed medical help, and was hoping for a rescue.

The nearest ship to Thorndike, the British frigate H.M.S. *Norfolk,* was located offshore about fifty miles from the Falkland Islands, too far from *Amelia* to receive its radio signal. But her yacht also carried a transceiver (radio transmitter-receiver) for a satellite-based communications system (Comsat Inmarsat C), which Thorndike had been using to send e-mail messages from her laptop computer to her home base in Seattle. When she sent a message for help to John Oman, who headed her support team, he furiously went to work on her rescue.

At first Oman tried to phone the Falkland Islands to alert a rescue ship, but all eighteen telephone lines on the island were not working because of the storm. The only way to communicate with the islands was by military satellite. Oman contacted Royal Navy headquarters in London, and an international distress call to rescue Thorndike was relayed by satellite to the *Norfolk.* Fortunately, the complicated process took only a matter of minutes.

Royal Navy performs rescue

The *Norfolk* steamed ahead, and reached Thorndike and *Amelia* early in the morning of February 3. The sick sailor was taken aboard and received medical treatment. The *Norfolk* then headed to Mare Naval Base in the Falklands, where Thorndike obtained additional care. Naval volunteers piloted *Amelia* back to Port Stanley.

By the time Thorndike and *Amelia* were ready to sail again it was April. Winter had already begun in the Southern Hemisphere, and it was too late to safely sail across the southern Atlantic and Indian oceans. Instead, Thorndike voyaged north to Mar del Plata, Argentina, arriving on May 6, 1997. There she waited out the winter, and resumed her world trip on November 1, heading east.

The voyage of Tania Aebi

On November 6, 1987, American Tania Aebi completed a two-and-a-half year voyage around the world in *Varuna,* a twenty-six-foot sloop. She was celebrated as the first American woman (and youngest person) to circumnavigate the globe. She wrote a book about her sailing adventures, *Maiden Voyage.*

More than a year after she completed the trip, Aebi was informed that she did not qualify for the American solo sailing honor. Without giving it much thought, she had let a friend come aboard her vessel in the South Pacific. The friend traveled with Aebi for about 80 miles (130 kilometers), keeping the sailor from making history. The feat would be left for another adventurer—Karen Thorndike—to accomplish.

Rounds great southern capes

With great difficulty, Thorndike rounded Africa's Cape of Good Hope, where *Amelia* was battered by a series of storms and giant waves that reached from thirty to fifty feet. Then the sailor headed for Australia, and arrived in Hobart, Tasmania, on February 5, 1998, following ninety-five days at sea. After a few weeks' rest, Thorndike was ready to round the last great cape of the Southern Hemisphere—the Southwest Cape. She set out for New Zealand on March 15. Off its southern coast she encountered sixty-five-knot winds that whipped up huge waves. They poured over *Amelia* as Thorndike frantically pumped water out.

Completes historic voyage

Still, Thorndike managed to round the cape, and headed for open seas. By May 21, she had crossed her outward route in the Pacific Ocean as she sailed south of Tahiti. She revis-

ited Hilo, Hawaii, arriving on June 25, 1998—625 days after her initial stop there. Then Thorndike set out on July 14 for the last leg of her voyage. A month later she arrived in San Diego, completing her historic trip.

In late September, Thorndike and *Amelia* set sail for the Washington coast and home. Memories of her departure from Port Angeles three years ago—when she had begun her circumnavigation odyssey—flooded her thoughts: how friends and family had lined the shore waving to her and had even shot off a gun to celebrate the launch of her dream. She was overwhelmed by their support, and also by the good wishes of thousands of strangers who had sent encouraging e-mails to her throughout her voyage (Thorndike's daily coordinates and the travel log she sent her support team appeared on the Internet at the Global Online Adventure Learning Site: GOALS).

Thorndike arrived in Port Angeles on October 19, where she was given a warm homecoming and a "Karen Thorndike Day" was declared by the mayor. Another honorary day was designated and more celebrations were enjoyed when she visited Seattle on October 23. Finally, on the evening of October 27, 1998, Thorndike arrived at the Washington port of Everett, where she kept *Amelia* docked. She decided to wait until morning to put her trusty vessel into its assigned slip. During the night, the boat moored next to that slip blew apart from a propane explosion, wrecking the dock. The lucky team of Thorndike and *Amelia* had dodged disaster once again.

Sources

Karen Thorndike and Amelia: A GOALS Sailing Adventure. [Online] Available http://goals.com/amelia/KarenB.htm, December 10, 1998.

The Seattle Times—Today's Top Stories. "Rescued Sailor Wants to Head Back to Sea." [Online] Available http://seattletimes.com/extra/browse/html97/altsail_021897.html, February 18, 1997.

The Week in Sailing. "Karen Thorndike Headed for Uruguay after Break in Severe Falkland Islands Weather." [Online] Available http://www.sailing.org/weekfortyeights/thorndike.html, October 16, 1998.

William of Rubruck

Born c. 1215, Rubruck, Flanders

Died c. 1295

William of Rubruck was a Franciscan friar who was sent on a religious mission to the court of Mongolia's Great Khan by King Louis IX of France.

Early in the thirteenth century, military leader Genghis Khan (c. 1162–1227) united the many scattered tribes of Mongolia into a powerful new nation. Over the next several decades his forces and those led by his sons and grandsons—some of whom would succeed him as the Great Khan (head military leader)—would sweep north into China and west into Europe, conquering most of Russia and crushing Hungarian and Polish armies. Mongol forces would invade Persia and overthrow the Islamic caliphate (domain) at Baghdad (what is now Iraq), creating a vast empire.

During this time, leaders of western Europe were fearful that the Mongols would expand farther west, into their territory. Their one great hope to avert this disaster was to convert the Mongols to Western Christianity. At the time of their greatest conquests, the Mongols practiced their native tribal religion. But as they came into contact with the rest of the world they became familiar with the beliefs and practices of Buddhism, Islamism, and Christianity.

In 1245 an Italian Franciscan friar, Giovanni da Pian del Carpini (c. 1180–1252), was sent by Pope Innocent IV (d. 1254) to visit the court of the Great Khan near the Mongolian capital of Karakorum. His mission was to establish diplomatic relations with the Mongol leader and to convert the ruler and his followers to Roman Christianity. Carpini returned to Europe in 1247, unsuccessful in his mission. In 1248 King Louis IX (1214–70) of France, who would later be made a saint, decided to launch another mission to convert the Great Khan. William of Rubruck, a Flemish Franciscan friar, would lead the expedition. Although the friar would encounter similar disappointments when trying to convert the Mongols, his account of the journey would provide valuable new information about Mongolian and Eastern culture and the geography of Russia and central Asia. His book, *The Journey of William of Rubruck to the Eastern Parts of the World, 1253–1255,* would come to be appreciated as one of the most valuable travel accounts written by a medieval Christian.

King Louis IX of France, who sent William of Rubruck on a mission to convert the Mongols to Christianity.

Not much is known about William's early life. He was born around 1215 in the village of Rubruck in Flanders (the site is now located in France). He entered the Franciscan order. In 1248 he was a member of a party that accompanied King Louis to Palestine (present-day Israel). The monarch was there to try to recover possession of the Holy Land for Christians, following its takeover by Muslims in 1187. The Crusade was going disastrously for Louis, and he was hoping to form an alliance with the Mongols to help him fight the forces of Islam. But it was unlikely that the Great Khan would help the French king until the Mongol leader had converted to Christianity. Therefore, when appointed to lead the next expedition to Mongolia, William was not made an official ambassador, although he did carry letters from the king. Instead, the

This page from a medieval manuscript shows William of Rubruck and his party en route to Mongolia in 1253.

friar and his small party approached the Great Kahn as missionaries, with their goal largely a religious one.

Begins eastern journey

In 1252 William left the port of Acre in northern Palestine and headed for Constantinople (now Istanbul, Turkey). On May 7, 1253, he embarked on his long journey to Karakorum—located in central Mongolia—accompanied by another Franciscan friar, Bartholomew of Cremona, as well as a clerk, an interpreter, and a few servants. The group sailed across the Black Sea to the great trading port of Soldaria (now Sudak) in the Crimea. From there, William and his party set out in ox-pulled carts and, within a few days, made their first contact with Mongolian tribesmen. Like many European explorers confronted with the unfamiliar, the travelers found the ways of these new people barbaric (uncivilized). The Mongols lived in tents made of felt called yurts, painted their faces, and ate peculiar foods, like kumis—fermented mare's milk.

Endures hardships and records important observations

The travelers continued eastward through the steppes (arid plains) of southern Russia. The trip was a difficult one, for the climate was harsh, food and water were scarce, and sometimes the Mongols they encountered were less than hospitable, taking anything of worth that the party possessed. The tribesmen even claimed the friars' religious vestments. All the while, William kept detailed records of everything he saw. He noted features of the countryside, native animals (he and his group were the first Europeans to observe the wild, long-horned mountain sheep), and the languages and practices of the different tribes he encountered. Later, in his book, William would describe Chinese writing, becoming the first European to do so. Similarly, he would be the first Westerner to identify the center of the silk trade (whose products were prized by wealthy Europeans): it was the land called Cathay (present-day China)—east of Mongolia.

Meets conqueror of Eastern Europe

Eventually, William and his party reached the camp of the great Mongolian general Batu, which was located on the Volga River. A grandson of Genghis Khan, Batu (d. 1255) was responsible for the conquest of Eastern Europe. The friar was hopeful that his religious message would be well received by this Mongol leader, for it was rumored that Batu's son, Sartach, had been converted to Christianity. But when William appeared before Batu and his court and urged them to be baptized as Christians, the Mongols burst into uproarious laughter. Apparently the information about Sartach had been untrue. Nonetheless, Batu did give William and his party permission to proceed to the court of the Great Khan—5,000 miles farther east—even providing them with horses and a guide.

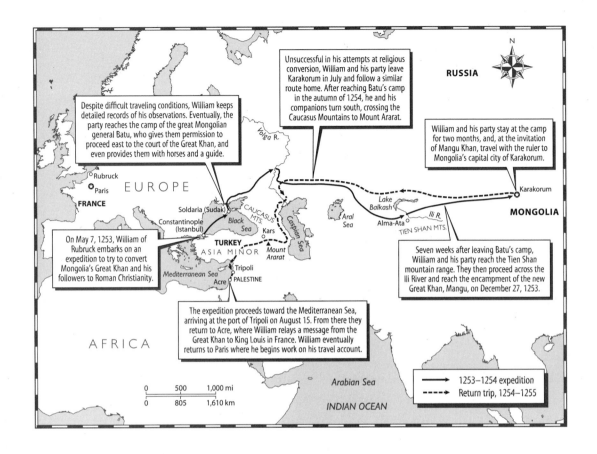

Despite difficult traveling conditions, William keeps detailed records of his observations. Eventually, the party reaches the camp of the great Mongolian general Batu, who gives them permission to proceed east to the court of the Great Khan, and even provides them with horses and a guide.

Unsuccessful in his attempts at religious conversion, William and his party leave Karakorum in July and follow a similar route home. After reaching Batu's camp in the autumn of 1254, he and his companions turn south, crossing the Caucasus Mountains to Mount Ararat.

William and his party stay at the camp for two months, and, at the invitation of Mangu Khan, travel with the ruler to Mongolia's capital city of Karakorum.

On May 7, 1253, William of Rubruck embarks on an expedition to try to convert Mongolia's Great Khan and his followers to Roman Christianity.

Seven weeks after leaving Batu's camp, William and his party reach the Tien Shan mountain range. They then proceed across the Ili River and reach the encampment of the new Great Khan, Mangu, on December 27, 1253.

The expedition proceeds toward the Mediterranean Sea, arriving at the port of Tripoli on August 15. From there they return to Acre, where William relays a message from the Great Khan to King Louis in France. William eventually returns to Paris where he begins work on his travel account.

→ 1253–1254 expedition
---- Return trip, 1254–1255

Reaches court of Great Khan

William and his party left Batu's camp on September 15, 1253, and continued on their eastward journey, acquiring fresh horses at Mongol camps along the way. They rode north of the Caspian and Aral seas, reaching the great Mongolian plains. (William would later correctly note in his book that the Caspian Sea was an enclosed body of water—not the gulf of a northern sea, as was believed at that time.) After seven weeks, the travelers came upon the great Tien Shan Mountain Range, probably in the region of the present-day city of Alma-Ata (in present-day Kazakstan). They proceeded across the Ili River. Finally, on December 27, 1253, they reached the encampment of the new Great Khan, Mangu (1208–59)—another grandson of Genghis Khan. William and his companions had to wait several days before they were presented to the Mongolian leader. When they at last received an audience, the meeting did not go well. It was obvious that Mangu was not interested in religious instruction, but rather in conquest, as he tried to extract from his visitors military information about France. William was forced to give evasive answers.

William and his party stayed in the camp for two months, until the worst of the winter was over. The friar used the time to closely study every aspect of Mongolian life: diet, dress, social structure, laws, customs, and religious beliefs. Then, at the invitation of Mangu Khan, he and his companions traveled with the ruler as he journeyed to Mongolia's capital city, Karakorum. In the great traveling march, William and his group encountered many other Westerners who had either been captured in various Mongol military campaigns or had attached themselves to the court. Political ambassadors from many Asian territories also joined them. William became one of several members of different religious groups—Buddhists, Muslims, Christians, and others—who vied for the favor of the Mongolian leader and looked to establish a stronghold in the new empire.

Attempts at religious conversion fail

Reaching Karakorum, William and his party found that the city was populated by men of every race and religion. In his book, the friar would later give Europe its first description of the small but cosmopolitan Mongolian capital. Since it had a Nestorian church (where an Eastern form of Christianity was practiced) as well as mosques and Buddhist temples, William was hopeful that he would succeed in his mission of spreading Roman Christianity there. In a final audience with Mangu Khan on May 31, 1254, William asked to remain in the royal court and give religious instruction to its members. The Mongolian leader refused the request, noting that just as God had created individual fingers on a single hand, he had given the world's inhabitants different customs and beliefs. Mangu gave the friar a letter to take back to King Louis. The message it conveyed was not a particularly encouraging one: While the Great Kahn invited the European monarch to send official ambassadors to Karakorum, it was primarily for the purpose of determining whether France wanted peace or war. The letter then reminded King Louis that no distance was great enough to protect him or his country from the might of the Mongols. (Fortunately for Europe—at the time of William's visit—the next targets of Mongolian conquest would be in Muslim territory.)

When William departed Karakorum in July, he left Brother Bartholomew behind since he was too sick to travel. William and his small party followed a return route similar to the one they had traveled on their outward journey. The friar reached Batu's camp in the autumn of 1254. From there he and his companions turned south, crossing the Caucasus Mountains to Mount Ararat. By February 15, 1255, the travelers had entered Asia Minor (now Turkey) near the city of Kars. They proceeded toward the Mediterranean Sea, arriving at the port of Tripoli (now in Lebanon) on August 15. They then returned to Acre in Palestine, where William hoped to meet with King Louis and report on his religious mission. But the monarch had already left the Holy Land and had returned to Paris. The Great Khan's message was relayed to him there.

After spending several months in a monastery in Acre, William returned to Paris as well, where he began work on his travel account. It is known that the friar met with the famous English Franciscan scholar Roger Bacon (c. 1220–92) there in 1257; the philosopher had apparently become interested in William's travel experiences and would later refer to them in his own writings. Following that, no further information can be found on William of Rubruck.

Sources

Baker, Daniel B., ed. *Explorers and Discoverers of the World.* Detroit: Gale Research, 1993.

Bohlander, Richard E., ed. *World Explorers and Discoverers.* New York: Macmillan, 1992.

Delpar, Helen, ed. *The Discoverers: An Encyclopedia of Explorers and Exploration.* New York: McGraw-Hill, 1980.

Explorers and Exploration, Volume 1: *The Earliest Explorers,* written by Nathaniel Harris. Danbury, CT: Grolier Educational, 1988.

Marshall Cavendish Illustrated Encyclopedia of Discovery and Exploration, Volume 2: *Beyond the Horizon,* written by Malcolm Ross MacDonald. Freeport, NY: Marshall Cavendish, 1990.

Waldman, Carl and Alan Wexler. *Who Was Who in World Exploration.* New York: Facts on File, 1992.

Hermann von Wissmann

Born September 4, 1853, Frankfurt, Germany

Died June 15, 1905, near Liezen, Austria

Hermann von Wissmann was a German explorer and colonial administrator in Africa during the last decades of the nineteenth century.

Before 1800 few Europeans had ventured into the interior of Africa. But by the close of that same century, much of the continent had been explored. A great deal had been learned about Africa's peoples, geography, and wealth of natural resources and trade opportunities. As a consequence—between 1880 and 1912—European powers rushed to lay claim to parts of the continent, to establish colonies or protectorates that operated under their influence. With the exception of the countries of Liberia and Ethiopia, all of Africa came under the control of France, Great Britain, Italy, Spain, Portugal, Belgium, and Germany. (By the 1970s, nearly all of the colonies and protectorates would have their independence.)

Travels through central Africa

Hermann von Wissmann was an explorer who helped such European nations in their quest to colonize Africa. Born in 1853 in Frankfurt, Germany, he later became an officer in the German army. Beginning in 1880, he went to work for the German Africa Society, exploring central Africa. That year he set off on a west-to-east transcontinental journey, starting out from Angola's capital city of Luanda, located on the Atlantic Coast. He journeyed along the Lulua and Kasai rivers, through the Congo River region. He made his way to Nyangwe, in what is now the central Democratic Republic of the Congo (formerly Zaire). He continued east, traveling by way of Lake Tanganyika and Lake Tabora until he reached Zanzibar on the Indian Ocean coast in 1882.

Explores Congo River region

With the French concentrating their colonial efforts in the northwest and west of Africa, and Great Britain spreading its influence primarily in the east and southeast, King Leopold II (1835–1909) of Belgium decided, in 1879, to colonize the extensive Congo River basin that runs through west-central and central Africa. (The Congo River is the second longest river in Africa, and one of the largest rivers in the world.) In the service of the Belgian king, Wissmann returned to the Congo region in 1883, and for the next two years explored the Kasai River—the Congo's main southern branch. Finding the Kasai mostly navigable, he investigated its tributaries, and came upon an undiscovered branch known as the Sankuru. In 1886–87 Wissmann also undertook an expedition to reach the Lomami River, which empties into the Congo River farther west, in what is now the north-central Democratic Republic of the Congo. In this mission he was unsuccessful.

King Leopold II of Belgium, who ordered the colonization of the Congo River basin. Wissmann explored the Congo region in service to the Belgian king.

In 1888 Wissmann led an expedition east beyond the Congo, to Lake Tanganyika and Lake Nyasa, and then on to the southeastern seaport of Quelimane (in present-day Mozambique). He skirted the area that Germany was attempting to

Colonial Africa
1880–1914

(Names of controlling nations in parentheses)

colonize on the east coast of Africa—what would be called German East Africa (comprised of what is now Tanzania and part of Kenya). For a time, in fact, Germany would have substantial holdings in Africa: roughly present-day Ghana, Cameroon, and Namibia on the west coast, as well as Tanzania and part of Kenya. These colonial possessions would be lost, of course, after World War I (1914–18), when they were divided among the Allies who had defeated Germany.

Serves in German East Africa

For the remainder of his time in Africa, Wissmann worked for the German government, helping establish its colony in East Africa. He served as colonial commissioner in German East Africa from 1889 to 1892, and during that time succeeded in suppressing an Arab revolt there; in the coastal area surrendered by the sultan of Zanzibar, he founded the settlement of Moshi on the slopes of Mount Kilimanjaro, the highest mountain on the continent. During that time Wissmann also brought the Masai people—a tribe particularly resistant to European control and who lived mostly in what is now Kenya and Tanzania—under German colonial authority.

Due in large part to Wissmann's work, the area between Lake Nyasa and Lake Tanganyika was brought under German colonial rule. He founded several settlements in the region, including Langenburg on Lake Nyasa. Wissmann served as governor of German East Africa briefly, from 1895 to 1896, before ill health forced him to return to Europe.

Wissmann wrote about his years in Africa. Some of his expedition experiences were recalled in *My Second Journey Through Equatorial Africa,* published in 1891. (Equatorial Africa refers to those countries, including Kenya, Tanzania, and the Democratic Republic of the Congo, located at or near the equator.) An important contributor to the European colonization of central Africa, Wissmann died in 1905.

Sources

Explorers and Exploration, Volume 8: *Africa and Arabia,* written by Geoffrey Nowell-Smith. Danbury, CT: Grolier Educational, 1998.

Waldman, Carl and Alan Wexler. *Who Was Who in World Exploration.* New York: Facts on File, 1992.

Chronology of Exploration

As an aid to the reader who wishes to trace the history of exploration or the explorers active in a particular location, the major expeditions within a geographical area are listed below in chronological order.

*Explorers with entries in Explorers and Discoverers, Volume 7 are in **boldface** and have page numbers following their names; explorers whose names are not in boldface appear in Volumes 1–4, Volume 5, or Volume 6.*

Africa: central

1802–14	Pedro João Baptista and Amaro José
1854–56	David Livingstone
1858–64	David Livingstone
1872–73	David Livingstone
1873–77	Henry Morton Stanley
1877–80	Hermenegildo de Brito Capelo and Roberto Ivens
1880–82	**Hermann von Wissmann 212**
1883–85	Hermann von Wissmann
1884–85	Hermenegildo de Brito Capelo and Roberto Ivens
1886–87	Hermann von Wissmann
1888–90	Henry Morton Stanley
1896–98	Jean-Baptiste Marchand
1903	May French Sheldon
1924–25	Delia Akeley

Africa: coast

c. 470 B.C.	**Hanno 107**
1416–60	Henry the Navigator
1487–88	Bartolomeu Dias
1500	**Pedro Álvares Cabral 37**
1765–68	James Bruce

Africa: east

c. 1493–92 B.C.	Hatshepsut (sponsored expedition)
1490–1526	Pero da Covilhã
1768–73	James Bruce

1812–13	Jean-Louis Burckhardt
1814	Jean-Louis Burckhardt
1848	Johannes Rebmann
1848–49	Johann Ludwig Krapf
1848–49	Johannes Rebmann
1849	Johannes Rebmann
1851	Johann Ludwig Krapf
1855–57	Alexine Tinné
1857–59	Richard Burton and John Hanning Speke (with Sidi Mubarak Bombay)
1860–63	John Hanning Speke and James Augustus Grant (with Sidi Mubarak Bombay)
1862–63	Alexine Tinné
1862–64	Samuel White Baker and Florence Baker
1865–71	David Livingstone
1869	Alexine Tinné
1870–73	Samuel White Baker and Florence Baker
1871–73	Henry Morton Stanley (with Sidi Mubarak Bombay)
1874–86	**William Junker 133**
1883–84	Joseph Thomson
1888	**Hermann von Wissmann 212**
1891	May French Sheldon
1905–06	Delia Akeley
1909–11	Delia Akeley
1930s–60s	Louis and Mary Leakey
1966–67	**Dervla Murphy 167**
1966–85	Dian Fossey
1968–	Richard Leakey

Africa: north

1763–65	James Bruce

1873	**William Junker 133**
1996	**Helen Thayer 188**

Africa: south

1849	David Livingstone
1850	David Livingstone
1850–51	**Carl Johan Andersson 1**
1851	Carl Johan Andersson
1851–52	David Livingstone
1851–55	Ida Pfeiffer
1853	Carl Johan Andersson
1859	Carl Johan Andersson
1866–67	Carl Johan Andersson
1990s	**Dervla Murphy 167**

Africa: west

1352–53	Abu Abdallah Ibn Battutah
1790–91	Daniel Houghton
1795–99	Mungo Park
1805	Mungo Park
1827–28	René Caillié
1850–55	Heinrich Barth
1854	**William Balfour Baikie 7**
1856–60	Paul Du Chaillu
1857–58	William Balfour Baikie
1861–76	Friedrich Gerhard Rohlfs
1863	Paul Du Chaillu
1867	Paul Du Chaillu
1875–78	Pierre Savorgnan de Brazza
1879	Henry Morton Stanley
1879–81	Pierre Savorgnan de Brazza
1883–85	Pierre Savorgnan de Brazza
1891–92	Pierre Savorgnan de Brazza
1893	Mary Kingsley
1894	Mary Kingsley
1903	May French Sheldon

1987	**Dervla Murphy 167**

Antarctica

1819–21	Fabian Gottlieb von Bellingshausen
1837–40	Jules-Sébastien-César Dumont d'Urville
1839–40	Charles Wilkes
1903–05	Jean-Baptiste Charcot
1907–09	Ernest Shackleton
1908–10	Jean-Baptiste Charcot
1910–12	Roald Amundsen
1914–16	Ernest Shackleton
1921–22	Ernest Shackleton
1928	Hubert Wilkins
1928–29	Richard Evelyn Byrd
1929	Hubert Wilkins
1933–34	Lincoln Ellsworth
1933–35	Richard Evelyn Byrd
1935–36	Lincoln Ellsworth
1937	Lincoln Ellsworth
1939–40	Richard Evelyn Byrd
1946–47	Richard Evelyn Byrd
1956	Richard Evelyn Byrd
1956–58	Vivian Fuchs
1989–90	Will Steger
1997	**Helen Thayer 188**

Arabia

25 B.C.	Aelius Gallus
1812–13	Hester Stanhhope
1814–15	Jean-Louis Burckhardt
1854–55	Richard Burton
1877–78	Anne Blunt and Wilfrid Scawen Blunt
1879–80	Anne Blunt and Wilfrid Scawen Blunt
1913	Gertrude Bell
1935–36	Freya Stark
1990	Nicholas Clapp
1991–92	Nicholas Clapp

Arctic (*see also* North America; Northwest Passage)

1827	Edward Parry
1850	**Elisha Kent Kane 138**
1853–55	Elisha Kent Kane
1858	Nils Adolf Erik Nordenskjöld
1860	Charles Francis Hall
1861	Nils Adolf Erik Nordenskjöld
1864	Nils Adolf Erik Nordenskjöld
1864–69	Charles Francis Hall
1868	Nils Adolf Erik Nordenskjöld
1871	Charles Francis Hall
1872	Nils Adolf Erik Nordenskjöld
1893–96	Fridtjof Nansen
1898–99	Bob Bartlett (with Robert Edwin Peary)
1902	Jean-Baptiste Charcot
1902	Robert Edwin Peary
1905–06	Bob Bartlett (with Robert Edwin Peary)
1905–06	Robert Edwin Peary (with Matthew A. Henson)
1906–07	Vilhjalmur Stefansson
1908–09	Bob Bartlett (with Robert Edwin Peary)
1908–09	Robert Edwin Peary (with Matthew A. Henson)
1908–12	Vilhjalmur Stefansson

1913–14	Bob Bartlett (with Vilhjalmur Stefansson)	1866–68	Francis Garnier
1913–18	Vilhjalmur Stefansson	1870–72	Nikolay Przhevalsky
1921–25	Vilhjalmur Stefansson	1876	Nikolay Przhevalsky
1925	Roald Amundsen	1883–85	Nikolay Przhevalsky
1925	Richard Evelyn Byrd	1893–95	Sven Hedin
1926	Roald Amundsen and Umberto Nobile	1895–97	Isabella Bird
		1899	Fanny Bullock Workman
1926	Louise Arner Boyd	1899–1901	Sven Hedin
1926	Richard Evelyn Byrd	1900	Aurel Stein
1926–27	Hubert Wilkins	1903–05	Sven Hedin
1928	Louise Arner Boyd	1906	Fanny Bullock Workman
1928	Hubert Wilkins	1906–08	Aurel Stein
1931	Hubert Wilkins	1913–15	Aurel Stein
1940	Louise Arner Boyd	1927–33	Sven Hedin
1955	Louise Arner Boyd	1932	Ella Maillart
1958	U.S.S. *Nautilus*	1934	Ella Maillart
1986	Will Steger	1934–36	Sven Hedin
1988	**Helen Thayer 188**	1953	Edmund Hillary
1992	Helen Thayer	1977	Edmund Hillary
1994	Helen Thayer		
1998	Helen Thayer		

Asia/Europe (*see* Eurasia)

Asia: east

Late 1960s	Freya Stark

Asia, south/China

629–645 B.C.	Hsüan-tsang
327–325 B.C.	**Nearchus 181**
138–126 B.C.	Chang Ch'ien
399–414	Fa-Hsien
672–82	I-Ching
1321–30s or c. 1354	Jordanus of Séverac
1405–07	Cheng Ho
1407–09	Cheng Ho
1409–11	Cheng Ho
1413–15	Cheng Ho
1417–19	Cheng Ho
1421–22	Cheng Ho

Asia: interior

1640–41	**Semyon Ivanovich Dezhnev 60**
1641–42	Semyon Ivanovich Dezhnev
1643	Semyon Ivanovich Dezhnev
1643–46	Vasily Danilovich Poyarkov
1647	Semyon Ivanovich Dezhnev
1648–62	Semyon Ivanovich Dezhnev
1649–50	Yerofey Pavlovich Khabarov
1650–54	Yerofey Pavlovich Khabarov

1433–35	Cheng Ho
1500–01	**Pedro Álvares Cabral 37**
1847–48	Ida Pfeiffer
1851–55	Ida Pfeiffer
1857–64	Robert Hermann Schomburgk
1868	Hari Ram
1871–72	Hari Ram
1873	Hari Ram
1885	Hari Ram
1935	Ella Maillart
1939	Ella Maillart
1949	Ella Maillart
1965	**Dervla Murphy 167**
1973	Dervla Murphy
1974	Dervla Murphy
1994	Ella Maillart

Australia

1605–06	Willem Janszoon
1642	Abel Tasman
1644	Abel Tasman
1770	James Cook
1798–99	Matthew Flinders
1801–02	Matthew Flinders
1801–02	Joseph Banks
1802–03	Matthew Flinders
1813	Gregory Blaxland
1839	Edward John Eyre
1840–41	Edward John Eyre
1860–61	Robert O'Hara Burke and William John Wills
1861–65	**Ernest Giles 100**
1869–70	John Forrest
1872	Ernest Giles
1873–74	Ernest Giles
1874	John Forrest

1875	Ernest Giles
1876	Ernest Giles
1876	John Forrest
1880	John Forrest
1882	Ernest Giles
1899–1940s	**Daisy Bates 14**

Aviation

1927	Charles Lindbergh
1928	Amelia Earhart
1930	Beryl Markham
1930	Amy Johnson
1931	Amy Johnson
1931	Wiley Post
1932	Amelia Earhart
1932	Amy Johnson
1933	Wiley Post
1935	Amelia Earhart
1936	Amelia Earhart
1936	Beryl Markham
1947	Chuck Yeager
1986	Dick Rutan and Jeana Yeager
1995	Steve Fossett
1996	Steve Fossett
1997	Steve Fossett
1997	**Linda Finch 77**

Central America

| 1523–26 | Pedro de Alvarado |

Circumnavigation

1525–36	Andrés de Urdaneta
1764–66	**John Byron 28**
1889–90	Nellie Bly
1996–98	**Karen Thorndike 197**

1997   **Linda Finch 77**

Eurasia (*see also* Tibet)

454–443 B.C. Herodotus
401–399 B.C. Xenophon
334–323 B.C. Alexander the Great
310–306 B.C. Pytheas
921–22   Ahmad Ibn Fadlan
1110s–40s   **Abu Abd-Allah Muhammed al-Sharif al-Idrisi 122**
1159–73   Benjamin of Tudela
1245–47   Giovanni da Pian del Carpini
1252–55   **William of Rubruck 204**
1271–95   Marco Polo
1280–90   Rabban Bar Sauma
1487–90   Pero da Covilhã
1492–93   Christopher Columbus
1497–99   Vasco da Gama
1502–03   Vasco da Gama
1537–58   Fernã o Mendes Pinto
1549–51   Saint Francis Xavier
1595–97   Cornelis de Houtman
1598–99   Cornelis de Houtman
1656–58   Johann Grüber
1661–64   Johann Grüber
1697–99   Vladimir Atlasov
1725–30   Vitus Bering
1733–41   Vitus Bering
1787   Jean François de Galaup, Comte de La Pérouse
1879–80   Nils Adolf Erik Nordenskjöld
1922–23   Marguerite Baker Harrison
1930s   Ella Maillart
1952–66   Freya Stark
1963   **Dervla Murphy 167**

Europe

1145–66   **Abu Abd-Allah Muhammed al-Sharif al-Idrisi 122**
1845   Ida Pfeiffer
1848   Ida Pfeiffer
1851   Ida Pfeiffer
1855   Alexine Tinné
1857   Alexine Tinné
1873   Heinrich Schliemann
1876–78   Heinrich Schliemann
1884–85   Heinrich Schliemann
1920   Marguerite Baker Harrison
1993   Barry Clifford

Greenland

982   Erik the Red
1853–55   **Elisha Kent Kane 138**
1870   Nils Adolf Erik Nordenskjöld
1871   Charles Francis Hall
1883   Nils Adolf Erik Nordenskjöld
1886   Robert Edwin Peary
1888   Fridtjof Nansen
1891–92   Robert Edwin Peary (with Matthew A. Henson)
1893–95   Robert Edwin Peary (with Matthew A. Henson)
1926–36   Jean-Baptiste Charcot
1931   Louise Arner Boyd
1933   Louise Arner Boyd
1937   Louise Arner Boyd
1938   Louise Arner Boyd

Middle East

334 B.C.   **Nearchus 181**
325–324 B.C. Nearchus

1765–68	James Bruce
1809–12	Jean-Louis Burckhardt
1815	Jean-Louis Burckhardt
1842–43	Ida Pfeiffer
1847–48	Ida Pfeiffer
1856	Alexine Tinné
1857	Alexine Tinné
1924	Marguerite Baker Harrison
1927	Freya Stark
1928	Freya Stark
1929–33	Freya Stark
1952–57	Kathleen M. Kenyon
1970s	**Thor Heyerdahl 113**

Muslim World

915–17	Abu al-Hasan 'Ali al-Mas'udi
918–28	Abu al-Hasan 'Ali al-Mas'udi
921–22	Ahmad Ibn Fadlan
943–73	Abu al-Kasim Ibn Ali al-Nasibi Ibn Hawkal
966–87	Muhammed ibn-Ahmad al-Muqaddasi
1325–49	Abu Abdallah Ibn Battutah

North America: coast

c. 566–573	**Saint Brendan 23**
1001–02	Leif Eriksson
1493–96	Christopher Columbus
1497	John Cabot
1498	John Cabot
1500	Gaspar Corte-Real
1501	Gaspar Corte-Real
1502	Miguel Corte-Real
1502–04	Christopher Columbus
1508	Sebastian Cabot
1513	Juan Ponce de León

1513–14	Vasco Núñez de Balboa
1518–22	Hernán Cortés
1519–22	Pedro de Alvarado
1524	Giovanni da Verrazano
1534	Jacques Cartier
1534–36	Hernán Cortés
1535–36	Jacques Cartier
1539	Hernán Cortés
1540–41	Pedro de Alvarado
1541–42	Jacques Cartier
1542–43	João Rodrigues Cabrilho
1584	Walter Raleigh
1585–86	Walter Raleigh
1587–89	Walter Raleigh
1603	Samuel de Champlain
1604–07	Samuel de Champlain
1606–09	John Smith
1608–10	Samuel de Champlain
1609	Henry Hudson
1610	Samuel de Champlain
1614	John Smith
1792–94	George Vancouver
1963–98	**Mel Fisher 83**
1976–	**National Air and Space Museum 175**

North America: interior

1618–20	Jean Nicollet
1620–29	Jean Nicollet
1634–35	Jean Nicollet
1666–71	Jacques Marquette
1673	Jacques Marquette
1674–75	Jacques Marquette
1678	Louis Hennepin
1679–80	Louis Hennepin (with René-Robert de La Salle)

| 1680–81 | Louis Hennepin |
| 1822 | William Henry Ashley |

North America: northwest

| 1805–06 | Simon Fraser |
| 1806–08 | Simon Fraser |

North America: southwest

1886	Nellie Bly
1987–	Biosphere 2
1997	**Helen Thayer 188**

North America: sub-Arctic

1654–56	Médard Chouart des Groselliers
1668	Médard Chouart des Groselliers
1668	Pierre Esprit Radisson
1670	Pierre Esprit Radisson
1679	Louis Jolliet
1682–83	Médard Chouart des Groselliers
1684	Pierre Esprit Radisson
1685–87	Pierre Esprit Radisson
1689	Louis Jolliet
1694	Louis Jolliet
1725–30	Vitus Bering
1733–41	Vitus Bering
1789	Alexander Mackenzie
1795	Aleksandr Baranov
1799	Aleksandr Baranov
1819–22	John Franklin
1825–27	John Franklin

North America: west

1527–36	Álvar Núñez Cabeza de Vaca (with Estevanico)
1538–43	Hernando de Soto
1539	Estevanico
1540–42	Francisco Vásquez de Coronado
1611–12	Samuel de Champlain
1613–15	Samuel de Champlain
1615–16	Samuel de Champlain
1615–16	Étienne Brulé
1621–23	Étienne Brulé
1657	Pierre Esprit Radisson
1659–60	Mé dard Chouart des Groselliers
1659–60	Pierre Esprit Radisson
1669–70	René-Robert Cavelier de La Salle
1672–74	Louis Jolliet
1678–83	René-Robert Cavelier de La Salle
1684–87	René-Robert Cavelier de La Salle
1769–71	Daniel Boone
1775	Daniel Boone
1792–94	Alexander Mackenzie
1792–97	David Thompson
1797–99	David Thompson
1800–02	David Thompson
1804–06	Meriwether Lewis and William Clark
1805–06	Sacagawea (with Meriwether Lewis and William Clark)
1805–06	Zebulon Pike
1806–07	Zebulon Pike
1807–11	David Thompson

1811–13	Wilson Price Hunt and Robert Stuart
1823	William Henry Ashley (with Jedediah Smith)
1823–25	Jedediah Smith
1824–25	William Henry Ashley
1824–25	Peter Skene Ogden
1825–26	Peter Skene Ogden
1826	William Henry Ashley
1826–27	Peter Skene Ogden
1826–28	Jedediah Smith
1828–29	Peter Skene Ogden
1829–30	Peter Skene Ogden
1842	John Charles Frémont
1843–44	John Charles Frémont
1845–48	John Charles Frémont
1848–49	John Charles Frémont
1850–51	Jim Beckwourth
1851–55	Ida Pfeiffer
1853–55	John Charles Frémont
1880–1940s	**Alice Eastwood 66**

North Pole (*see* Arctic)

Northeast Passage

1607	Henry Hudson
1878–79	Nils A. E. Nordenskjöld
1918–20	Roald Amundsen
1931	Lincoln Ellsworth

Northwest Passage

1610–13	Henry Hudson
1776–79	James Cook
1819–20	Edward Parry
1821–23	Edward Parry
1824–25	Edward Parry

1845–47	John Franklin
1850–54	Robert McClure
1903–06	Roald Amundsen
1969	**S.S. *Manhattan* 159**

Oceans

c. 566–573	**Saint Brendan 23**
1872–76	H.M.S. *Challenger*
1901	Jean-Baptiste Charcot
1912	R.M.S *Titanic*
1921	Jean-Baptiste Charcot
1925–27	S.S. *Meteor*
1942–42	Jacques Cousteau
1948	August Piccard
1949–	**Eugenie Clark 44**
1954	August Piccard
1960s–	Sylvia Earle
1960	Jacques Piccard
1968–80	*Glomar Challenger*
1969	Jacques Piccard
1969	**Thor Heyerdahl 113**
1970	Thor Heyerdahl
1984	Barry Clifford
1985	R.M.S. *Titanic*
1996–98	**Karen Thorndike 197**

South America: coast

1498–1500	Christopher Columbus
1499–1500	Alonso de Ojeda
1499–1500	Amerigo Vespucci
1500	**Pedro Álvares Cabral 37**
1501–02	Amerigo Vespucci
1502	Alonso de Ojeda
1505	Alonso de Ojeda
1509–10	Alonso de Ojeda
1519–20	Ferdinand Magellan

1526–30	Sebastian Cabot
1527	Giovanni da Verrazano
1528	Giovanni da Verrazano
1534	Pedro de Alvarado
1594	Walter Raleigh
1595	Walter Raleigh
1615	Willem Corneliszoon Schouten
1615	Pedro de Teixeira
1615–16	**Jacob Le Maire 151**
1617–18	Walter Raleigh
1735–43	Charles-Marie de La Condomine
1740–44	**John Byron 28**
1743–44	Charles-Marie de La Condomine
1764–65	John Byron
1831–34	Charles Darwin
1847–48	Ida Pfeiffer
1851–55	Ida Pfeiffer

South America: interior

1524–25	Francisco Pizarro
1526–27	Francisco Pizarro
1531–41	Francisco Pizarro
1536–39	**Gonzalo Jiménez de Quesada 126**
1540–44	Álvar Núñez Cabeza de Vaca
1541–42	Francisco de Orellana
1569–72	Gonzalo Jiménez de Quesada
1620s	Pedro de Teixeira
1629	Pedro de Teixeira
1637–38	Pedro de Teixeira
1639	Pedro de Teixeira
1743	Charles-Marie de La Condomine

1760–62	José Celestino Mutis
1769–70	Isabel Godin des Odonais
1777–78	José Celestino Mutis
1782–92	José Celestino Mutis
1799–1803	Alexander von Humboldt
1835–36	Robert Hermann Schomburgk
1836–37	Robert Hermann Schomburgk
1838–40	Robert Hermann Schomburgk
1841–44	Robert Hermann Schomburgk
1900–06	Cândido Rondón
1903	Annie Smith Peck
1904	Annie Smith Peck
1906–09	Cândido Rondón
1908	Annie Smith Peck
1911	Hiram Bingham
1912	Hiram Bingham
1913–14	Cândido Rondón
1915	Hiram Bingham
1915–19	Cândido Rondón
1927–30	Cândido Rondón
1978	**Dervla Murphy 167**
1995	**Helen Thayer 188**

South Pacific

671	I-Ching
682–95	I-Ching
1519–22	Ferdinand Magellan
1526–35	Andrés de Urdaneta
1564–65	Andrés de Urdaneta
1577–80	Francis Drake
1616	**Jacob Le Maire 151**

1616	Willem Corneliszoon Schouten
1642–43	Abel Tasman
1721–22	Jacob Roggeveen
1765	**John Byron 28**
1766–68	Samuel Wallis
1766–69	Philip Carteret
1767–69	Louis-Antoine de Bougainville
1768–71	James Cook (with Joseph Banks)
1772–75	James Cook
1776–79	James Cook
1785–88	Jean François de Galaup, Comte de La Pérouse
1791	George Vancouver
1826–29	Jules-Sébastien-César Dumont d'Urville
1834–36	Charles Darwin
1838–39	Jules-Sébastien-César Dumont d'Urville
1838–42	Charles Wilkes
1847–48	Ida Pfeiffer
1851–55	Ida Pfeiffer
1871–74	**Luigi Maria D'Albertis 52**
1875	Luigi Maria D'Albertis
1876	Luigi Maria D'Albertis
1877	Luigi Maria D'Albertis
1923	Evelyn Cheesman
1928–30	Evelyn Cheesman
1930	Michael J. Leahy
1931	Michael J. Leahy
1932–33	Michael J. Leahy
1933–42	Evelyn Cheesman
1936–38	**Thor Heyerdahl 113**
1947	Thor Heyerdahl
1971–	**Birute Galdikas 92**

1995	**Helen Thayer 188**

Space

1957	*Sputnik*
1958–70	*Explorer 1*
1959–72	*Luna*
1961	Yury Gagarin
1962	John Glenn
1962–75	*Mariner*
1963	Valentina Tereshkova
1967–72	*Apollo*
1969	Neil Armstrong
1975–83	*Viking*
1977–90	*Voyager 1* and *2*
1983	Sally Ride
1986	Christa McAuliffe
1987	Mae Jemison
1990–	Hubble Space Telescope
1992	Mae Jemison
1986–	*Mir* space station

Tibet (*see also* Asia, south/China; Eurasia)

1624–30	Antonio de Andrade
1661	Johann Grüber
1811–12	Thomas Manning
1865–66	Nain Singh
1867–68	Nain Singh
1871	Hari Ram
1879–80	Nikolay Przhevalsky
1880–84	**Kintup 145**
1885	Hari Ram
1892–93	Annie Royle Taylor
1898	Susie Carson Rijnhart
1901	Sven Hedin
1915–16	Alexandra David-Neel

1923–24   Alexandra David-Neel

West Indies

Late 1980s   **Mel Fisher 83**

Explorers by Country of Birth

If an expedition was sponsored by a country other than the explorer's place of birth, the sponsoring country is listed in parentheses after the explorer's name.

Explorers with entries in Explorers and Discoverers, Volume 7 *are in **boldface** and have page numbers following their names; explorers whose names are not in boldface appear in Volumes 1–4, Volume 5, or Volume 6.*

Angola

Pedro João Baptista (Portugal)
Amaro José

Australia

John Forrest
Michael J. Leahy
Hubert Wilkins
William John Wills

Austria

Johann Grüber
Ida Pfeiffer

Belgium

Louis Hennepin (France)

Brazil

Cândido Rondón

Canada

Bob Bartlett
Alice Eastwood 66
Louis Jolliet
Peter Skene Ogden
Susie Carson Rijnhart
Vilhjalmur Stefansson

Carthage

Hanno 107

China

Rabban Bar Sauma

Chang Ch'ien
Cheng Ho
Fa-Hsien
Hsüan-Tsang
I-Ching

Denmark
Vitus Bering (Russia)

Ecuador
Isabel Godin des Odonais

Egypt
Hatshepsut

England
Samuel White Baker
Joseph Banks
Gertrude Bell
Isabella Bird
Gregory Blaxland
Anne Blunt
Wilfrid Scawen Blunt
Richard Burton
John Byron 28
Philip Carteret
H.M.S. *Challenger*
Evelyn Cheesman
James Cook
Charles Darwin
Francis Drake
Edward John Eyre
Matthew Flinders
John Franklin
Vivian Fuchs

Ernest Giles 100
Henry Hudson (Netherlands)
Amy Johnson
Kathleen M. Kenyon
Mary Kingsley
Mary Leakey
Thomas Manning
Beryl Markham (Kenya)
Edward Parry
Walter Raleigh
John Smith
John Hanning Speke
Hester Stanhope
Freya Stark
Annie Royle Taylor
David Thompson
R.M.S. *Titanic* (built in Belfast, Ireland)
George Vancouver
Samuel Wallis

Estonia
Fabian Gottlieb von Bellingshausen
   (Russia)

Finland
Nils Adolf Erik Nordenskjöld (Sweden)

Flanders
William of Rubruck 204

France
Louis-Antoine de Bougainville
Étienne Brulé
René Caillié
Jacques Cartier

Samuel de Champlain
Jean-Baptiste Charcot
Médard Chouart des Groselliers
Paul Du Chaillu (United States)
Jacques Cousteau
Alexandra David-Neel
Jules-Sébastien-César Dumont d'Urville
Francis Garnier
Jordanus of Séverac
Charles-Marie de La Condamine
Jean François de Galaup, Comte de La
    Pérouse
René-Robert Cavelier de La Salle
Jean-Baptiste Marchand
Jacques Marquette
Jean Nicollet
Pierre Esprit Radisson

Germany

Heinrich Barth (Great Britain)
Birute Galdikas 92
Alexander von Humboldt
Johann Ludwig Krapf
Johannes Rebmann
Friedrich Gerhard Rohlfs
Heinrich Schliemann
Robert Hermann Schomburgk (Great Britain)
Hermann von Wissmann (and Belgium)
    212

Greece

Alexander the Great
Herodotus
Nearchus 181
Pytheas
Xenophon

Hungary

Aurel Stein (Great Britain)

Iceland

Leif Eriksson

India

Hari Ram (Great Britain)
Kintup (Great Britain) **145**
Nain Singh

Iraq

Abu al-Kasim Ibn Ali al-Nasibi Ibn Hawkal
Ahmad Ibn Fadlan
Abu al-Hasan 'Ali al-Mas'udi

Ireland

Daisy Bates 14
Saint Brendan 23
Daniel Houghton
Robert O'Hara Burke (Australia)
Robert McClure
Dervla Murphy 167
Ernest Shackleton

Italy

Pierre Savorgnan de Brazza (France)
John Cabot (Great Britain)
Sebastian Cabot (England, Spain)
Giovanni da Pian del Carpini
Christopher Columbus (Spain)
Luigi Maria D'Albertis 52
Marco Polo
Giovanni da Verrazano (France)

Amerigo Vespucci (Spain, Portugal)

Kenya

Louis S. B. Leakey

Richard Leakey

Malawi

Sidi Mubarak Bombay (Great Britain)

James Chuma (Great Britain)

Morocco

Abu Abdallah Ibn Battutah

Estevanico

Abu Abd-Allah Muhammed al-Sharif al-Idrisi (royal geographer/cartographer in Sicily) **122**

The Netherlands

Willem Barents

Cornelis de Houtman

Willem Janszoon

Jacob Le Maire (with Willem Corneliszoon Schouten) **151**

Jacob Roggeveen

Willem Corneliszoon Schouten

Abel Tasman

Alexine Tinné

New Zealand

Edmund Hillary

Helen Thayer 188

Norway

Roald Amundsen

Erik the Red (Iceland)

Thor Heyerdahl 113

Fridtjof Nansen

Palestine

Muhammed ibn-Ahmad al-Muqaddasi

Portugal

Antonio de Andrade

Pedro Álvares Cabral (with Bartolomeu Dias) **37**

Hermenegildo de Brito Capelo

João Rodrigues Cabrilho (Spain)

Gaspar Corte-Real

Miguel Corte-Real

Pedro da Covilhã

Bartolomeu Dias

Vasco da Gama

Henry the Navigator

Roberto Ivens

Ferdinand Magellan (Spain)

Fernão Mendes Pinto

Pedro de Teixeira

Romania

Florence Baker

Rome

Aelius Gallus

Russia (see also Union of Soviet Socialist Republics)

Vladimir Atlasov

Aleksandr Baranov

Semyon Ivanovich Dezhnev 60

William Junker 133

Yerofey Pavlovich Khabarov
Vasily Danilovich Poyarkov
Nikolay Przhevalsky

Scotland

William Balfour Baikie 7
James Bruce
David Livingstone
Alexander Mackenzie
Mungo Park
Robert Stuart (United States)
Joseph Thomson

Spain

Pedro de Alvarado
Benjamin of Tudela
Álvar Núñez Cabeza de Vaca
Francisco Vásquez de Coronado
Hernán Cortés
Gonzalo Jiménez de Quesada 126
José Celestino Mutis
Vasco Núñez de Balboa
Alonso de Ojeda
Francisco de Orellana
Francisco Pizarro
Juan Ponce de León
Hernando de Soto
Andrés de Urdaneta
Saint Francis Xavier

Sweden

Carl Johan Andersson 1
Sven Hedin

Switzerland

Jean-Louis Burckhardt (Great Britain)
Ella Maillairt
Auguste Piccard
Jacques Piccard

Union of Soviet Socialist Republics

Yury Gagarin
Luna
Mir space station
Sputnik
Valentina Tereshkova

United States of America

Delia Akeley
Apollo
Neil Armstrong
William Henry Ashley
Jim Beckwourth
Hiram Bingham
Nellie Bly
Daniel Boone
Louise Arner Boyd
Richard Evelyn Byrd
Nicholas Clapp
Eugenie Clark 44
William Clark
Barry Clifford
Sylvia Earle
Amelia Earhart
Lincoln Ellsworth
Explorer 1
Linda Finch 77
Mel Fisher 83

Steve Fossett
Dian Fossey
Simon Fraser (Canada)
John Charles Frémont
John Glenn
Glomar Challenger
Charles Francis Hall
Marguerite Baker Harrison
Matthew A. Henson
Hubble Space Telescope
Wilson Price Hunt
Mae Jemison
Elisha Kent Kane 138
Meriwether Lewis
Charles Lindbergh
S.S. *Manhattan* 159
Mariner
Christa McAuliffe
National Air and Space Museum 175
National Geographic Society
U.S.S. *Nautilus*

Robert Edwin Peary
Annie Smith Peck
Zebulon Pike
Wiley Post
Sally Ride
Dick Rutan
Sacagawea
May French Sheldon
Jedediah Smith
Will Steger
Karen Thorndike 197
Viking
Voyager 1 and *2*
Charles Wilkes
Fanny Bullock Workman
Chuck Yeager
Jeana Yeager

Wales

Henry Morton Stanley (United States)

Cumulative Index to Volumes 1-7

Boldface indicates main entries in Volume 7 and their page numbers; *1–4:* refers to entries in the four-volume base set; *5:* refers to entries in Volume 5; *6:* refers to entries in Volume 6; *7:* refers to entries in Volume 7; (ill.) following a page number refers to photos, drawings, and maps.

A

A-erh-chin Shan-mo mountains *1–4:* 421, 706

Abadan *6:* 139

Abandoned Shipwreck Act *7:* 90

Abd al-Hamid II *1–4:* 105

Abominable Snowman *1–4:* 453

Aborigines *1–4:* 147–148, 260, 302, 356–357, 367, 487, 857; *5:* 58–60

Abu Simbel, Egypt *5:* 156; *6:* 37, 38, 38 (ill.)

Abyssinia *1–4:* 287, 289, 503, 789; *6:* 27, 112

Académie Française *1–4:* 286; *5:* 90

Acadia *1–4:* 212, 214–215

Acapulco, Mexico *1–4:* 481; *6:* 191–193

Accra, Ghana *1–4:* 416

Acoma, New Mexico *1–4:* 271

Acre, Israel *1–4:* 786; *6:* 139; *7:* 47, 206, 210

Acropolis *1–4:* 656

Across the Tian Shan to Lop-Nor *1–4:* 706

Adam's Peak *1–4:* 79

Addis Ababa, Ethiopia *7:* 172

Adelaide, Australia *1–4:* 144, 355, 357, 362; *5:* 59, 60; *7:* 14, 22, 101, 105

Adelaide Island *1–4:* 853; *5:* 31, 32

Adélie Coast *1–4:* 328–329

Adelie Land *5:* 33

Aden, Yemen *1–4:* 289, 290, 503–504, 772–773, 775; *6:* 23

Admiralty Islands *1–4:* 127, 190

Adriatic Sea *1–4:* 157, 184, 186

Advance *7:* 140–142

Adventure *1–4:* 261–264, 298, 300

Adwa *1–4:* 503

Aebi, Tania *7:* 201

Aegean Islands *1–4:* 433

Aegean Sea *1–4:* 6, 96, 325

"Aeroplane Girl" *1–4:* 492

African Association *1–4:* 52, 54–55, 632, 635; *6:* 35, 36, 38, 40, 41, 101–104

African Society *1–4:* 501

Agadez, Niger *1–4:* 71

Agamemnon *5:* 138

Agena *1–4:* 36–37

Agesilaus II *1–4:* 870

Agona *1–4:* 196

Agra, India *1–4:* 23; *6:* 74

Aguarico River *1–4:* 629

Aguilar, Jeronimo de *1–4:* 276

Ahaggar Mountains *1–4:* 80

Ahmad, Muhammad *7:* 135, 136

Ahvaz, Iran *1–4:* 595, 597

Ain Humran, Oman *5:* 45

Ainu *1–4:* 40, 42, 105

Air Mountains *1–4:* 71

Aitchison, Sarah Jane *7:* 3, 4

Akan (tribe) *5:* 49

Akeley, Carl *1–4:* 1–2

Akeley, Delia *1–4:* 1–4

Aksum, Ethiopia *7:* 172

Al-Jazira, Syria *1–4:* 416

Al-Kufrah *1–4:* 738

Al-Kusayr *6:* 29

Ala Tau Mountains *1–4:* 706

Alabama River *1–4:* 770

Aladdin *6:* 185

Alamut *6:* 184

Alarcón, Hernando de *1–4:* 270

Alazeya River *7:* 61

Albany, Australia *1–4:* 356–357

Albany, New York *1–4:* 226

Albaza *6:* 122

Alberga River *5:* 60; *7:* 101

Albert Einstein Planetarium *7:* 177

Albi *1–4:* 508

Albigensian heresy *1–4:* 95

Albuquerque, Afonso de *1–4:* 291

Aldan River *5:* 134

Aldrin, Edwin "Buzz," Jr. *1–4:* 29, 37–38

Aleppo, Syria *1–4:* 108, 596; *6:* 36

Aleutian Islands *1–4:* 266, 600, 612; *5:* 23

Alexander *1–4:* 639

Alexander Aegus *1–4:* 13

Alexander Archipelago *1–4:* 63

Alexander I *1–4:* 63, 91

Alexander I Land *1–4:* 92

Alexander the Great *1–4:* 5–13, 218, 808; *6:* 186; *7:* 181–186, 182 (ill.)

Alexander VII *6:* 75

Alexandretta, Syria *1–4:* 108

Alexandria, Egypt *1–4:* 7, 76, 97, 152, 289, 785, 789

Alfonso (of Portugal) *1–4:* 287

Alfora (tribe) *5:* 129

Algerian Memories *1–4:* 862

Algiers, North Africa *1–4:* 281, 737; *5:* 159; *6:* 27

Algonquin (tribe) *1–4:* 216–217, 765; *6:* 148, 149

Ali Baba *6:* 185

Alice River *7:* 56

Alima River *1–4:* 134

Allah *6:* 138

Allahabad *1–4:* 462

Alling, Abigail K. *6:* 15

Allumette Island *1–4:* 216; *6:* 148

Alma-Ata, China *5:* 100; *7:* 208

Almagro, Diego de *1–4:* 628, 670

Almagro, Francisco *1–4:* 673

Almanzor *1–4:* 571

Aloha *6:* 53

Alps *1–4:* 87, 408, 450, 475, 654; *7:* 53, 168

Altai Mountains *1–4:* 185, 219, 707

Alvarado, Hector de *1–4:* 271–272

Alvarado, Pedro de *1–4:* 176, 275–276, 279, 672; *5:* 1–5, 1 (ill.), 3 (ill.); *6:* 190

Alvin *5:* 166

Amazar River *6:* 122

Amazon Basin *1–4:* 337
Amazon River *1–4:* 304,
409–410, 413, 474, 477, 481,
627–629, 631; *5:* 85, 87–89,
150–154; *6:* 144, 153–155,
158, 173, 174; *7:* 193
Amazonas *6:* 155
Amelia 7: 197–203, 202 (ill.)
Ameralik Fjord *1–4:* 606
American Fur Company *1–4:* 82
American Geographical Society
1–4: 132
American Highlands *1–4:* 339
American Indians in the Pacific
7: 117
American Museum of Natural
History *1–4:* 2, 3; *7:* 45, 46,
47
American Philosophical Society
1–4: 529
American Relief Administration
6: 84, 86
American Revolution *1–4:* 120,
127, 192, 508, 529
American River *1–4:* 760
American Samoa *1–4:* 510
Amiens, France *6:* 23
Amirante Islands *1–4:* 392
Amon-Ra *1–4:* 7; *6:* 91
Amritsar, India *1–4:* 105
Amsterdam, The Netherlands
1–4: 455, 458, 486; *5:* 14, 16,
135; *6:* 176, 179; *7:* 152, 157
Amu Darya River *1–4:* 8, 808;
5: 101
Amundsen, Roald *1–4:* 14–22,
56, 130, 158, 160, 337, 429,
641, 747, 859; *7:* 159
Amundsen Gulf *1–4:* 17; *7:* 165
Amundsen-Scott Base *1–4:* 377,
804
Amur River *5:* 22, 131–133; *6:*
121–124
"Amy, Wonderful Amy" *1–4:*
492
Anabasis 1–4: 868, 870
Anadyr River *1–4:* 41; *7:* 62, 63
Añasco Bay *1–4:* 248
Ancient Greeks *5:* 135
Andalusia, Spain *1–4:* 287

Andaman Islands *1–4:* 693
Anders, William *1–4:* 28
Anderson, Rudolph M. *5:* 147
Anderson, William R. *1–4:* 611,
613
Andersson, Carl Johan *7:* 1–6,
1 (ill.), 5 (ill.)
Andes Mountains *1–4:* 99, 101,
157, 174, 299–301, 409, 479,
654, 768; *5:* 4, 88, 152; *6:*
143; *7:* 116
Andrade, Antonio de *1–4:*
23–25
Andrews, Jimmy *7:* 101
Andronicus II *1–4:* 67
Andronicus III *1–4:* 77
Andros Island *1–4:* 697
Anegada *6:* 170
Angareb River *1–4:* 45
Angediva Island *1–4:* 390; *7:* 41
Angkor, Cambodia *1–4:* 395
Angmagssalik, Greenland *1–4:*
342
Angostura *1–4:* 479
Aneityum *5:* 37, 38
Annam, Vietnam *1–4:* 394
Annapolis Royal, Nova Scotia
1–4: 214
Anson, George *7:* 29, 30, 33
Antanarivo, Madagascar *5:* 130
Antarctic Circle *1–4:* 91, 262; *5:*
32
Antarctic Peninsula *1–4:* 92–93,
803, 853
Antarctic Treaty *1–4:* 340
Anticosti Island *1–4:* 194–195,
498
Antioch, Syria *1–4:* 97, 220, 598
Antivari, Yugoslavia *1–4:* 186
Anual (tribe) *7:* 63
Apalachen *1–4:* 769
Aparia *1–4:* 629, 630
Apollo 1–4: 26–33, 37, 402, 558
Apollo 11 7: 178
Appalachian Mountains *1–4:*
118, 529, 770
Appenine Mountains *1–4:* 31
Apuré River *1–4:* 478
Aqualung *1–4:* 282–284
Arab Bureauscuba *1–4:* 89

Arabian Desert *5:* 127; *6:* 140
Arabian Nights 6: 182, 185
Arabian Peninsula *1–4:* 108, 223, 772; *5:* 40, 42; *6:* 39, 139, 184; *7:* 185, 186
Arabian Sea *1–4:* 435; *6:* 75; *7:* 121, 183, 185, 186
Aral Sea *1–4:* 78, 597
Arawak (tribe) *1–4:* 248–249
Archimedes Crater *1–4:* 556
Archives of the Indies *7:* 85
Arctic Circle *1–4:* 328, 612, 640; *6:* 44
Arctic Ocean *1–4:* 14, 21, 469, 509, 801, 821, 857; *5:* 13, 120, 123, 131, 147; *7:* 61, 62, 141, 161, 193
Arctic Researches and Life Among the Esquimaux 5: 71
Ardfert, Ireland *7:* 24
Arellano, Alonso de *6:* 192
Arequipa, Peru *1–4:* 99
Areta (tribe) *1–4:* 384
Arfak Mountains *7:* 53, 55
Argh˜un *1–4:* 67
Argo 5: 166
Arguin Island *1–4:* 426
Arias, Pedro *1–4:* 767
Arikara (tribe) *1–4:* 483, 532
Aristotle *1–4:* 5, 9; *6:* 52
Ark of the Covenant *7:* 172
Arkansas (tribe) *1–4:* 516
Arkansas River *1–4:* 83, 372, 497, 662, 663, 761
Armstrong, Neil *1–4:* 29, 34–39, 523, 558; *6:* 126
Arnhem Land *1–4:* 812
Around the World in Eighty Days 1–4: 700; *6:* 18, 22
Arrian *7:* 186
Arrillaga, José de *1–4:* 834
Artaxerxes *1–4:* 867
Arteaga, Melchor *1–4:* 100
Artemisia (of Greece) *1–4:* 434
Artocarpus *1–4:* 478
Aru Island *1–4:* 487
Aruwimi River *1–4:* 797
Ascension Island *1–4:* 127, 190, 302
Ash Shisur, Oman *5:* 44

Ashango (tribe) *1–4:* 323
Ashburton River *5:* 61
Ashley, William Henry *1–4:* 758–759; *5:* 6–11, 7 (ill.), 9 (ill.)
Ashquelon, Israel *1–4:* 787
Asian Antiquities Museum *1–4:* 807
Asolo, Italy *6:* 181, 186
Assam, India *1–4:* 752; *7:* 146–149
Assassins *1–4:* 97; *6:* 184
Assiniboine River *1–4:* 823
Astin Tagh mountains *1–4:* 706–708
Astor, John Jacob *1–4:* 64, 483–484, 824; *5:* 162
Astoria, Oregon *1–4:* 535
Astrolabe 1–4: 326–328
Astronauts *5:* 80–84, 109, 111–114
Asunción, Paraguay *1–4:* 167
Aswan, Egypt *1–4:* 76; *5:* 156; *6:* 29, 31, 33
Asyut, Egypt *5:* 156
Atahualpa *1–4:* 672, 768
Atbara River *1–4:* 45
Athabaska Pass *1–4:* 824
Athabaska River *1–4:* 823
Athens, Greece *1–4:* 434, 785, 870; *5:* 74, 138
Athi Plains *1–4:* 1
Athi River *1–4:* 505
Atlantic Anomaly *1–4:* 352
Atlantic Ocean *1–4:* 4, 210, 407, 472–473, 493, 500, 509, 598; *5:* 33, 64, 161, 162; *6:* 43, 44, 47, 131, 134; *7:* 7, 23–29, 178, 198
Atlantic Richfield Company *7:* 159, 160
Atlantic Ridge *1–4:* 211
Atlantis 5: 114
Atlas Mountains *1–4:* 79, 182, 435, 828, 861
Atlasov, Vladimir *1–4:* 40–42
Atlasova Island *1–4:* 40
Atocha. See Nuestra Señora de Atocha
Attock, Pakistan *1–4:* 434

Auckland, New Zealand *1–4:* 449, 453

Augusta Victoria 6: 23

Augustus *1–4:* 383

Aujila *1–4:* 738

Aurora Borealis *1–4:* 352

Austin, Horatio *1–4:* 368

Australian Company *7:* 152

Autissier, Isabelle *7:* 198

Autolycus Crater *1–4:* 556

Avavares *1–4:* 166, 347

Avila, Pedro Arias de *1–4:* 617

Awdaghost, Mali *1–4:* 416

Axel Heiberg Glacier *1–4:* 20

Axumite empire *7:* 172

Ayres, Harry *1–4:* 450

Aymara (tribe) *7:* 120

Azemmou, Morocco *1–4:* 566

Azevado, Francisco de *1–4:* 25

Azores *1–4:* 246, 390

Aztec (tribe) *1–4:* 276–279; *5:* 1, 2; *7:* 113, 126, 129

Azua, Dominican Republic *1–4:* 275

B

Baalbek, Lebanon *1–4:* 97, 787

Baalbek, Syria *1–4:* 597

Back, George *1–4:* 366, 367

Back River *1–4:* 368

Bacon, Roger *7:* 210

Bactria, Afghanistan *1–4:* 8–9, 219, 461; *7:* 182

Badakhshan, Afghanistan *1–4:* 690

Badrinath, India *1–4:* 24

Baffin Bay *1–4:* 368, 603, 645; *7:* 160, 161

Baffin Island *1–4:* 525, 640–642; *5:* 70, 71, 74; *6:* 4, 7

Bafuka, Zaire *1–4:* 4

Bagamoyo *1–4:* 773, 792, 794

Baghdad, Iraq *1–4:* 67, 76, 88–89, 97, 108, 110, 184, 490; *5:* 75, 76, 78, 128; *6:* 182, 184–186

Baghdad Sketches 184

Bahia, Brazil *1–4:* 303

Bahía Bariay, Cuba *1–4:* 245

Bahia Blanca, Argentina *1–4:* 297–298

Bahia dos Vaqueiros *1–4:* 312

Bahía San Miguel *1–4:* 616

Bahr al-Ghazal River *1–4:* 582; *5:* 158, 159

Bahr al-Jebel River *5:* 158

Bahr-el-Salam River *1–4:* 45

Baikie, William Balfour *7:* **7–13,** 7 (ill.), 11 (ill.)

Baikonur Space Center *1–4:* 380, 778, 818

Baja, California *1–4:* 28, 177, 281, 834

Baker, Florence *1–4:* 43–51, 114, 156, 776

Baker, Norman *7:* 119

Baker, Samuel White *1–4:* 43–51, 114, 156, 580, 776; *5:* 158

Bakhtiari (tribe) *6:* 86

Bakongo (tribe) *1–4:* 581

Baku, Azerbaijan *1–4:* 418

Balboa, Vasco Núñez de. *See* Núñez de Balboa, Vasco

Balchen, Bernt *1–4:* 338

Baliem River *1–4:* 522

Balkan Peninsula *1–4:* 5–6, 44

Balkan Wars *1–4:* 856

Balkh *1–4:* 462

Ballard, Robert *5:* 117, 165–167, 165 (ill.), 169

Balloons *5:* 62, 64–67

Baltistan (Little Tibet) *7:* 173

Balugani, Luigi *6:* 27, 28, 30, 31, 33

Bamako, Mali *1–4:* 634, 636

Bamian, Afghanistan *1–4:* 462; *7:* 169

Bancroft, Ann *1–4:* 802

Banda Sea *1–4:* 487

Bangala (tribe) *1–4:* 796

Bangkok, Thailand *1–4:* 491, 666; *6:* 174

Bangui *1–4:* 581

Banks, Joseph *1–4:* 52–56, 91, 257, 262, 360, 575, 601,

Boldface indicates main entries in Volume 7 and their page numbers; *1–4:* refers to entries in the four-volume base set; *5:* refers to entries in Volume 5; *6:* refers to entries in Volume 6; *7:* refers to entries in Volume 7; (ill.) following a page number refers to photos, drawings, and maps.

239 | Index

632–633, 635, 638; *5:* 25; *6:* 35, 36, 101

Banks Island *1–4:* 601–602

Bantam *1–4:* 456–457, 486–487

Baptista, Pedro Joâo *1–4:* 57–60, 139

Bar Sauma, Rabban *1–4:* 65–68

Baranof Island *1–4:* 63

Baranov, Aleksandr *1–4:* 61–64

Baranov, Peter *1–4:* 62

Barbosa, Duarte *1–4:* 571

Barcelona, Spain *1–4:* 95, 247

Barents, Willem *5:* 13–18, 14 (ill.), 15 (ill.), 120

Barents Sea *5:* 13, 14

Bari *1–4:* 50

Barka Khan *1–4:* 688

Barker, Frederick *1–4:* 794

Barotse *1–4:* 548

Barrow, John *1–4:* 638–639

Barrow, Alaska *7:* 165

Barrow Point *7:* 165

Barrow Strait *1–4:* 639

Barrow Submarine Canyon *1–4:* 612

Barth, Heinrich *1–4:* 69–74, 737; *7:* 8, 9, 9 (ill.)

Bartholomew of Cremona *7:* 206

Bartlett, Bob *1–4:* 430–431, 648, 652; *5:* 148; *6:* 1–8, 1 (ill.), 4 (ill.), 7 (ill.)

Barton, Otis *6:* 53

Basel, Switzerland *1–4:* 503–504

Bashkirs *5:* 77

Basra, Iraq *1–4:* 77, 89, 416–417

Bass, George *1–4:* 360

Bass Strait *1–4:* 360

Basundi (tribe) *1–4:* 581

Batak (tribe) *5:* 129

Batavia, Dutch East Indies *1–4:* 64, 261, 733, 810; *6:* 179; *7:* 34, 156

Bates, Daisy *7:* 14–22

Bates, Henry Walter *1–4:* 304

Bates, John *7:* 16, 17, 20

Bathori, Sigismund *1–4:* 763

Bathurst, Australia *1–4:* 302

Bathurst Island *7:* 162

Bathurst Plains, Australia *5:* 26

"Battle" of Cahuenga *1–4:* 83

Battle of Coruña *1–4:* 784

Battle of Las Salinas *1–4:* 673

Battle of New Orleans *1–4:* 365

Battle of Okeechobee *1–4:* 83

Battle of Omdurman *1–4:* 583

Battle of Trafalgar *1–4:* 365

Battle of Wounded Knee *1–4:* 532

Batu *1–4:* 184–186

Baudin, Nicolas *1–4:* 362

Bauer, Ferdinand *1–4:* 361

Baxter, John *1–4:* 356, 357

Bay of Arguin *1–4:* 426

Bay of Bengal *1–4:* 693; *6:* 107; *7:* 149

Bay of Fundy *1–4:* 213–215; *5:* 64

Bay of Guayaquil *1–4:* 671

Bay of San Julián *1–4:* 568

Bay of Santa Cruz *1–4:* 569

Bay of the Horses *1–4:* 165

Bay of Whales *1–4:* 19, 160, 339

H.M.S. *Beagle* *1–4:* 292–294, 296–305

Beagle Channel *1–4:* 297, 299

Bean, Alan *1–4:* 30

Bear Flag Revolt *1–4:* 373

Bear Island *5:* 13, 16

Bear Lake *1–4:* 760

Bear River *1–4:* 620

Beardmore Glacier *1–4:* 746

Beas River *1–4:* 9

Beaufort Sea *1–4:* 600; *5:* 148; *7:* 193

Beccari, Odouardo *7:* 53

Beckwith, James Pierson. *See* Beckwourth, Jim

Beckwourth, Jim *1–4:* 81–85

Beckwourth Pass *1–4:* 84

Bedouin (tribe) *1–4:* 107–109, 111, 786

Beebe, William *6:* 53; *7:* 45, 47, 50

Beechey Island *1–4:* 368

Beecroft, John *7:* 8

Beethoven, Ludwig von *1–4:* 474

Beijing, China *1–4:* 65–66, 184, 394, 397, 577, 688, 705, 755; *6:* 71, 85

Beirut, Lebanon *5:* 156, 157

Beja, Abraham de *1–4:* 290

Belcher, Edward *1–4:* 368, 603

Belém, Brazil *1–4:* 304, 410

Belém, Portugal *1–4:* 392

Belerium (Land's End) *1–4:* 710

Belgian Congo (Zaire) *1–4:* 3; *5:* 144

Belgica 1–4: 15

Belgrade, Yugoslavia *7:* 168

Bell, Gertrude *1–4:* 86–89

Bella Coola (tribe) *1–4:* 564

Bella Coola River *1–4:* 563

Bellamy, Black Sam *5:* 47, 48

Bellingshausen, Fabian Gottlieb von *1–4:* 90–93, 853

Bellingshausen Sea *1–4:* 92

Bena Bena *1–4:* 521–522

Benares, India *6:* 74

Bengal, India *1–4:* 79, 223

Benghazi *1–4:* 738

Benguela, Angola *1–4:* 138

Benin, Africa *1–4:* 157

Benjamin of Tudela *1–4:* 94–97

Bennett, Floyd *1–4:* 160

Bennett, James Gordon, Jr. *1–4:* 789, 792

Benton, Thomas Hart *1–4:* 371, 373

Benue River *7:* 9, 10

Beothuk (tribe) *6:* 45

Berber, Sudan *6:* 31

Berbera, Somalia *1–4:* 153, 773

Berbice, Guyana *6:* 169, 172

Bering, Vitus *5:* 19–23, 19 (ill.), 21 (ill.), 22 (ill.), 124; *7:* 63

Bering Island *5:* 19, 23

Bering Sea *1–4:* 41, 612, 701; *5:* 23

Bering Strait *1–4:* 600; *5:* 20, 124; *6:* 5, 6; *7:* 60, 63

Berlin, Germany *1–4:* 475, 482, 701–703; *5:* 99, 138, 139

Berlin Conference (1884–85) *1–4:* 796

Berlin Geographical Society *1–4:* 419

Berrio 1–4: 387, 390

Bessus 1–4: 8

Beyond Horizons 1–4: 339

Bibliothèque Nationale *1–4:* 175

Bibbulmun (tribe) *7:* 20

Bié Plateau *1–4:* 138

Big Lead *1–4:* 649

Bijagós Islands *7:* 110

Billings, Montana *1–4:* 536

Bingham, Hiram *1–4:* 98–102

Bios-3 *6:* 15

Biosphere 1 *6:* 10

Biosphere 2 *6:* 9–17, 9 (ill.), 11 (ill.), 14 (ill.), 16 (ill.)

Biospherians *6:* 12–16, 14 (ill.)

Bird, Isabella *1–4:* 103–106, 863

Bird Woman's River *6:* 165

Birú *1–4:* 670

Biscoe, John *1–4:* 853

Bishop, John *1–4:* 105

Bisland, Elizabeth *6:* 23, 24

Bismarck, North Dakota *1–4:* 532

Bitter Root River *1–4:* 535

Bitterroot Range *1–4:* 534

Bjaaland, Olav *1–4:* 19

Black, Campbell *1–4:* 593

Black, Tom Campbell *1–4:* 591

Black Death *1–4:* 80

Black Flags *1–4:* 398

Black Sea *1–4:* 44–45, 67, 91, 597, 694, 763, 869; *5:* 99; *7:* 206

Blackbeard *5:* 50, 52

Blackfoot (tribe) *1–4:* 82, 483, 535

Blackwell's Island *6:* 21, 22

Blaha, John *5:* 111, 114

Blaxland, Gregory *1–4:* 55; *5:* 24–27, 24 (ill.), 25 (ill.)

The Blessing of Burntisland 5: 52

Bligh, William *1–4:* 54, 189, 264, 359

Blom, Kristin *5:* 44

Blom, Ron *5:* 42–44

Blue Mountains *1–4:* 484; *5:* 24–27

Blue Nile River *1–4:* 54; *5:* 158; *6:* 26

Boldface indicates main entries in Volume 7 and their page numbers; *1–4:* refers to entries in the four-volume base set; *5:* refers to entries in Volume 5; *6:* refers to entries in Volume 6; *7:* refers to entries in Volume 7; (ill.) following a page number refers to photos, drawings, and maps.

241 | Index

Blunt, Anne *1–4:* 107–111

Blunt, Wilfrid Scawen *1–4:* 107–111

Bly, Nellie *6:* 18–25, 18 (ill.), 22 (ill.)

Bobadilla, Francisco de *1–4:* 251

Bobonaza River *1–4:* 411, 412

Boca del Sierpe *1–4:* 251

Bodega y Quadra, Francisco de la *1–4:* 833

Bodleian Library *6:* 31, 32, 32 (ill.)

Bogotá, Colombia *1–4:* 99, 479; *6:* 143–146

Bohol *6:* 191

Bolivar, Simon *1–4:* 99

Bolling Advanced Weather Station *1–4:* 161

Boma, Zaire *1–4:* 4, 795

Bombay, India *1–4:* 112; *7:* 172

Bombay, Sidi Mubarak *1–4:* 112–116, 153–155, 231, 233, 773, 790

Bomokandi River *1–4:* 4

Bonner, T. D. *1–4:* 84

Bonpland, Aimé *1–4:* 474, 476–480, 482; *6:* 146

Book of Joshua *6:* 114

Book of Ser Marco Polo 1–4: 687, 694

Boone, Daniel *1–4:* 117–121, 531

Boone, Daniel Morgan *1–4:* 121

Boone, Rebecca Bryan *1–4:* 117

Boonesboro, Kentucky *1–4:* 119–120

Boothia Peninsula *1–4:* 368

Bora Bora *5:* 36

Bora Island *1–4:* 733

Bordeaux, France *1–4:* 68

Borman, Frank *1–4:* 28

Bornu, Nigeria *1–4:* 71

Bororo (tribe) *6:* 154

Boston, Massachusetts *1–4:* 227

Botany Bay *1–4:* 260, 360, 510–511

Botletle *1–4:* 546

Bou-Am *1–4:* 736

Boudeuse 1–4: 123, 127, 190

Bougainville, Louis-Antoine de *1–4:* 122–128, 190, 510; *7:* 32, 32 (ill.)

Bougainville Island *1–4:* 126

Bougainvillea 1–4: 122

Boulogne, France *1–4:* 151

Bounty 1–4: 54, 188

Boxer Rebellion *1–4:* 584

Boyarsky, Victor *1–4:* 803

Boyd, Louise Arner *1–4:* 129–132

Bozeman Pass *1–4:* 536

BP Oil *7:* 160

Braddock, Edward *1–4:* 117

Brahe, William *1–4:* 145–148

Brahmaputra River *1–4:* 421, 752; *7:* 145–147, 149

Brandagee, Katharine *7:* 70, 71

Brandegee, Townsend Stith *7:* 70

Bransfield, Edward *1–4:* 91

Brattahlid, Greenland *1–4:* 343, 524

Braun, Wernher von *1–4:* 27, 352

Brava, Somalia *1–4:* 223

Brazza, Pierre Savorgnan de *1–4:* 133–136, 581

Brazzaville, Congo *1–4:* 135, 580, 795

Breder, Charles M. Jr. *7:* 45, 46

Brendan, Saint *7:* **23–27,** 23 (ill.), 25 (ill.)

Brendan the Navigator *7:* 27

Brewster, Samantha *7:* 198

Bridgeport, Connecticut *1–4:* 493

Bridger, James *1–4:* 758

Brindamour, Rod *7:* 94, 98

Bristol, England *1–4:* 170, 171

British Air League *1–4:* 489

British Antarctic Survey *1–4:* 377

British Cape Province *7:* 3

British Foreign Office *7:* 8, 9, 12

British Hudson's Bay Company *1–4:* 530

British Ministry of Information *6:* 185

British Museum *1–4:* 52, 857

British Museum of Natural History *5:* 36

British School of Archaeology *6:* 115, 119

British South African Company *1–4:* 828

British Survey Department *7:* 146, 147, 149

Brito Capelo, Hermenegildo de *1–4:* 137–140

Brittany *1–4:* 508

Broach, Persia *6:* 111

Bronx Zoo *6:* 4

Brooklyn Museum *1–4:* 3

Brooks Army Base *1–4:* 538

Brooks Mountain Range *7:* 196

Broome, Australia *7:* 18, 21

Broughton, William *1–4:* 833

Brown, Robert *1–4:* 361

Bruce, James *1–4:* 54; *6:* 26–34, 26 (ill.), 28 (ill.), 30 (ill.)

Bruce, Michael *1–4:* 785

Brulé, Étienne *1–4:* 141–143

Bruni d'Entrecasteaux *1–4:* 511

Bryan's Station, Kentucky *1–4:* 121

Bryon, John *1–4:* 123

Bubonic plague *1–4:* 80

Buchan, David *1–4:* 365

Buchanan, James *1–4:* 374

Buddh Gaya *5:* 56

Buddha *1–4:* 462; *5:* 56

Buddhas *7:* 169, 169 (ill.)

Buddhism *1–4:* 25, 307, 460, 463, 693, 728; *5:* 56, 57; *6:* 73, 106, 108; *7:* 204

Budington, Sidney *5:* 72

Buenaventura River *1–4:* 759, 760

Buenos Aires, Argentina *1–4:* 99, 157, 296, 299, 482; *5:* 30, 31

Bugungu, Africa *1–4:* 47–48

Bukhara, Uzbekistan *1–4:* 78, 184; *5:* 101; *6:* 139, 141

Bukhara River *1–4:* 808

Bulgars *1–4:* 597

Bulolo River *1–4:* 520

Bumbire Island *1–4:* 794

Bungo *1–4:* 865–866

Bunkeya, Zaire *1–4:* 139

Bunyoro, Africa *1–4:* 46–47, 49–50, 776

Burckhardt, Jean-Louis *6:* 35–41, *6:* 35 (ill.), 39 (ill.)

Bureau of Indian Affairs *6:* 166

Burke, Robert O'Hara *1–4:* 144–149

Burmese Technical Institute *1–4:* 491

Burmese–Thai wars *1–4:* 667

Burns Island *1–4:* 770

Burntisland, Scotland *5:* 51, 52

Burr, Aaron *1–4:* 662

Burrard Inlet *1–4:* 833

Burton, Isabel Arundell *1–4:* 151, 153, 156–157

Burton, Richard *1–4:* 45, 74, 113–114, 150–157, 502, 506, 551, 580, 722, 772–777, 792; *6:* 34, 41

Burton Medal *6:* 184

Busch Stadium, St. Louis, Missouri *5:* 65

Bussa Rapids *1–4:* 637; *7:* 10

Bykovsky, Valeri *1–4:* 819

Bylot, Robert *1–4:* 473

Byrd, Richard Evelyn *1–4:* 22, 158–163, 332, 338, 800, 859; *5:* 116

Byron, George Gordon (Lord Byron) *7:* 35, 35 (ill.)

Byron, John *1–4:* 187, 785; **7: 28–36,** 28 (ill.), 31 (ill.)

Byron Island *7:* 34

Byzantine Empire *1–4:* 95, 869

C

Cabeza de Vaca, Alvar Núñez *1–4:* 164–168, 270, 346, 348

Cabo da Roca, Portugal *1–4:* 247

Cabot, John *1–4:* 169–171, 172; *6:* 44

Cabot, Sebastian *1–4:* 170, 172–175

Cabot Strait *1–4:* 194

Boldface indicates main entries in Volume 7 and their page numbers; *1–4:* refers to entries in the four-volume base set; *5:* refers to entries in Volume 5; *6:* refers to entries in Volume 6; *7:* refers to entries in Volume 7; (ill.) following a page number refers to photos, drawings, and maps.

243 | Index

Cabral, Pedro Álvares *1–4:*
313, 391, 840; *7:* **37–43,** 37
(ill.), 39 (ill.), 40 (ill.)

Cabrilho, Joao Rodrigues *1–4:*
176–178

Cache Valley *1–4:* 759

Cadamosto, Alvise da *1–4:* 426

Cádiz, Spain *1–4:* 248, 250, 252,
320, 710, 716; *6:* 143

Caillié, René *1–4:* 73, 179–182,
736

*Caillié Travels through Central
Africa to Timbuktoo 1–4:* 182

Caingangue (tribe) *6:* 155

Cairo, Egypt *1–4:* 45, 49, 51, 55,
76, 89, 111, 114, 152, 289,
416, 506, 578, 583, 591, 721,
786; *5:* 127, 156, 157, 159; *6:*
28, 31, 33, 35, 37, 40, 102; *7:*
137

Cajamarca, Inca empire *1–4:*
481, 672, 768; *7:* 173

Cajon Pass *1–4:* 621

Calais, France *1–4:* 320

Calcutta, India *1–4:* 421, 491,
575, 577, 755, 807

Calicut, India *1–4:* 78, 222–223,
289, 389–392; *7:* 41, 42

California Academy of Sciences
7: 66, 70, 71, 73–75

California Gold Rush *1–4:* 81,
83; *5:* 136

Caliph al-Muktadir, Abbasid *5:*
75

Callao, Peru *7:* 116

Callisthenes *1–4:* 9

Callisto *1–4:* 848

Caloris 588

Calypso 1–4: 285

Cambridge, England *1–4:* 499

Cambridge Bay *1–4:* 17

Cambridge University *5:* 92; *6:*
36, 61

Camden, Arkansas *1–4:* 770

Cameahwait *6:* 165

Camelford, Baron *1–4:* 835

Cameron, Verney Lovett *1–4:*
116, 234

Camp Leakey *7:* 94, 96, 98

Camp VIII *1–4:* 451

Canaan *6:* 114

Canadian Arctic Archipelago *7:*
160

Canadian Arctic Expedition *1–4:*
856; *5:* 147; *6:* 1, 5

Canadian Rockies *1–4:* 701

Canary Islands *1–4:* 174, 244,
248, 288, 426, 455, 500, 568,
631; *6:* 143

Canberra, Australia *7:* 22

Cannanore, India *1–4:* 289; *7:*
42

Canton, China *1–4:* 79, 105,
577, 667, 866; *5:* 57, 128; *6:*
107, 109

Cañar *1–4:* 481

Cao, Diogo *1–4:* 311

Cap Haitien, Haiti *1–4:* 246

Capara *1–4:* 696

Cape Blanco *1–4:* 426

Cape Bojador *1–4:* 425

Cape Breton Island *1–4:* 170; *6:*
2

Cape Canaveral, Florida *1–4:*
26, 28–29, 37, 353, 725; *5:* 82

Cape Chelyuskin *5:* 124

Cape Cod, Massachusetts *1–4:*
213–215; *5:* 47

Cape Columbia *1–4:* 430, 431,
650, 652; *6:* 3

Cape Cross *1–4:* 311

Cape Dan *1–4:* 605

Cape Delgado *1–4:* 505

Cape Dezhnev *7:* 62

Cape Disappointment *1–4:* 832

Cape Fear, North Carolina *1–4:*
837–838

Cape Hatteras *1–4:* 837

Cape Haze Marine Laboratory *7:*
44, 48, 49

Cape Haze Peninsula *7:* 47

Cape Hecla *1–4:* 648, 650

Cape Hood *1–4:* 832

Cape Horn *1–4:* 258, 297, 510,
732, 834, 853; *5:* 128; *6:* 178;
7: 29, 30, 155, 157, 197, 199

Cape Leeuwin *1–4:* 361

Cape Maria van Diemen *1–4:*
811

Cape Mendocino *1–4:* 178

Cape Musandam *7:* 185

Cape of Good Hope *1–4:* 116, 127, 190, 192, 241, 258, 260–262, 265, 288, 311, 313–314, 319, 386, 388, 390, 455, 566, 666, 832, 865; *5:* 129; *6:* 176, 190; *7:* 30, 37, 38, 40–42, 152, 197, 201

Cape of Masts *1–4:* 426

Cape of the Virgins *1–4:* 569

Cape Parry *5:* 147

Cape Race, Newfoundland *1–4:* 170, 540

Cape Royds *1–4:* 746, 747

Cape Sheridan *1–4:* 650; *6:* 2, 3

Cape Town, South Africa *1–4:* 92, 302, 493, 501, 544, 548, 578, 829; *5:* 129; *7:* 3–5, 34

Cape Verde Islands *1–4:* 174, 294, 319, 387, 426, 455, 572, 631; *7:* 38, 42

Cape Wolstenholme *1–4:* 472

Cape York *1–4:* 647

Cape York Peninsula *1–4:* 487

Capelo, Hermenegildo de Brito. *See* Brito Capelo, Hermenegildo de

Caracas, Venezuela *1–4:* 99, 476, 477

Carantouan, New York *1–4:* 142

Caravel *6:* 44, 44 (ill.)

Caravelas, Brazil *7:* 39

Cárdenas, Garcia Lopez de *1–4:* 271

Carib (tribe) *1–4:* 248, 838

Caribbean Sea *1–4:* 192, 247, 600, 616, 713, 831, 855

Carlos IV *1–4:* 476

Carlyle, Thomas *1–4:* 358

Carmathians *1–4:* 597

Caroline Islands *1–4:* 326, 328

Caroni River *1–4:* 715, 716

Carpathia 5: 163, 164

Carpathian Mountains *1–4:* 475

Carpentaria *1–4:* 147

Carpenter, William B. *1–4:* 209

Carpini, Giovanni da Pian del *1–4:* 183–186; *7:* 205

Carranca, Andrés Dorantes de *1–4:* 346

Carrel, Alexis *1–4:* 541

Carson, Kit *1–4:* 372, 758

Carson Lake *1–4:* 621

Carstenszoon, Jan *1–4:* 488

Cartagena, Juan de *1–4:* 567

Cartagena, Colombia *1–4:* 319, 479, 615, 625; *5:* 87; *6:* 143

Carteret, Philip *1–4:* 126, 127, 187–192

Carthage *7:* 107, 108, 111

Cartier, Jacques *1–4:* 193–196, 526

Carvajal, Gaspar de *1–4:* 629–630

Casati, Gaetano *1–4:* 797; *7:* 135

Cascade Falls *1–4:* 535

Cascade Mountains *1–4:* 620; *7:* 189, 195

Casement, Roger *1–4:* 136

Casiquiare Canal *1–4:* 474, 479; *6:* 173

Caspian Sea *1–4:* 13, 97, 185, 418, 435, 597; *5:* 76, 77; *6:* 184; *7:* 208

Cassai River *1–4:* 58

Cassini, Jacques *5:* 85

Castilla 6: 143

Castillo, Alonso de *1–4:* 165–166, 347–348

Cathay *7:* 207

Catherine of Aragon *1–4:* 316

Caucasus Mountains *1–4:* 219, 597; *5:* 99, 128; *7:* 210

Caves of the Thousand Buddhas, *1–4:* 806–807

Cayenne, French Guiana *1–4:* 410, 411, 413; *5:* 89

Cayman Islands *1–4:* 253

Cayuga (tribe) *1–4:* 215

Cayuse (tribe) *1–4:* 622

Cebu Island *1–4:* 570, 571; *6:* 191

Celebes, Indonesia *1–4:* 190

Central Overland Telegraph Line *5:* 60

Centrites River *1–4:* 868

Cernan, Eugene *1–4:* 29, 32

Cerne Island *7:* 109, 111

Cerro de Guadalupe *6:* 144

Boldface indicates main entries in Volume 7 and their page numbers; *1–4:* refers to entries in the four-volume base set; *5:* refers to entries in Volume 5; *6:* refers to entries in Volume 6; *7:* refers to entries in Volume 7; (ill.) following a page number refers to photos, drawings, and maps.

245 Index

Cervantes, Miguel de *7:* 131

Cesar River *7:* 127

Cessna airplane *7:* 81

Ceuta, Morocco *1–4:* 425

Ceuta, Spain *1–4:* 79

Ceylon (Sri Lanka) *5:* 57; *6:* 23

Chabot, Philippe de *1–4:* 838

Chaffee, Roger *1–4:* 27

Chagga *1–4:* 505, 719

Chaillé-Long, Charles *1–4:* 580

Chalcedon. *1–4:* 869

Chalcidice *1–4:* 6

Chaleur Bay *1–4:* 194

Challenger (space shuttle) *1–4:*
    39, 467, 725–726; *5:* 42; *6:*
    125, 129–132, 132 (ill.)

H.M.S. *Challenger* *1–4:*
    209–211, 406

Challenger Flight 51-L *6:* 129

Chalybes *1–4:* 868

Champlain, Samuel de *1–4:*
    141–143, 212–217; *6:*
    147–149, 148 (ill.)

Ch'ang-an *1–4:* 460–461

Chang Ch'ien *1–4:* 218–220

Channel Islands *1–4:* 178; *6:*
    193

Charbonneau, Pomp *1–4:* 532,
    534, 536; *6:* 163, 167, 168

Charbonneau, Toussaint *1–4:*
    532; *6:* 162, 163, 165–167

Charcot, Jean-Baptiste *5:* 28–34,
    28 (ill.), 29 (ill.)

Charcot Land *5:* 33

Charles I (of England) *5:* 51

Charles I (of Spain) *1–4:* 168,
    175, 629–630, 768; *6:* 189

Charles II (of England) *1–4:* 227

Charles III (of Spain) *1–4:* 123;
    6: 142

Charles V (of Spain) *1–4:* 277,
    280–281, 567, 570, 573, 671

Charles X (of France) *1–4:* 326

Charlesbourg, Quebec *1–4:* 196

Charlie *7:* 188, 190, 192, 193,
    196

Charlotte Harbor *1–4:* 697

Charlotte Waters, Australia *7:*
    101, 103

Charlottesville, Virginia *1–4:*
    120, 528

Charters Towers, Australia *7:* 15

Charlton Island *1–4:* 472

Chasseloup-Laubat, Marquis de
    1–4: 395

Chatham *1–4:* 832

Chatham Island *1–4:* 301

Cheesman, Evelyn *5:* 35–38, 35
    (ill.), 37 (ill.)

Cheirosophus *1–4:* 868–869

Chen Tsu-i *1–4:* 222

Cheng Ho *1–4:* 221–224

Ch'eng-tu *1–4:* 460

Cherokee *1–4:* 118, 119

Chesapeake Bay *1–4:* 142, 470,
    764–765

Chester, Pennsylvania *7:*
    159–161

Cheyenne (tribe) *1–4:* 85

Cheyenne Peak *1–4:* 663

Chiaha *1–4:* 770

Chibcha (tribe) *1–4:* 479; *7:*
    126, 128–131

Chicago River *5:* 107

Chickahominy River *1–4:* 764

Chickasaw (tribe) *1–4:* 770

Chiengmai, Thailand *6:* 174

Chihuahua, Mexico *1–4:* 348,
    663

Childersburg, Alabama *1–4:* 770

Children's Crusade *1–4:* 96

Chillicothe, Ohio *1–4:* 120

Chiloe Island *1–4:* 300

Chimbu Valley *1–4:* 521

Chin-liu, China *1–4:* 460

China Illustrata *6:* 75

China Inland Mission *1–4:* 814

China Sea *6:* 149, 150, 152

Chinese Nationalists *5:* 98

Chira River *1–4:* 672

Chiriguaná, Colombia *7:* 127

Chirikov, Alexei Ilyich *5:* 22, 23

Chitambo *1–4:* 554

Cho Oyu *1–4:* 450

Chobe River *1–4:* 547–548

Choctaw Bluff, Alabama *1–4:*
    770

Chojnowska-Liskiewicz, Krysty-
    na *7:* 197

Cholon (Saigon, Vietnam) *1–4:* 394

Cholula, Mexico *1–4:* 278

Choqquequirau, Peru *1–4:* 99

Chouart des Groseilliers, Médard *1–4:* 225–230

Christa McAuliffe Fellowship *6:* 133

Christian, Fletcher *1–4:* 189

Christmas Island *1–4:* 265

Chryse Planitia *1–4:* 845

Chu Chan-chi *1–4:* 223

Chu Ti *1–4:* 222

Ch'üan-chou, China *1–4:* 79

Chukchi (tribe) *6:* 6

Chukchi Peninsula *1–4:* 62

Chukchi Sea *1–4:* 611

Chukotski Peninsula *7:* 62

Chuma, James *1–4:* 116, 231–237, 552, 554, 826

Church Missionary Society *1–4:* 503, 505

Church of England *1–4:* 316

Church of Rome *7:* 23

Church of Vidigueira *1–4:* 392

Churchill, Winston *1–4:* 748

Churchill River *1–4:* 561

Cíbola. *See* Seven Cities of Cíbola)

Cilicia, Turkey *1–4:* 88

Cimarron River *1–4:* 761

Ciudad Bolivar *1–4:* 479

Clapp, Nicholas *5:* 40–46, 40 (ill.), 41 (ill.)

Clapperton, Hugh *1–4:* 72, 637

Clark, Eugenie *7:* **44–51,** 44 (ill.), 46 (ill.)

Clark, George Rogers *1–4:* 119, 529

Clark, William *1–4:* 485, 528–537; *5:* 6; *6:* 64, 161–168, 163 (ill.)

Clearwater River *1–4:* 534

Cleopatris, Egypt *1–4:* 384

Cleveland, Ohio *1–4:* 702

Clifford, Barry *5:* 47–53, 47 (ill.), 48 (ill.), 49 (ill.), 50 (ill.)

Clinch River *1–4:* 118

Clinch River valley *1–4:* 119

Clitus *1–4:* 9

Clonfert, Ireland *7:* 24

The Coast of Northeast Greenland 1–4: 132

Coats Land *1–4:* 748

Cochin, India *1–4:* 394, 397; *7:* 42

Cochran, Elizabeth *6:* 18, 19

Cocos Islands *1–4:* 302

Coelho, Nicolau *1–4:* 387; *7:* 38

Coen, Jan Pieterszoon *7:* 156

Cofitachequi *1–4:* 769

Coiba *1–4:* 615

Collins, Michael *1–4:* 29, 37

Collinson, Richard *1–4:* 17, 368, 600, 602

Colorado River *1–4:* 166, 270–271, 530, 621, 759–760

Columba, Saint *7:* 26

Columbia 1–4: 37, 38, 725, 832

Columbia River *1–4:* 372, 483–484, 530, 534–535, 621–622, 821, 824, 832; *6:* 165

Columbia River Valley *1–4:* 824

Columbia University *6:* 17

Columbum *6:* 111

Columbus, Bartholomew *1–4:* 239, 241, 249, 251–252

Columbus, Christopher *1–4:* 169–170, 238–254, 275, 288, 313, 386, 487, 614, 623, 695, 796, 839; *6:* 42; *7:* 27, 27 (ill.)

Columbus, Diego *1–4:* 238, 240, 251, 254, 696

Columbus, Ferdinand *1–4:* 239, 241, 252

Comanche (tribe) *1–4:* 761

Committee for Research and Exploration *5:* 116, 117

Communists *5:* 98; *6:* 84

Comogre *1–4:* 616

Compagnie des Cent-Associés (Company of One Hundred Associates) *1–4:* 217; *6:* 149

Compagnie du Nord *1–4:* 229

Compagnie van Verre *1–4:* 455

Compostela, Mexico *1–4:* 270

Concepción 1–4: 567, 571

Concepción, Chile *1–4:* 300

Concord High School *6:* 127

Boldface indicates main entries in Volume 7 and their page numbers; *1–4:* refers to entries in the four-volume base set; *5:* refers to entries in Volume 5; *6:* refers to entries in Volume 6; *7:* refers to entries in Volume 7; (ill.) following a page number refers to photos, drawings, and maps.

247 | Index

Confederate Air Force *7:* 78

The Congo and the Founding of Its Free State *1–4:* 799

Congo Free State *1–4:* 135, 136, 548, 796–797

Congo River *1–4:* 116, 133–136, 138, 580, 792, 796, 798; *7:* 133–135, 213

Congo River Basin *7:* 134, 213

Congress of Vienna *1–4:* 482

Congressional Medal of Honor *1–4:* 160

Conquistadors *1–4:* 274, 281; *5:* 1, 2, 4, 5

Conrad, Pete *1–4:* 30

Conshelf *1–4:* 286

Constanta, Romania *1–4:* 44

Constantinople (Istanbul, Turkey) *1–4:* 44, 66–67, 77, 95–96, 108, 687–688, 694, 763, 785; *5:* 86; *7:* 206

Continental Congress *1–4:* 119

Contributions to the Theory of Natural Selection *1–4:* 304

Cook, Frederick Albert *1–4:* 429, 645, 650, 652

Cook, James *1–4:* 52–55, 91, 255–267, 475, 488, 509, 561, 796, 832, 834; *5:* 25, 124

Cook Inlet *1–4:* 62, 266, 834

Cook Islands *1–4:* 265

Cook Strait *1–4:* 327

Cooktown, Australia *1–4:* 260

Cooley, W. D. *1–4:* 720

Cooper, Merian *6:* 86, 88

Cooper's Creek *1–4:* 145–147

Coorg, India *7:* 172

Coos Bay *1–4:* 318

Coosa River *1–4:* 770

Copiapó, Peru *1–4:* 301

Cophas (Kappar, Pakistan) *7:* 184, 185

Coppermine River *1–4:* 366–367, 641

Coptic Christians *1–4:* 598

Coptos, Egypt *6:* 92

Coquivacoa *1–4:* 624

Coqville *1–4:* 326

Cordillera Mountains *1–4:* 299

Cordoba, Francisco Hernandez de *1–4:* 275, 767

Córdoba, Spain *1–4:* 241, 415

Corinthian War *1–4:* 870

Cornwall, England *7:* 24

Cornwallis Island *1–4:* 368; *7:* 190

Coronado, Francisco Vásquez de *1–4:* 164, 167, 176, 268–273, 281, 345, 349; *5:* 5

Coronation Gulf *5:* 147

Corps of Discovery *6:* 161, 163–165, 168

Corrective Optics Space Telescope Axial Replacement (COSTAR) *1–4:* 468

Corrigan, Sharon Christa. *See* McAuliffe, Christa

Corroborree dance *7:* 19 (ill.)

Corte-Real, Gaspar *1–4:* 171; *6:* 42–47, 43 (ill.)

Corte-Real, Joäo Vaz *6:* 42

Corte-Real, Miguel *6:* 42–47, 43 (ill.)

Cortés, Hernán *1–4:* 176–177, 274–281, 669, 672; *5:* 1, 2; *7:* 126

Coryndon Memorial Museum *5:* 92

Cosa, Juan de la *1–4:* 623

Cosa *1–4:* 770

Cosmonauts *5:* 109, 113

Cosmopolitan *1–4:* 332; *6:* 85

Cossacks *1–4:* 40–42, 421; *5:* 19, 128, 131, 133

Cotee, Kay *7:* 198

Council of Clermont (1095) *1–4:* 96

Courantyne River *6:* 174

Coureur de bois (forest runner) *6:* 147, 149

Cousteau, Jacques *1–4:* 282–286; *5:* 116; *6:* 53

The Cousteau Almanac of the Environment *1–4:* 285

Covilha, Pero da *1–4:* 287–291

Cozumel, Cuba *1–4:* 275–276

Craterus *1–4:* 11, 12

Cree (tribe) *1–4:* 227

Crèvecoeur *1–4:* 514

Crichton, Michael *5:* 76, 79

Crimea, Ukraine *1–4:* 77, 433, 773

Crimean War *1–4:* 153, 773; *5:* 136

Crippen, Robert *1–4:* 725

Crocker, George *1–4:* 649

Crocker Land *1–4:* 649

Crocola (Karachi, Pakistan) *7:* 184

Crooked Island, Bahama Islands *1–4:* 245

The Crossing of Antarctica 1–4: 377

Crow *1–4:* 81–82, 85

Crown Point, New York *1–4:* 215

Croydon Airfield *1–4:* 490

Crusades *1–4:* 96–97, 186, 424

Cuauhtémoc *1–4:* 279

Cubagua Island *1–4:* 630–631

Cueva, Beatriz de la *5:* 5

Cuiabá, Argentina *6:* 154

Culiacán, Mexico *1–4:* 167, 270

Cumaná *1–4:* 476

Cumberland 1–4: 363

Cumberland Gap *1–4:* 118, 119

Cumberland Peninsula *1–4:* 525

Cumberland valley *1–4:* 119

Cundinamarca, Colombia *7:* 129

Cunene River *1–4:* 139; *7:* 4, 5

Cunningham, Walter *1–4:* 28

Curaçao Island *1–4:* 624; *6:* 143

Curtiss Field *1–4:* 539

Custer, George Armstrong *1–4:* 789

Cutler, W. E. *5:* 92

Cuzco, Peru *1–4:* 99, 627, 672, 768; *7:* 173

Cyrene, Libya *1–4:* 434

Cyrus *1–4:* 867–868

D

D'Albertis, Luigi Maria *7:* **52–59,**, 52 (ill.), 55 (ill.), 57 (ill.)

D'Estaing, Jean Baptiste Charles Henri Hector *7:* 35

D'Orville, Albert *6:* 70, 71, 73, 74

Dahar-June *1–4:* 787

Dahe, Qin *1–4:* 803

Daily Mail 1–4: 492

Dakar, Senegal *1–4:* 426

Dalai Lama *1–4:* 307–309, 575–577, 753

The Dalles, Oregon *1–4:* 621

Damaraland, Namibia *7:* 5

Damascus, Syria *1–4:* 76, 88, 97, 109, 157, 597

Damietta, Egypt *1–4:* 97

Dampier Peninsula *7:* 17

Danube River *1–4:* 44

Dardanelles *1–4:* 6

Darién *1–4:* 616

Darien Peninsula *1–4:* 625, 670

Darius I (of Persia) *1–4:* 434; *7:* 181

Darius II (of Persia) *1–4:* 867

Darius III (of Persia) *1–4:* 7, 8; *7:* 181, 182

Darjeeling, India *7:* 147

Darling, William *1–4:* 357

Darling River *1–4:* 145, 147; *7:* 101

Dartmouth, England *1–4:* 472

Dartmouth College *5:* 148

Darwin, Charles *1–4:* 292–305, 474; *7:* 100

Darwin, Erasmus *1–4:* 292

Darwin, Australia *1–4:* 491–492

Daurians *5:* 133; *6:* 122

David, Edgeworth *1–4:* 747

David, T. W. E. *7:* 163

David-Neel, Alexandra *1–4:* 306–310

Davis, John *1–4:* 458

Davis Strait *1–4:* 472, 525; *6:* 44

Dawson, Yukon Territory *7:* 74, 193

De Haven, Edwin Jesse *7:* 139

De Long, George Washington *1–4:* 606; *6:* 5

De Pere, Wisconsin *5:* 107

De Soto, Hernando. *See* Soto, Hernando de

Boldface indicates main entries in Volume 7 and their page numbers; *1–4:* refers to entries in the four-volume base set; *5:* refers to entries in Volume 5; *6:* refers to entries in Volume 6; *7:* refers to entries in Volume 7; (ill.) following a page number refers to photos, drawings, and maps.

Dead Sea *1–4:* 597; *6:* 114
Dean Channel *1–4:* 564
Death Valley, California *7:* 75
Deccan, India *1–4:* 596
Deena *1–4:* 633
Deep Flight 6: 55, 56
Deep Ocean Engineering *6:* 54
Deep Rover 6: 54, 54 (ill.), 55
Deep Sea Drilling Project *1–4:* 406
Deganawidah *1–4:* 215
Deimos *1–4:* 587
Delabarre, Edmund B. *6:* 45, 47
Delaware Bay *1–4:* 470
Delaware River *1–4:* 470
Delft 1–4: 487
Delhi, India *1–4:* 23; *6:* 75; *7:* 168, 170
Demerara, Guyana *6:* 169
Denbei *1–4:* 42
Denmark Strait *6:* 44
Denver, Colorado *1–4:* 84; *7:* 67, 69–71, 86
Derb-el-Haj *1–4:* 76
Derendingen *1–4:* 502
Descartes Mountains *1–4:* 32
Déscription de la Louisiane 6: 99
A Description of New England 1–4: 765
Desideri, Ippolito *1–4:* 576
Detroit, Michigan *1–4:* 120, 485, 538
Detroit Arctic Expedition *1–4:* 857
Devil's Ballroom *1–4:* 20
Devon Island *1–4:* 16; *7:* 139
Dezhnev, Semyon Ivanovich 7: 60–65, 61 (ill.)
Dhofar Mountains *5:* 42
Dias, Bartolomeu *1–4:* 241, 288, 311–314, 386, 388, 426; *7:* 37, 38, 41
Dias, Dinis *1–4:* 426
Días, Melchor *1–4:* 270, 271
Dickson, James *1–4:* 633, 635
Diderot, Denis *1–4:* 127
Diebetsch, Josephine *1–4:* 645
Diemen, Anthony van *1–4:* 810
Dieppe, France *1–4:* 837
Diestel, Bernard *6:* 70

Dietrich, Rosine *1–4:* 504
Digges Island *1–4:* 473
Digging Up Jericho 6: 119
Dighton, Massachusetts *6:* 45
Dighton Rock *6:* 45–47, 46 (ill.)
Dingri, Tibet *6:* 78, 79
Diomede Islands *5:* 20
Dione, moon *1–4:* 849
Discoverie of Guiana 1–4: 715
Discovery 1–4: 264–266, 464, 472–473, 830–833
Discovery: The Autobiography of Vilhjalmur Stefansson 5: 149
Disko Bay *5:* 125
Dispatch 6: 19–21
District of Orleans *1–4:* 536
Diyarbakir *1–4:* 77
Djakarta, Indonesia *1–4:* 127, 190
Djenné, Mali *1–4:* 180, 579
Dnieper River *1–4:* 41
Dolak Island *1–4:* 487
Dolphin 1–4: 188, 190, 191, 257; *7:* 31, 34
Don Juan 7: 35
Don Quixote de la Mancha 7: 131
Donkya Pass *7:* 147
Donn River *1–4:* 41
Donnacona *1–4:* 194, 195
Dorantes, Andres *1–4:* 165–166, 347–348
Doudart de Lagrée, Ernest *1–4:* 396
Draa River Valley *7:* 194
Drake, Francis *1–4:* 315–320; *7:* 31, 152
Druid 1–4: 296
Druses *1–4:* 786–787
Druze *1–4:* 87
Dry Tortugas *1–4:* 697
Du Chaillu, Paul *1–4:* 321–324
Du Pont, François Gravé *1–4:* 213
Dubois River *1–4:* 530
Dudh Kosi River *1–4:* 752; *6:* 79
Duifken 1–4: 486–487
Duke, Charles *1–4:* 32
Dulhut, Daniel Greysolon *6:* 98

Dulles Center *7:* 179

Duluth, Minnesota *1–4:* 142, 823

Dumont d'Urville, Jules-Sébastien-César *1–4:* 325–329, 511, 853

Dundee Island *1–4:* 339

Dunhuang, China *5:* 55

Dunkerque, France *7:* 168

Dupuis, Jean *1–4:* 396–398

Dusky Sound *1–4:* 263

Dutch East India Company *1–4:* 454–455, 469, 486, 732, 809–810; *6:* 175, 176, 179, 180; *7:* 151, 152, 156, 157

Dutch West India Company *1–4:* 470, 732

Dwyer, Michael *1–4:* 520

Dyak (tribe) *5:* 129

Dza-chu River *1–4:* 706

Dzungaria *1–4:* 707

E

Eagle 1–4: 37–38

Eagle, Alaska *1–4:* 18

Eaglet 1–4: 227

Eannes, Gil *1–4:* 426

Earhart, Amelia *1–4:* 330–335, 493; *7:* 77–82

Earle, Sylvia *6:* 45–56, 48 (ill.), 50 (ill.), 55 (ill.)

Earp, Wyatt *1–4:* 337

Earthwatch *7:* 98

East Denver High School *7:* 69, 71

East India Company *1–4:* 151, 564, 575, 811, 733

Easter Island *1–4:* 263, 732

Eastman, Charles *6:* 166

Eastwood, Alice *7:* **66–76,** 66 (ill.), 68 (ill.), 72 (ill.)

Eastwoodia elegans 7: 71, 72 (ill.)

Eaters of the Dead 5: 76

Ebierbing *5:* 70, 71, 73

Ebro River *1–4:* 94

Ecbatana (Hamadan, Iran) *1–4:* 220

Edmonton, Alberta *1–4:* 701, 703

Edward I (of England) *1–4:* 68

Edward VI (of England) *1–4:* 175

Edwards Air Force Base *1–4:* 726, 742, 872, 874

Edy, Montana *1–4:* 759

Eendracht 6: 176, 178–180; *7:* 154–157

Effie M. Morrissey 7, 8

Eielson, Carl *1–4:* 858

Eight Feet in the Andes 7: 173

Eight Years' Wanderings in Ceylon 1–4: 44

Einstein Cross *1–4:* 467

Eisele, Don *1–4:* 28

Eisenhower, Dwight D. *1–4:* 428, 542

El Carmen, Patagonia *1–4:* 298

El Dorado *7:* 127, 130, 131

El Haura, Arabia *1–4:* 384

El-Mahdi *1–4:* 580, 582, 583

El Misti *1–4:* 654

Elburz Mountains *6:* 184

Elcano, Juan Sebastián de *1–4:* 571–573; *6:* 189

Electra. *See* Lockheed Electra 10E

Elephant Island *1–4:* 748–749

Eletrophorus electricus 1–4: 477

Elgon, Mount *1–4:* 828

Elizabeth I (of England) *1–4:* 316–319, 712–713

Elizabeth II (of England) *1–4:* 452

Ellengowan 7: 54, 56

Ellesmere Island *1–4:* 159, 647–650, 802–803; *6:* 2, 7; *7:* 139, 141

Ellsworth, Lincoln *1–4:* 21, 130, 336–340, 859–860

Ellsworth Land *1–4:* 336, 339

Emin Pasha Relief Expedition *1–4:* 796, 799, 828

Emir of Nupe *7:* 12

Enceladus *1–4:* 849

Boldface indicates main entries in Volume 7 and their page numbers; *1–4:* refers to entries in the four-volume base set; *5:* refers to entries in Volume 5; *6:* refers to entries in Volume 6; *7:* refers to entries in Volume 7; (ill.) following a page number refers to photos, drawings, and maps.

251 | Index

Enciso, Martín Fernandez de *1–4:* 615, 617

Encounter Bay *1–4:* 362

Endeavour 1–4: 53, 257–261, 467

Endurance 1–4: 747–748

Engastromenos, Sophia *5:* 138

Englewood, Florida *7:* 47

English Channel *1–4:* 316, 320, 716; *5:* 62, 66

The Englishwoman in America 1–4: 104

Enlightenment *1–4:* 529; *6:* 142

Enriquez de Harana, Beatriz *1–4:* 239, 241

Enterprise 1–4: 600

Entomology *5:* 36

Epirus *1–4:* 6

Equatoria *7:* 135, 137

Equatorial Nile Basin *1–4:* 43, 49–50

Equinoctial Plants 6: 146

Erebus 1–4: 368

Eredia, Manuel Godhino de *1–4:* 487

Erhardt, Jakob *1–4:* 721

Erik the Red *1–4:* 341–344, 524–525, 527

Erik the Red's Saga 1–4: 524

Erik's Island *1–4:* 342

Eriksfjord *1–4:* 524

Erzurum *1–4:* 868

Esmeraldas River *5:* 87

Esperance Bay *1–4:* 357

Espinosa, Gonzalo Gómez de *1–4:* 571, 573

Espiritu Pampa *1–4:* 98, 101–102

Espiritu Santo, Vanuatu *1–4:* 263

Essaouira, Morocco *7:* 108

Essay on the Principle of Population 1–4: 304

Essequibo, Guyana *6:* 169, 170, 172–174

Essequibo River *6:* 172

Essex 1–4: 35

Estevanico *1–4:* 166, 268, 270, 345–350

Etah, Greenland *1–4:* 429, 649–650; *6:* 2

Eternity Mountains *1–4:* 339

Etienne, Jean-Louis *1–4:* 803

Etoile 1–4: 124, 127

Etosha Pan, Namibia *7:* 2

Eucla, Australia *1–4:* 356; *7:* 21

Euphrates River *1–4:* 8, 11, 88, 108, 597; *6:* 94; *7:* 186

European Space Agency *1–4:* 465; *5:* 109

Evans, George William *5:* 26

Evans, Ronald *1–4:* 32

Everett, Washington *7:* 203

Excavations at Jericho 6: 119

Expedition Whydah *5:* 51

Explorations and Adventures in Equatorial Africa 1–4: 322

Explorations in Australia 5: 60

Explorer 1 1–4: 351–354

Explorer 2 1–4: 354

Explorers' Club *1–4:* 428, 432, 523, 652

Explorers Hall *5:* 117, 119

Exxon Valdez 6: 56

Eyre, Edward John *1–4:* 355–358; *5:* 59

Eyre Peninsula *1–4:* 356

F

Fa-Hsien *5:* 54–57, 55 (ill.); *6:* 106

The Faerie Queene 1–4: 714

Faeroe Islands *7:* 26

Faidherbe 1–4: 582

Fairbanks, Alaska *1–4:* 701, 857

Faisal I (of Arabia) *1–4:* 87, 89

Falkland Islands *1–4:* 123, 187, 256, 299, 328, 732; *7:* 28, 32, 199, 200, 203

Falkland Islands Dependencies Survey *1–4:* 375

Falklands War *1–4:* 123; *7:* 32

Falls of St. Anthony *1–4:* 662

Fan (tribe) *1–4:* 323, 500

Fars, Iran *1–4:* 416, 595, 597

Farthest North 1–4: 608

Fashoda Incident *1–4:* 578, 582–583

Fatiko, Africa *1–4:* 50, 51

Fatimids *1–4:* 416

Fatouma, Ahmadi *1–4:* 636–637

Fatu Hiva (Marquesas Islands) *7:* 114, 115

Federmann, Nikolaus *7:* 130

Femme Osage, Missouri *1–4:* 121, 531

Ferdinand (of Spain) *1–4:* 241, 247, 250–251, 386, 616–617, 624, 697

Fergana, Uzbekistan *1–4:* 219

Fernandes, Alvaro *1–4:* 426

Fernández, Juan *6:* 49, 178

Fernando Po Island *1–4:* 157; *7:* 8

Ferrelo, Bartolomé *1–4:* 177–178

Fez, Morocco *1–4:* 79–80

Field Museum of Natural History *1–4:* 1–2

Fiennes, Ranulph *5:* 43

Fifth Dalai Lama *6:* 73

Fiji Island *1–4:* 328, 809, 811, 854

Filchner Ice Shelf *1–4:* 376

Finch, Linda *7:* **77–82,** 77 (ill.), 79 (ill.), 81 (ill.)

Finke River *7:* 101, 105

Finley, John *1–4:* 118

Finlay River *1–4:* 563

The Fiord Region of East Greenland *1–4:* 131

First Kamchatka Expedition *5:* 20

First Steps in Africa *1–4:* 775

Firth of Forth, Scotland *5:* 51, 52

Fischer, Gustav Adolf *1–4:* 827

Fish River *5:* 26

Fisher, Mel *7:* **83–91,** 83 (ill.), 85 (ill.), 88 (ill.)

FitzRoy, Robert *1–4:* 293–294, 296–302

Fitzroy River *5:* 61

Five Nations *1–4:* 215

Flandro, Gary *1–4:* 847

Flat, Alaska *1–4:* 703

Flathead (tribe) *1–4:* 534

Flathead Lake *1–4:* 620

Flathead Post *1–4:* 759

Fleming, Peter *5:* 98, 101

Flinders, Matthew *1–4:* 55, 359–363, 364

Flinders Ranges *1–4:* 355, 361

Flinders River *1–4:* 146

Florida Keys National Marine Sanctuary *7:* 89

Florida State University *6:* 49

Floyd Bennett *1–4:* 160–161

Floyd Bennett Field *1–4:* 703

Floyd River *1–4:* 531

Fly River *7:* 52, 53, 55, 58

"Flying Sweethearts" *1–4:* 493

Flying the Arctic *1–4:* 860

F.N.R.S. 2 *1–4:* 659

Fo-Kwe-Ki *5:* 57

Foale, Michael *5:* 112–114

Fogg, Phileas *6:* 18, 22, 24

Forbidden Journey *5:* 103

Ford, Edsel *1–4:* 160

Ford, Gerald *7:* 176

Ford, Henry *1–4:* 542

Formidable *1–4:* 508

Forrest, John *5:* 58–61, 58 (ill.), 59 (ill.); *7:* 103

Forster, Georg *1–4:* 475

Fort Chipewyan, Lake Athabasca *1–4:* 561, 563–564; *6:* 65

Fort Clatsop *1–4:* 535; *6:* 167

Fort Conger, Ellesmere Island *1–4:* 647

Fort Conti *6:* 96

Fort Crèvecoeur *1–4:* 514, 516; *6:* 96

Fort Enterprise, Canada *1–4:* 366

Fort Franklin *1–4:* 367

Fort Fraser *6:* 66

Fort Frontenac *1–4:* 514; *6:* 96

Fort George *6:* 66, 67

Fort Kootenay *1–4:* 824

Fort Mandan *1–4:* 532

Fort McLeod *6:* 65

Fort New Archangel, Alaska *1–4:* 63

Fort of Ilimsk *6:* 124

Fort of Kumarsk *6:* 124

Boldface indicates main entries in Volume 7 and their page numbers; *1–4:* refers to entries in the four-volume base set; *5:* refers to entries in Volume 5; *6:* refers to entries in Volume 6; *7:* refers to entries in Volume 7; (ill.) following a page number refers to photos, drawings, and maps.

253 | Index

Fort Pierce, Florida *7:* 86

Fort Presépio *5:* 151, 152

Fort Prud'homme *1–4:* 516

Fort Ross, California *1–4:* 64

Fort St. James *6:* 66

Fort St. Louis *1–4:* 518

Fort Vancouver, Washington
1–4: 761

Fossett, Steve *5:* 62–67, 62 (ill.),
63 (ill.)

Fossey, Dian *5:* 117; *6:* 57–63,
57 (ill.), 60 (ill.), 62 (ill.); *7:*
93, 94

Foster, Stephen *6:* 19

"Foul Weather Jack" *7:* 35

Foweira, Africa *1–4:* 49

Fowler's Bay *7:* 21

Fox, Jack *1–4:* 522

Fox, Luke *1–4:* 640

Fox, Tom *1–4:* 522

Fox River *1–4:* 496; *5:* 106; *6:*
152

Foxe Basin *1–4:* 640

Fra Mauro Highlands *1–4:* 31

Fraehn, C. M. *5:* 78

Fram 1–4: 18, 19, 21, 607–608

Framingham State College *6:* 126

Français 5: 29–31

Francia, José *1–4:* 482

Francis of Assisi *1–4:* 183

Franciscana *5:* 153

Franciscans *6:* 95

Franco-Prussian War *1–4:* 134,
397

François I (of France) *1–4:*
193–196, 837–838

Frankincense *5:* 40, 42, 44–46

Frankincense trade route *5:* 40,
45

Franklin, Jane Griffin *1–4:*
367–368; *7:* 143

Franklin, John *1–4:* 14, 361,
364–369, 599, 639; *5:* 68; *7:*
138–141, 143

Franklin Strait *1–4:* 16, 368

Franz Josef Land *1–4:* 130, 607

Fraser, Simon *1–4:* 563; *6:*
64–68, 64 (ill.), 68 (ill.)

Fraser River *1–4:* 563; *6:* 64, 67,
67 (ill.)

Frederick the Great (of Prussia)
1–4: 474

Free Svanetia *5:* 99

Freetown, Sierra Leone *1–4:*
180, 500

Freiburg, Germany *1–4:* 475

Frémont, Jessie Benton *1–4:*
371, 374

Frémont, John Charles *1–4:*
370–374

Fremont Peak *1–4:* 372

French and Indian War *1–4:*
117, 122, 508

French Antarctic Expedition *5:*
32, 33

French Equatorial Expedition *5:*
87

French Foreign Legion *1–4:* 736

French Geographical Society
1–4: 182, 329

French Legion of Honor *1–4:*
326

French Revolution *1–4:* 511

French River *1–4:* 142, 216; *6:*
150

The Friendly Arctic 5: 148

Friendship 1–4: 332, 402–404

Frobisher, Martin *1–4:* 344, 472;
5: 70

Frobisher Bay *5:* 70

Frontenac, Count de *1–4:* 496,
513

Frozen Strait *1–4:* 640

Fuchs, Vivian *1–4:* 375–377,
452–453, 801

Fulbright scholarship *7:* 47

*Full Tilt: Ireland to India With a
Bicycle 7:* 169, 174

Funatsu, Keizo *1–4:* 803–804

Fur trade *5:* 6, 8

Furneaux Islands *1–4:* 360

Fury 1–4: 641–642

Fury Strait *1–4:* 641

Futuna Islands *6:* 178; *7:* 155

G

Gabet, Joseph *1–4:* 814

Gabon, West Africa *1–4:* 135, 321–322, 500

Gades, Phoenicia *1–4:* 710

Gagarin, Yuri *1–4:* 378–382, 402, 559, 782, 818

Gagnan, Emile *6:* 53

Galapagos Islands *1–4:* 301, 303; *5:* 36; *6:* 49

Galdikas, Birute *7:* **92–99,** 92 (ill.), 95 (ill.)

Galfridus of Langele *1–4:* 68

Galileo *1–4:* 32, 464

Galla (tribe) *1–4:* 503–504

Gallatin, Albert *1–4:* 533

Gallatin River *1–4:* 533

Gallus, Aelius *1–4:* 383–385

Galton, Francis *7:* 2, 3

Galveston Island *1–4:* 165, 166, 346

Gama, Paolo da *1–4:* 387

Gama, Vasco da *1–4:* 224, 288, 313, 386–392; *7:* 37–39, 42–43

Gambia River *1–4:* 426, 633; *6:* 103; *7:* 109

Gandak River *6:* 78

Ganges River *1–4:* 24, 453, 462–463, 598; *5:* 56; *6:* 107, 108; *7:* 149, 182

Ganymede *1–4:* 848

Garhwal, India *1–4:* 24

Garnier, Francis *1–4:* 393–399

Garstang, John *6:* 115

Gaspé Bay *1–4:* 194

Gaspé Peninsula *1–4:* 194–195, 214

Gatty, Harold *1–4:* 700–702

Gaugamela, Assyria *1–4:* 8

Gauhati *1–4:* 463

Gautama, Siddhartha. *See* Siddhartha Gautama

Gaza *1–4:* 7

Gedrosia *1–4:* 12

Gemini 6 1–4: 28

Gemini 8 1–4: 36, 37

Genesee River *1–4:* 142

Genesis Rock *1–4:* 32

Geneva, Switzerland *5:* 98, 99

Genghis Khan *1–4:* 66, 67, 184; *7:* 169, 204, 207, 208

Genoa, Italy *1–4:* 95, 694

Geodesy *5:* 86

Geographical Magazine 1–4: 755

George III (of England) *1–4:* 53; *6:* 33

Georges River *1–4:* 360

Georgetown, British Guiana *6:* 170, 173

Georgian Bay *1–4:* 142; *6:* 148, 151

Geraldton, Australia *5:* 60

Gerlache, Adrien de *1–4:* 15

German Africa Society *7:* 213

German Atlantic Expedition *6:* 134, 136

German East Africa *7:* 214, 215

Ghat, Libya *1–4:* 71

Gibney, Matthew *7:* 17

Gibson, Alfred *7:* 101–105

Gibson Desert *5:* 60; *7:* 100, 101, 104, 105

Gila River *1–4:* 271

Gilbert, Humphrey *1–4:* 712

Gilbert Island *1–4:* 326

Giles, Ernest *7:* **100–106,** 100 (ill.), 104 (ill.)

Gilgit, Pakistan *5:* 56; *7:* 169

Gilgit range *1–4:* 807

Ginuha Genoa, Italy *1–4:* 67

Gjöa 1–4: 16–18

Gjöa Haven *1–4:* 16–17

Gladstone, William *1–4:* 105

Glenn, John *1–4:* 31, 400–405; *6:* 126

Global Positioning System (GPS) *7:* 80

Glomar Challenger 1–4: 406–408

Gloster Meteor 1–4: 872

Glover, J. H. *7:* 10

Goa, India *1–4:* 25, 289, 636, 666, 667–668, 865–866

Gobabis, Namibia *7:* 2, 3

Gobi Desert *1–4:* 308, 420, 461, 691, 705, 707; *6:* 86

Godin des Odonais, Isabel *1–4:* 409–414

Godin des Odonais, Jean *1–4:* 409–411, 413–414

Boldface indicates main entries in Volume 7 and their page numbers; *1–4:* refers to entries in the four-volume base set; *5:* refers to entries in Volume 5; *6:* refers to entries in Volume 6; *7:* refers to entries in Volume 7; (ill.) following a page number refers to photos, drawings, and maps.

255 | Index

Godthaab, Greenland *1–4:* 606; *5:* 122

Goering, Hermann *1–4:* 703

Goethe, Johann Wolfgang von *1–4:* 475

Golashkerd, Persia *7:* 185

Golden Gate Park *7:* 74

Golden Hind 1–4: 318, 319

Gombe National Park *5:* 117; *6:* 58

Gomes, Diogo *1–4:* 427

Gomez, Fernao *1–4:* 291

Gonçalves, Antao *1–4:* 426

Gonam River *5:* 132, 133

Gondar, Ethiopia *6:* 29–31; *7:* 172

Gondokoro, Sudan *1–4:* 45, 48–51, 114, 156, 776–777; *5:* 158

Góngora, Antonio Caballero y *6:* 145

Goodall, Jane *5:* 117; *6:* 58–60; *7:* 93–95

Gordon, Charles "Chinese" *1–4:* 51, 580, 796; *7:* 135

Gordon, George *1–4:* 358

Gordon, Richard *1–4:* 30

Goree Island *1–4:* 636; *6:* 102

Gorgan, Iran *1–4:* 416

Gorges, Ferdinando *1–4:* 765

Gorillas in the Mist 6: 61

Goroka Valley *1–4:* 521

Gouda *1–4:* 454

Graf Zeppelin 1–4: 338

Graham Land *1–4:* 15; *5:* 31

Graham Peninsula *1–4:* 328, 375, 859

Granada, Spain *1–4:* 79, 242, 251, 767

Grand Canyon *1–4:* 268, 271

Grand Cayman *7:* 50

Grand Tetons, Wyoming *1–4:* 484

Grandmaison, Pedro de *1–4:* 411–413

Grandmaison y Bruna, Isabela de *1–4:* 409

Granicus River *1–4:* 6

Grant, James Augustus *1–4:* 45, 114, 156, 776; *5:* 158

Grant, Robert *1–4:* 293

Grass 6: 88

Gray, Charles *1–4:* 145–147

Gray, Robert *1–4:* 832

Gray's Harbor *1–4:* 833

Grays Peak, Colorado *7:* 70

Great Australian Bight *1–4:* 361; *5:* 59

Great Barrier Reef *1–4:* 125, 260, 362

Great Basin *1–4:* 760

Great Bear Lake *1–4:* 367

Great Dark Spot *1–4:* 850

Great Divide *6:* 165

Great Dividing Range *5:* 24

Great Falls, Montana *1–4:* 533

Great Fish River *1–4:* 312

Great Inagua Island *1–4:* 245

Great Khan *7:* 204, 205, 207, 208, 210

Great Lakes *1–4:* 141–142, 214, 216–217, 496, 514, 518, 600; *5:* 104, 105; *6:* 96, 147, 150

Great Northern Expedition *5:* 21

Great Plains *1–4:* 272, 664; *6:* 162

Great Red Spot *1–4:* 848

Great Salt Lake *1–4:* 372, 373, 620, 759; *5:* 11

Great Slave Lake *1–4:* 366, 561

Great southern continent *1–4:* 188, 256–257, 487, 731, 810

Great Trigonometrical Survey *1–4:* 751; *7:* 145

Great Victoria Desert *7:* 100, 102, 104

Great Wall of China *1–4:* 666, 691; *6:* 71

Great Western Highway *5:* 27

Greek city-states *7:* 181

Greek History 1–4: 870

Greely, Adolphus Washington *7:* 143

Green Bay, Wisconsin *1–4:* 216, 496–497; *5:* 106, 107; *6:* 149, 151

Green Harbor, Spitsbergen *1–4:* 858

Green River *1–4:* 759; *5:* 6, 8–11

Greene, Henry *1–4:* 473

Greenland Ice Cap *1–4:* 159, 644

Greenland Sea *1–4:* 611

Greenlanders' Saga 1–4: 524, 526

Greenville 1–4: 256

Grenville, Richard *1–4:* 713

Grierson, John *1–4:* 592

Griffon 1–4: 514; *6:* 96

Grijalba, Juan de *1–4:* 275–276

Grinnell, Henry *5:* 70; *7:* 138–140, 143

Griper 1–4: 639–640

Griper Bay *1–4:* 640

Grissom, Virgil "Gus" *1–4:* 27, 28, 402

Grizzly Gultch, Colorado *7:* 70

Gros Ventre (tribe) *1–4:* 535

Groseilliers, Médard Chouart des. *See* Chouart des Groseilliers, Médard

Grüber, Johann *1–4:* 576; *6:* 70–75, 74 (ill.)

Grytviken *1–4:* 749

Guadeloupe Island *1–4:* 248, 838

Guam Island *1–4:* 569

Guaraní *1–4:* 167, 168

Guaviare River *7:* 131

Guayaquil *1–4:* 628; *5:* 87

Guggenheim, Benjamin *5:* 162

Gulf of Anadyr *7:* 63

Gulf of California *1–4:* 270, 280, 496, 621

Gulf of Carpentaria *1–4:* 145, 146, 362, 487, 812

Gulf of Guinea *1–4:* 55, 157, 387, 636, 735, 737; *7:* 7, 8

Gulf of Maracaibo *1–4:* 615

Gulf of Mexico *1–4:* 496–497, 516–517, 529; *5:* 104, 106; *6:* 12, 43, 49, 161

Gulf of Oman *1–4:* 434; *7:* 185

Gulf of Paria *1–4:* 251, 624

Gulf of St. Lawrence *1–4:* 193, 194, 498, 539

Gulf of Suez *1–4:* 384

Gulf of Taranto *1–4:* 434

Gulf of Tonkin *1–4:* 396

Gulf of Urabá *1–4:* 615, 625, 670

Gulf St. Vincent *1–4:* 362

Gunnbjörn's Skerries *1–4:* 342

Gurgan, Persia *6:* 139

Gustav V (of Sweden) *1–4:* 422

Güyük *1–4:* 185, 186

Gwadar, Pakistan *1–4:* 10

Gyala Sindong, Tibet *7:* 147

Gymnias *1–4:* 868

H

Ha-mi *1–4:* 461

Haakon VII (of Norway) *1–4:* 19, 130

Hab River *1–4:* 10; *7:* 184

Hadhramaut, Yemen *1–4:* 384; *6:* 184, 185

Hadjui *1–4:* 736

Hagia Sophia *1–4:* 67, 96

The Hague, the Netherlands *5:* 18, 155

Hail, Saudi Arabia *1–4:* 88

Haiphong, Vietnam *1–4:* 398

Haise, Fred *1–4:* 30

Half Moon 1–4: 469–470

Halicarnassus *1–4:* 6

Hall, Charles Francis *5:* 68–74, 69 (ill.); *7:* 143

Hall, F. C. *1–4:* 700

Hall Land *5:* 72

Hallett, Goody *5:* 47

Hamadan, Iran *1–4:* 8

Hamburg, Germany *1–4:* 16; *6:* 134

Hamid, Abdul *1–4:* 751

A Handbook of the Trees of California 7: 73

Hankow, China *1–4:* 396, 397

Hanoi, Vietnam *1–4:* 393, 398–399

Hanno 7: 107–112, 110 (ill.)

Hanssen, Helmer *1–4:* 19

Harana, Diego de *1–4:* 246

Harar, Ethiopia *1–4:* 153

Harbor Grace, Newfoundland *1–4:* 333

Boldface indicates main entries in Volume 7 and their page numbers; *1–4:* refers to entries in the four-volume base set; *5:* refers to entries in Volume 5; *6:* refers to entries in Volume 6; *7:* refers to entries in Volume 7; (ill.) following a page number refers to photos, drawings, and maps.

257 | Index

Hari Ram *1–4:* 752; *6:* 76–79, 77 (ill.)

Harrison, Marguerite Baker *6:* 81–89, 81 (ill.), 85 (ill.), 87 (ill.)

Harrison, Thomas Bullitt *6:* 82

Harrison, William Henry *1–4:* 82

Hartog, Dirk *1–4:* 488

Hartstene, H. J. *7:* 143

Hassel, Sverre *1–4:* 19

Hatshepsut *6:* 90–94, 90 (ill.), 93 (ill.)

Hatton, Denys Finch *1–4:* 590

Hauptmann, Bruno *1–4:* 541

Hausa (language) *7:* 11

Havana, Cuba *7:* 84, 138, 143

Hawaiian Islands *1–4:* 104, 255, 265, 408, 484, 510, 542, 832, 834, 854

Hawikuh, New Mexico *1–4:* 270, 349

Hawkes, Graham *6:* 53–55

Hayes, Isaac Israel *7:* 141, 142

Headhunting *7:* 54

Hearne, Samuel *1–4:* 509, 821

The Heart of the Antarctic *1–4:* 747

Hebard, Grace *6:* 166

Hebrides Islands *7:* 24

Hebron, Jordan *1–4:* 97

Hecla *1–4:* 639–642

Hecla Bay *1–4:* 640

Hecla Strait *1–4:* 641

Hedges, George *5:* 43, 45

Hedin, Sven *1–4:* 418–423, 728, 807

Heemskerk, Jacob van *5:* 16, 17

Heemskerk *1–4:* 810

Hejaz, Saudi Arabia *6:* 39

Helena Island *7:* 192

Heligoland Island *1–4:* 711

Hellenism *1–4:* 5, 12

Heller, John *7:* 48

Henderson, Richard *1–4:* 118–119

Hendrik, Hans *5:* 73

Hennepin, Louis *1–4:* 513–514; *6:* 95–100, 95 (ill.), 97 (ill.), 99 (ill.)

Henrietta Bird Hospital *1–4:* 105

Henry, Andrew *5:* 6

Henry IV (of France) *1–4:* 213, 215

Henry VII (of Norway) *1–4:* 170

Henry VIII (of England) *1–4:* 316

Henry the Navigator *1–4:* 239, 387, 424–427

Henslow, John *1–4:* 293, 294, 301

Henson, Matthew A. *1–4:* 18, 158, 428–432, 645–651; *6:* 3

Heraclides *1–4:* 13

Herald Island *6:* 6

Herat, Afghanistan *1–4:* 690

Herbert, Wally *1–4:* 652

Hercules Inlet *7:* 195

Herero (tribe) *7:* 4

Herjolfsson, Bjarni *1–4:* 524, 525

Herodotus *1–4:* 6, 433–435

Herschel, John *1–4:* 302

Herschel Island *1–4:* 18; *5:* 146; *6:* 5

Heyerdahl, Thor *7:* 113–121, 113 (ill.), 117 (ill.), 119 (ill.)

Hiawatha *1–4:* 215

Hickok, Wild Bill *1–4:* 789

Hidatsa (tribe) *6:* 162

Hieroglyphics *6:* 92, 92 (ill.)

High Atlas Mountains *7:* 194

Hillary, Edmund *1–4:* 376–377, 449–453, 801

Hilo, Hawaii *7:* 202

Hilton, James *1–4:* 522

Himalaya Mountains *1–4:* 24, 309, 450–451, 453, 522, 751–752, 755, 772; *6:* 73, 76, 78, 106, 187; *7:* 145, 146, 169, 170, 173

Himyarite (tribe) *1–4:* 384, 385

Hindu Kush Mountains *1–4:* 8, 9, 78, 434, 462; *7:* 169

Hingol River *1–4:* 10; *7:* 184

Hinkler, Bert *1–4:* 490–491

Hispaniola *1–4:* 245–246, 249, 251, 615, 623

History *1–4:* 433–434

Hit, Iraq *1–4:* 597

Hitler, Adolf *1–4:* 423; *5:* 139
Hobart, Indiana *7:* 83, 85
Hobart, Tasmania *1–4:* 328–329; *7:* 201
M.S. *Hobby* *1–4:* 130
Hochelaga (Montreal, Quebec) *1–4:* 195–196
Hog Cay, Bahama Islands *1–4:* 245
Hokkaido, Japan *1–4:* 104
Hollandia *1–4:* 455
Hollick-Kenyon, Herbert *1–4:* 339
Holston River valley *1–4:* 118
Holy Land (Palestine) *5:* 156; *7:* 205, 210
Homer *5:* 135, 137–139
Homo erectus *5:* 96
Honan province, China *6:* 109
Honda, Colombia *6:* 145
Honolulu, Hawaii *1–4:* 600
Honorato da Costa, Francisco *1–4:* 58
Hoorn *6:* 176, 178; *7:* 154
Hoorn, The Netherlands *6:* 175, 176, 178; *7:* 154, 155
Hopewell, New Jersey *1–4:* 483
Hopi (tribe) *1–4:* 271
Hormuz, Iran *1–4:* 10, 12, 223, 289–290, 666, 689–690
Hornemann, Friedrich *1–4:* 55
Hornet *1–4:* 39
Hotien *1–4:* 463
Hottentot (tribe) *1–4:* 388
Houghton, Daniel *1–4:* 55, 632–633; *6:* 101–104, 102 (ill.)
House Committee on Indian Affairs *5:* 11
Houtman, Cornelis de *1–4:* 454–459, 486
Houtman, Frederik de *1–4:* 455, 458–459
How I Found Livingstone in Central Africa *1–4:* 793, 798
Howitt, Alfred *1–4:* 148
Howland Island *7:* 77
Howse Pass *1–4:* 824
Hsi-ning, Tsinghai *1–4:* 728; *6:* 71

Hsiung-nu *1–4:* 219
Hsüan-tsang *1–4:* 460–463; *6:* 106
Huadquina, Peru *1–4:* 100
Huascar *1–4:* 671
Huascarán *1–4:* 655–656
Hubbard, Gardiner Greene *5:* 116
Hubble, Edwin P. *1–4:* 464
Hubble Space Telescope *1–4:* 464–468
Huc, Evariste Regis *1–4:* 814
Huckleberry Finn *1–4:* 801
Hudson, Henry *1–4:* 469–473
Hudson, John *1–4:* 472
Hudson Bay *1–4:* 173, 225–227, 229, 366, 368, 472–473, 497, 508, 640; *6:* 149
Hudson River *1–4:* 470; *6:* 149
Hudson Strait *1–4:* 472
Hudson's Bay Company *1–4:* 225, 227, 230, 366, 564, 618–619, 622, 759, 761, 821–823
Hulagu Khan *1–4:* 688
Humber River *1–4:* 142
Humble Oil & Refining Company *7:* 159, 160
Humboldt, Alexander von *1–4:* 293, 474–482, 505; *6:* 145, 145 (ill.), 146, 173
Humboldt, Alexander von (son) *1–4:* 474
Humboldt, Wilhelm von *1–4:* 474–475
Humboldt Current *1–4:* 481
Humboldt Glacier *7:* 141
Humboldt River *1–4:* 620
Humboldt Sink *1–4:* 620–621
Humphreys, Jack *1–4:* 492
Hunt, John *1–4:* 451
Hunt, Wilson Price *1–4:* 483–485
Hupei *5:* 54, 57
Huron (tribe) *1–4:* 141–143, 215–217, 226; *6:* 151
Hwang Ho River *1–4:* 707
Hyksos people *6:* 91

I

I-Ching *6:* 106–109, 108 (ill.)

Iberian Peninsula *1–4:* 95; *6:* 138

Ibn Abdullah, Ibrahim *6:* 36

Ibn Battutah, Abu Abdallah 75–80, 181

Ibn Fadlan, Ahmad *5:* 75–79, 77 (ill.), 78 (ill.)

Ibn Hawkal, Abu al-Kasim Ibn Ali al-Nasibi *1–4:* 415–417

Ice Fjord *1–4:* 131

Ice Haven *5:* 17, 18

Ictis Island, St. Michael's Mount, Cornwall *1–4:* 710

Id-al-Khabir *1–4:* 152

Iditarod *5:* 62

Idrisi, Abu Abd-Allah Muhammed al-Sharif al- *7:* **122–125,** 123 (ill.)

Igloolik Island *1–4:* 641

Iguaçu Falls *1–4:* 168

Il-Khan Abaga *1–4:* 67–68, 693

Ile-a-la-Crosse *1–4:* 561, 619

Ili River *1–4:* 219; *7:* 208

Iliad 5: 135, 137, 138

Illinois (tribe) *5:* 104, 107

Illinois River *1–4:* 497, 516; *5:* 107; *6:* 96, 98, 152

Illyria *1–4:* 6

Imperial Herbarium *5:* 159

In Darkest Africa 1–4: 799

In Ethiopia With a Mule 7: 172, 174

Inca (tribe) *7:* 113, 115, 126, 129, 173

Inca Empire *1–4:* 98–102, 174, 627, 669, 671, 768; *5:* 5

Independence Bay *1–4:* 429, 647

Indian Ocean *1–4:* 10, 11, 456, 488, 504, 598; *6:* 49; *7:* 38, 41, 186, 213

Indica 7: 186

Indigirka River *7:* 61

Indus River *1–4:* 5, 9, 11, 78, 421, 434–435, 463, 598, 754–755, 808; *5:* 56; *6:* 75; *7:* 182, 183

Indus Valley *1–4:* 9, 596; *7:* 121

Innocent IV *1–4:* 183; *7:* 205

Inquisition *1–4:* 95

Inside Passage, Alaska *1–4:* 834

International Botanical Congress *7:* 75

International Date Line *1–4:* 573

International Geophysical Year *1–4:* 93, 340, 351, 376, 801; *6:* 136

International Memorial *5:* 168

International Space Station (ISS) *5:* 109, 110, 114

International Trans-Antarctica Expedition *1–4:* 803

International Women's Peace Congress *1–4:* 820

Inuit (tribe) *1–4:* 344, 368, 428–432, 473, 498, 641, 645, 647–648, 650; *5:* 68, 70, 71, 73, 74, 122, 145–147; *6:* 1–3, 6; *7:* 141, 143, 190

Investigator 1–4: 361–364, 600–603

Investigator Strait *1–4:* 362

Iona Island *7:* 27

Iraq Museum *1–4:* 89

Irish Sea *1–4:* 711

Irixana River *7:* 193

Irkutsk *1–4:* 701, 703

Iron Gates *1–4:* 461

Iroquois (tribe) *1–4:* 142, 194–196, 215, 217, 225–227, 513, 765; *6:* 148, 152

Iroquois Confederacy *1–4:* 142, 215

Irwin, James *1–4:* 31

Isabela, Dominican Republic *1–4:* 248–249

Isabella (of Spain) *1–4:* 241–243, 247, 250, 251, 254, 386, 616

Isenberg, C. W. *1–4:* 503

Isfahan, Iran *1–4:* 77

Iskander *1–4:* 290

Iskenderun, Turkey *1–4:* 7

Isla de los Estados *6:* 178; *7:* 154

Isla Mujeres *7:* 50

Islam *1–4:* 75; *5:* 75; *7:* 136, 204, 205
Island of Thule *1–4:* 711
Islands of the Blessed *7:* 25
Isna, Egypt *6:* 37, 38
Israelites *6:* 114, 116
Issus, Turkey *1–4:* 7
Issyk-Kul *1–4:* 461
Istanbul, Turkey *1–4:* 96, 490, 687, 869. *See also* Constantinople
Isthmus of Darien *1–4:* 615–616
Isthmus of Kra *6:* 174
Isthmus of Panama *1–4:* 317–318, 615, 617; *5:* 87
Isthmus of Suez *5:* 127
Italia 1–4: 22
Ithaca *5:* 138
Ituri forest *1–4:* 797
Ituri River *1–4:* 3–4
Ivens, Roberto *1–4:* 137–140
Ivory *7:* 4–5, 9, 10 (ill.), 60, 62–64, 64 (ill.)
Ivory Coast *1–4:* 579; *5:* 49
Izmir, Turkey *6:* 70
Iztaccíhuatl *1–4:* 278

J

Jackson, Frederick *1–4:* 608
Jackson, Thomas "Stonewall" *1–4:* 374
Jackson Hole, Wyoming *1–4:* 484
Jaén *1–4:* 481
Jaette Glacier *1–4:* 131
Jahangir, Emperor *1–4:* 23
Jalan, Pak Bohap bin *7:* 98
Jalapa, Mexico *1–4:* 277
Jamaica Channel *1–4:* 253
James I (of England) *1–4:* 712, 716
James II (of England) *1–4:* 229
James, Naomi *7:* 197
James Bay *1–4:* 472
James River *1–4:* 764
Jameson, Robert *1–4:* 293
Jamestown, Virginia *1–4:* 763

Jan Mayen Island *1–4:* 469
Janszoon, Willem *1–4:* 486–488
Japan Current *6:* 192, 193
Jaquare River *7:* 193
Jarra *1–4:* 633
Jarrat, Jim *6:* 51
Jarvis, Gregory B. *6:* 129
Jason 1–4: 490, 492
Jason Junior (JJ) *5:* 166
Jauf, Saudi Arabia *1–4:* 110
Java *1–4:* 222–223, 457, 486, 488, 667, 862
Java Man *5:* 91
Jeannette 1–4: 606; *6:* 5
Jebel Dinka *5:* 158
Jefferson, Thomas *1–4:* 482, 528–530, 533, 536; *6:* 161
Jefferson River *1–4:* 533
Jemison, Mae *5:* 80–84, 80 (ill.), 82 (ill.)
Jemison Group *5:* 84
Jericho, Jordan *6:* 114–119
Jersey City, New Jersey *6:* 23, 24
Jersey Island, English Channel *1–4:* 716
Jerusalem, Israel *1–4:* 65, 76, 87, 96–97, 597, 786; *5:* 127; *6:* 115, 119, 138
Jessup, Morris K. *1–4:* 647
Jesuit missionaries *1–4:* 23–25, 494, 498, 512, 668, 866; *6:* 71
Jet Propulsion Laboratory *1–4:* 847; *5:* 42
Jhansi *1–4:* 491
Jhelum River *1–4:* 9, 11; *7:* 182
Jidda, Saudi Arabia *1–4:* 76, 152, 290; *6:* 29, 39, 40
Jih-k'a-tse, Tibet *1–4:* 308, 753
"Jim suit" *6:* 48, 50, 51
Jiménez de Quesada, Gonzalo *7:* **126–132,** 126 (ill.), 129 (ill.),
Jinja, Uganda *1–4:* 3
Jiparaná River *6:* 155
Jivaro (tribe) *7:* 54
Johansen, Hjalmar *1–4:* 607
John A. Macdonald 7: 161
John Bishop Memorial Hospital *1–4:* 105

Boldface indicates main entries in Volume 7 and their page numbers; *1–4:* refers to entries in the four-volume base set; *5:* refers to entries in Volume 5; *6:* refers to entries in Volume 6; *7:* refers to entries in Volume 7; (ill.) following a page number refers to photos, drawings, and maps.

261 | Index

John F. Kennedy Space Center *1–4:* 402, 587
John I (of Portugal) *1–4:* 240, 247, 288, 424, 425
John II (of Portugal) *1–4:* 288, 290, 291, 311, 313, 386
John III (of Portugal) *1–4:* 864
John XXII (Pope) *6:* 111
John of Monte Corvino *1–4:* 68; *6:* 110
Johns Hopkins University *1–4:* 337
Johnson, Amy *1–4:* 333, 489–493
Johnson, Lyndon B. *1–4:* 404
Johnson, Samuel *6:* 33
Johnson Space Center *5:* 114; *6:* 128, 132
Johnston, Keith *1–4:* 235, 236, 826
Johore *1–4:* 458
Joinville Land *1–4:* 328
Joliba 1–4: 636, 637
Jolliet, Louis *1–4:* 494–498, 513, 516; *5:* 104, 106–108
Jordan River *6:* 37, 114
Jordan Valley *1–4:* 597
Jordanus of Séverac *6:* 110–112, 112 (ill.)
José, Amaro *1–4:* 57–60, 139
Josephine Ford 1–4: 160
Joshua era *6:* 115, 116
A Journey in Ashango Land 1–4: 324
Journal of a Voyage by Order of the King to the Equator 5: 89
Journal of the Royal Geographical Society 6: 170
"J.T.": The Biography of an African Monkey 1–4: 2
Juan Fernández Islands *1–4:* 124, 188, 569, 732; *6:* 49, 178; *7:* 32, 155
Juba, Somalia *1–4:* 223
Juba, Sudan *1–4:* 591; *5:* 160
Jumano (tribe) *1–4:* 347
Jumla, Nepal *6:* 78
Jungle Portraits 1–4: 4
Junker, Wilhelm *7:* **133–137,** 133 (ill.), 134 (ill.)

Junkers, Hugo *1–4:* 422
Jupiter *1–4:* 464, 468, 847–850
Jupiter Inlet *1–4:* 697
Jur River *1–4:* 582

K

Ka-erh *1–4:* 754–755
Ka'abah *1–4:* 152
Kabalega Falls *1–4:* 43
Kabara *1–4:* 636; *6:* 59
Kabul, Afghanistan *1–4:* 8, 434, 808
Kabul River *1–4:* 434, 462; *5:* 56
Kabylia campaigns *1–4:* 736
Kadiköy *1–4:* 869
Kafu River *1–4:* 47
Kagoshima *1–4:* 667
K'ai-feng *1–4:* 687
Kai Island *1–4:* 487
Kailas Mountains *1–4:* 421
Kalahari Desert *1–4:* 544, 546; *7:* 2, 2 (ill.), 3
Kalami River *1–4:* 10
Kalgan, China *1–4:* 705
Kalimantan *7:* 94
Kalomo River *1–4:* 549
Kalongosi River *1–4:* 553
Kamalia *1–4:* 634
Kamchadals *1–4:* 42
Kamchatka Mountains *1–4:* 41
Kamchatka Peninsula *1–4:* 40–42, 267, 510; *5:* 20
Kamchatka River *1–4:* 41, 42
Kamehameha (of Hawaii) *1–4:* 64, 832, 834
Kanawha valley *1–4:* 121
Kanbaya, port *1–4:* 596
Kan-chou River *1–4:* 808
Kane, Elisha Kent *1–4:* 644; *5:* 71, 72; *7:* **138–144,** 138 (ill.), 140 (ill.), 142 (ill.)
Kane Basin *7:* 141
Kangaroo Island *1–4:* 362
Kannauj *1–4:* 462
Kano, Nigeria *1–4:* 71; *7:* 10
Kanpur *1–4:* 462

Kansas (tribe) *1–4:* 662
Kansu *5:* 102
Kapuas River *5:* 129
Kara Sea *5:* 16
Karachi, Pakistan *1–4:* 10, 434,
   491
Karagwe *1–4:* 776
Karakorum, Mongolia *1–4:*
   184–185
Karakorum Mountains *1–4:*
   862–863; *7:* 173, 205, 206,
   209, 210
Karankawa (tribe) *1–4:* 518
Karbala, Iraq *1–4:* 88
Karisoke Research Centre *6:* 59,
   61, 62
Karlsefni, Thorfinn *1–4:* 527
Karluk 6: 5, 6
Karnak, Egypt *6:* 91
Kars, Turkey *7:* 210
Karuma Falls *1–4:* 48
Karun River *6:* 87; *7:* 186
Kasai River *1–4:* 548–549; *7:*
   213
Kasanje, Africa *1–4:* 58–59
Kashgar, China *1–4:* 419–421,
   463, 690, 808; *5:* 56, 102
Kashmir, India *1–4:* 24, 105,
   462, 755, 807, 862; *5:* 98, 102
Kasonia, Gascony, France *1–4:*
   67
Kassange *1–4:* 549
Katanga *1–4:* 58
Katmandu, Nepal *1–4:* 452, 753;
   6: 73, 78; *7:* 171
Katsina, Nigeria *1–4:* 72
Kauai, Hawaii *1–4:* 64
Kayak Island *5:* 23
Kazeh *1–4:* 553, 774, 790
Kazembe, Zambia *1–4:* 58–59,
   233
Kealakekua Bay *1–4:* 266
Kearny, Stephen W. *1–4:* 373
Keeling Atoll *1–4:* 302
Kellett, Henry, Captain *1–4:*
   602–603
Kemys, Lawrence *1–4:* 716–717
Kenai Peninsula *5:* 23
Kennedy, John F. *1–4:* 26, 34,
   402, 404

Kennedy Channel *7:* 141
Kennedy Space Center *5:* 82,
   83; *6:* 130
Kentucky River *1–4:* 118–119
Kenyon, Frederic *6:* 115
Kenyon, Kathleen M. *6:*
   114–119, 114 (ill.), 117 (ill.)
Kerguelen Island *1–4:* 265
Kerman *1–4:* 12
Key West, Florida *7:* 83, 87, 88,
   90
Keyzer, Pieter de *1–4:* 455–456
Khabarov, Yerofey Pavlovich *6:*
   121–124, 123 (ill.)
Khabarovsk *1–4:* 701–703; *6:*
   124
Khadija (of Maldive Islands)
   1–4: 78
Khanbalik *1–4:* 688, 691–693
Kharashahr *1–4:* 461
Khartoum, Sudan *1–4:* 4, 45,
   49–50, 591, 776; *5:* 156, 158,
   159; *6:* 31; *7:* 135, 136
Khawak Pass *1–4:* 8
Khazars *1–4:* 597; *5:* 77
Kheidir, Iraq *1–4:* 88
Khojali *1–4:* 582
Khon Rapids *1–4:* 395
Khorasan, Iran *1–4:* 66; *6:* 139
Khotan, China *1–4:* 420, 463,
   690, 708, 807
Khrushchev, Nikita *1–4:* 381,
   779, 818
Khubilai Khan *1–4:* 184
Khumbu Glacier *1–4:* 451
Khurasan *1–4:* 596
Khuzestan, Iran *1–4:* 416–417,
   595
Khwarizm, Persia *1–4:* 78
Khyber Pass *1–4:* 9
Kiangsu *1–4:* 692
Kiev, Ukraine *1–4:* 184, 186
Kikuyu (tribe) *1–4:* 719, 827; *5:*
   91
Kilimane *1–4:* 551
Kilwa, Tanzania *1–4:* 289, 392;
   7: 41
Kim 1–4: 151
Kimangelia, Tanzania *5:* 142
King Christian Island *7:* 189

King George Islands *7:* 34

King George Sound *1–4:* 302, 361, 832

King William Island *1–4:* 16, 368; *5:* 70, 71

King William's Cataract *6:* 170

Kingsley, Charles *1–4:* 499

Kingsley, George *1–4:* 499

Kingsley, Henry *1–4:* 499

Kingsley, Mary *1–4:* 499–501

Kingston, Ontario *1–4:* 513–514

Kinshasa, Zaire *1–4:* 4, 581, 795

Kintup *1–4:* 752; *7:* **145–150,** 147 (ill.)

Kipfer, Paul *1–4:* 658

Kircher, Athanasius *6:* 75

Kirghiz (Kazakh) *5:* 100

Kiribati Islands *1–4:* 733

Kisangani, Zaire *1–4:* 4, 795

Kisulidini *1–4:* 721, 722

Kisumu *1–4:* 3

Kitchener, Horatio Herbert *1–4:* 583; *7:* 136

Kitty Hawk, North Carolina *1–4:* 837; *7:* 178

Kitui *1–4:* 505

Kivoi, King *1–4:* 506

Klamath Lake *1–4:* 621

Klamath River *1–4:* 620

Kmeri (of Usambara) *1–4:* 504

Knife River *6:* 162

Knorr *5:* 165

Knox Coast *1–4:* 853

Kodiak Island, Alaska *1–4:* 62–63

Koko Nor *1–4:* 705, 707, 728, 752

Kolobeng *1–4:* 544, 548

Kolyma River *7:* 62

Kon-Tiki *7:* 115

Kon-Tiki *7:* 116, 117, 117 (ill.)

Konstantinou, Ilias *7:* 47, 48

Kootenay (tribe) *1–4:* 824

The Koran *6:* 36, 138

Korean War *1–4:* 35, 401

Korntal *1–4:* 506, 507

Korolov, Sergei *1–4:* 380, 778–779

Korosko *5:* 158

Koryaks *1–4:* 41, 42

Kosmos *1–4:* 482

Koundian *1–4:* 579

Kouroussa, Guinea *1–4:* 180

Krapf, Johann Ludwig *1–4:* 152, 502–507, 718, 721–722, 827

Krestovka River *1–4:* 41

Kronshlot, Russia *1–4:* 91, 93

Kublai Khan *1–4:* 65–66, 687–689, 691–693

Kucha *1–4:* 461

Kukawa, Nigeria *1–4:* 72–74, 737

Kukukuku (tribe) *1–4:* 521

Kuldja *1–4:* 706

Kumara River *6:* 124

Kumbum *1–4:* 728

Kun Lun Shan mountains *1–4:* 219, 707, 807

K'un-ming, China *1–4:* 221, 396, 692

Kurdistan, Turkey *5:* 128

Kurdistan Mountains *1–4:* 868

Kuril Islands *1–4:* 40; *5:* 22

Kuruman *1–4:* 544

Kuskov, I. A. *1–4:* 64

Kuti Pass *6:* 78

Kwango River *1–4:* 138, 549

Kyakhta, Russia *1–4:* 420, 705

Kyasha *1–4:* 667

Kyi-Chu River *1–4:* 753

Kyirong *1–4:* 753

Kyoto, Japan *1–4:* 865

Kyushu *1–4:* 667, 865–866

Kyzyl Kum Desert *5:* 101

L

L. S. B. Leakey Foundation *7:* 98

La Boussole *1–4:* 509, 511

La Concepción de Urbana *1–4:* 478

La Condamine, Charles-Marie de *1–4:* 409–410, 476–477, 481; *6:* 144

La Coruña, Spain *6:* 189

La Dauphine *1–4:* 837–838

La Guajira *1–4:* 624–625

La Hogue *1–4:* 638

La Motte, Dominique *1–4:* 513

La Navidad (Limonade-Bord-de-Mer, Haiti) *1–4:* 246, 248

La Paz, Bolivia *1–4:* 654

La Paz Bay *1–4:* 280–281

La Pérouse, Jean-François de Galaup, comte de *1–4:* 326, 508–511

La Pérouse Strait *1–4:* 510

La Relación y Comentarios 1–4: 168

La Rochelle, France *1–4:* 766; *5:* 87

La Salle, René-Robert Cavelier de *1–4:* 512–518; *6:* 95, 100

La Salle, Illinois *1–4:* 516

Labrador *1–4:* 173, 338, 432, 498, 526, 652; *6:* 4, 45

Lacerda, Francisco José de *1–4:* 57–58

Lachine Rapids *1–4:* 142, 195, 497

Ladakh, India *1–4:* 105, 755

Lado, Sudan *7:* 135

Lady Alice 1–4: 794–795

The Lady and the Sharks 7: 49

Lady With a Spear 7: 47

A Lady's Life in the Rocky Mountains 1–4: 104

A Lady's Second Journey Round the World 5: 130

A Lady's Voyage Round the World 5: 129

Lae, New Guinea *1–4:* 520

Laetoli, Tanzania *5:* 95

Lagos, Portugal *1–4:* 239, 737

Lagrée, Ernest Doudart de *1–4:* 395

Lahore, Pakistan *6:* 75

Laidley, John *6:* 103

Laing, Alexander Gordon *1–4:* 181

Lairdsport (trading station) *7:* 10

Lake Alakol *1–4:* 185

Lake Albert *1–4:* 3, 43, 47–48, 50, 794, 798; *7:* 135

Lake Amadeus *7:* 101, 105

Lake Athabaska *1–4:* 822; *6:* 65

Lake Baikal *5:* 22; *6:* 124

Lake Bangweulu *1–4:* 232–234, 551–552, 554

Lake Chad *1–4:* 69–72, 136, 737; *7:* 118

Lake Chala *5:* 143

Lake Champlain *1–4:* 215

Lake Chilwa *1–4:* 550

Lake Courte Oreille *1–4:* 226

Lake Dilolo *1–4:* 548

Lake Edward *1–4:* 798

Lake Erie *1–4:* 142, 513–514; *6:* 96

Lake Eyre *1–4:* 356; *5:* 60; *7:* 101

Lake Huron *1–4:* 142, 216, 496, 514; *6:* 96, 148, 150

Lake Illiwarra *1–4:* 360

Lake Issyk-Kul *1–4:* 419

Lake Itasca *1–4:* 662

Lake Kazembe *1–4:* 233

Lake Leopold *1–4:* 796

Lake Malawi *1–4:* 550–552, 826

Lake Manitoba *1–4:* 823

Lake Maracaibo *1–4:* 624

Lake Michigan *1–4:* 216, 496–497, 514; *5:* 106, 107; *6:* 96, 147, 149–151

Lake Mweru *1–4:* 552

Lake Naivasha *1–4:* 827

Lake Ngami *1–4:* 544, 546; *7:* 2–4

Lake Nipissing *1–4:* 142, 216; *6:* 149, 150

Lake No *5:* 158

Lake Nyasa *1–4:* 112, 231–232, 236, 505, 773, 789, 826; *7:* 213, 215

Lake of the Woods *1–4:* 823

Lake Ontario *1–4:* 513; *6:* 96

Lake Parima *1–4:* 479

Lake Raeside *5:* 59

Lake Rukwa *1–4:* 826

Lake Simcoe *1–4:* 142

Lake Superior *1–4:* 142, 225–227, 823; *5:* 106; *6:* 151

Lake Tabora *7:* 213

Lake Tahoe, Nevada *1–4:* 104

Lake Tana *6:* 30

Lake Tanganyika *1–4:* 113, 115–116, 155–156, 233–234,

Boldface indicates main entries in Volume 7 and their page numbers; *1–4:* refers to entries in the four-volume base set; *5:* refers to entries in Volume 5; *6:* refers to entries in Volume 6; *7:* refers to entries in Volume 7; (ill.) following a page number refers to photos, drawings, and maps.

265 | Index

236, 551–553, 774, 790, 792, 794, 826; *7:* 213, 215

Lake Texcoco *5:* 2

Lake Titicaca *7:* 120

Lake Torrens *1–4:* 356; *7:* 104

Lake Turkana *5:* 95, 96

Lake Victoria *1–4:* 3, 45, 113–114, 155–156, 435, 772, 775–777, 794, 798, 828; *6:* 26, 34; *7:* 135

Lake Winnipeg *1–4:* 823

Lamaism *1–4:* 574

Lambaréné, Gabon *1–4:* 134, 322

Lamego, Joseph de *1–4:* 290

Lancaster Sound *1–4:* 16, 639, 642; *7:* 162, 165

Lanchou *1–4:* 691

Land of Punt *6:* 90–92, 94

The Land of the Sherpas 5: 103

Landells, George *1–4:* 145

Lander, Richard *1–4:* 637

Land's End, Belerium *1–4:* 710

Landsat 5: 44

Langenburg (settlement) *7:* 215

Langle, Paul-Antoine de *1–4:* 509–510

Langtang, Nepal *7:* 171

L'Anse aux Meadows, Newfoundland *1–4:* 526

Las Conchas, Argentina *1–4:* 299

Las Palmas, Canary islands *1–4:* 244

Lassen Volcanic National Park *1–4:* 83

L'Astrolabe 1–4: 509–511

Latakia, Syria *1–4:* 787

Lavaca River *1–4:* 518

Lawrence, T. E. *1–4:* 87, 89; *5:* 41

Lawrence, Wendy *5:* 114

Lawrence of Arabia. *See* Lawrence, T. E.

Lazarev, Mikhail *1–4:* 91

Le Bourget Field *1–4:* 540

Le Havre, France *5:* 30, 32

Le Jeune, Paul *6:* 149

Le Maire, Daniel *7:* 157

Le Maire, Isaac *6:* 176, 181; *7:* 152, 154, 157

Le Maire, Jacob *6:* 179–181; *7:* **151–158,** 153 (ill.)

Le Maire Strait *6:* 180; *7:* 157

League of Nations *1–4:* 522

Leahy, Dan *1–4:* 521–523

Leahy, Michael J. *1–4:* 519–523

Leahy, Patrick "Paddy" *1–4:* 521

Leakey, Louis S. B. *5:* 91–97, 91 (ill.), 94 (ill.); *6:* 58, 58 (ill.), 59; *7:* 93

Leakey, Mary *5:* 91–97, 92 (ill.), 94 (ill.), 117; *6:* 58

Leakey, Richard *5:* 91–97, 93 (ill.), 94 (ill.)

"Leakey's Angels" *7:* 93

Ledyard, John *1–4:* 55, 632; *6:* 101

Leech Lake *1–4:* 662

Leeward Islands *1–4:* 357

Legazpi, Miguel Lopez de *6:* 191, 192

Legion of Honor *1–4:* 128, 579

Leh, India *1–4:* 421, 755

Leicester, England *6:* 115

Leichhardt, Friedrich Wilhelm Ludwig *5:* 58

Leif Eriksson *1–4:* 251, 343, 524–527

Leifrsbudir *1–4:* 526–527

Leif's Booths *1–4:* 526

Leigh, Linda *6:* 15

Leith (Edinburgh, Scotland) *5:* 51

Lemhi River *1–4:* 533–534

Lena River *5:* 124, 131, 134; *7:* 61

Lennon, Patrick *1–4:* 296

Leopold II (of Belguim) *1–4:* 134–136, 738, 796–797, 799; *7:* 213, 213 (ill.)

Lesseps, Jean de *1–4:* 510

Leticia, Colombia *6:* 158

Lett River *5:* 26

Levant *1–4:* 787

Lewis, Meriwether *1–4:* 458, 528–537; *5:* 6; *6:* 64, 65, 161–163, 162 (ill.), 165–168

Lhasa, Tibet *1–4:* 24, 306, 308–309, 421, 574–577, 707, 727–729, 753, 813–815; *6:* 71–73, 72 (ill.); *7:* 147, 148, 149

Liang-chou *1–4:* 461

Liber Tatarorum 1–4: 186

Libreville, Gabon *1–4:* 135–136

Liegnitz, Poland *1–4:* 184

The Life and Adventures of James P. Beckwourth, Mountaineer, Scout, Pioneer, and Chief of the Crow Nation 1–4: 84

Lillooet, British Columbia *6:* 66

Lima, Rodrigo da *1–4:* 291

Lima, Peru *1–4:* 99, 157, 481, 627, 673; *5:* 88

Lincoln, Abraham *1–4:* 374

Lincoln, Nebraska *1–4:* 538

Lindbergh, Ann Morrow *1–4:* 542

Lindbergh, Charles *1–4:* 160, 492, 538–542, 592, 743; *7:* 178

Linenger, Jerry *5:* 114

Linnaean Society *1–4:* 304

Linnaeus, Carolus *1–4:* 53; *6:* 144, 145; *7:* 75

Linschoten, Jan Huyghen van *1–4:* 455; *5:* 14—17

Linyanti *1–4:* 549

Lippershey, Hans *1–4:* 464

Lisa, Manuel *1–4:* 483

Lisbon, Portugal *1–4:* 239, 241, 312–313, 387, 390, 454–455, 666, 668; *6:* 43–45, 190; *7:* 29, 38, 42, 43

Lisiansky, Yuri *1–4:* 63

Little Abbai River *6:* 30

Little America 1–4: 160–161

Little America II 1–4: 338–339

Little Cornwallis Island *7:* 190

Little Falls, Minnesota *1–4:* 538

Livingstone, David *1–4:* 60, 74, 115–116, 134, 231–236, 397, 502, 543–554, 718, 777, 789–793, 798, 825; *7:* 2

Livingstone, Mary *1–4:* 551

Livingstone Falls *1–4:* 795

Liv's Glacier *1–4:* 160

Llanos *1–4:* 479

Loango, French Congo *1–4:* 581

Loaysa, Francisco Garcia Jofre de *6:* 189

Lockheed Electra 10E *7:* 77, 78, 81

Loire River *1–4:* 710

Loja, Bonpland *1–4:* 481

Lokoja (trading station) *7:* 10–12

Lolo Pass *1–4:* 534

Lomami River *7:* 213

Lombok *1–4:* 304

London, England *5:* 27, 35, 36, 39, 70, 71, 91, 102, 130, 140, 141, 144; *6:* 27, 33, 35, 36, 101, 146, 181

London Daily Mail 1–4: 492

London Ethnological Society *1–4:* 323

London Missionary Society *1–4:* 297, 543, 548, 550

London *Times 5:* 101, 148; *7:* 15, 17

"The Lone Dove," *1–4:* 492

Long Island, Bahama Islands *1–4:* 245

Long Island, New York *1–4:* 539

Longfellow, Henry Wadsworth *1–4:* 215

Lono *1–4:* 266

Lop Nor, China *1–4:* 219, 420–421, 706, 708

Lop Nor Lake *1–4:* 807

Los Angeles, California *1–4:* 83, 177

Los Angeles-Chicago Bendix Trophy Race *1–4:* 700

Los Majos Islands *1–4:* 834

Los naufragios 1–4: 168

Los Patos, Peru *1–4:* 301

Lost Horizon 1–4: 522

Lou Lan, Tibet *1–4:* 421, 807

Louis IV (of France) *1–4:* 513

Louis IX (of France) *1–4:* 186; *7:* 204, 205, 205 (ill.)

Louis XIII (of France) *1–4:* 216

Louis XIV (of France) *1–4:* 474; *6:* 95

Louis XV (of France) *1–4:* 123

Boldface indicates main entries in Volume 7 and their page numbers; *1–4:* refers to entries in the four-volume base set; *5:* refers to entries in Volume 5; *6:* refers to entries in Volume 6; *7:* refers to entries in Volume 7; (ill.) following a page number refers to photos, drawings, and maps.

267   Index

Louis XVI (of France) *1–4:* 509
Louisiade Archipelago *1–4:* 126
Louisiana Territory *1–4:* 497,
517, 529–530, 536; *6:* 161
Louis-Philippe *1–4:* 327
Louis Philippe Land *1–4:* 328
Louisville, Kentucky *1–4:* 119,
530
Louvre Museum *1–4:* 326
Lovell, James *1–4:* 28, 30
Loyalty Islands *1–4:* 329; *5:* 38
Loyola University *5:* 65
Lualaba River *1–4:* 134, 233,
552, 553, 792, 794, 796, 826
Luanda, Angola *1–4:* 59, 500,
549
Luang Prabang, Laos *1–4:* 395,
667
Luapula River *1–4:* 139–140
Lubianka Prison *6:* 83, 83 (ill.),
84
Lucas, Simon *1–4:* 55, 632; *6:*
101
Lucid, Shannon *5:* 111, 112, 114
Lucma, Peru *1–4:* 100
Ludington, Michigan *5:* 107
Lugo, Alonso Luis de *7:* 131
Lugo, Pedro Fernández de *7:* 127
Lukuga River *1–4:* 116, 826
Luna 1–4: 555–559
Luo-yang *1–4:* 460
Luque, Hernando de *1–4:* 670
Luristan, Persia *6:* 182, 183
Lurs people *6:* 182, 183
Lusar *1–4:* 728
Luta N'Zige *1–4:* 46, 47
Luttig, John *6:* 166
Luvironza *1–4:* 774
Luxor, Egypt *5:* 156; *6:* 91
Lycia (Turkey) *7:* 182, 186
Lyell, Charles *1–4:* 302
Lygdamis (of Greece) *1–4:* 434
Lyon, Eugene *7:* 84, 87
Lyons, France *1–4:* 186

M

Ma-Robert 1–4: 550

Maamba Aboriginal Reserve *7:*
20
Mababe River *1–4:* 547
Mabotsa *1–4:* 544
Macao *1–4:* 510; *6:* 70
MacCallum, Taber Kyle *6:* 15
Macdonald 7: 162, 164
Macdonnell Mountain Ranges *7:*
101
Mach, Ernst *1–4:* 872
Machiparo *1–4:* 630
Machu Picchu *1–4:* 98, 100, 102
Mackenzie, Alexander *1–4:* 367,
560–565, 834; *6:* 65, 66
Mackenzie, Charles Frederick
1–4: 231
Mackenzie Bay *5:* 146
Mackenzie Delta *1–4:* 601
Mackenzie Pass *1–4:* 563
Mackenzie River *1–4:* 18, 367,
560, 562, 601, 801; *5:* 146
Mackinac *1–4:* 496, 514
Macquarie Island *1–4:* 92
Mactan Island *1–4:* 570
Madeira Islands *1–4:* 19, 239,
425; *7:* 24
Madeira River *1–4:* 630
Madison, James *1–4:* 533
Madison River *1–4:* 533
Madras, India *6:* 110
Madrid, Spain *6:* 142, 146
Madura *1–4:* 457
Magadha, India *1–4:* 462; *5:*
56; *6:* 108
Magdalen Islands *1–4:* 194
Magdalena River *1–4:* 479, 615;
6: 143, 145, 146; *7:* 127, 128
Magellan, Ferdinand *1–4:* 174,
566–573; *6:* 189
Magomero, Africa *1–4:* 231
Maharashtra *1–4:* 463
Mahdia, Tunisia *1–4:* 415
Maiden Voyage 7: 201
Maigaard, Christian *1–4:* 645
Maillart, Ella *5:* 98–103, 98
(ill.), 100 (ill.)
Makale, Ethiopia *7:* 172
Makatéa Island *1–4:* 733
Makololo *1–4:* 546–550

Makran Coast, Pakistan *1–4:* 10–11

Malabar Coast *6:* 111; *7:* 38, 41

Malacca, Malaya *1–4:* 223, 667, 865

Malaga, Spain *1–4:* 79

Malagarasi River *1–4:* 790

Malakal, Sudan *1–4:* 591; *7:* 134

Malange, Angola *1–4:* 138

Malay Archipelago *1–4:* 327, 459, 666, 742, 865

Malay Peninsula *1–4:* 105, 666, 692; *6:* 109, 174

Maldive Islands *1–4:* 78, 223

Maldonado, Pedro Vicente *5:* 87, 88

Malheur River *1–4:* 620

Malindi, Kenya *1–4:* 223, 290, 389–390

Malta Island *1–4:* 785

Malthus, Thomas

Mambirima Falls *1–4:* 140

Mana, India *1–4:* 24

Mana Pass *1–4:* 24, 754

Manacupuru *5:* 152

Manaus, Brazil *6:* 155; *7:* 193

Manco *1–4:* 672

Manco II *1–4:* 99

Mancos, Colorado *7:* 71

Mandan (tribe) *1–4:* 532, 823; *6:* 162, 167

Mandarin *1–4:* 460

Mandingo language *6:* 102, 103

Mangu Khan *7:* 209

Manhattan *1–4:* 470

S.S. *Manhattan* *1–4:* 17; *7:* **159–166,** 159 (ill.), 161 (ill.), 162 (ill.), 164 (ill.)

Manila, Philippines *6:* 193

Manila Galleon *6:* 193

Mankinga (of the Chagga) 719–721

Manning, Thomas *1–4:* 574–577

Manta *5:* 87

Manoa, South America *1–4:* 715

Manuel Comnenus *1–4:* 95, 96

Manuel I (of Portugal) *1–4:* 313, 386, 390–391; *6:* 42; *7:* 37, 38

Manuel II *1–4:* 566

Maori (tribe) *1–4:* 259, 260, 302, 810

A Map of Virginia, 1–4: 764

Mar del Plata, Argentina *7:* 200

Maragheh, Azerbaijan *1–4:* 66

Marañón River *1–4:* 411, 413; *5:* 88, 89

Marchand, Jean Baptiste *1–4:* 136, 578–584

Marcos, Fray *1–4:* 176

Mare Crisium *1–4:* 559

Mare Imbrium *1–4:* 556

Mare Naval Base *7:* 200

Margarita 7: 84, 85, 87

Margarita Island *1–4:* 251, 624

Margarita, Venezuela *1–4:* 630

Mariame (tribe) *1–4:* 347

Mariana Islands *1–4:* 569, 573; *6:* 191

Mariana Trench *1–4:* 211, 659

Marias River *1–4:* 533

Mar'ib, Yemen *1–4:* 384

Marie Byrd Land *1–4:* 160

Marie Galante Island *1–4:* 248

Marina (Malinche) *1–4:* 276, 278

Mariner 1–4: 585–588

Mariquita, Colombia *6:* 145, 146

Markham, Beryl *1–4:* 333, 589–594

Markham, Mansfield *1–4:* 590

Markland, Labrador *1–4:* 526–527

Marooned in Moscow 6: 84

Marpung, Tibet *7:* 148, 149

Marques, Manuel *1–4:* 23–24

Marquesa Island *1–4:* 263

Marquesas Islands *5:* 36

Marquesas Keys, Florida *7:* 85

Marquette, Jacques *1–4:* 494, 496, 497, 513, 516; *5:* 104–108, 104 (ill.), 105 (ill.)

Marrakech, Morocco *7:* 194

Mars *1–4:* 586–587, 843–846, 850

Mars 2 1–4: 587

Marshall Islands *1–4:* 401

Martelli, Dean *7:* 17

Martha's Vineyard, Massachusetts *1–4:* 214

Boldface indicates main entries in Volume 7 and their page numbers; *1–4:* refers to entries in the four-volume base set; *5:* refers to entries in Volume 5; *6:* refers to entries in Volume 6; *7:* refers to entries in Volume 7; (ill.) following a page number refers to photos, drawings, and maps.

269 | Index

Martin, James *1–4:* 827
Martinez, Juan *1–4:* 715
Martinique *5:* 36, 87
Martyr, Peter *1–4:* 173
Marvin, Ross *1–4:* 430
Mary Kingsley Hospital *1–4:* 501
Marysville, California *1–4:* 84
Marzuq, Libya *1–4:* 71, 737
Mas Afuera *1–4:* 188
Mas'ada, Aba al-Hasan 'Ala al- *1–4:* 595–598
Masai (tribe) *1–4:* 825, 827–828; Masai (tribe) *5:* 143; *7:* 215
Masaki *1–4:* 719
Masasi, Tanzania *1–4:* 235
Mascoutens, Wisconsin *6:* 152
Mashhad, Iran *1–4:* 419
Mason, James *1–4:* 854
Massa'ot 1–4: 94, 97
Massassa Rapids *1–4:* 795
Massawa, Ethiopia *6:* 29; *7:* 172
Massawomeke (tribe) *1–4:* 765
Matagorda Bay *1–4:* 518
Matavai Bay *1–4:* 258
Mato Grosso, Brazil *6:* 153–155, 158
Matoaka (Pocahontas) *1–4:* 764
Matterhorn *1–4:* 653
Matthew 1–4: 170
Mattingly, Thomas *1–4:* 32
Maud 1–4: 21
Maui, Hawaii *1–4:* 542
Mauna Loa *1–4:* 854
Maupertius, Pierre Moreau de *5:* 87 *5:* 87
Mauritius 1–4: 455; *5:* 130
Mauritius *1–4:* 127, 302, 363, 810
Mawson, Douglas *1–4:* 746; *7:* 163
Maya (tribe) *1–4:* 275; *5:* 1, 3; *7:* 113
Mayflower 6: 47
Maysville, Kentucky *1–4:* 121
Mbomu Rapids *1–4:* 581
McAuliffe, Christa *1–4:* 726; *6:* 125–133, 125 (ill.), 128 (ill.)
McAuliffe, Steve *6:* 127

McClintock, Francis *1–4:* 368, 602; *5:* 69; *7:* 143
McClure, Robert *1–4:* 368, 599–603, 640; *7:* 138
McDivitt, James *1–4:* 29
McGregor River *1–4:* 563
McMurdo Sound *1–4:* 19, 376, 377, 746
McNair, Ronald E. *6:* 129
Mecca, Saudi Arabia *1–4:* 75–77, 110, 151, 152, 290, 597; *6:* 35, 38–41, 138, 139, 139 (ill.), 141
Medal of Freedom *1–4:* 39, 286
Medina, Woolli *1–4:* 633
Medina, Saudi Arabia *1–4:* 75, 76, 152, 290, 597; *6:* 35, 40, 41, 103, 104
Mediterranean Sea *1–4:* 11, 67, 108, 282, 286, 408, 476, 591, 596, 735, 774, 786–787, 837; *6:* 23; *7:* 107, 210
Meknes *1–4:* 736
Mekong *1–4:* 706
Mekong River *1–4:* 393–395
Melbourne, Australia *1–4:* 19, 145, 148–149, 355, 362
Melchior, Simone *1–4:* 284
Melian, Francisco Núñez *7:* 84, 85
Melville Island *1–4:* 600, 639–640
Melville Peninsula *1–4:* 641
Melville Sound *1–4:* 601–602, 640
Memphis, Tennessee *1–4:* 516, 770
Mendaña, Alvaro de *1–4:* 126, 189
Mendez, Diego *1–4:* 253, 254
Mendoza, Antonio de *1–4:* 167, 176–177, 268, 270, 272–273, 280, 348–349
Menindee, Australia *1–4:* 145, 147–148
Merchant Adventurers *1–4:* 175
Mercury *1–4:* 481, 587–588, 850
Mercury 1–4: 31, 401
Mercury 5 1–4: 28

"Mercury Seven" *1–4:* 401, 404

Mercy Bay *1–4:* 602–603

Méré *1–4:* 582

Meru *1–4:* 3

Meryon, Charles *1–4:* 784–785, 787

Merz, Alfred *6:* 134

Mesa de Juan Díaz, Colombia *6:* 145

Mesawa *1–4:* 503

Messina, Sicily *1–4:* 97

Mestiza 1–4: 479

S.S. *Meteor 6:* 134–137, 135 (ill.)

Metternich, Clemens von *1–4:* 475

Metzenbaum, Howard *1–4:* 405

Mexico City, Mexico *1–4:* 167, 270, 272, 273, 541; *5:* 2; *6:* 188, 190, 191; *7:* 90

Miami, Florida *7:* 77

Michel, Jean-Louis *5:* 165

Michilimackinac *1–4:* 216, 496, 516; *6:* 98

Middle Ages *6:* 37, 110, 112, 138, 141; *7:* 27, 122, 124

Midjökull *1–4:* 342

Mikkelsen, Ejnar *5:* 146

Miletus *1–4:* 6

Military Intelligence Division (MID) *6:* 82

Mill, John Stuart *1–4:* 358

Minab River *1–4:* 10; *7:* 185

Minaret of Djam *6:* 186

Minas del Sapo, Brazil *6:* 144, 145

Mindanao Island *1–4:* 571

Minnetaree (tribe) *1–4:* 532, 534

Mir space station *5:* 109–114, 109 (ill.), 110 (ill.), 112 (ill.)

Mir/Shuttle rendezvous program *5:* 109

Mirabilia (Book of Marvels) 6: 110–112

Mirambo *1–4:* 790

Miranda *1–4:* 850

Mirnyi 1–4: 91–92

Miss Boyd Land *1–4:* 131

Mission San Gabriel *1–4:* 760

Mississippi River *1–4:* 165, 494, 496–497, 513–518, 529–530, 661–662, 767, 770, 823; *5:* 6, 104; *6:* 95, 98, 100, 161

Mississippi Valley *1–4:* 517

Missoula, Montana *1–4:* 620

Missouri (tribe) *1–4:* 531

Missouri River *1–4:* 483, 496, 516, 530–533, 535–536, 759, 823; *5:* 6–9, 106; *6:* 161, 164, 165, 167

Mitchell, Edgar *1–4:* 31

Míxton War *6:* 190

Mocha, Yemen *1–4:* 666

Mock, Geraldine *7:* 81

Moffat, Robert *1–4:* 544

Mogadishu, Somalia *1–4:* 223

Mohawk (tribe) *1–4:* 215, 225

Mohi, Hungary *1–4:* 184

Mojave (tribe) *1–4:* 621, 760

Mojave Desert *1–4:* 760; *7:* 194

Mojave River *1–4:* 760

Môle St. Nicolas, Haiti *1–4:* 245

Mollison, Jim *1–4:* 492, 493, 592

Moluccas (Spice Islands) *1–4:* 127, 174, 318, 457, 567, 570–571, 573, 733, 865; *6:* 179, 189; *7:* 156

Mombasa, Kenya *1–4:* 3, 113, 223, 289, 389, 504, 718, 828; *5:* 140, 141, 144

Möngkhe *1–4:* 184

Mongol Empire *1–4:* 688

Mongolia *1–4:* 704–705; *6:* 86

Mongolia and the Tangut Country 1–4: 706

Mongols *1–4:* 65–67, 77, 97, 183, 185, 576, 687, 691–693; *6:* 184

Moniz, Felipa Perestrello de *1–4:* 238

Montana *1–4:* 484, 533; *6:* 167, 168

Monte Pascoal (Mount Pascal) *7:* 39

Monterey, California *1–4:* 83, 510, 761, 834

Montevideo, Uruguay *1–4:* 296, 299

Boldface indicates main entries in Volume 7 and their page numbers; *1–4:* refers to entries in the four-volume base set; *5:* refers to entries in Volume 5; *6:* refers to entries in Volume 6; *7:* refers to entries in Volume 7; (ill.) following a page number refers to photos, drawings, and maps.

271 | Index

Montezuma *1–4:* 274–276, 278, 279
Montgomerie, Thomas George *1–4:* 751
Monticello *1–4:* 482
Montpelier, France *1–4:* 95
Montreal, Quebec, Canada *1–4:* 195, 226, 483–484, 497, 512–513, 516, 518; *6:* 65
Monts, Pierre de *1–4:* 214
Moore, John *1–4:* 784
Moors *1–4:* 241–242, 424; *6:* 27, 104
Morant Bay *1–4:* 357
Morel, Edmund *1–4:* 136
Morgan, Barbara *6:* 128–130, 128 (ill.)
Moriussaw, Greenland *1–4:* 432
Morocco *1–4:* 106, 287, 736, 763, 861; *6:* 102
Morovejo, Evaristo *1–4:* 100–101
Morozko, Luka *1–4:* 41
Morrow, Ann *1–4:* 541
Morton, William *7:* 141
Moscoso, Luis de *1–4:* 771
Moscow, Russia *1–4:* 184, 701, 703; *5:* 99, 100, 113, 114, 131, 134, 139; *6:* 83, 84, 86, 122, 124; *7:* 60, 64, 65, 133
Moshi (settlement) *7:* 215
Moskvitin, Ivan *5:* 133
Mossel Bay *1–4:* 312, 388
Mosul (Iraq) *5:* 128
Mount Aconcagua *1–4:* 99, 101, 654
Mount Albert *1–4:* 506
Mount Ararat *1–4:* 689; *7:* 210
Mount Blaxland *5:* 26
Mount Brown *1–4:* 361
Mount Cameroon *1–4:* 500; *7:* 111
Mount Chimborazo *1–4:* 480
Mount Cook *1–4:* 450; *7:* 189
Mount Desert Island *1–4:* 214
Mount Egmont *1–4:* 450; *7:* 188
Mount Elgon *1–4:* 828
Mount Erebus *1–4:* 746
Mount Etna *1–4:* 67

Mount Everest *1–4:* 450–451, 752; *5:* 116; *6:* 56, 76–79, 79 (ill.)
Mount Fuji *1–4:* 450
Mount Gardner *1–4:* 832
Mount Hagen *1–4:* 521–522
Mount Herschel *1–4:* 453
Mount Hood *1–4:* 833
Mount Hopeless *1–4:* 147
Mount Huascarán *1–4:* 653, 654
Mount Idinen *1–4:* 71
Mount Illampu *1–4:* 654
Mount Kakulima *7:* 111
Mount Kenya *1–4:* 3, 505, 827
Mount Kilimanjaro *1–4:* 505, 718–720, 827; *5:* 142; *7:* 215
Mount Koser Gunge *1–4:* 862
Mount McKinley *7:* 189
Mount Olympus *1–4:* 870
Mount Orizaba *1–4:* 654
Mount Palomar *1–4:* 465
Mount Rainier *1–4:* 833
Mount Roraima *6:* 172, 173
Mount Royal *1–4:* 195
Mount Ruapehu *1–4:* 449
Mount Shasta, California *1–4:* 620, 654
Mount Sinai *6:* 40
Mount St. Elias *5:* 23
Mount Tapuaenuku *1–4:* 450
Mount Taveta *1–4:* 827
Mount Weld *5:* 59
Mount Whitney *7:* 72
Mount William *1–4:* 506
Mount York *5:* 26
Mountain Green *1–4:* 620
Mountain men *1–4:* 758; *5:* 6, 10, 11
Mountains of the Moon *1–4:* 798
Mozambique *1–4:* 57–58, 137, 223, 388–389, 392, 505, 550, 865
Muddy Pass *1–4:* 372
Muhammad *6:* 40, 138
Muhammad Tughluql *1–4:* 78
Mukden, Manchuria *1–4:* 106
Mukut Parbat *1–4:* 450
Multan, India *1–4:* 11
Multan, Pakistan *1–4:* 78

Mundus Novus *1–4:* 841

Munster, Ireland *1–4:* 713

al-Muqaddasi, Muhammed ibn-Ahmad *6:* 138–141, 140 (ill.)

Murchison Falls *1–4:* 48

Murchison River *5:* 60

Murphy, Dervla *7:* 167–174, 167 (ill.), 171 (ill.)

Murray, Mungo *1–4:* 546

Muruj adh-Dhahab *1–4:* 595

Museum of Science and Industry *5:* 83

Muslims *1–4:* 389, 424; *6:* 38, 104, 111, 138, 139, 185, 186; *7:* 135, 136, 205, 209

Mussolini, Benito *1–4:* 22

Mustang Island *1–4:* 346

Mutis, José Celestino *1–4:* 479; *6:* 142–146, 142 (ill.), 143 (ill.)

Mweru, Lake *1–4:* 232

My Life with the Eskimo *5:* 148

My Second Journey Through Equatorial Africa *7:* 215

Mycenae, Greece *5:* 135, 138

Myrrh *5:* 40

Mystic Seaport, Connecticut *6:* 8

N

Nablus *1–4:* 597

Nachtigal, Gustav *1–4:* 737

Nafud Desert *1–4:* 110

Nagasaki, Japan *1–4:* 866

Nagchu *1–4:* 707

Nagchuka *1–4:* 729

Nain *1–4:* 754

Nairobi *5:* 91, 92, 95, 96

Najaf, Iraq *1–4:* 77

Najran, Saudi Arabia *1–4:* 384

Nalanda *1–4:* 462, 463; *6:* 108, 109

Nama (tribe) *7:* 5

Nambikwara (tribe) *6:* 154

Namibe, Angola *1–4:* 139

Nan Shan mountains *1–4:* 707; *5:* 55

Nanking, China *1–4:* 222–223; *5:* 57

Nansemond River *1–4:* 765

Nansen, Fridtjof *1–4:* 15, 18–19, 604–609, 645; *5:* 125

Naples, Italy *1–4:* 95

Napo River *1–4:* 627–629; *5:* 153

Napoléon Bonaparte *1–4:* 474, 528, 784–785

Napoleonic Wars *1–4:* 56, 365, 476, 482, 638, 831

Nares, George *1–4:* 209, 210; *5:* 74

Narragansett Bay *1–4:* 838

The Narrative of the Honourable John Byron *7:* 30

Narrative of the United States Exploring Expedition *1–4:* 854

Narváez, Pánfilo de *1–4:* 165, 176, 278, 346

NASA. *See* National Aeronautics and Space Administration (NASA)

NASA Space Flight Center *1–4:* 466

Nass River *1–4:* 622

Natchez (tribe) *1–4:* 516

Natchitoches, Louisiana *1–4:* 664

National Aeronautics and Space Administration (NASA) *1–4:* 26, 29, 31, 36, 39, 465–467, 660, 723–724, 726, 780, 847; *5:* 42, 46, 81, 82, 84, 109, 112–114; *6:* 125–128, 130, 133

National African Company *1–4:* 828

National Air and Space Museum *1–4:* 743, 845; *7:* **175–180,** 176 (ill.), 179 (ill.)

National Air and Space Museum Archives *7:* 177

National Air Museum *7:* 175

National Geographic Society *1–4:* 159, 377, 652; *5:* 66, 95, 115–119, 115 (ill.); *6:* 8, 59; *7:* 51, 93, 98, 99

National Geographic magazine
  5: 115, 117
National Indian Museum *6:* 159
National Mall *7:* 175, 177
National Science Foundation *7:* 48
National Service for the Protection of Indians *6:* 155
National Space Development Agency of Japan (NASDA) *5:* 82
Native American *1–4:* 470, 478, 495–496, 514, 516, 518, 527–528, 530, 532, 534–536; *5:* 11, 104, 106
The Native Tribes of Western Australia 7: 19
U.S.S. *Nautilus 1–4:* 610–613, 859
Navasota, Texas *1–4:* 518
Navidad, Mexico *1–4:* 177
Navigatio Sancti Brendani (The Voyage of Saint Brendan) 7: 24–26
Nduye, Zaire *1–4:* 4
Neah Bay *7:* 198
Nearchus *1–4:* 10–13; *7:* **181–187,** 183 (ill.)
Nearest the Pole: A Narrative of the Polar Expedition of the Peary Arctic Club 1–4: 652
Nebraska *6:* 168
Necho, King *1–4:* 435
Needles, California *1–4:* 621
A Negro at the North Pole 1–4: 432
Negros Island *1–4:* 571
Nehsi *6:* 92, 93
Nelson, Horatio *1–4:* 359
Nelson, Mark *6:* 15
Nelson River *1–4:* 229
Neptune *1–4:* 847, 849–850
Nerchinsk, Russia *6:* 124
Nestorians *1–4:* 65, 66; *6:* 111
Nestorius *1–4:* 66
Netsilik *1–4:* 16
Neva 1–4: 63; *7:* 55–58
Nevado Coropuna *1–4:* 99, 101
New Archangel, Alaska *1–4:* 64

New Caledonia *1–4:* 264; *5:* 38; *6:* 65
New England Institute for Medical Research *7:* 48
New France (Canada) *1–4:* 141, 212, 216–217, 225, 494, 496, 497, 512–513, 516; *6:* 95, 96, 148
New Granada (Colombia) *6:* 142, 143, 145
New Guinea: What I Did and What I Saw 7: 59
New Hanover *6:* 179; *7:* 156
New Hebrides *5:* 36, 37
New Holland *1–4:* 488, 812
New Ireland *1–4:* 127, 190; *6:* 179; *7:* 156
New London *5:* 70, 71
New London Company *1–4:* 763
New Sarai, Russia *1–4:* 77
New South Wales, Australia *1–4:* 359, 511, 643; *5:* 24–27; *7:* 16, 55, 57, 58, 101
New Spain (Mexico) *1–4:* 176, 280, 517; *6:* 142, 188
New World *6:* 42, 142, 145, 146
New York, New York *6:* 4, 8, 17, 21
New York Aquarium *7:* 45
New York Harbor *1–4:* 470, 837–838; *6:* 2
New York University *7:* 45–47
Newport Harbor *1–4:* 838
News From Tartary 5: 103
Newton, Isaac *1–4:* 465; *5:* 85, 88
Nez Percé (tribe) *1–4:* 534; *6:* 165
Ngounié River *1–4:* 322
Niagara Falls *6:* 96
Niagara River *1–4:* 142, 513–514; *6:* 96
Nicaragua *1–4:* 627, 767
Nichol, Mary. *See* Leakey, Mary
Nicholas II *1–4:* 420–421
Nicholas IV *1–4:* 68
Nicholls, Henry *1–4:* 55
Nicobar Islands *6:* 107

Nicollet, Jean *1–4:* 216, 217, 371; *6:* 147–152, 147 (ill.), 150 (ill.), 151 (ill.)

Niger 1–4: 53

Niger River *1–4:* 52, 54–55, 72, 416, 579, 632–636, 737, 828; *5:* 66; *6:* 35–38, 101, 103, 104; *7:* 7–12

Nihavend, Persia *6:* 183

Nikolayev, Andriyan *1–4:* 819, 820

Nikumaroro Atoll *1–4:* 335

Nile River *1–4:* 11, 45–47, 51, 76, 113–114, 150, 152–153, 155, 435, 502, 506, 551, 553, 578, 582–583, 591, 598, 721–722, 772, 774–777, 792, 798; *5:* 155, 156; *6:* 26–28, 30, 36, 37, 102; *7:* 118, 133–136

Niles, Blair 88, 88 (ill.)

Nimrod 1–4: 746–747

Niña 1–4: 243, 246, 247, 250, 487

Nioro, Mali *6:* 104

Nipissing (tribe) *6:* 148–150

Nixon, Richard M. *1–4:* 30, 38

Niza, Marcos de *1–4:* 268, 270–271, 348

Njoro, Kenya *1–4:* 590

Nobel Peace Prize *1–4:* 609; *6:* 159

Nobile, Umberto *1–4:* 22, 130, 337, 859

Noe, Lewis *1–4:* 789

Noel, Anne Isabella *1–4:* 107

Noga *1–4:* 814–815

Nombre de Dios, Panama *1–4:* 316

Nome, Alaska *1–4:* 18, 21, 701

Noonan, Frederick *1–4:* 334, 335; *7:* 77

Noort, Oliver van *1–4:* 458

Nootka Convention *1–4:* 831

Nootka Sound *1–4:* 833–834

Nordaustlandet *5:* 123

Nordenskiöld, Nils Adolf Erik *1–4:* 21, 418, 605, 645; *5:* 13, 120–125, 120 (ill.), 122 (ill.)

Nordenskjöld, Otto *5:* 29

H.M.S. *Norfolk 1–4:* 360; *7:* 200

Norfolk Island *1–4:* 360, 510

Norgay, Tenzing *1–4:* 451–452

Norge 1–4: 22, 337, 859

Normandy *1–4:* 512, 540

Noronha, Fernando de *1–4:* 58

Norsemen *1–4:* 524–527; *5:* 147

North Atlantic Ocean *5:* 28, 117, 161, 162; *6:* 42, 43, 47

North Cape *5:* 124

North Frisian Islands *1–4:* 711

North Holland *1–4:* 454

North Island (New Zealand) *1–4:* 259, 302, 327, 449, 811

North Magnetic Pole *1–4:* 15–16, 600, 642; *7:* 162, 163, 188–192, 194

North Pole *1–4:* 18, 21–22, 158–160, 428, 431–432, 606, 608, 610–612, 644, 647–652, 801, 803, 859; *5:* 16, 66, 68, 71, 85, 116, 117, 121, 123; *6:* 1–3; *7:* 140, 141, 143, 189

The North Pole: Its Discovery Under the Auspices of the Peary Arctic Club 1–4: 652

North West Company *1–4:* 561, 564, 619, 822–824; *6:* 64, 65, 67

North Saskatchewan River *1–4:* 823

North Sea *5:* 14, 51

Northeast Passage *1–4:* 21, 175, 469; *5:* 13, 14, 16–18, 120, 123, 124

Northern Sea Route *5:* 120

Northward over the "Great Ice" 1–4: 652

Northwest Passage *1–4:* 14, 16–17, 52, 56, 170, 173, 214, 217, 264–265, 280, 364, 368, 470, 472, 509, 599, 601, 603, 639–640, 642, 832, 834; *5:* 68, 70, 120; *7:* 31, 138, 159, 166

The Northwest Passage 1–4: 18

Nossob River *7:* 3

Nothing Venture, Nothing Win 1–4: 453

Boldface indicates main entries in Volume 7 and their page numbers; *1–4:* refers to entries in the four-volume base set; *5:* refers to entries in Volume 5; *6:* refers to entries in Volume 6; *7:* refers to entries in Volume 7; (ill.) following a page number refers to photos, drawings, and maps.

Nouveau voyage 6: 100
Nouvelle découverte 6: 100
Novaya Zemlya 5: 14–18
Novosibirsk 1–4: 701, 703
Ntem, West Africa 1–4: 323
Nubia region, Sudan 6: 37
Nubian Desert 6: 31
Nueva Andalucía 1–4: 625
Nuestra Señora de Atocha 7:
    83–89
Nullarbor Plain 1–4: 356; 7: 21
Nun Kun Range 1–4: 862
Núñez de Balboa, Vasco 1–4:
    253, 614–617, 625, 670
Nyangwe (Democratic Republic
    of the Congo) 1–4: 795; 7:
    213
Nyoros 1–4: 46, 51
Nyul-nyul (tribe) 7: 17

O

Oahu, Hawaii 6: 51, 55
Oakland, California 7: 77
Oakland International Airport 7:
    77, 81
Oaxaca, Mexico 1–4: 176
Ob River 5: 123
Oberon 1–4: 850
Ocean Everest 6: 56
Ocean of Storms 1–4: 30, 557
Ocean World 1–4: 285
Oceanic 6: 23
Oceanographic Museum of
    Monaco 1–4: 285
Oceanus Procellarum 1–4: 557
Odoric of Pordenone 1–4: 24, 576
Odysseus 5: 138
Office of Naval Research 7: 47,
    48
Ogden, Peter Skene 1–4:
    618–622
Ögedei 1–4: 184, 185
Oghuz Turks 5: 76
Ogooué River 1–4: 133–134,
    322, 500
Ohio River 1–4: 119, 496–497,
    513, 516, 530

Ojeda, Alonso de 1–4: 171, 249,
    615, 623–626, 670, 840; 7: 39,
    40
Okavango River 1–4: 139
Okhotsk, Siberia 1–4: 62–63; 5:
    20–22, 131, 133
Okinawa, Japan 1–4: 874
Olaf I (Norway) 1–4: 524
Old Jericho 6: 115, 118
Old Testament 6: 37, 114
Olduvai Gorge, Tanzania 5: 93,
    95, 117; 6: 58
Olenek River 7: 65
Olgas (monoliths) 7: 101, 102
    (ill.)
Ollantaitambo, Peru 1–4: 99
Olympias 1–4: 5–6
Olympic Games (1924) 5: 99
Olympic Games (1936) 1–4: 423
Omagua Indians 5: 89, 153
Omaha (tribe) 1–4: 531
Oman, John 7: 200
Omanum Emporium 5: 42, 43
On a Shoestring to Coorg: An
    Experience of Southern India
    7: 172
On the Ocean 1–4: 709
On the Shape of the World 1–4:
    415
Oneida (tribe) 1–4: 215
Onizuka, Ellison S. 6: 129
Onondaga (tribe) 1–4: 215
Onondaga, New York 1–4: 226
Ooldea, Australia 7: 21
Open polar sea 7: 140, 141
Operation Highjump 1–4: 163
Opium War 1–4: 544
Oracle, Arizona 6: 9
Oran 1–4: 737
Orangutan Foundation Interna-
    tional 7: 98
Orangutans 7: 92–99, 94 (ill.)
Orchomenus, Greece 5: 138
Order of Christ 1–4: 425; 7: 38
Ordos Desert 1–4: 705; 6: 71
Oregon River 1–4: 530
Oregon Trail 1–4: 372, 484, 485
Orellana, Francisco de 1–4:
    627–631; 5: 152

Organization of African Unity *5:* 83

The Origin of Species *1–4:* 304–305

Orinoco River *1–4:* 251, 476–479, 715–717; *6:* 173; *7:* 131

Orkney Islands *1–4:* 711

Ormuz, Persia *6:* 70, 75, 111

Ormuz Island *7:* 186

Oromo *1–4:* 503

Orteig Prize *1–4:* 539

Ortiz, Juan *1–4:* 770

Osage (tribe) *1–4:* 662

Oscar (of Sweden and Norway) *1–4:* 608

Oscar II (of Sweden) *1–4:* 419; *5:* 123

Oslo, Norway *1–4:* 16, 19

Oswell, William Colton *1–4:* 546–548

Oto (tribe) *1–4:* 531

Ottawa (tribe) *1–4:* 226–227

Ottawa River *1–4:* 142, 195, 216; *6:* 148

Ottoman Empire *1–4:* 44, 49; *6:* 70

Otumba *1–4:* 279

Ouango *1–4:* 581

Oudry, Brigitte *7:* 197

Ouessant Island *1–4:* 710

Ouezzane *1–4:* 736

Ovando, Nicolás de *1–4:* 252–254

Overland Telegraph Line *7:* 100, 101

Overweg, Adolf *1–4:* 70, 72

Ovimbundu *1–4:* 58

Oxford University *6:* 31, 32, 47, 89, 115, 187

Oxus River *1–4:* 416

Oyster Bay, New York *6:* 3

Ozark Mountains *1–4:* 770

P

Pacific Ocean *1–4:* 28, 39, 210, 408, 472, 511, 529–530, 535; *5:* 4, 13, 19–21, 62–64, 104, 124, 131–133; *6:* 51, 64–67, 84, 121, 161, 165, 167, 178, 188; *7:* 29, 32, 47, 52, 60, 62, 80, 114, 115, 117, 155, 199, 201

Padilla, Juan de *1–4:* 271

Paez, Pedro *6:* 30

Pai River *1–4:* 394

Paiva, Afonso de *1–4:* 288, 290

Pakistan *1–4:* 462, 808

Palau *1–4:* 318, 573

Palembang, Sumatra *6:* 107, 109

Palermo, Sicily *1–4:* 417; *7:* 123

Palmer, Nathaniel *1–4:* 91–92

Palmer Archipelago *5:* 31, 32

Palmer Peninsula *1–4:* 93, 748

Palmyra, Syria *1–4:* 87, 109, 385, 597, 786; *6:* 37

Palo de vaca *1–4:* 477

Palos de la Frontera, Spain *1–4:* 240, 243

Pamir Mountains *1–4:* 419, 420, 807–808; *5:* 56

Pamir Plateau *1–4:* 690

Pamlico Sound *1–4:* 837

Panama *1–4:* 253, 627, 670–671; *5:* 36, 51, 87, 130

Panama City, Panama *5:* 87

Panchen Lama *1–4:* 308, 753

Pánuco, Mexico *1–4:* 165, 166

Pangu La Pass, Tibet *6:* 79

Papakonstantinou, Ilias. *See* Konstantinou, Ilias

Papua *1–4:* 520–523

Papua (tribe) *1–4:* 520

Papua New Guinea *5:* 37

Pará, Brazil *5:* 89, 151–154

Paraguay *6:* 154

Paraguay River *1–4:* 164, 168

Paraná River *1–4:* 168, 174

Parc National des Virungas *6:* 59

Parc National des Volcans *6:* 61

Paria Peninsula *1–4:* 842

Parintin (tribe) *6:* 155

Paris, France *1–4:* 67, 482, 511–512, 539–540

Park, Mungo *1–4:* 55, 632–637; *6:* 35, 104, 104 (ill.); *7:* 10

Parmenion *1–4:* 7, 9

Boldface indicates main entries in Volume 7 and their page numbers; *1–4:* refers to entries in the four-volume base set; *5:* refers to entries in Volume 5; *6:* refers to entries in Volume 6; *7:* refers to entries in Volume 7; (ill.) following a page number refers to photos, drawings, and maps.

277 | Index

Parry, (William) Edward *1–4:* 56, 600–601, 638–643

Parry Channel *1–4:* 17

Parry Islands *1–4:* 639

Parsnip River *1–4:* 563

Pasha, Emin *1–4:* 580, 796; *7:* 135, 137, 137 (ill.)

Pasha 1–4: 316

The Passing of the Aborigines 7: 22

Pastaza River *1–4:* 413

Patagonia *1–4:* 296, 299–300, 568; *6:* 178; *7:* 30, 32, 154

Patani *1–4:* 666

Patapsco *1–4:* 765

Patapsco River *1–4:* 764

Patna, India *6:* 74

Patrick, Saint *7:* 23

Patuxent River *1–4:* 765

Paul E. Garber Preservation, Restoration and Storage Facility *7:* 179

Paulet Island *1–4:* 748

Pawnee (tribe) *1–4:* 82, 759

Pawtucket *1–4:* 838

Peace Corps *5:* 81

Peace River *1–4:* 563

Peake telegraph station *7:* 105

Pearl Islands *1–4:* 616

Pearl River *1–4:* 866

Peary, Josephine *1–4:* 429, 646

Peary, Robert Edwin *1–4:* 18, 158, 428–432, 644–652, 654, 800, 802; *5:* 116, 117; *6:* 1–3, 6, 8; *7:* 143

Peary Arctic Club *1–4:* 647

Peary Channel *1–4:* 645

Peary Land *1–4:* 645

"Peary system" *6:* 1, 6

Peck, Annie Smith *1–4:* 653–656, 862

Pecos River *1–4:* 272

Pedro II (Brazil) *6:* 154

Peel Sound *1–4:* 368

Peel Strait *1–4:* 16

Peking (Beijing, China) *5:* 91, 98, 101; *6:* 71

Peking Man *5:* 91

Peloponnesian War *1–4:* 434

Peregrinaçïo 1–4: 665

Pereira, Gonçalo *1–4:* 59

"Periplus of Hannon" *7:* 108

Perowne, Stewart *6:* 186

Persepolis, Persia *1–4:* 8, 595

Persia (Iran) *1–4:* 5–6, 8, 65–67, 77–78, 97, 105, 184, 219, 433, 690, 808; *5:* 40, 45, 75, 128; *6:* 70, 75, 86, 111, 139, 181–183

Persian Gulf *1–4:* 10–12, 110, 289, 434; *6:* 56, 70, 75, 86, 184; *7:* 121, 183, 185, 186

Persian Pictures, A Book of Travels 1–4: 87

Persian Wars *7:* 181

Perth, Australia *1–4:* 403; *5:* 58–60; *7:* 17, 20, 21, 100, 104, 105, 197

Peshawar, Pakistan *1–4:* 219, 462; *5:* 56

Petchenegs (tribe) *5:* 77

Peter I *1–4:* 42

Peter I Island *1–4:* 92, 859

Peter the Great *5:* 19, 20

Petermann Island *5:* 32

Petermann Mountain Ranges *7:* 102

Petherick, John *1–4:* 45–46, 776

Petra, Jordan *1–4:* 385; *6:* 37

Petropavlovsk, Russia *5:* 22, 23

Petropavlovsk-Kamchatski *1–4:* 510

Petropolis, Brazil *5:* 127

Pfeiffer, Ida *5:* 126–130, 126 (ill.), 127 (ill.)

Philadelphia Academy of Natural Sciences *1–4:* 322

Philip I (of Spain) *1–4:* 173

Philip II (of Macedonia) *1–4:* 5–6; *7:* 181

Philip II (of Spain) *1–4:* 317, 319, 570; *5:* 150; *6:* 188, 191

Philip IV (of France) *1–4:* 67

Philippines *1–4:* 3, 570, 742, 809; *6:* 188, 191–193

Phillip, Arthur, 511

Phobos *1–4:* 587

Phoenix 1–4: 63

Piacenza *1–4:* 689

Piccard, Auguste *1–4:* 657–660; *6:* 53

Piccard, Jacques *1–4:* 657–660

Piccard, Jean *1–4:* 657

Pichincha *1–4:* 480

Piegan (tribe) *1–4:* 822–824

Pierre, South Dakota *1–4:* 532

Pike, Zebulon *1–4:* 661–664

Pikes Peak *1–4:* 663

Pillars of Hercules *1–4:* 710

Pim, Bedford *1–4:* 603

Pindar *1–4:* 6

Piner's Bay *1–4:* 853

Pinta 1–4: 243–246, 487

Pinto, Fernïo Mendes *1–4:* 665–668

Pinzón, Martín Alonso *1–4:* 245

Pinzón, Vicente Yáñez *7:* 40

The Pirate Prince: Discovering the Priceless Treasure of the Sunken Ship Whydah 5: 51

Pirates *5:* 47, 50, 52

Pir-Sar *1–4:* 9

Pirthiganj, India *5:* 65

Pisa, Italy *1–4:* 95

Pisania *1–4:* 633, 635, 636

Pitcairn Island *1–4:* 188, 189

Pitt, William *1–4:* 784, 835

Pittsburgh, Pennsylvania *6:* 19, 20

Pittsburgh *Dispatch 6:* 19

Pizarro, Atahualpa *1–4:* 671

Pizarro, Francisco *1–4:* 99, 481, 615–617, 625, 627–629, 669–673, 767–768; *5:* 4; *7:* 126

Pizarro, Hernando *1–4:* 673

A Place Apart 7: 173

Plateau of Manz *7:* 172

Plateau of Tibet *1–4:* 421

Platte River *1–4:* 485, 531, 759

Pleiad 7: 8, 9

Pluto *1–4:* 850–851

Pnompenh, Cambodia *1–4:* 395

Po Me, Tibet *7:* 148

Pocahontas *1–4:* 762, 764

Pocatello, Idaho *1–4:* 620

Pocock, Edward *1–4:* 794

Pocock, Frank *1–4:* 794–795

Podang, India *1–4:* 309

Point Arena, California *1–4:* 178

Point Barrow, Alaska *1–4:* 18, 22, 266, 600, 612, 703, 801, 857–858; *5:* 147

Point Conception, California *1–4:* 177

Point Loma Head *1–4:* 178

Poland *1–4:* 492

Polar Dream 7: 192, 196

Polar Star 1–4: 339

Polaris 5: 71–74

Polo, Maffeo *1–4:* 687–688

Polo, Marco *1–4:* 65, 184, 687–694, 706

Polo, Niccolò *1–4:* 687–688

Polybias *1–4:* 709

Polynesia *1–4:* 92, 327, 732; *6:* 178

Pompey's Rock *1–4:* 536; *6:* 167

Ponce de León, Juan *1–4:* 695–698, 768

Pond, Peter *1–4:* 561

Pontianak, Borneo *5:* 129

Popocatépetl *1–4:* 278

Popov, Fyodor Alekseyev *7:* 62

Popovich, Pavel *1–4:* 819

A Popular Flora of Denver, Colorado 7: 71

Porpoise 1–4: 329, 363

Port Angeles, Washington *7:* 198, 202, 203

Port Augusta, Australia *1–4:* 361; *7:* 100, 103

Port Desire *1–4:* 299; *6:* 178; *7:* 32

Port Said *6:* 23

Port Sudan *1–4:* 4

Port Suez, Egypt *1–4:* 152

Portland, Oregon *1–4:* 761; *6:* 66, 168

Portneuf River *1–4:* 620

Pôrto Seguro *7:* 39

Portobelo, Panama *1–4:* 317

Porus (of India) *1–4:* 9

Post, Wiley *1–4:* 699–703

Potala *1–4:* 309, 575–576, 753

Potala palace *6:* 71, 73

Potawotomi (tribe) *1–4:* 513

Potomac River *1–4:* 764

Boldface indicates main entries in Volume 7 and their page numbers; *1–4:* refers to entries in the four-volume base set; *5:* refers to entries in Volume 5; *6:* refers to entries in Volume 6; *7:* refers to entries in Volume 7; (ill.) following a page number refers to photos, drawings, and maps.

279 | Index

Pourquoi-Pas? *5:* 31–33

Powell River *1–4:* 118

Powhatan (tribe) *1–4:* 764

Poyarkov, Vasily Danilovich *5:* 131–134, 132 (ill.); *6:* 121

Poytner, Jane Elizabeth *6:* 15

Pratt & Whitney *7:* 79–81

Press On: Further Adventures of the Good Life 1–4: 874

Prester John *1–4:* 287–290, 425

Priam's Treasure *5:* 137–139

Price, W. Salter *1–4:* 116

Prince Edward Island *1–4:* 194, 265

Prince of Wales Strait *1–4:* 601

Prince of Wales Sound *7:* 165

Prince Regent Inlet *1–4:* 642

Prince William Sound *1–4:* 62, 63; *6:* 56

Princess Martha Coast *1–4:* 91

Principles of Geology 1–4: 294

Project Mohole *1–4:* 406

Project Vanguard *1–4:* 352, 353

Prudhoe Bay *7:* 159

Prussian Geographical Society *1–4:* 74

Przewalski's horse *1–4:* 707

Przhevalsky, Nikolay *1–4:* 418–419, 704–708

Ptolemy *1–4:* 798; *5:* 42, 43; *7:* 124, 124 (ill.)

Pueblo (tribe) *1–4:* 347

Pueblo, Colorado *1–4:* 83, 663

Puerto de los Reyes, Paraguay *1–4:* 168

Puget, Peter *1–4:* 835

Puget Sound *1–4:* 832

Pulitzer, Joseph *6:* 21, 22

Pundit-explorers *6:* 76; *7:* 45–49

Pundits *1–4:* 751–753

Punjab, India *1–4:* 462, 754

Punjab Plains *5:* 56

Punta Alta, Argentina *1–4:* 297

Puquiura, Peru *1–4:* 100

Purari River *1–4:* 520

Pushkin Museum *5:* 139

Putnam, George Palmer *1–4:* 332

Pygmies *1–4:* 1, 4, 321, 324, 797

Pyrenees Mountains *1–4:* 872

Pytheas *1–4:* 709–711

Q

Qagssiarssuk, Greenland *1–4:* 343

Quapaw *1–4:* 497

Quebec City, Quebec *1–4:* 195, 215, 494; *7:* 30

Quebrabasa Falls *1–4:* 549

Quebrabasa Rapids *1–4:* 550

Queen Charlotte Islands *1–4:* 834

Queen Charlotte Sound *1–4:* 259, 263–264, 833

Queen Maud Gulf *1–4:* 17

"Queen of the Air," *1–4:* 492

Queensland, Australia *1–4:* 360, 520, 523

Quelimane, Mozambique *1–4:* 140, 232, 550; *7:* 213

Quesada, Gonzalo Jimenez de *1–4:* 479

Quetzalcoatl *1–4:* 276, 278

Qui Nhon, Vietnam *1–4:* 222

Quindio Pass *1–4:* 480

Quiros, Pedro Fernandez de *1–4:* 125

Quito, Ecuador *1–4:* 410, 479–480, 628; *5:* 4, 5, 85, 87–89, 152, 153

Quixote, Don *7:* 131, 168

Qumis *1–4:* 596

R

Ra 7: 118–120

Ra II 7: 120

Rabai *1–4:* 721, 828

Rabbai Mpia *1–4:* 504–506

Radcliffe-Brown, Alfred Reginald *7:* 21

Radisson, Pierre Esprit *1–4:* 225–230

Rae, John *1–4:* 368

Raleigh, Walter *1–4:* 712–717

Ram, Hari *1–4:* 752

Ramotobi *1–4:* 546

Ramsay, William *1–4:* 88

Ramses II *5:* 157; *6:* 37, 38

Ramu *1–4:* 520

Ranavola, Queen *5:* 130

Rangpur, Bangladesh *1–4:* 575

Rappahannock River *1–4:* 764, 765

Ras Michael of Tigre *6:* 29, 30

Reagan, Ronald *6:* 125, 127, 132

Rebmann, Johannes *1–4:* 113, 504–505, 718–722

Recife, Brazil *1–4:* 174

Red River *1–4:* 396, 398, 662–663; *6:* 67

Red Sea *1–4:* 4, 13, 76, 285, 290, 384, 503, 580, 583, 584, 666, 773; *5:* 86, 156; *6:* 23, 29, 39, 40, 92, 139, 184; *7:* 47, 49, 51, 186

Reflections of Eden: My Years with the Orangutans of Borneo *7:* 97, 99

Reisen in Afrika 1875–86 (Travels in Africa 1875–86) *7:* 137

Rejaf, Sudan *5:* 158

Reliance *1–4:* 360

Repulse Bay *1–4:* 640

Research Institute for the Exploration of the Sea (IFREMER) *5:* 165, 168

Resolute Bay *7:* 190, 191

Resolution *1–4:* 261–264, 266, 830

Resolution Island *1–4:* 472

Resource Analysts *7:* 88

Restello, Portugal *1–4:* 392

Return Reef *1–4:* 367

Revillagigedo Island *1–4:* 834

Revolt in the Desert *1–4:* 87

Reyer, Ida. *See* Pfeiffer, Ida

Reynier Pauw *1–4:* 454

Rhages, Iran *1–4:* 8

Rhea *1–4:* 849

Rhine River *1–4:* 475

Rhodes, Cecil *1–4:* 828

Rhodes, Greece *1–4:* 289

Richardson, James *1–4:* 70, 72

Richelieu, Cardinal de *1–4:* 217

Richelieu River *1–4:* 215

Ride, Sally *1–4:* 723–726

The Rifle and Hound in Ceylon *1–4:* 44

The Right Stuff *1–4:* 874

Rihla *1–4:* 80

Rijnhart, Petrus *1–4:* 727–730

Rijnhart, Susie Carson *1–4:* 420, 727–730

Rijp, Jan Cornelizoon *5:* 16, 17

Rincon, New Mexico *1–4:* 167

Rio Branco River *6:* 173

Rio Colorado *1–4:* 298

Rio Conejos *1–4:* 663

Rio de Janeiro, Brazil *1–4:* 59, 91, 93, 123, 296, 568, 841; *5:* 127; *6:* 153–155, 159; *7:* 31, 39

Río de la Plata *1–4:* 167, 172, 174, 568, 841

Río de Oro *1–4:* 426; *7:* 109

Rio dos Bons Sinais *1–4:* 388

Rio Grande *1–4:* 167, 272, 347, 348, 517, 663

Rio Grande Valley *1–4:* 271

Rio Negro River *1–4:* 478, 630; *5:* 152; *6:* 173; *7:* 193

Rio Nunez *1–4:* 180, 181

Rio Plata *1–4:* 298

Rio Santa Cruz *1–4:* 299

Riobamba, Ecuador *1–4:* 411

Ripon Falls *1–4:* 776

Ritter, Karl *1–4:* 70

River Forth *5:* 51

River of Doubt *6:* 153, 155, 156, 158

Riyadh, Saudi Arabia *1–4:* 88

R.M.S Titanic, Inc. *5:* 168, 169

Roanoke Island *1–4:* 714

Roberval, Jean-François de La Rocque, Sieur de *1–4:* 196

Robinson, John *1–4:* 662–663

Robinson Crusoe *1–4:* 359

Rock of Aronos, Pakistan *1–4:* 808

Rockefeller, John D. *1–4:* 160

Rocky Mountain Fur Company *1–4:* 761; *5:* 6, 8

Rocky Mountains *1–4:* 51, 104, 373, 484–485, 529–530, 663,

Boldface indicates main entries in Volume 7 and their page numbers; *1–4:* refers to entries in the four-volume base set; *5:* refers to entries in Volume 5; *6:* refers to entries in Volume 6; *7:* refers to entries in Volume 7; (ill.) following a page number refers to photos, drawings, and maps.

281 | Index

758–759, 821, 823–824; *5:* 8, 10; *6:* 64, 65, 161, 162, 165, 166; *7:* 68, 70, 75

Roger II (of Sicily) *7:* 123

Rogers, Will *1–4:* 703

Roggeveen, Jacob *1–4:* 731–734; *7:* 34

Rogue River *1–4:* 178

Rohlfs, Friedrich Gerhard *1–4:* 735–738

Rolfe, John *1–4:* 764

Roman Christianity *7:* 205, 209

Rome, Italy *1–4:* 95; *6:* 71, 74, 75, 95, 100, 186

Rome on the Euphrates 6: 186

Rondón, Cândido *6:* 153–159, 157 (ill.)

Roosa, Stuart *1–4:* 31

Roosevelt, Eleanor *1–4:* 333

Roosevelt, Franklin D. *1–4:* 542

Roosevelt, Theodore *6:* 2, 3, 153, 156, 156 (ill.), 158

Roosevelt River *6:* 153

Roosevelt-Rondón Scientific Expedition *6:* 156, 158

Roosevelt 1–4: 430–431

Ros Sharsba *6:* 118

Rosas, Juan Manuel *1–4:* 298

Rose, Louise *1–4:* 452

Ross, Alexander *1–4:* 759

Ross, James Clark *1–4:* 16, 56, 328, 368, 600, 642; *7:* 138, 163

Ross, John *1–4:* 368, 639

Ross Ice Barrier *1–4:* 160

Ross Ice Shelf *1–4:* 19, 20, 452, 746

Ross Island *1–4:* 746

Ross Sea *1–4:* 339, 747

Rousseau, Jean-Jacques *1–4:* 127

Rowley, Henry *1–4:* 231

Royal Academy of Science *5:* 87

Royal Asiatic Society *6:* 184

Royal Botanical Gardens *1–4:* 54, 363; *6:* 142

Royal Geographical Society *1–4:* 48, 55, 60, 105, 112, 114–115, 138, 152–153, 156, 231, 235, 237, 303, 324, 546, 550–552, 637, 652, 747, 750, 754, 756, 775–776, 789, 792, 826–828, 859, 863; *5:* 103, 144; *6:* 169, 170, 173, 184; *7:* 4, 10, 105

Royal Gorge *1–4:* 663

Royal Navy *7:* 8, 29, 30, 34, 35, 200

Royal Society *1–4:* 52–54, 209, 256–257, 305, 360, 366, 575, 601, 638

Royal Society of London for Improving Natural Knowledge *6:* 33

Rozier, Pilatre de *5:* 66

Rozinante (bicycle) *7:* 168

Rub al Khali (Empty Quarter) *5:* 42, 43

Ruiz, Bartolomé *1–4:* 671

Ruiz, Hipólito *1–4:* 476

Rum Cay, Bahama Islands *1–4:* 245

Rupununi River *6:* 170

Rus (Vikings) *5:* 77

Russell, Israel C. *5:* 116

Russian America *1–4:* 61, 63

Russian Empire *5:* 19, 121

Russian Mission Control Center *5:* 114

Russian Revolution *1–4:* 857; *5:* 99

Russo-Turkish War *1–4:* 93

Rustichello *1–4:* 694

Rutan, Burt *1–4:* 739

Rutan, Dick *1–4:* 739–743

Ruvuma River *1–4:* 551, 826

Ruwenzori Range *1–4:* 798

Ruzizi River *1–4:* 155, 553, 774, 792

Ryukyu Islands *1–4:* 223, 667

S

Sabians *1–4:* 597

Sabos (of the Bedouins) *1–4:* 384

Sacagawea *1–4:* 532–536; *6:* 161–168, 161 (ill.), 164 (ill.)

Sacagawea Peak *6:* 168

Safi, Morocco *7:* 118, 120

Sagres, Portugal *1–4:* 425

Saguenay River *1–4:* 195, 213

Sahara Desert *1–4:* 69–71, 79,
    416, 435, 455, 861; *5:* 155,
    159; *7:* 8–10, 108, 194

Saigon, Vietnam *1–4:* 105, 394,
    398

Saint Brendan. *See* Brendan,
    Saint

Saint Columba. *See* Columba,
    Saint

Saint Croix River *1–4:* 214

Saint Elias Mountains *1–4:* 510

Saint Elmo's fire *1–4:* 296

Saint Helena Bay *1–4:* 388

Saint-Malo, France *1–4:* 127

Saint Patrick. *See* Patrick, Saint

Sakhalin *1–4:* 510

Sakhalin Island *5:* 133

Salapunco, Peru *1–4:* 99

Salcado, Felipe de *6:* 192

Samana Cay, Bahama Islands
    1–4: 245

Samaná Bay *1–4:* 246

Samar Island *1–4:* 570; *6:* 191

Samaria, England *6:* 115

Samaritans *1–4:* 97

Samarkand, Uzbekistan *1–4:* 78,
    461; *5:* 101

Samudra, Sumatra *1–4:* 79

Samuel P. Langley IMAX The-
    ater *7:* 177

San Antonio 1–4: 567, 569

San Antonio, Texas *1–4:* 166,
    539; *7:* 78

San Antonio Bay *1–4:* 347

San Bernardino, California *1–4:*
    621

San Diego, California *1–4:* 539,
    760; *6:* 12, 55; *7:* 197, 198,
    202

San Diego Bay *1–4:* 177

San Diego Harbor *1–4:* 178

San Domingo, Cuba *1–4:* 319

San Fernando de Apuré *1–4:*
    478

San Francisco, California *1–4:*
    104; *5:* 63, 130; *6:* 24, 57; *7:*
    66, 70, 73, 75

San Francisco Bay *1–4:* 832,
    834

San Germain, Puerto Rico *1–4:*
    696

San Gerónimo, Mexico *1–4:* 270

San'a, Yemen *1–4:* 597

San Joaquin Valley *1–4:* 372,
    621, 760

San Jose, Trinidad *1–4:* 715

San Juan, Puerto Rico *1–4:* 671,
    696, 698

San Kuri *1–4:* 3

San Lucas 6: 192

San Luis Rey *1–4:* 537

San Miguel, California *1–4:* 83,
    672; *6:* 191

San Miguel Island *1–4:* 177

San Pedro 6: 192

San Salvador, Bahama Islands
    1–4: 176, 245, 696

San Sebastián *1–4:* 615

San Tomás *1–4:* 717

Sancti Spiritus, Argentina *1–4:*
    174

Sandwich Islands *1–4:* 510

Sandy Hook *1–4:* 470

Sangha (monks) *5:* 56

Sangre de Cristo Mountains *1–4:*
    373, 663

Sanlúcar de Barrameda *1–4:*
    568, 573

Sansanding *1–4:* 634, 636

Sanskrit *1–4:* 462–463; *6:*
    107–109, 107 (ill.)

Santa Barbara Channel *1–4:* 177

Santa Catalina Island *1–4:* 177

Santa Catalina Mountains *6:* 9

Santa Cruz *1–4:* 511, 697

Santa Cruz Islands *1–4:* 189

Santa Fe, Argentina *1–4:* 299

Santa Fe, New Mexico *1–4:*
    662–664, 761

Santa Fé de Bogotá, Colombia *7:*
    130, 131

Santa Fe Trail *1–4:* 83

Santa Margarita 7: 84

Santa Maria 1–4: 243, 245–246, 248

Santa Maria de la Antigua del Darién *1–4:* 615

Santa Maria Island *1–4:* 246

Santa Marta, Colombia *7:* 127, 128, 130, 131

Santangel, Luis de *1–4:* 242

Santiago 1–4: 567, 569

Santiago, Chile *7:* 29

Santiago, Cuba *1–4:* 275

Santiago Island *1–4:* 572

Santo Domingo, Dominican Republic *1–4:* 165, 249, 251–254, 274, 615, 625, 696, 840; *6:* 174

Santos, Brazil *1–4:* 157

Sao Gabriel 1–4: 387, 390

Sâo Jorge da Mina, Benin *1–4:* 239

São Luís do Maranhão, Brazil *5:* 150, 151, 154

São Paulo, Brazil *6:* 155, 158

Sao Rafael 1–4: 387, 390

Sao Tiago *1–4:* 294

Sarasota, Florida *7:* 47–49

Sarawak, Borneo *5:* 129

Sargasso Sea *1–4:* 244; *7:* 26

Saskatchewan, Canada *1–4:* 561, 822–823; *5:* 63

Sasquatch *1–4:* 453

Saturn *1–4:* 464, 467, 847, 849–850

Saturn 1–4: 37

Saturn V 1–4: 27

Sault Ste. Marie, Michigan *5:* 105; *6:* 151

Savannah River *1–4:* 769

Savitskaya, Svetlana *1–4:* 723

Sawyer, Herbert *1–4:* 105

Say, Nigeria *1–4:* 72

Scandinavia *5:* 65, 76, 127

Schaller, George B. *6:* 58, 59, 61

Schariar *6:* 185

Scheherezade *6:* 185

Schenectady, New York *1–4:* 225

Schiller, Friedrich *1–4:* 475

Schirra, Walter "Wally" *1–4:* 28

Schliemann, Heinrich *5:* 135–139, 135 (ill.), 136 (ill.)

Schmitt, Harrison *1–4:* 32

Schoedsack, Ernest *6:* 86, 88

Schomburgk, Robert Hermann *6:* 169–174, 169 (ill.), 171 (ill.)

Schomburgk Line *6:* 173

School of Mines *1–4:* 475

Schouten, Jan *6:* 176, 178; *7:* 154, 156

Schouten, Willem Corneliszoon *6:* 175–179, 177 (ill.); *7:* 152–157

Schumacher, Raoul *1–4:* 593

Schurke, Paul *1–4:* 801

Schweickart, Russell *1–4:* 29

Schweinfurth, Gerog *1–4:* 4

Schweitzer, Albert *1–4:* 134

Scillus *1–4:* 870

Scobee, Francis R. (Dick) *6:* 129, 131

Scoresby, William *1–4:* 56

Scoresby Sound *5:* 33

Scotland *1–4:* 484, 493, 525, 711; *5:* 51

Scott, David *1–4:* 29, 31, 36

Scott, Robert Falcon *1–4:* 19, 21, 453, 744

Scott, Walter *1–4:* 635

Scott Base *1–4:* 452, 453

Scottish Geographical Society *1–4:* 745

Scripps Institute of Oceanography *7:* 46

SCUBA *6:* 49, 53

Scurvy *5:* 22, 23

Scylax of Caryanda *1–4:* 434–435

Sea of Crises *1–4:* 557

Sea of Galilee *6:* 114

Sea of Japan *1–4:* 510

Sea of Marmara *1–4:* 6

Sea of Okhotsk *1–4:* 510, 701; *5:* 20, 131, 133

Sea of Plenty *1–4:* 558

Sea of Tranquility *1–4:* 37

Seal Nunataks *1–4:* 803

Sealab *1–4:* 286

Seaman, Robert L. *6:* 24

Seattle, Washington *1–4:* 18, 857; *7:* 74, 198, 200, 203

Sebituane *1–4:* 547

Second Kamchatka Expedition *5:* 21

Second U.S. Grinnell Expedition *7:* 140

Sedgwick, Adam *1–4:* 293

Ségou *1–4:* 579, 634

Seine River *1–4:* 540

Seistan *1–4:* 596

Sekelutu *1–4:* 548–550

Seleucia-Ctesiphon, Iraq *1–4:* 220

Seminole (tribe) *1–4:* 83

Seneca (tribe) *1–4:* 142, 215, 513

Senegal River *1–4:* 426; *7:* 109

Sennar, Sudan *6:* 31

Seoul, Korea *5:* 62

Serengeti Plain *5:* 95

Serpa Pinto, Alexandre Alberto da Rocha de *1–4:* 138

Sesheke *1–4:* 547

Sesostris II *6:* 92

Setúbal *1–4:* 666

Seuthe *1–4:* 870

Seven Cities of Cíbola *1–4:* 164, 167, 270, 281, 345, 348, 349, 768; *5:* 5

Seven Pillars of Wisdom 1–4: 87

Seven Years' War *1–4:* 187, 255, 410, 508

Seville, Spain *1–4:* 254; *6:* 190

Shackleton, Ernest *1–4:* 20, 375, 744–749, 857

Shackleton Base *1–4:* 376, 452

Shackleton Ice Shelf *1–4:* 854

Shanapur, India *1–4:* 231

Shang-ch'uan Island *1–4:* 866

Shang-tu *1–4:* 691

Shanghai, China *1–4:* 397, 399, 692, 728; *6:* 23

Shantung Peninsula *5:* 57

Sharks *7:* 44–51

Shaw, T. E. *1–4:* 87

Shawnee (tribe) *1–4:* 118, 120

Sheffield University *1–4:* 489

Sheldon, May French *5:* 140–144, 140 (ill.), 141 (ill.)

Shelekhov, Gregory *1–4:* 62

Shendi, Sudan *6:* 38, 39

Shensi *1–4:* 692

Shepard, Alan *1–4:* 31, 402; *6:* 126

Shepard, Sam *1–4:* 874

Sherpa *1–4:* 451, 453

Shetland Islands *7:* 24

Shewa, Ethiopia *1–4:* 290, 503

Shi'ite Muslims *1–4:* 77, 88

Shigatse, Tibet *1–4:* 421; *6:* 78

Shipton, Eric *1–4:* 450

Shiraz, Iran *1–4:* 77; *6:* 139

Shire River *1–4:* 550

Shoemaker-Levy 9 *1–4:* 468

Shoshone (tribe) *1–4:* 532–534; *6:* 162, 165, 166

Shuga Mountains *6:* 71

Shuttle Imaging Radar (SIR) *5:* 25, 42, 68–70, 74, 85

Siam *1–4:* 812

Sian *1–4:* 461, 463, 692

Sicily, Italy *1–4:* 67, 95, 434, 710

Sidayu *1–4:* 457

Siddhartha Gautama *1–4:* 307; *5:* 56

Siebe, Augustus *6:* 52

Sierra de Quareca *1–4:* 616

Sierra Leone *1–4:* 387, 426; *5:* 58, 81; *6:* 176

Sierra Nevada *1–4:* 83, 372–373, 621, 760

Sierra Nevada de Santa Marta Mountains *7:* 127

Siesta Key, Florida *7:* 48

Sijilmasa, Morocco *1–4:* 416

Sikkim *1–4:* 308, 751, 814, 816; *6:* 78

The Silent World 1–4: 285

Silk Road *1–4:* 218, 220

Silla *1–4:* 634

Silverstein, Abe *1–4:* 26

Silverstone, Sally *6:* 15

Simbing *1–4:* 633

Simla, India *1–4:* 105

Simon Fraser University *7:* 98

Simonstown *1–4:* 501

Simpson, George *1–4:* 619

Simpson Strait *1–4:* 17

Boldface indicates main entries in Volume 7 and their page numbers; *1–4:* refers to entries in the four-volume base set; *5:* refers to entries in Volume 5; *6:* refers to entries in Volume 6; *7:* refers to entries in Volume 7; (ill.) following a page number refers to photos, drawings, and maps.

Sinai, Egypt *1–4:* 290
Sinai Desert *1–4:* 97
Sinai Peninsula *1–4:* 76; *6:* 37, 40
Sinaloa, Mexico *1–4:* 281
Sinbad *6:* 185
Sind, Pakistan *1–4:* 151, 434
Singapore *1–4:* 105, 491; *5:* 129; *6:* 23
Singh, Duleep *1–4:* 44
Singh, Kalian *1–4:* 754
Singh, Kishen *1–4:* 752
Singh, Mani *1–4:* 751, 753–754
Singh, Nain *1–4:* 750–756; *7:* 146
Singh, Nem *7:* 146
Sinkiang Uighur, China *1–4:* 66, 704–706; *5:* 56, 101, 102
Sino-Japanese War *1–4:* 106
Sino-Swedish Scientific Expedition *1–4:* 422
Sinta, Pedro de *1–4:* 426
Sioux (tribe) *1–4:* 227, 532; *6:* 98
Sioux City, Iowa *1–4:* 531
Siple, Paul A. *1–4:* 163
Sitka Island *1–4:* 63
Six Months in the Sandwich Islands *1–4:* 104
Skagway, Alaska *7:* 74
Skate *1–4:* 860
Sketches Awheel *1–4:* 862
Skraelings *1–4:* 527
Sky Roads of the World *1–4:* 493
Slave River *1–4:* 561
"Sleeping" sharks *7:* 49, 50
Slidell, John *1–4:* 854
Smith, Edward J. *5:* 162
Smith, Jedediah *1–4:* 620–621, 757–761; *5:* 8
Smith, John *1–4:* 470, 762–766
Smith, Michael J. *6:* 129, 131
Smith Sound *5:* 71; *6:* 2; *7:* 139, 140
Smithsonian Institution *1–4:* 743; *7:* 74, 175
Smoky River *1–4:* 563
Snaefellsnes *1–4:* 342
Snake River *1–4:* 372, 484, 534, 619–620

Snook, Neta *1–4:* 331
Society Islands *1–4:* 733
Society of Geography *1–4:* 138
Society of Women Geographers *6:* 88
Socrates *1–4:* 867, 870
Sofala, Mozambique *1–4:* 289, 392; *7:* 41
Soko (tribe) *1–4:* 796
Sokoto, Nigeria *1–4:* 72
Soldaria *7:* 206
Solis, Juan Diaz de *1–4:* 173, 568
"Solo Challenger" *5:* 64
Solomon Islands *1–4:* 126, 189–190, 326, 328, 511; *7:* 32, 156
Somali Desert *1–4:* 3
Somaliland *1–4:* 773
Somers, Geoff *1–4:* 803
Somerset Island *1–4:* 16
Songkhla, Thailand *1–4:* 491
Son-tay, Vietnam *1–4:* 398
Sonora, Mexico *1–4:* 167
Sonoran Desert *7:* 194
SOS *5:* 164
Soto, Hernando de *1–4:* 164, 167, 767–771
South *1–4:* 749
South Atlantic *6:* 134, 136, 137
South China Sea *1–4:* 222
South East Cape *7:* 197
South Georgia Island *1–4:* 91, 749
South Island, New Zealand *1–4:* 259, 263, 327, 449, 810–811
South Magnetic Pole *1–4:* 328, 747; *7:* 163
South Orkney Islands *1–4:* 328
South Pacific *5:* 35, 36, 38; *7:* 34, 47, 152, 201
South Pass, Wyoming *1–4:* 372, 485, 757; *5:* 10
South Peak *1–4:* 451
South Pole *1–4:* 14, 18–20, 158, 160–161, 163, 338, 377, 452–453, 744, 746–747, 804, 859; *5:* 116; *7:* 194
South Seas *1–4:* 509, 513; *7:* 47

South Shetland Islands *1–4:* 92, 93, 328; *5:* 32

Southampton, England *5:* 161, 162; *6:* 23; *7:* 198

The Southern Gates of Arabia 6: 185

Southern Rhodesia *6:* 115

Southwest Cape *7:* 198, 201

Soviet Army *5:* 139

Soviet Space Commission *1–4:* 818

Soyuz I 1–4: 382

Space Biospheres Ventures (SBV) *6:* 9, 15

Space shuttle *5:* 42, 80–82, 109, 114

Space Telescope Science Institute (Baltimore, Maryland) *1–4:* 466

Spacelab *5:* 82

Spanish-American War *1–4:* 158

Spanish Armada *1–4:* 315, 319–320, 714

Spanish Inquisition *1–4:* 241

Spanish Trail *1–4:* 372

Sparta *1–4:* 870

Speke, John Hanning *1–4:* 45–46, 112, 113–114, 153–156, 502, 551, 580, 722, 772–777, 794; *5:* 158; *6:* 34

Spencer, Herbert *1–4:* 358

Spencer Gulf *1–4:* 355, 356, 361, 362; *7:* 103

Spice Islands *1–4:* 127, 174, 318, 457, 567, 570–571, 573, 733, 865

Spiess, Wilhelm *6:* 134

Spirit of St. Louis 1–4: 539, 542; *7:* 178

Spitsbergen, Norway *1–4:* 21, 22, 337, 365, 611–612, 858

Spitsbergen Island *1–4:* 130, 160, 642; *5:* 13, 16, 121, 123

Springs of Geesh *6:* 30

Spruce, Richard *1–4:* 481

Sputnik 1–4: 26, 36, 351, 353, 379, 555, 557, 778–782

Srinigar, India *1–4:* 105, 406

St. Ann's Bay *1–4:* 253

St. Anthony's Falls *6:* 98

St. Augustine, Florida *1–4:* 319, 696

St. Croix, Virgin Islands *1–4:* 248

St. Francis Xavier Mission *5:* 107

St. Helena *1–4:* 302, 834

St. Ignace *1–4:* 496; *5:* 106, 107

St. John, New Brunswick *5:* 64

St. John's, Newfoundland *1–4:* 196; *6:* 1, 45

St. Joseph, Missouri *1–4:* 483

St. Lawrence Island *5:* 20

St. Lawrence River *1–4:* 193, 195, 212–213, 215, 227, 255, 497–498, 526; *5:* 105; *6:* 149

St. Louis, Missouri *1–4:* 483–485, 530–531, 536, 539–540, 662; *6:* 161, 168

St. Paul, Minnesota *1–4:* 662

St. Peter 5: 23

St. Petersburg, Russia *1–4:* 420, 705, 708; *5:* 20, 21, 23, 135

St. Thomas Christians *6:* 111

St. Vincent, West Indies *1–4:* 357

Stadacona (Quebec City, Quebec) *1–4:* 195–196

Stadukhin, Mikhail *7:* 61, 62

Stafford, Thomas *1–4:* 29

Stag Lane *1–4:* 489

Stalin, Joseph *1–4:* 779

Stanhope, Hester *1–4:* 783–787

Stanislaus River *1–4:* 760

Stanley, Henry Morton *1–4:* 115, 134–135, 138, 233, 236, 553, 788–799, 828; *5:* 141; *7:* 137

Stanley Falls *1–4:* 795

Stanley Pool *1–4:* 134–135, 795

Star City, Russia *5:* 112, 113

Star II 6: 51, 53

Stark, Freya *6:* 181–187, 181 (ill.), 183 (ill.)

Station Camp Creek, Kentucky *1–4:* 118

Stead, William Thomas *7:* 17

Boldface indicates main entries in Volume 7 and their page numbers; *1–4:* refers to entries in the four-volume base set; *5:* refers to entries in Volume 5; *6:* refers to entries in Volume 6; *7:* refers to entries in Volume 7; (ill.) following a page number refers to photos, drawings, and maps.

287 | Index

Stefansson, Vilhjalmur *1–4:* 857; *5:* 145–149, 145 (ill.), 146 (ill.); *6:* 5, 8
Stefansson Collection *5:* 148
Stefansson Island, Northwest Territories *5:* 148
Steger, Will *1–4:* 800–805
Steger International Polar Expedition *1–4:* 802
Stein, Aurel *1–4:* 806–808
Stephen of Cloyes *1–4:* 96
Steward, Roger *7:* 161, 162 (ill.)
Stewart, James *1–4:* 542
Stingray Point *1–4:* 764
Stirlingshire, Scotland *6:* 26, 27
Stockton, Robert F. *1–4:* 373
Strabo *1–4:* 384
Strait of Belle Isle *1–4:* 194, 526
Strait of Georgia *1–4:* 833; *6:* 66
Strait of Gibraltar *1–4:* 408, 415, 710; *7:* 108
Strait of Hormuz *1–4:* 223
Strait of Juan de Fuca *1–4:* 832, 854
Strait of Magellan *1–4:* 124, 174, 188, 300, 318–319, 327, 458, 569, 600; *5:* 32; *6:* 176, 178, 180, 189; *7:* 29, 32, 152, 154, 156, 157
Straits of Florida *7:* 84
Straits of Mackinac *1–4:* 514; *5:* 106
Straits of Malacca *1–4:* 459; *6:* 107
Straits of Mackinac *6:* 96, 98, 151
Stratobowl (Rapid City, South Dakota) *5:* 64
Straus, Isidor *5:* 162
Streaky Bay *1–4:* 356
Stuart, John McDouall *1–4:* 144, 146, 149
Stuart, Robert *1–4:* 483–485
Stuart Lake *6:* 66
Suakin, Ethiopia *6:* 39
Suali, India *6:* 111
Submarine Force Museum *1–4:* 613
Sudan *5:* 156, 158–160; *6:* 31, 35, 37, 38, 41
Sué River *1–4:* 582

Suez Canal *6:* 23
Suffren 1–4: 394
Sulpicians *1–4:* 513
Sun 6: 82, 84
Sunda Strait *1–4:* 456
Sungari River *6:* 123
Surabaja, Indonesia *1–4:* 457, 491
Surat, India *6:* 70, 111
Surumu River *6:* 172
Surveyor III 1–4: 30
Susa, Persia *1–4:* 8, 10, 12; *7:* 186
Susi, David *1–4:* 115, 231, 233–236, 552, 554, 790
Susquehanna (tribe) *1–4:* 141, 142
Susquehannah River *1–4:* 142, 765
Sutlej River *1–4:* 421, 754
Sutter's Fort, California *1–4:* 372, 373
Svalbard Islands *1–4:* 469
Sverdrup, Otto *1–4:* 18, 606
Swahili *1–4:* 504, 720, 828
Swallow 1–4: 188–190
Swan 1–4: 316
Swan River *1–4:* 356
Swedish Academy of Science *5:* 121
Swedish Geographical Society *1–4:* 418
Sweetwater River *1–4:* 485
Swigert, John *1–4:* 30
Sydney, Australia *1–4:* 92, 302, 326, 355, 363, 510–511, 853; *5:* 24–27; *7:* 53, 57, 198
Sydney, New Zealand *1–4:* 452
Sydney Harbor *1–4:* 362
Syr Darya River *1–4:* 185
Syrian Desert *1–4:* 108, 109; *6:* 37
Szechwan, China *1–4:* 106, 219, 460, 692, 814

T

Tabasco, Cuba *1–4:* 276
Tabasco, Mexico *1–4:* 276

Tabora, Tanzania *1–4:* 113–116, 155, 233–234, 554, 774–776, 790, 792, 826

Tabriz, Kurdistan (Iran) *5:* 128

Tadoussac, Quebec *1–4:* 213–214

Tagus River *1–4:* 247, 387, 390, 668

Taino (tribe) *1–4:* 245

Takla Makan *1–4:* 420, 690, 706, 708, 807–808; *5:* 55

Talavera Commission *1–4:* 241

Tallahassee, Florida *1–4:* 165

Taloi Mountains *1–4:* 11

Talon, Jean *1–4:* 496

Tamar 7: 31, 34

Tampa Bay, Florida *1–4:* 165, 769

Tamralipti *1–4:* 463; *5:* 56; *6:* 107, 108

Tana River *1–4:* 3, 506

Tangier, Morocco *1–4:* 79, 426, 736

Tanjung Puting swamp *7:* 94, 98, 99

Tankar, China *1–4:* 420

Tao-chou *1–4:* 814

Taos, New Mexico *1–4:* 83

Tapirapuã, Brazil *6:* 155, 156

Tarim Basin *1–4:* 420–421, 706

Tashkent, Uzbekistan *1–4:* 419, 461; *5:* 101

Tasman, Abel *1–4:* 258–259, 809–812

Tassili-n-Ajjer Plateau *1–4:* 71

Ta-T'ang Si-Yu-Ki 1–4: 463

Tatar Straits *1–4:* 510

Tatars *1–4:* 41, 666

Taunton River *6:* 45, 47

Taveta *5:* 142

Tawang *1–4:* 755

Taxila, Pakistan *1–4:* 9, 462

Taylor, Annie Royle *1–4:* 813–816

Taylor, Jim *1–4:* 521–523

Tecla Haimanot *6:* 29

Tegulet, Ethiopia *1–4:* 290

Tehachapi Mountains *1–4:* 760

Tehran, Iran *1–4:* 87, 105, 419

Teixeira, Pedro de *5:* 150–154, 151 (ill.)

Tekeze River *1–4:* 45

Tektite II *6:* 49

Telefomin *1–4:* 522

Tenerife Island *1–4:* 568

Tengri Nor Lake *1–4:* 755

Tennessee River *1–4:* 770

Tennyson, Alfred *1–4:* 358

Tenochtitlán (Mexico City, Mexico) *1–4:* 276–279; *5:* 1, 2

Tensas (tribe) *1–4:* 516

Tereshkova, Valentina *1–4:* 723, 817–820

Terhazza, Mali *1–4:* 80

Ternate (outpost) *1–4:* 304; *6:* 179, 190; *7:* 156

Terra Australis *1–4:* 188, 256–257, 487, 731, 810; *7:* 30

Terra Verde (Newfoundland) *6:* 44, 45

Terror 1–4: 368

Tete, Africa *1–4:* 58–59, 550

Teton Sioux (tribe) *1–4:* 532

Thagard, Norman *5:* 114

Thames River *1–4:* 493, 835

Thana, Salsette Island *6:* 111

Thank God Harbor *5:* 72

Thar Desert *1–4:* 463

Thayer, Bill *7:* 189, 196

Thayer, Helen *7:* **188–196,** 188 (ill.), 191 (ill.), 194 (ill.)

Thebes, Egypt *1–4:* 6, 95; *5:* 138; *6:* 91

Theodore Roosevelt 1–4: 648–649, 652; *6:* 2–4, 2 (ill.)

There's Always Tomorrow 6: 89

Thessaly *1–4:* 6

Thok Jalung, Tibet *1–4:* 754

Thomas, Bertram *5:* 42

Thompson, David *1–4:* 821–824

Thompson Springs, Utah *7:* 71

Thomson, Charles Wyville *1–4:* 209–210

Thomson, Joseph *1–4:* 231, 235–236, 825–829

Thorndike, Karen *7:* **197–203,** 197 (ill.), 199 (ill.), 202 (ill.)

Thousand and One Nights 6: 185

Thrace *1–4:* 6, 433, 870

Through the Dark Continent
   1–4: 798
Thucydides, Historian *1–4:* 870
Thurii, Greece *1–4:* 434
Thutmose I *6:* 91
Thutmose II *6:* 91
Thutmose III *6:* 94
Thuzkan, Tuscany, Italy *1–4:* 67
Thymiaterium (Mehdia) *7:* 108
Tib, Tippu *1–4:* 794–795, 797
Tibetan Buddhism *1–4:* 307, 576, 689
Tibetan Pioneer Mission *1–4:* 816
Tibetan Plateau *6:* 71
Tider, Morocco *1–4:* 426
Tidore Island *1–4:* 571, 573; *6:* 190
Tien Shan Mountain Range *1–4:* 419, 461, 706–708; *5:* 100; *7:* 208
Tierra del Fuego *1–4:* 53, 258, 264, 296–297, 299–300; *6:* 176, 178; *7:* 152, 154, 157
Tietkins, William *7:* 101–103
Tigeux, New Mexico *1–4:* 271
Tigeux War *1–4:* 272
Tigris River *1–4:* 108, 110, 868; *5:* 128
Tikrït, Iraq *1–4:* 596
Timbuktu, Mali *1–4:* 69, 73, 80, 179–181, 634, 636, 737; *6:* 35, 36, 40, 101, 103, 104; *7:* 9
Timor, Malay Archipelago *1–4:* 189, 491
Tinareh, Egypt *6:* 37
Tinian Island *1–4:* 192
Tinné, Alexine *5:* 155–160, 155 (ill.), 157 (ill.)
Tintellust *1–4:* 71
Tinto River *1–4:* 243
Tiribazus *1–4:* 868
Tiryns, Greece *5:* 138
Tissaphernes *1–4:* 868
Tississat Falls *6:* 30
Titan *1–4:* 849
Titania *1–4:* 850
R.M.S. *Titanic* *5:* 117, 161–168, 161 (ill.), 163 (ill.), 165 (ill.), 167 (ill.)

Titanic Historical Society *5:* 167
Titov, Gherman *1–4:* 380
Tlaxcala, Mexico *1–4:* 277–279
Tlingit-Haida *1–4:* 63
Tobolsk (settlement) *7:* 61
Tockwough (tribe) *1–4:* 765
Tonga Island *6:* 178
Tongkyuk Dzong *7:* 148
Tokugawa *1–4:* 866
Tom Thumb *1–4:* 360
Tonga Island *1–4:* 265, 328, 809, 811
Tongariro National Park *1–4:* 449
Tonquin *1–4:* 484
Tonty, Henri de *1–4:* 513, 514, 516
Tookolito *5:* 70, 71, 73
Toowoomba *1–4:* 520
Tora (Barrancabermeja, Colombia) *7:* 128
Töregene *1–4:* 185
Torell, Otto *5:* 121
Torres, Luis Vaez de *1–4:* 126, 261, 488
Torres Strait *1–4:* 126, 261, 362, 487; *7:* 53
Toulon, France *1–4:* 182, 282, 326, 659
Tovar, Pedro de *1–4:* 271
Tower of London *1–4:* 714, 716
Townsville, Australia *7:* 15
Trabzon *1–4:* 694, 869
Traits of American-Indian Life and Character *1–4:* 618
Trans-Siberian Railroad *1–4:* 701
Transantarctic Mountains *1–4:* 20
Transcontinental Air Transport *1–4:* 541
Transylvania Company *1–4:* 119
Trapezus *1–4:* 869
Travancore, India *1–4:* 865
Travels in West Africa *1–4:* 501
Travels to Discover the Source of the Nile *6:* 33
Treasure Salvors, Inc. *7:* 87

Treaty of Tordesillas *1–4:* 386,
567; *5:* 150; *6:* 175, 188, 191;
7: 39, 83, 151
Treaty of Versailles *6:* 134
Trebizond, Greece *1–4:* 67
Trent Affair *1–4:* 854
Trevanion, Sophia *7:* 35
Triana, Rodrigo de *1–4:* 244
Trieste 1–4: 659; *6:* 53
Trieste, Italy *1–4:* 157, 659
Trinidad 1–4: 567, 571, 573
Tripoli, Libya *1–4:* 55, 70, 71,
737; *5:* 159; *6:* 27, 101; *7:* 9,
210
Triton 1–4: 850
Trois-Rivières, Canada *1–4:*
226–227; *5:* 105
Trojan War *5:* 135, 138
Trombetas River *6:* 174
Tromsö, Norway *5:* 123
Trondheim, Norway *1–4:* 711
Tropic of Capricorn *7:* 105
Troy, Greece *1–4:* 6; *5:*
135–139
True Relation of Virginia 1–4:
764
Trujillo, Peru *1–4:* 627, 481
Truman, Harry S *1–4:* 428
Tsaidam, China *1–4:* 219, 705
Tsangpo River *1–4:* 752, 753; *7:*
145–149
Tsaparang, Tibet *1–4:* 24–25
Tswana *1–4:* 544
Tuakau, New Zealand *1–4:* 449
Tuamotu Archipelago *1–4:* 92,
124, 189, 191, 733; *6:* 178; *7:*
33, 155
Tuamotu Islands *7:* 117
Tuat, Algeria *1–4:* 737
Tübingen *1–4:* 502
Tucker, HL *1–4:* 101
Tudela, Spain *1–4:* 94, 97
Tukulors *1–4:* 579
Tulloch, George *5:* 168
Tumba Lake *1–4:* 796
Tumbes *1–4:* 671, 672
Tun-huang *1–4:* 691, 807
Tunis, Africa *1–4:* 307; *6:* 27
Tunja *7:* 129
Touré, Samory *1–4:* 579

Turkestan Solo 5: 101
Turks *6:* 29
Turktol *5:* 101
Turtle Lake *1–4:* 823
Tuscaloosa, Chief *1–4:* 770
Tutuila *1–4:* 510
Tutankhamen *6:* 119
Tuvalu Islands *1–4:* 733
*Twenty Thousand Leagues under
the Sea 1–4:* 610
Tyre, Lebanon *1–4:* 7, 433
Tyson, George *5:* 72–74

U

Ubangi River *1–4:* 581; *7:* 134
Ubar *5:* 40–46
Uele River *7:* 134, 135
Ugogo *1–4:* 774
Ujiji, Tanzania *1–4:* 115–116,
233, 552–553, 774, 790
Ukambani *1–4:* 505–506
Ulan Bator *1–4:* 705
Ulfsson, Gunnbjörn *1–4:* 342
Ulloa, Francisco de *1–4:* 281
Ulya River *5:* 133
Umbriel *1–4:* 850
Umivik Fjord *1–4:* 605
Umpqua (tribe) *1–4:* 761
Umpqua River *1–4:* 761
Unalakleet River Basin *7:* 196
Unalaska, Aleutian Islands *1–4:*
62
Unbeaten Tracks in Japan 1–4:
105
*The Undersea Odyssey of the
"Calypso" 1–4:* 286
United States Biological Survey
1–4: 337
University of Colorado at Boulder
7: 71
University of Heidelberg *6:* 134
Unyanyembe *1–4:* 773
Upernavik, Greenland *7:* 143
Ural Mountains *5:* 121
Uranus *1–4:* 847, 849, 850
Urban II *1–4:* 96

Boldface indicates main entries in Volume 7 and their page numbers; *1–4:* refers to entries in the four-
volume base set; *5:* refers to entries in Volume 5; *6:* refers to entries in Volume 6; *7:* refers to entries in
Volume 7; (ill.) following a page number refers to photos, drawings, and maps.

291 | Index

Urdaneta, Andrés de *6:* 188–193, 189 (ill.)

Urdaneta's Passage *6:* 188, 193

Urga *1–4:* 705

Urubamba River *1–4:* 99, 100

Uruguay River *1–4:* 174

U.S. Bureau of Indian Affairs *6:* 166

U.S. Congress *5:* 167

The U.S. Grinnell Expedition in Search of Sir John Franklin 7: 140

U.S. Navy *6:* 6, 8

U.S. Virgin Islands *6:* 49

Usambara *1–4:* 504, 506

Ussuri River *1–4:* 705

V

Vaca, Ívar Núñez Cabeza de. *See* Cabeza de Vaca, Ívar Núñez

Valdez, Alaska *7:* 166

Valenzuela, Eloy *6:* 145

Valladolid, Spain *1–4:* 254; *6:* 190

Valles Marineris *1–4:* 587

Valley of Añaquito *1–4:* 480

Valley of Mexico *1–4:* 278, 279

Valley of Taurus-Littrow *1–4:* 32

The Valley of the Assassins 6: 184

Valparaíso, Chile *1–4:* 300, 301, 328; *7:* 29

Valparaíso, Spain *1–4:* 318

Van Allen radiation belts *1–4:* 352, 376

Van Diemen's Land *1–4:* 810

Van Thillo, Mark *6:* 15

Vancouver, George *1–4:* 62, 263–264, 361, 564, 830–835

Vancouver, British Columbia *6:* 66

Vancouver Island *1–4:* 833

Vanderbilt, William H. *7:* 47

Vanguard 1 1–4: 351, 353, 354

Vanikoro Island *1–4:* 511

Vanuatu Archipelago *1–4:* 125, 263, 328

Varanasi *1–4:* 462

Varuna 7: 201

Vasconcelos, Lués Aranha de *5:* 151

Vega 5: 124

Velázquez, Diego *1–4:* 275, 277, 278; *5:* 1

Velho, Alvaro *1–4:* 390

Venera 1–4: 781

Venus *1–4:* 256, 259, 585, 587–588, 781–782

Venus de Milo 1–4: 325–326

Ver-sur-Mer, France *1–4:* 160

Veracruz, Mexico *1–4:* 277

Veranzano, Girolamo da *1–4:* 837

Verkhne-Kamchatsk *1–4:* 42

Verne, Jules *1–4:* 610, 658; *6:* 18, 23, 24

Verón, Pierre Antoine *1–4:* 123, 126

Verrazano, Giovanni da *1–4:* 193, 470, 836–838

Verrazano-Narrows Bridge *1–4:* 836

Versailles Treaty *6:* 82

Verulamium, England *6:* 115

Veslekari 1–4: 131

Vespucci, Amerigo *1–4:* 623–624, 839–842; *7:* 40, 42

Vestfold Hills *1–4:* 860

Victoria (of England) *7:* 12

Victoria 1–4: 567, 571, 573

Victoria Falls *1–4:* 549

Victoria Island *1–4:* 17; *5:* 146, 147

Victoria Land *1–4:* 163, 377

Victoria-Maui International Yacht Race *7:* 40

Victoria Nile *1–4:* 48, 50, 794

Vidin, Bulgaria *1–4:* 44

Vienna, Austria *1–4:* 184; *5:* 126–128, 130, 157, 159

Vientiane, Laos *1–4:* 395

Viking 1–4: 843–846; *7:* 176

Viking (ship) *1–4:* 604

Viking Lander Atlas of Mars 1–4: 846

Vikings *5:* 17, 77, 147; *6:* 47; *7:* 27

Vilcabamba mountains *1–4:* 99
Vilcabamba River *1–4:* 99–100
Villa-Lobos, Heitor *6:* 158, 159, 159 (ill.)
Ville de Bruges 1–4: 581
Ville de Paris 1–4: 638
Vilyui River *7:* 65
Vincennes 1–4: 853
Vinland *1–4:* 524, 526–527
Virgin River *1–4:* 759
Virginia *1–4:* 529, 713, 763
Viroconium-Bath, England *6:* 115
Virunga Mountains *6:* 58
Visconti, Teobaldo *1–4:* 689
Viscount Melville Sound *1–4:* 639; *7:* 163, 165
Visscher, Frans Jacobszoon *1–4:* 810–811
Vitcos *1–4:* 98–102
Vogel, Edward *1–4:* 73
Volga Bulgars *5:* 75
Volga River *1–4:* 77, 184, 688, 818; *5:* 75–77; *7:* 207
Vostok 1–4: 91–92, 380, 402, 559, 781, 818–819
Vostok Island *1–4:* 92
A Voyage of Discovery to the North Pacific Ocean and Round the World 1–4: 835
Voyage of the Vega Round Asia and Europe 5: 125
Voyage to Terra Australis 1–4: 363
Voyager (airplane) *1–4:* 740–743
Voyager 1 and *2 1–4:* 847–851
Voyages 1–4: 227
Voyages to the Frozen and Pacific Oceans 1–4: 564
The Voyages and Adventures of Fernïo Mendes Pinto 1–4: 668

W

Wabag Valley *1–4:* 521
Wad Dra (tribe) *7:* 108

Wager 7: 29
Wagner, Johannes *1–4:* 721
Wahgi Valley *1–4:* 521
Wainwright, Jacob *1–4:* 234
Wakamba *1–4:* 505–506
Walford, Roy L. *6:* 15
Walker, Alan *5:* 96
Walker Lake *1–4:* 760
Walla Walla (tribe) *6:* 167
Walla Walla, Washington *1–4:* 620–622
Wallace, Alfred Russell *1–4:* 304–305; *7:* 70
Wallace Line *1–4:* 304
Waller, Horace *1–4:* 235
Wallis, Samuel *1–4:* 124, 187–192, 257
Wallis Islands *1–4:* 192
Walsh, Donald *1–4:* 659
Walvis Bay *1–4:* 312; *7:* 2–5
Wamba, Zaire *1–4:* 4
Wampanoag (tribe) *6:* 47
War of 1812 *1–4:* 64, 365
War of the Austrian Succession *1–4:* 187
Washington, D.C. *1–4:* 466, 536, 538, 764; *5:* 116–118; *6:* 88, 127, 168
Watauga Treaty *1–4:* 119
Wateita (tribe) *1–4:* 719
The Water Babies 1–4: 499
Wau, Sudan *1–4:* 582; *5:* 159
Wayne, Anthony *1–4:* 528
Weaver, Sigourney *6:* 62
Weddell, James *1–4:* 263, 327–328
Weddell Island *1–4:* 328
Weddell Sea *1–4:* 163, 747
Wedgwood, Josiah *1–4:* 292
Wekotani *1–4:* 231, 232
West India Company *1–4:* 733
West Palm Beach, Florida *1–4:* 660
West Road River *1–4:* 563
West with the Night 1–4: 593, 594
Westall, William *1–4:* 361
Whales *7:* 184, 185 (ill.)
Whiddon, Jacob *1–4:* 715
Whiskey Rebellion *1–4:* 528

White, Edward *1–4:* 27; *6:* 126

White, Isobel *7:* 19, 22

White, John *1–4:* 714

White Nile River *1–4:* 50, 136, 582, 776, 798; *5:* 158, 159; *7:* 134, 135

White Star Line *5:* 161

Whitehorse, Alaska *7:* 74

Whydah 5: 47–50, 48 (ill.), 50 (ill.)

Wilkes, Charles *1–4:* 329, 852–855

Wilkes Land *1–4:* 853

Wilkins, (George) Hubert *1–4:* 337–338, 749, 856–860; *5:* 148

Wilkins-Hearst Expedition *1–4:* 859

Wilkinson, James *1–4:* 661–664

Willamette River *1–4:* 761

William I (of Sicily) *7:* 125

William Henry Ashley's Missouri Fur Company *1–4:* 536

William of Rubruck *7:* 204–211, 204 (ill.), 206 (ill.), 208 (ill.)

Williams, Roger *1–4:* 838

Wills, William John *1–4:* 144–149

Wilson, Edward *1–4:* 744

Wind River *1–4:* 484, 761

Wind River Range *1–4:* 372

Windhoek, Namibia *7:* 2

Windward Islands *7:* 35

Windward 6: 1

Windward Passage *1–4:* 245

Winnebago (tribe) *1–4:* 216; *6:* 150

Winnie Mae 1–4: 700–702

Wirilya, Australia *7:* 21

Wisconsin River *1–4:* 496; *5:* 106; *6:* 98, 152

Wissmann, Hermann von *7:* 212–215, 212 (ill.), 214 (ill.)

Wisting, Oskar *1–4:* 19

Wolf, David *5:* 114

Wolfe, Tom *1–4:* 874

Wollongong, Australia *1–4:* 360

Wood, Maria *1–4:* 533

Woods Hole Oceanographic Institution *1–4:* 660; *5:* 165

Worden, Alfred *1–4:* 31

Workman, Fanny Bullock *1–4:* 656, 861–863

Workman, William Hunter *1–4:* 861

The World 6: 21, 23, 24, 94

World Flight 1997 *7:* 78, 80–82

The World of Silence 1–4: 285

World War I *1–4:* 3, 87, 89, 337, 422, 519, 748; *6:* 6, 24, 81, 82, 134, 136, 181; *7:* 178, 214

World War II *1–4:* 27, 132, 162, 375, 401, 449, 493, 520, 522, 658, 780, 860; *5:* 92, 138, 148; *6:* 8, 136, 137, 185; *7:* 45, 86

World Wildlife Fund *7:* 98

Wrangel Island *5:* 148; *6:* 6

Wright, Orville *1–4:* 35, 743

Wright, Wilbur *1–4:* 35, 743

Wright, William *1–4:* 145, 147

Wright 1903 Flyer 7: 178

Wu-Ti *1–4:* 218, 219

X

X-1 1–4: 872, 873

X-1A 1–4: 874

Xanadu *1–4:* 691

Xavier, Saint Francis *1–4:* 497, 667–668, 864–866

Xenophon *1–4:* 867–870

Xingu River *5:* 151; *6:* 159

Xining, China *5:* 55

Xocotla, Mexico *1–4:* 277

XS-1 project *1–4:* 872

Y

Yadkin valley *1–4:* 118–119

Yakutat Bay *1–4:* 63, 510

Yakutsk, Russia *5:* 131, 134; *6:* 121, 122; *7:* 61, 64

Yana River *7:* 61

Yang-chou *1–4:* 692

Yangtze River *1–4:* 106, 222, 396, 692, 728

The Yangtze River and Beyond 1–4: 106

Yanomami (tribe) *7:* 193

Yao (tribe) *1–4:* 112, 231

Yaqui *1–4:* 167

Yaqui River *1–4:* 270

Yarkand, China *1–4:* 421, 690, 755

Yarmuk *6:* 118

Yarqui plains *5:* 88

Yatung, Sikkim *1–4:* 816

Yauri, Hausa 636–637

Yeager, Chuck *1–4:* 871–874

Yeager, Jeana *1–4:* 739–743

Yeager 1–4: 874

Yelcho 1–4: 749

Yellow River *1–4:* 460, 691; *6:* 71

Yellowstone River *1–4:* 533, 536; *6:* 167

Yenbï, Saudi Arabia *1–4:* 152; *6:* 40

Yenisei River *1–4:* 482; *5:* 123; *6:* 121

Yeti *1–4:* 453

Yokohama, Japan *1–4:* 106; *5:* 63, 124; *6:* 23

Yongden *1–4:* 308–310

York *1–4:* 530, 534, 664

York Factory, Canada *1–4:* 366

Young, Brigham *1–4:* 372

Young, John *1–4:* 29, 32

Younghusband, Francis *1–4:* 577

Yucatán Peninsula *1–4:* 275; *7:* 49, 50

Yucay, Peru *1–4:* 99

Yüeh-chih *1–4:* 218

Yukagirs *1–4:* 41

Yukon Arctic coast *5:* 147

Yukon River *1–4:* 18, 801

Yule, Henry *1–4:* 750

Yule Island *7:* 53

Yuma, Arizona *1–4:* 271

Yung-lo *1–4:* 222–223

Yungay *1–4:* 654

Yunnan, China *1–4:* 396, 692

Z

Zagros Mountains *6:* 182

Zambezi *1–4:* 547, 549–550

Zambezi River *1–4:* 58, 139–140, 232

Zanzibar, Tanzania *1–4:* 112–116, 153–154, 156, 223, 234–236, 504, 552, 776, 789, 792, 795–796, 798, 826–827; *5:* 141

Zanzibar Island *1–4:* 721

Zardeh Kuh mountain *6:* 87

Zarins, Juris *5:* 43

Zaysan *1–4:* 707

Zeehaen 1–4: 810

Zeeland *1–4:* 458

Zeila, Somalia *1–4:* 77, 290

Zelée 1–4: 327, 328

Zen Buddhism *1–4:* 307

Zenag *1–4:* 523

Zenobia *1–4:* 786

Zeya River *5:* 132; *6:* 124

Zinga *1–4:* 581

Zinjanthropus 5: 95

Zionists *6:* 186

Zoar *1–4:* 498

Zoe 7: 71

Zond 5 *1–4:* 557

Zond 6 *1–4:* 557

Zoroastrianism *1–4:* 596

Zumaco *1–4:* 628

Zumbo, Mozambique *1–4:* 140

Zungomero *1–4:* 773

Zuni (tribe) *1–4:* 270, 345, 349–350

Zvedochka *1–4:* 782

Boldface indicates main entries in Volume 7 and their page numbers; *1–4:* refers to entries in the four-volume base set; *5:* refers to entries in Volume 5; *6:* refers to entries in Volume 6; *7:* refers to entries in Volume 7; (ill.) following a page number refers to photos, drawings, and maps.

295 | Index

Smita Manjunath

Marketing
Management

TWELFTH EDITION

Welcome Kevin Lane Keller.

I'm thrilled to introduce Professor Kevin Lane Keller as my co-author on the twelfth edition of *Marketing Management*. Kevin is acknowledged as one of the top academics of his generation. Currently the E.B. Osborn Professor of Marketing at the Tuck School of Business at Dartmouth, he received his Ph.D. from Duke University's Fuqua School of Business. His path-breaking research and writings on brands, branding, and brand equity have been widely cited and received numerous awards. He is also actively involved with industry as a popular speaker and marketing confidant to such top companies as Accenture, American Express, Disney, Ford, Intel, Levi-Strauss, Procter & Gamble, and Starbucks. Thanks to his tireless efforts, I am confident we've crafted the best edition yet.

We hope you enjoy reading the twelfth edition as much as we enjoyed writing it, and that it serves as a practical resource during your education and career.